AF513843

BRITISH LABOUR LEADERS

BRITISH LABOUR LEADERS

EDITED BY

Charles Clarke and Toby S. James

This revised edition published in Great Britain in 2025 by
Biteback Publishing Ltd, London

ISBN 978-1-78590-950-4

10 9 8 7 6 5 4 3 2 1

A CIP catalogue record for this book is available from the British Library.

Set in Bulmer

Printed and bound in Great Britain by
CPI Group (UK) Ltd, Croydon CR0 4YY

CONTENTS

Preface vii

List of tables and figures ix

Author biographies xi

PART I: FRAMEWORKS FOR ASSESSING LEADERS

Chapter 1 Introduction: political leadership, Britain and the Labour Party – *Toby S. James* 3

Chapter 2 Statecraft: a framework for assessing Labour Party leaders – *Toby S. James and Jim Buller* 23

Chapter 3 Measuring the success or failure of Labour leaders: the general election test – *Charles Clarke* 39

Chapter 4 Assessing the policy and societal impact of Labour leaders – *Toby S. James* 63

PART II: ASSESSMENTS OF LABOUR LEADERS

Chapter 5 Keir Hardie – *Kenneth O. Morgan* 83

Chapter 6 George Nicoll Barnes and William Adamson – *William W. J. Knox* 101

Chapter 7 John Robert Clynes – *Phil Woolas* 119

Chapter 8 Ramsay MacDonald – *David Howell* 135

Chapter 9 Arthur Henderson – *Chris Wrigley* 153

Chapter 10 George Lansbury – *John Shepherd* 173

Chapter 11 Clement Attlee – *Nicklaus Thomas-Symonds* 195

Chapter 12 Hugh Gaitskell – *Brian Brivati* 213

Chapter 13 Harold Wilson – *Thomas Hennessey* 229

Chapter 14 James Callaghan – *Peter Kellner* 245

Chapter 15 Michael Foot – *Kenneth O. Morgan* 259

Chapter 16 Neil Kinnock – *Martin Westlake* 275

Chapter 17 John Smith – *Mark Stuart* 297

Chapter 18 Tony Blair – *John Rentoul* 311

Chapter 19 Gordon Brown – *Steve Richards* 327

Chapter 20 Ed Miliband – *Tim Bale* 343

Chapter 21 Jeremy Corbyn – *Peter Dorey* 361

Chapter 22 Keir Starmer – *Patrick Diamond* 377

PART III: LEADERSHIP PERSPECTIVES

Chapter 23 Brexit and the Labour Party: squaring the circle – *Victoria Honeyman* 401

Chapter 24 Neil Kinnock on leadership, the Labour Party and statecraft theory – *Neil Kinnock, Toby S. James and Charles Clarke* 417

Chapter 25 Tony Blair on leadership, New Labour and statecraft theory – *Tony Blair, Toby S. James and Charles Clarke* 439

Bibliography 453

Index 483

PREFACE

Sometimes history goes very slowly. And then suddenly it goes really fast. The first edition of *British Labour Leaders* was published in 2015. Events in the ten years since include an EU referendum, the UK's eventual departure from the EU, three general elections, the death of the UK's longest-living monarch, the Covid pandemic, Donald Trump being elected twice, AI becoming mainstream, major land war returning to Europe following the full-scale invasion of Ukraine by Russia, the end of the post-Cold War period and the global resurgence of autocracy. All of these events have reshaped British politics in profound ways.

This updated volume includes new chapters on the Labour leaders to have held office during these times, Jeremy Corbyn and Keir Starmer, and a new chapter on Brexit and the Labour Party. We have provided updated statistics for the 'league tables' in the opening chapters, which rank the performance of political leaders since the formation of the Labour Party.

Concerns about incumbent leaders centralising power in countries such as India, Israel, Turkey and the US reveal the dangers inherent in and the darker side of political leadership. Good political leadership is ever-more important if democratic societies are to navigate safely and successfully the pressing problems that they face. Leaders need to win elections and retain office to respond to these challenges. However, there are also dangers in rewarding leaders purely in terms of whether they maximised power and held office. This volume therefore also includes a revised introduction and a new chapter examining the broader effects of leaders and the threats to democracy that they now face.

As with the first edition, we are grateful to Olivia Beattie at Biteback for her support with the project. We are also grateful to Catriona Allon for her support with the second edition. It has been a pleasure to work with them. Finally, we would like to thank our families, who have supported us throughout.

Charles Clarke and Toby S. James
Cambridge and Norwich, September 2025

LIST OF TABLES AND FIGURES

Figure 1.1: The Labour Party's vote share (votes cast for the party as a proportion of registered electors), voting-age population share (votes cast for the party as a proportion of all eligible electors) and seat share in the House of Commons at general elections 1900–2024.

Figure 1.2: The overlap between conscientious and cunning leadership.

Table 1.1: Labour leaders: statecraft successes and failures 1900–2025.

Table 2.1: Contextual factors to be considered when assessing leaders.

Table 3.1: Labour performances in each of the thirty-two general elections 1906–2024.

Table 3.2: Labour performances in terms of votes gained or lost in each of the thirty-two general elections 1906–2024.

Table 3.3: Labour performances in each of the thirty-two general elections 1906–2024, ranked by seats gained or lost.

Table 3.4: Labour performances in each of the thirty-two general elections 1906–2024, ranked by share of vote gained or lost.

Table 3.5: Labour performances in each of the thirty-two general elections 1906–2024, ranked by votes gained or lost.

Table 3.6: Overall cumulative Labour leaders' performances in the thirty-two general elections 1906–2024, ranked by seats gained or lost.

Table 3.7: Overall cumulative Labour leaders' performances in the thirty-two general elections 1906–2024, ranked by share of vote gained or lost.

Table 3.8: Overall cumulative Labour leaders' performances in the thirty-two general elections 1906–2024, ranked by votes gained or lost.

Table 3.9: Labour leaders' 'league table', ranked by seats gained or lost.

Table 3.10: Performances of Labour leaders of the opposition.

Table 3.11: Labour leaders in subjective rankings of British prime ministers.

Figure 4.1: The layered framework for understanding policy change.

Table 8.1: Labour Party performance in general elections, 1922–29.

Table 8.2: Labour Party performance in general elections, 1931–35.

Table 16.1: The 1983, 1987 and 1992 general election results.

Table 16.2: Labour leaders of the opposition, 1937–2015.

AUTHOR BIOGRAPHIES

TIM BALE graduated from Gonville & Caius College, Cambridge, completed a Master's at Northwestern University and earned his PhD from Sheffield. He specialises in political parties and elections in the UK and Europe. Tim's media work includes writing for multiple newspapers and websites in the UK and overseas. He also appears on radio, television, and podcasts to talk about politics. He is the author and co-author of several books, most recently, *The Conservative Party after Brexit: Turmoil and Transformation*; *The British General Election of 2024*; and the fifth edition of *European Politics: a Comparative Introduction*, all published in 2025.

TONY BLAIR was Prime Minister of Great Britain and Northern Ireland from May 1997 to June 2007. He was also the leader of Britain's Labour Party from 1994 to 2007 and the Member of Parliament for Sedgefield, England, from 1983 to 2007.

BRIAN BRIVATI is executive director at the Balfour Project. He has published extensive work on contemporary British politics, with an emphasis on the political history of the British Labour Party. His biography of Hugh Gaitskell received ten book-of-the-year selections. He has also written a biography of Lord Goodman and edited *The Uncollected Michael Foot: Essays, Old and New, 1953–2003*; Alan Bullock's single-volume edition of *Ernest Bevin*; *Guiding Light: The Collected Speeches of John Smith*; *The Labour Party: A Centenary History*; Michael Foot's single-volume edition of *Aneurin Bevan, 1897–1960*; and *New Labour in Power: Precedents and Prospects*.

JIM BULLER is a secondary school teacher of English at Huntington School, York. He was previously senior lecturer in politics at the University of York. He has a PhD from the University of Sheffield and has previously worked in the department of political science and international studies at the University of Birmingham. He has written widely on the subject of British politics and public policy, including recent articles in the *New Political Economy*, *British Journal of Politics and International Relations*, *West European Politics*, *Contemporary European Politics* and *British Politics*.

CHARLES CLARKE was Member of Parliament for Norwich South from 1997 to 2010. He served as a minister in the Department for Education and then the Home Office before joining the Cabinet as Minister Without Portfolio and Labour Party chair. From 2002 to 2004 he was Secretary of State for Education and Skills and then Home Secretary until 2006. He now holds visiting professorships at Lancaster University and King's College London and co-leads the Baltic Geopolitics Programme at Cambridge University.

PATRICK DIAMOND is professor of British politics and public policy at Queen Mary University of London, a visiting fellow at Kellogg College, Oxford, and an associate member of Nuffield College. He was previously a local councillor in the London Borough of Southwark and chair of the think tank Policy Network. He is the former head of policy planning at 10 Downing Street. His recent books include *After the Third Way*, *Governing Britain: Power, Politics and the Prime Minister* and *The British Labour Party in Opposition and Power: 1979-2019*.

PETER DOREY is professor of British politics in the School of Law and Politics at Cardiff University. He has authored, co-authored and edited eighteen books and published more than 100 book chapters and journal articles. His books include *The Labour Party and Constitutional Reform*, *The Labour Governments 1964-1970* (editor), and *Comrades in Conflict: Labour, the Trade Unions, and 1969's In Place of Strife*.

THOMAS HENNESSEY is a professor of modern British and Irish history at Canterbury Christ Church University. After completing his doctorate,

Hennessey was a junior research fellow at the Institute of Irish Studies, Queen's; a research officer at the Centre for the Study of Conflict, University of Ulster; a research assistant at the think tank Democratic Dialogue; and a research fellow at the School of Politics, Queen's. He was also a member of the Ulster Unionist Party's talks team during the negotiation of the Belfast Agreement (Good Friday Agreement) in 1998. Hennessey joined the history team at Canterbury Christ Church that same year. He is the author of *Optimist in a Raincoat: Harold Wilson, 1964–70*, among many other publications.

VICTORIA HONEYMAN is professor of British politics at the University of Leeds. She served as chair of the British International Studies Association Foreign Policy Specialist Group between 2014 and 2018. She is co-chair of the Political Studies Association's Learning and Teaching Network and was a member of the Subject Benchmark Statement Working Group. Victoria provides analysis for BBC News and Breakfast, Channel 5, Al Jazeera, France 24, Radio 5 Live and Radio 4, among others, and has written for the UK in a Changing Europe Group, the Foreign Policy Centre and the Conversation website. She has written extensively on the foreign policy objectives of both the Conservative and Labour parties and is the author of two books on Richard Crossman, plus several journal articles and chapters in edited collections.

DAVID HOWELL is a professor emeritus of politics at the University of York. He has written extensively on the British labour movement. His publications include *MacDonald's Party: Labour Identities and Crisis 1922–31*, and he is an editor of the *Dictionary of Labour Biography*. His latest book is *Mosley and British Politics 1918–32: Oswald's Odyssey*.

TOBY S. JAMES is professor of politics and public policy at the University of East Anglia and visiting professor at the London School of Economics. He currently serves as co-director of the Electoral Integrity Project and editor-in-chief of the journal *Policy Studies*. He has written widely on democracy, electoral integrity, political leadership and the policy process. Toby's books include: *Elite Statecraft and Election Administration*; *The Trump Administration*; *The Effects of Wars: Lessons from the War in Ukraine*; *Oxford Handbook of Electoral Integrity*; and *Electoral Reform: Democratic Principles and Global Practice*. He has worked with many major national and international organisations involved in promoting and delivering elections.

PETER KELLNER is an award-winning journalist and pollster. He was chairman of YouGov from 2001–7 and then its president until 2016. He has written for *The Times*, *Sunday Times*, *The Observer*, *The Independent*, *New Statesman*, Prospect and other publications. He has also been the political editor of BBC *Newsnight* and an on-screen analyst on five BBC general election night results programmes. He is co-author of *Callaghan: The Road to Number Ten*.

NEIL KINNOCK was Member of Parliament for Bedwellty (then Islwyn) in south Wales from 1970 until 1995, and leader of the Labour Party from 1983 until 1992. He then served as a European Commissioner from 1995 to 2004, and, in 2004, became a peer.

WILLIAM W. J. KNOX (Bill Knox) is an honorary senior lecturer at the Institute for Scottish Historical Research, University of St Andrews, and the author of a number of books and articles on the labour movement in Scotland. In this field, his major publications include: *Scottish Labour Leaders, 1918–1939: A Biographical Dictionary*; *Industrial Nation: Work, Culture and Society in Scotland, 1800–Present*; *Jimmy Reid: A Clyde-Built Man*; and *Women and Scottish Society 1700-2000*. He has also written on a wide variety of other subjects, including women's history, American multi-nationals in post-1945 Scotland and crime, protest and policing in nineteenth-century Scotland.

KENNETH O. MORGAN, Lord Morgan, was a fellow and tutor at The Queen's College, Oxford, 1966–89, vice-chancellor at the University of Wales, 1989–95 and is now visiting professor at King's College London. He has lectured at universities in the US, Canada, France, the Netherlands, Germany,

Italy, Spain, Latvia, South Africa, India, Malaysia and Singapore. He has been a fellow of the British Academy since 1983 and a Labour peer since 2000. His thirty-four books include: *Wales in British Politics*; *Consensus and Disunity*; *Wales: Rebirth of a Nation*; *Labour in Power 1945–51*; *The Oxford Illustrated History of Britain*; *Labour People*; *The People's Peace*; *Revolution to Devolution*; and biographies of Lloyd George, Keir Hardie, Lord Addison, James Callaghan and Michael Foot.

JOHN RENTOUL is chief political commentator for the *Independent on Sunday*, visiting professor at King's College London and author of *Tony Blair: Prime Minister*, a new edition of which was published in 2013. He has written about Blair since publishing an early biography in 1995 – the year after Blair became Labour leader. At King's, he teaches a Master's course in politics and government called 'The Blair Government'.

STEVE RICHARDS is established as one of the most influential political commentators in the country. He became *The Independent*'s chief political commentator in 2005, having been political editor of the *New Statesman* and a BBC political correspondent. He has presented Radio 4's *Week in Westminster* and ITV's *Sunday Programme*. He is the author of *Whatever It Takes: The Real Story of Gordon Brown and New Labour*.

JOHN SHEPHERD was a visiting professor of modern British history at the University of Huddersfield. He was one of the founders of the Labour History Research Unit at Anglia Ruskin University. He had published extensively on British political and Labour history, and is the author of *George Lansbury: At the Heart of Old Labour*.

MARK STUART was assistant professor in the faculty of social sciences at the University of Nottingham. He is the author of *John Smith: A Life* and has published in journals including *Political Studies* and *British Journal of Politics and International Relations*.

NICKLAUS THOMAS-SYMONDS was appointed Paymaster General and Minister for the Cabinet Office (Minister for the Constitution and European Union Relations) in July 2024. He was elected as Labour MP for Torfaen at the 2015 general election, having served as the secretary of the Blaenavon branch of the Labour Party, and as secretary of the Torfaen Constituency Labour Party. Prior to his election to Parliament, he was a practising barrister at Civitas Law, Cardiff. A fellow of the Royal Historical Society, he often writes articles on UK politics, and has been a regular newspaper reviewer on BBC Radio Wales. He is the author of *Attlee: A Life in Politics* and *Nye: The Political Life of Aneurin Bevan*.

MARTIN WESTLAKE has published widely on the European institutions and on European and British politics, and is the author of *Kinnock: The Biography*. He is currently a visiting professor at the College of Europe (Bruges) and a senior visiting fellow at the European Institute of the London School of Economics.

PHIL WOOLAS was Labour MP for Oldham East & Saddleworth for thirteen years. He served as parliamentary private secretary to Lord Gus MacDonald, as Minister of State for Transport, as Lord Commissioner of the Treasury, as Deputy Leader of the House of Commons, as Minister of State for Local Government and Regeneration, as Minister of State for Civil Contingency, as Minister of State for the Environment, and as Minister of State for Immigration and Customs. He also served as a regional minister for the north-west of England. Prior to his time in Parliament, Phil served as a national official for the GMB trade union. His early career was in television, where he worked for ITV, *Newsnight* and *Channel 4 News*. He has published numerous articles and essays and is a fellow of the Royal Society of Arts. He is currently writing a biography of John Robert Clynes.

CHRIS WRIGLEY was a professor of modern British history at Nottingham University (1991–2012) and is now professor emeritus. He was a University of

East Anglia undergraduate 1965–68, president of the Historical Association 1996–99, chair of the Society for the Study of Labour History 1997–2001, and a vice-president of the Royal Historical Society 1997–2001. He was leader of the Labour Group on Leicestershire county council 1986–89, and a parliamentary candidate in 1983 and 1987. His books include biographies of Henderson, Lloyd George, Churchill and A. J. P. Taylor, as well as studies of Lloyd George and Labour, British trade unions and British industrial relations.

PART I

FRAMEWORKS FOR ASSESSING LEADERS

CHAPTER 1

INTRODUCTION: POLITICAL LEADERSHIP, BRITAIN AND THE LABOUR PARTY

TOBY S. JAMES

Political leaders matter. The decisions and actions they take can have decisive effects for the future of both their party and wider society. However, they often confront challenging contexts. This introductory chapter places the contemporary challenges facing Labour leaders in the long-term political context and outlines the different kinds of leadership they can strive for. It differentiates leadership by political cunning, which involves winning elections and maintaining power, and leadership by conscience, which involves achieving ethical goals. The complete leader should achieve both, while also upholding the principles of democracy.

• • •

Keir Starmer's victory in the 2024 general election was labelled by many pundits as 'historic'.[1] The party won 411 of 650 seats and the Conservatives, the governing party, were obliterated to only 121 MPs – losing over 200. It gave the party an unquestionable dominance in the Commons in terms of parliamentary arithmetic. Two-thirds of the famous green benches would be red Labour MPs who could vote through any legislation that they wished, provided they could remain united.

1 George Parker, Jim Pickard, Lucy Fisher and Rafe Uddin, 'Keir Starmer enters Downing Street as UK prime minister after historic victory,' *Financial Times*, last updated 5 July 2024, accessed 23 July 2025 (https://www.ft.com/content/9ddccaa8-4b63-4a7a-8192-c65b7318c16e).

And yet a closer look at the vote tallies shows a much more fragile situation for Starmer and Labour. The vote share for Labour was only 33.7 per cent – only up slightly on the 32.1 per cent in 2019. A total of 9.7 million people voted for Starmer, 3 million less than the 12.8 million who voted for Corbyn in 2017. The low amount of support for Labour is further hidden by the way the UK press reports voting statistics and the quirks of the electoral franchise. Votes from less than 10 million adults is a narrow support base to govern a country nearly 70 million strong in population.[2] Support for Labour had been in long-term decline – a problem facing many mainstream parties in democracies around the world – and this continued under Starmer (see Figure 1.1). The landslide victory in 2024 owed much to the rise of Reform UK, which split the Conservative vote, tactical voting at local level and the nature of the UK electoral system. The crop of seats won was the most disproportionate yield from votes on record.[3]

Major economic, social and geopolitical shifts are posing major challenges for the new Labour Prime Minister. Economic growth had been sluggish in the UK for decades and national debt was high following the Covid pandemic. Technology and AI have been much-heralded as a means to increase productivity. However, there are dangers that technology could lead to job losses just as much as it might create new jobs.[4] There are record low levels

---

2 The usual practice is to publish votes received as a proportion of all votes counted. This disguises the real sentiment in the country because it ignores those who do not cast a vote – and those who are not even registered, of which there were 7–8 million in 2023. See Electoral Commission, 'Accuracy and completeness of electoral registers', 2023, accessed 23 July 2025 (https://www.electoralcommission.org.uk/research-reports-and-data/electoral-registration-research/accuracy-and-completeness-electoral-registers). Calculating votes received as a proportion of the voting-age population therefore provides a better assessment of support. This measure is used in many other countries. See Michael P. McDonald and Samuel L. Popkin, 'The Myth of the Vanishing Voter', *American Political Science Review*, 95(4), 2001, pp. 963–74.

3 Marta Miori and Jane Green, 'The Most Disproportionate UK Election: How the Labour Party Doubled its Seat Share with a 1.6-Point Increase in Vote Share in 2024', *Political Quarterly*, 96(1), 2025, pp. 37–64.

4 Nick Srnicek and Alex Williams, *Inventing the Future: Postcapitalism and a World Without Work*, London, Verso, 2015; Institute for Public Policy Research, 'Up to 8 million UK jobs at risk from AI unless government acts, finds IPPR', last updated 27 March 2024, accessed 23 July 2025 (https://www.ippr.org/media-office/up-to-8-million-uk-jobs-at-risk-from-ai-unless-government-acts-finds-ippr).

of satisfaction in the NHS, with long waiting times for patients.[5] Schools and many local governments are under financial stress. Geopolitical upheaval is underway, with more aggressive international environments illustrated by Russia's invasion of Ukraine, Trump's declaration of trade wars and the global retreat of democracy.[6] This has made strategic alliances uncertain, led to inflationary hikes and made access to vital commodities and energy more difficult. Social media platforms have become a source of misinformation and interference in national politics, from owners such as Elon Musk (who used his platform to call the Prime Minister 'Two-Tier Keir')[7] and from foreign governments.[8] Meanwhile, global warming has become a reality, giving rise to demands for environmental action and posing new threats to UK infrastructure – but building on the green belt and farmland to improve sources of renewable energy has been met with opposition too.

Contemporary leaders may often feel like they have been dealt a more difficult hand than their predecessors. The immediacy of problems makes them feel worse. However, these are times of great uncertainty and disruption. Starmer's leadership matters enormously for the future of the Labour Party and for the people of the UK and beyond.

The central argument of this book is that leadership matters in all circumstances. It has mattered since the formation of the Labour Party – and

---

5 Danielle Jefferies, Dan Wellings, Jessica Morris, Mark Dayan and Cyril Lobont, 'Public satisfaction with the NHS and social care in 2023: Results of the British Social Attitudes Survey', King's Fund, last updated 27 March 2024, accessed 23 July 2025 (https://www.kingsfund.org.uk/insight-and-analysis/reports/public-satisfaction-nhs-social-care-2023).

6 Pierre Bocquillion, Suzanne Doyle, Toby S. James, Ra Mason, Soul Park and Matilde Rosina, 'The Effects of Wars: Lessons from the War in Ukraine', *Policy Studies*, 45(3–4), 2024, pp. 261–81.

7 Faye Brown, 'Elon Musk brands Starmer "two-tier Keir" and asks "is this Britain or Soviet Union?" over Facebook comment arrest video', Sky News, last updated 6 August 2024, accessed 23 July 2025 (https://news.sky.com/story/elon-musk-brands-starmer-two-tier-keir-and-asks-is-this-britain-or-soviet-union-over-facebook-comment-arrest-video-13191898).

8 Benjamin Little and Alison Winch, *The New Patriarchs of Digital Capitalism: Celebrity Tech Founders and Networks of Power*, London, Routledge, 2021; Sally Broughton Micova, 'Systemic Risk in Digital Services: Benchmarks for Evaluating the Management of Risks to Electoral Processes', Centre on Regulation in Europe (CERRE), last updated 24 May 2024, accessed 23 July 2025 (https://cerre.eu/publications/systemic-risk-in-digital-services-benchmarks-for-evaluating-the-management-of-risks-to-electoral-processes/).

will continue to do so long beyond Starmer's time as Prime Minister. To better understand leadership, it is important that we look backwards as well as forwards. We should identify the challenges faced by former leaders and how they overcame them or failed to. We should also be clear on some of the terminology and frameworks that we use to assess leaders. This chapter introduces the different types of leadership that those in positions of power can seek to achieve. It then introduces the remainder of the book, which will provide more detailed yardsticks to evaluate leadership and will assess each leader in turn, from the founding of the Labour Party to the modern day.

FIGURE 1.1: THE LABOUR PARTY'S VOTE SHARE (VOTES CAST FOR THE PARTY AS A PROPORTION OF REGISTERED ELECTORS), VOTING-AGE POPULATION SHARE (VOTES CAST FOR THE PARTY AS A PROPORTION OF ALL ELIGIBLE ELECTORS) AND SEAT SHARE IN THE HOUSE OF COMMONS AT GENERAL ELECTIONS 1900–2024.

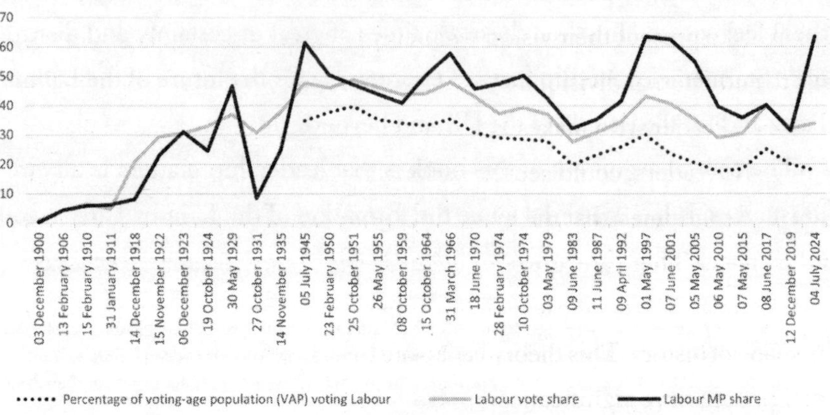

Source: Based on information in Colin Rallings and Michael Thrasher, *British Electoral Facts*, London, Routledge, 2006, pp. 3–58, 59, 61–2, 85–92; Richard Cracknell, Elise Uberoi and Matthew Burton, 'UK Election Statistics: 1918–2023: A century of elections', House of Commons Library, last updated 9 August 2023, accessed 23 July 2025 (https://commonslibrary.parliament.uk/research-briefings/cbp-7529/); BBC News, 'UK General election 2024 Results', 2024, accessed 30 January 2025 (https://www.bbc.co.uk/news/election/2024/uk/results). Voting-age population data taken from International IDEA Voter Turnout Database, 22 January 2025.

LEADERS MATTER

Party leaders are commonly the focal point for discussion about politics and policy in Britain, as they are in many countries. Elections, conference seasons, manifesto launches, TV debates, Prime Minister's Questions – in nearly every aspect of practical politics, the media zooms its lens on the leader. Among the public, 'Starmer', 'Johnson', 'Thatcher', 'Blair' and 'Farage' are easy proxies for discussing the credibility of the parties, when they often know less about policy detail. Behind closed doors, leaders play a vital role in shaping the policy platform of their party, agree votes on parliamentary bills, negotiate post-election coalitions and pacts with their opponents, deal with rogue backbenchers and represent their country in meetings with overseas leaders and international organisations.

Party leaders therefore matter. The fortunes of their party, their members and their country depend on them. A party leader without the communication skills to present their vision will never be taken seriously. A leader who fails to end internal divisions could leave their party out of power for a generation. A leader who makes key strategic errors, or blunders in meetings with world leaders, could see the national interest damaged.

It is often claimed that the history of the world is the history of great men and women.[9] There are 'great' individuals who are innovators and demonstrate courage or strategic leadership. They can have a decisive influence on the shape of history. This theory is implausible and elitist because the actions of all people have significance. It also overemphasises the transformative capacities that all leaders can have. Leaders face constraints. Not all are capable of delivering change, leading an ill-disciplined party to electoral victory or reversing the course of history by themselves. But even in the most challenging of circumstances, they can make a difference, if only in steadying a ship. Political leaders hold positions of significant power and responsibility.

9 Originally from Thomas Carlyle, *On Heroes, Hero-Worship & the Heroic in History*, London, Chapman and Hall, 1840.

To ignore how a skilled leader can reshape their time is to misunderstand history, politics and society in Britain.

WHO WAS BEST?

It therefore follows that assessing political leaders is an important task in any country. Citizens should do this in a democracy, to hold their elected representatives to account and to ensure that their voices are heard. Parties should do this carefully to make sure that their electoral prospects are maximised and they have a programme for improving the lives of people. These questions are ever-more important at a time when public disillusionment with politics and the political process has increased – and when the UK faces serious geopolitical, economic and other challenges.

But who have been the 'great' leaders? How can we make a claim that they are 'great' objectively and impartially? What can political parties and future leaders learn from past successes and mistakes? In this book, we address these questions by assessing British Labour Party leaders from the time that the party was founded to Keir Starmer. Who was the most successful Labour Party leader of all time? And who was the worst?

If we were to just count general election victories, Harold Wilson comes top with four wins. But does this tell the whole story? Clement Attlee frequently comes top of polls of the public, academics and even parliamentarians.[10] Tony Blair's record of three consecutive electoral victories must put him in good stead. And then there are also the many other forgotten leaders. Take, for example, George Lansbury, who was described by Jon Cruddas as the 'greatest ever Labour leader' and the 'unsung father of blue Labour'.[11]

---

10 See Royal Holloway Group PR3710, 'The Good, the Not so Good, and Liz Truss: MPs' Evaluations of Postwar Prime Ministers,' *Political Quarterly*, 95(2), 2024, pp. 315–23; Kevin Theakston and Mark Gill, 'The Postwar Premiership League', *Political Quarterly*, 82(1), 2011, p 67–80.

11 Jon Crudas, 'George Lansbury: the unsung hero of blue Labour,' Labour Uncut, last updated 5 August 2011, accessed 29 May 2015 (http://labour-uncut.co.uk/2011/05/08/george-lansbury-the-unsung-father-of-blue-labour/).

Moreover, many Labour figures have, on occasion, praised Tory leaders. Keir Starmer praised Margaret Thatcher for setting loose Britain's 'natural entrepreneurialism'.[12] So, are there characteristics of opposition leaders that the Labour Party leader should emulate?

Drawing conclusions is made harder because even those leaders we may think of as great have their critics. Winston Churchill described Attlee as 'a modest man with much to be modest about'.[13] Wilson was criticised for having 'neither political principle' nor a 'sense of direction' by Denis Healey.[14] Blair is considered a 'warmonger' for his decision to go to war in Iraq and a leader who too readily accepted free-market principles by many on the left. Beatrice Webb, a contemporary of Lansbury, described him as having 'no bloody brains to speak of'.[15]

THE TWO 'C'S OF LEADERSHIP: CONSCIENCE AND CUNNING

It is suggested here that there are two ways in which we can try to evaluate leaders. Much confusion comes about because spectators confuse the two approaches or are not explicit about the approach that they have in mind and the contradictions between them.[16]

The first approach is to evaluate political leaders in terms of whether they have aims, use methods and bring about outcomes that are principled and

12 Sam Francis and Hannah Miller, 'Keir Starmer defends praising Thatcher in pitch for Tories', BBC News, last updated 3 December 2023, accessed 23 July 2025 (https://www.bbc.co.uk/news/uk-politics-67604830).

13 Cited in Chris Wrigley, *Winston Churchill: A Biographical Companion*, Santa Barbara, CA, ABC-CLIO, 2002, p. 32.

14 Cited in Kevin Hickson, *The IMF Crisis of 1976 and British Politics*, London, Tauris Academic Studies, 2005, pp. 48–9.

15 See Chapter 10.

16 Toby S. James, 'Political Leadership as Statecraft? Aligning Theory with Praxis in Conversation with British Party Leaders', *British Journal of Politics and International Relations*, 20(3), 2018, pp. 555–72.

morally good, defined here as leadership driven by the leader's *conscience*.[17] This involves an ethical and normative judgement about whether the leader's imprint on the world has been positive. Leaders are 'better,' for example, if they strive to reduce poverty, increase economic growth or prevent human suffering; less so if they bring about needless war, cause economic decline or fail to improve the lives of the impoverished. A leader led by their conscience will resist opportunities to further their own private position, be it the allure of office, prestige or power, if it is at the detriment of the public good. Leadership led by moral conscience can be interchangeably termed *conscientious* leadership.

Evaluations of Labour leaders in terms of conscience are ever-present because of the history of the party. It grew out of the trade union movement and socialist political parties of the nineteenth century to represent the interests of the urban proletariat, some of whom had been newly enfranchised for the first time. The 1900 Labour Party manifesto therefore pledged maintenance for the aged poor, public provision of homes, work for the unemployed, graduated income taxes and more.[18] The party sought to, in Keir Hardie's later words, bring 'progress in this country … break down sex barriers and class barriers … [and] lead to the great women's movement as well as to the great working-class movement'.[19]

Evaluations of whether leaders aimed to achieve conscience-orientated goals are found in this volume. For example, Kenneth O. Morgan praises Keir Hardie for setting out policy platforms on unemployment, poverty, women's rights, racial equality and more. Phil Woolas praises John Robert Clynes for his 'selfless political ego' and commitment to improving the lives of millions

---

17 This discussion builds on the distinction made by Joesph Nye, *The Powers to Lead*, Oxford and New York, Oxford University Press, 2008, pp. 111–14.

18 The Labour Party, 'The Labour Party General Election Manifesto 1900: Manifesto of the Labour Representation Committee', in Iain Dale (ed.), *Labour Party General Election Manifestos, 1900–1997*, London, Routledge, 2000, p. 9.

19 Keir Hardie, 'The Sunshine of Socialism', speech delivered at the twenty-first anniversary of the formation of the Independent Labour Party in Bradford, 11 April 1914, last updated 11 April 2014, accessed 29 May 2015 (http://labourlist.org/2014/04/keir-hardies-sunshine-of-socialism-speech-full-text/).

of impoverished Britons. Brian Brivati heralds Hugh Gaitskell for not treating the Labour Party as 'a vote-maximising machine' and considers him to be 'the last great democratic socialist leader of the Labour Party'.

Many leaders have faced criticism for supposedly deviating from conscience-orientated goals. The Labour Party's history is full of accusations of 'betrayal' of the roots of the party – by the workers, unions or voters. These criticisms accumulated as the twentieth century progressed, when the party moved to the centre ground and leaders began to accept economic orthodoxy. During the Second World War, in contempt of the stock and strategy of British politicians on the left, George Orwell blasted that the 'Labour Party stood for a timid reformism … The Labour leaders wanted to go on and on, drawing their salaries and periodically swapping jobs with the Conservatives.'[20] Such evaluations are well documented in this book. David Howell describes how the decision of Ramsay MacDonald, as Labour Prime Minister, to accept unemployment benefits cuts led to him being demonised for careerism, class betrayal and treachery. Neil Kinnock, as he himself describes in Chapter 24, was roundly criticised for having 'electionitis'. For the Bennite left he was 'the great betrayer'.[21] Even Ed Miliband, who was criticised for being 'too left wing', as Tim Bale asserts, was denounced for severing the link between the unions and the Labour Party. Left Unity accused him of betraying the roots of the party.[22] Of course, conscience-orientated criticism has also come from the right. The pursuit of socialist goals might stifle economic opportunity, insist liberals, conservatives and even some social democrats.

A second approach involves assessing leadership in terms of political *cunning*, which requires us to appraise leaders in terms of whether they have

20 George Orwell, *The Lion and the Unicorn: Socialism and the English Genius: Part 3, The English Revolution*, London, Secker & Warburg, 1941.

21 Francis Beckett, 'Neil Kinnock: the man who saved Labour', *New Statesman*, last updated 25 September 2014, accessed 23 July 2025 (https://www.newstatesman.com/long-reads/2014/09/neil-kinnock-man-who-saved-labour).

22 Bianca Todd, 'Labour has betrayed its roots by distancing itself from the unions', *The Guardian*, last updated 3 March 2014, accessed 29 May 2015 (http://www.theguardian.com/commentisfree/2014/mar/03/labour-party-unions-left-unity-ed-miliband).

been successful in winning power, office and influence. This forces us to introduce a degree of political realism into our evaluations. Leaders operate in a tough, cut-throat environment, where the costs of electoral defeat are usually their job and their party's prospects of power. To survive, a leader's goals can never be solely altruistic. They need to win elections and bolster their own position within their party and government if they are to realise the grander aims that they may have first set out into the field of politics to achieve. In trying to achieve policy objectives, they are operating in an environment that can be hugely challenging. Some policy goals might have to be dropped as part of horse-trading within Parliament so that other legislation can be passed. 'Accommodating' the electorate by dropping policies which are an 'electoral liability' might not be heroic in the sense of conscientious leadership but can be astute leadership in the cunning sense.

There exists a tension between conscience and cunning when we consider the *means* that leaders use to achieve their goals. Those concerned with conscientious leadership might not want leaders to be underhand, break promises to the electorate or be disloyal to their parliamentary party or (shadow) Cabinet. But those concerned with cunning leadership might, at least on occasion, recognise that these are necessary means to other ends if they are to secure their long-term goals. Those concerned with conscientious leadership might warn us that 'whoever fights monsters should see to it that in the process he does not become a monster'.[23]

Lastly, there is also a tension between conscience and cunning in terms of the *consequences* of political leaders' terms in office. Whose interests should leaders pursue? Those concerned with conscience leadership would demand that leaders should further the interests of the whole polity. They should not put any private interest, such as those of the individual, Cabinet or party, above those of the country. Those concerned with cunning leadership, however, would champion the importance of furthering the interests of a particular group or section of society. The Labour Party, we should remember, like

23 Friedrich Nietzsche, *Beyond Good and Evil*, New York, Random House, 1966[1886], sec. 146.

similar parties that were forged from the flames of industrialisation across western Europe and much of the rest of world, did not form to promote the general welfare of a nation. It began as a trade union movement, promoting the welfare and interests of its own members. These were members of a particular class, based predominantly in manufacturing industries: invariably, those who were exposed to the harshest living and working conditions and, in many cases, to absolute poverty. They defined their aims and interests in open opposition to those of employers and landowners. The policies they promoted may have benefited the national interest, but that was not how labour politics was framed.[24] Further, leaders might be successful in maintaining their own position of power – this too would be cunning leadership.

CONSCIENTIOUS VERSUS CUNNING LEADERSHIP

Which is more important? Conscientious or cunning leadership? Our instincts are perhaps that conscientious leadership is more important. A perception that leaders endlessly pursue the interests of their party above those of the country has arguably contributed towards public distrust of politicians, political leaders and politics. Yet the reality of politics is that it does involve compromise and strategy. Evaluating leaders in terms of conscientious leadership alone is therefore obviously problematic.

The case for evaluating leaders in terms of cunning leadership is three-fold. Firstly, such evaluations are easier to conduct in objective terms. Discussions about what constitutes conscientious leadership are inevitably normative. After all, is the conscientious economic policy one that limits environmental degradation or promotes economic growth to alleviate poverty? Is it one that promotes state provision of health care or private enterprise? Each of

24 Over time, of course, the party evolved to develop a broader appeal as class cleavages were perceived to have declined. Ed Miliband rebranded the party as 'One Nation Labour' in 2012. See Roy Hattersley and Kevin Hickson, *The Socialist Way: Social Democracy in Contemporary Britain*, London, I.B. Tauris, 2013, p. 213.

these requires difficult judgements that should be considered in detail elsewhere. They require the tools of the economist, the philosopher and more.

Secondly, nothing can be achieved without power and office. The Labour Party took twenty-four years to be in government after it was founded. It was out of office for eighteen years after James Callaghan was defeated in 1979. And it was out for another fourteen years after Gordon Brown lost the election in 2010. During these times of political wilderness, leaders are typically incapable of bringing about progressive social change because of the 'winner-takes-all' nature of British government. It is therefore necessary for political parties who are trying to choose their leaders and decide upon a future political strategy to think about leadership in terms of political cunning.

Thirdly, there are also advantages for the citizen in evaluating leaders in this way. If *all* parties are sufficiently politically competent, democratic politics should be a more competitive process, giving the voter better choice. As Neil Kinnock remarks in Chapter 24, leaders of the opposition play a vital role in servicing democracy by providing an alternative government.

Moreover, if civil society better understands the challenges leaders face, why they were (un)successful in winning office and how any imperfections and injustices in democratic politics bring about this outcome, it will be better positioned to prescribe democratic change and support more conscientious leaders. Civil society is not always equipped with knowledge about the inner workings of government in the way that elite politicians and parties are. Evaluating leaders in cunning terms can therefore encourage us to think about the health of democratic politics and redress shortcomings. Of the poor leader who still won elections, we think how did they get away with it? Of the good leader who overcame numerous challenges, we think how did they manage that?

THE THIRD 'C' OF LEADERSHIP: COMPLETE LEADERSHIP

Conscientious and cunning leadership are, of course, not mutually exclusive. Theoretically, leaders can achieve their goals of conscience with political cunning. This, however, is no small feat. To manage a political party, develop policies, pass legislation, outmanoeuvre the opposition and form electoral coalitions when necessary without compromising their goals of conscience, using unscrupulous methods or putting their personal or party interest above the interest of the nation might be infeasible. But theoretically it is possible, and we can think of leaders who achieve this as being *complete* leaders (Figure 1.2).

FIGURE 1.2: THE OVERLAP BETWEEN CONSCIENTIOUS AND CUNNING LEADERSHIP.

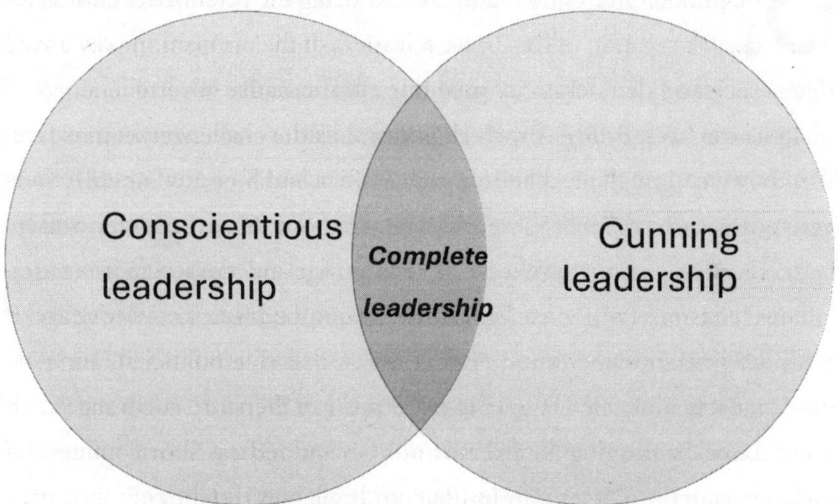

Since the Labour Party was founded, leaders have been under increased pressure to achieve both conscientious and cunning leadership. In 1900, the franchise was limited to men with wealth and levels of education were comparatively low. A winning electoral strategy could therefore be wilfully neglectful of much of the country. Today, all citizens can vote, and the free press allows ideas to be exchanged and debated. In a democracy, being a conscience-focused leader should therefore deliver you electoral dividends. As Charles Clarke argues in Chapter 3, a general election is in many ways a fair test of the leader.

But there are flaws in British democracy. The media is often thought to have undue influence, electoral laws can give advantage to certain political parties, corporate power gives uneven political influence, citizens have limited knowledge of and interest in politics and policy, and incumbency gives a government the opportunity to use the state for political purposes. An unscrupulous leader might win office because of these injustices.

POLITICAL LEADERSHIP AND DEMOCRACY

One prominent trend around the world, which has become clear since the first edition of this book was published, has been the decline of democracy and democratic norms. It is often said that we live in an era of 'democratic backsliding', in which political leaders have sought to extend their powers through mechanisms such as promissory coups (where leaders grab power through force to 'defend democracy'), executive aggrandisement (where leaders weaken the checks on their power) and the strategic manipulation of elections (where leaders change electoral rules to their advantage).[25] This is a phenomenon found even in the so-called 'established democracies' – most notably the United States.[26] President Donald Trump started his second term by purging the federal bureaucracy, defying federal judges and continuing to push voter reforms that erode electoral integrity.[27]

---

25 Nancy Bermeo, 'On Democratic Backsliding', *Journal of Democracy*, 27(1), 2016, pp. 5–19.

26 Steven Levitsky and Daniel Ziblatt, *How Democracies Die*, New York, Penguin, 2018.

27 Steven Levitsky, 'The New Authoritarianism', *The Atlantic*, last updated 10 February 2025, accessed 23 July 2025 (https://www.theatlantic.com/ideas/archive/2025/02/trump-competitive-authoritarian/681609/); Roberto Stefan Foa and Yascha Mounk, 'America after Trump: From "Clean" to "Dirty" Democracy?', *Policy Studies*, 42(5–6), 2021, pp. 455–72; Steven Levitsky, 'Right Now, the U.S. Is Ceasing to Be a Democracy', *Der Spiegel*, last updated 24 March 2025, accessed 23 July 2025 (https://www.spiegel.de/international/world/harvard-professor-steven-levitsky-right-now-the-u-s-is-ceasing-to-be-a-democracy-a-d6595df5-68a5-4b74-ab09-1dbf5179ddbd).

The UK has not been immune to democratic backsliding.[28] The Johnson government strengthened its power over the judiciary by reducing the scope of judicial review in the Judicial Review and Courts Act 2022. The Elections Act 2022 made photographic voter identification compulsory for local elections. Significant concerns were raised by parliamentarians, academics and campaigners that this was a disproportionate measure which would prevent many people from voting. The Police, Crime, Sentencing and Courts Act 2022 widened the power of the police to stop protests that involved 'significant impact on people or cause serious disruption to the activities of organisations in the vicinity'. Concerns were raised that this effectively reduced the right to protest.

The possibility of democratic backsliding brings the tension between cunning leadership and leadership by conscience to the fore. Cunning leadership may be praised on its own terms for being politically astute – but only within the boundaries of democratic politics. No leadership that breaks the conventions, norms and guardrails of democracy can be praised. These include but are not limited to:[29]

- freedom of speech and conditions for deliberation and discussion across society
- free and fair elections in which voter participation is encouraged
- mutual toleration and respect of the political opposition
- rule of law
- professional, neutral public administration

---

28 Toby S. James, *UK Democracy Under Strain: Democratic Backsliding and Strengthening 2019–2023*, London, Unlock Democracy, 2023.

29 Toby S. James, 'Real Democracy: A Critical Realist Approach to Democracy and Democratic Theory', *New Political Science*, 46(3), 2024, pp. 228–58.

- constitutional protections for citizens
- the absence of racism, patriarchy, homophobia, transphobia or discriminatory discourses against specific religious groups
- basic education, health and standard of living

These have not always been present during the period this volume covers – and cannot be taken for granted in future. This line must be drawn. Those who cross it are committing undemocratic leadership – regardless of the general election result that gave them a mandate to be in office.

THE BOOK AHEAD

Having now introduced the puzzle, in the next chapter of this book, Jim Buller and I introduce a framework for evaluating leaders. This suggests that we should assess leaders by whether they achieve statecraft – the art of winning elections and achieving a semblance of governing competence in office. Not all Labour leaders were prime ministers; some did not stay in power long enough to fight a general election and for others, winning office was never likely. But we can still assess them in terms of whether they moved their party in this direction. The statecraft approach also defines the key things leaders need to achieve in order to win elections. This is helpful because it allows us to consider where they might have gone wrong. The approach focuses firmly on cunning leadership.

After the statecraft framework is outlined in Chapter 2, Charles Clarke then evaluates the success (or otherwise) of Labour Party leaders at general elections in Chapter 3. Using data on the seats and votes that they have won or lost, he compiles league tables to identify those who have been successful and those who have not. This gives us an important overview of the electoral fortunes of Labour leaders since the party was founded. Chapter 4 considers the policy impact that political leaders have had. It therefore extends the analysis beyond cunning leadership to also consider conscientious leadership.

Subsequent chapters then provide individual assessments of each of the Labour leaders. The authors of each chapter are all leading biographers of their subject. Biographers were deliberately invited to contribute towards the volume, as they can paint a picture of the context of the times and the political circumstances of each Labour leader. The biographers were not asked to directly apply the statecraft approach but to describe the leader's background, their path towards the position of leader, the challenges they faced and how successful they were in electoral and statecraft terms. Many assessments go beyond examining the political cunning of their leadership and also include judgements in conscience terms. They therefore collectively provide a rich set of evaluations from leading scholars and commentators.

Table 1.1 provides a summary of the authors' (and not necessarily the editors') assessments in statecraft terms. Many of the early leaders were deemed to be a success. Keir Hardie is praised for being a pragmatic strategist who concentrated political efforts on increasing Labour representation in Parliament, which laid the road to power. John Robert Clynes was at the helm for the great breakthrough in 1922 and Ramsay MacDonald became the first Labour Prime Minister. Of the modern leaders, Thomas Hennessey argues that Harold Wilson has an almost unrivalled electoral record. Tony Blair, asserts John Rentoul, had an intuitive feel for public opinion, natural communication skills and devised a successful winning electoral strategy. Keir Starmer, according to Patrick Diamond, was undeniably successful in winning office for his party but, at the time of writing, Diamond expresses uncertainty about whether this success will follow in office.

Gaitskell, Callaghan, Michael Foot, Brown, Miliband and Corbyn, the chapter authors generally accept, were failures in statecraft terms. Claims for success, if there are any, instead lie largely in conscience terms (in the case of Gaitskell and Foot) or their contribution before they were leader (in the case of Callaghan and Brown). Brown received widespread praise for his management of the financial crisis but was unsuccessful at the ballot box in

2010. Jeremy Corbyn, meanwhile, could claim to have substantially grown the party membership and Labour vote share in 2017 but was ultimately unable to win office after two attempts.

Clement Attlee is perhaps a surprise inclusion in those leaders who are given a more mixed assessment. Nicklaus Thomas-Symonds provides a robust argument in favour of Attlee in conscience terms – it was under Attlee that the modern welfare state and the National Health Service were created – but he failed to provide leadership on issues such as the devaluation crisis of 1949 and had a naive approach to electoral boundaries. This undermined his statecraft.

TABLE 1.1: LABOUR LEADERS: STATECRAFT SUCCESSES AND FAILURES 1900–2025.

Great	Mixed	Poor
Keir Hardie	George Nicoll Barnes	Hugh Gaitskell
John Robert Clynes	William Adamson	James Callaghan
Ramsay MacDonald	Arthur Henderson	Michael Foot
Harold Wilson	George Lansbury	Gordon Brown
Tony Blair	Clement Attlee	Ed Miliband
Keir Starmer	Neil Kinnock	Jeremy Corbyn
	John Smith	

In the final part of the book, we take an original approach by asking leaders for their own perspectives on leading the Labour Party. There are two exclusive original interviews with Neil Kinnock, who led the Labour Party from 1983 to 1992 and Tony Blair, leader from 1994 to 2007. In the interviews we ask them about their path towards the office of leader, the challenges that they faced, whether they think the statecraft framework is a 'fair' test of a leader and how they would rate themselves using the model. These interviews are of important historical value for those wanting to understand past leaders' tenures. They also provide lessons for future leaders. Moreover, they allow politicians to join in conversation with academics, whose ideas might otherwise be developed and left in 'ivory towers'. This type of conversation can only improve our understanding of the quality of leadership and leaders' understanding of the scholarship on it.

One of the major issues facing the leadership of the party has been Brexit. Victoria Honeyman considers how recent leaders have confronted the challenge posed by EU membership and Brexit, warning that this particular challenge is unlikely to recede.

CHAPTER 2

STATECRAFT: A FRAMEWORK FOR ASSESSING LABOUR PARTY LEADERS

TOBY S. JAMES AND JIM BULLER

Assessing party leaders is not an easy task. In this chapter, Toby S. James and Jim Buller discuss the challenges we face in trying to do so and suggest a framework that can be used to assess leadership. Leaders can be assessed in terms of whether they achieve statecraft – the art of winning elections and demonstrating a semblance of governing competence to the electorate. To achieve statecraft, however, leaders need to achieve five core tasks. They need to devise a winning electoral strategy, establish a reputation for governing competence, ensure effective party management, win the battle of ideas over key policy issues and manage the constitution so their electoral prospects are intact. This chapter outlines what these tasks involve and considers some of the contextual factors that might make them more or less difficult to achieve.

• • •

We live in an age where objective agreement seems increasingly difficult. The public is often said to be more divided and polarised on political issues. Disagreements between 'Remainers' and 'Leavers' have become enduring political divisions, which continue to shape viewpoints years after the EU referendum.[30] 'Culture wars' are said to be underway on issues such as abortion, LBGTQ+ rights, 'cancel culture' and post-colonialism. The advent of social media has contributed towards an age of 'post-truth', where disinformation and misinformation can spread quickly, science is rejected and the guarantors of information quality are undermined.[31]

The assessment of political leaders is an important exercise, as Chapter 1 set out. It is vitally important that, as citizens, we evaluate the performance of those in power, especially during an age of so-called democratic backsliding. Parties need effective leaders to keep them competitive in electoral politics and capable of bringing change for society.

Assessing political leaders, however, is not easy, given the divisions in contemporary political debate. There are at least three problems that must be faced. Firstly, we should reflect on whether this is just a subjective process in which we will all have our own favourite. Can even the most detached observer really claim to make objective, scientific judgements about who was 'best'? Or will our own political views and values prevent us making a fair assessment? For example, could a left-leaning observer ever recognise Margaret Thatcher's leadership qualities or a right-leaning one acknowledge the achievements of Clement Attlee? The benchmarks for success and failure need to be made clear. Unless we nail down some firm criteria, ideological disagreement will always get in the way.

Secondly, who is the Labour leader in question anyway? During the early years of the Labour Party, there was no formal position of leader and leadership came more from the chairman. So, who should be the focus of our analysis? And there is a bigger problem. Assessing the party leader implies that the focus should be on assessing one single person. Leadership is often, however, a task discharged by more than one individual. A single person will not have the time and resources to manage a party alone and they will always

30 James Tilley and Sara Hobolt, 'Brexit as an Identity: Political Identities and Policy Norms', *PS: Political Science & Politics*, 54(4), 2023, pp. 546–52.

31 Matthew d'Ancona, *Post-Truth: The New War on Truth and How to Fight Back*, London, Ebury Press, 2017.

therefore rely on key advisors and allies. This is not to suggest that a party leader will make decisions entirely collegially with their (shadow) Cabinet, but there is a case for evaluating the leadership of a small group of two or three individuals, who act in a united way, rather than just one person.

Thirdly, aren't a leader's fortunes influenced by whether they have to govern in difficult or favourable times? Clement Attlee's 1945 landslide general election victory has ranked, for many at least, as one of the greatest moments for the party. The result came as a great shock because of Winston Churchill's heroic status, but Attlee led the party to a 145-seat majority and the greatest Labour vote ever recorded at that moment in time. James Chuter Ede, who later became Attlee's Home Secretary, said that he 'began to wonder if I should wake up to find it all a dream' when he heard the results coming in over the radio.[32] The King, when asking Attlee to form a government, was struck that Attlee himself was 'very surprised that his Party had won'.[33] Meanwhile, the *Daily Herald* and *Daily Worker* proclaimed the result as the 'People's Victory' that would 'stand out for all time as a great act of leadership in the building of the peace'.[34] Subsequent historians considered the election as 'one of the most important turning points in modern British political history, comparable with the events of 1832 and 1906'.[35]

However, a different analysis of Attlee's 1945 victory may cause us to reassess him. Many historians have argued that 1945 was a moment at which the popular mood had changed. Ralph Miliband argued that the war 'caused the emergence of a new popular radicalism, more widespread than at any time in the previous hundred years', which was 'eager for major, even fundamental

32 Gary McCulloch, 'Labour, the Left, and the British General Election of 1945', *Journal of British Studies*, Vol. 24, 1985, pp. 465–89.

33 Henry Pelling, 'The 1945 General Election Reconsidered', *Historical Journal*, 23(2), 1980, pp. 399–414, p. 399.

34 Steven Fielding, 'What did "the people" want?: The meaning of the 1945 general election', *Historical Journal*, 35(3), 1992, pp. 623–39, p. 624.

35 Fielding, op. cit., 1992, p. 623.

change in British society after the war'.[36] The public found itself decisively pro-Soviet because of the wartime media coverage.[37] The Labour Party, argued historian Henry Pelling, benefited from securing credit for the Beveridge Report, but this was somewhat accidental.[38] Meanwhile, the Conservative Party was perceived to be tired and disorganised, with Churchill making many presentational mistakes.[39] The historian Robert Pearce has gone so far as to suggest that victory therefore 'owed little to Attlee'.[40]

Labour leaders who were 'unsuccessful' often faced difficult challenges. Brown was defeated at the ballot box, but he inherited an unpopular party after it had been in power for ten years. He also took power only months before the global financial crisis of 2007–8 hit Britain, considered by many economists to have been the worst since at least the Great Depression.[41] The economy was sent into recession, and Brown, who had worked to establish a reputation as the 'Iron Chancellor', was faced with very difficult waters from which to rescue the party's reputation for economic management.[42] Michael Foot is commonly derided by contemporaries for his strategy in the 1983 general election. His manifesto was described as 'the longest suicide note in history' by Labour MP Gerald Kaufman. But could any Labour leader have defeated Thatcher in 1983 off the back of victory in the Falklands War and an upswing in the economy? Factoring in such circumstances is clearly important when we make judgements about Labour leaders. Jeremy Corbyn,

---

36 Ralph Miliband, *Parliamentary Socialism: A Study in the Politics of Labour*, London, Merlin Press, 1972.

37 Pelling, op. cit., 1980, p. 412.

38 Pelling, op. cit., 1980, pp. 411–12.

39 Stephen Brooke, 'The Labour Party and the 1945 general election', *Contemporary Record*, Vol. 9, 1995, pp. 1–21; Michael David Kandiah, 'The Conservative Party and the 1945 general election', *Contemporary Record*, Vol. 9, 1995, pp. 22–47.

40 Robert Pearce, 'Clement Attlee', in Kevin Jefferys ed., *Leading Labour: From Keir Hardie to Tony Blair*, London, I.B. Tauris, 1999, p. 88.

41 Paul Krugman, *End This Depression Now!*, New York, W. W. Norton & Company, 2012.

42 Jim Buller and Toby S. James, 'Integrating Structural Context into the Assessment of Political Leadership: Realism, Gordon Brown and the Great Financial Crisis', *Parliamentary Affairs*, 68(1), 2015, pp. 77–96.

meanwhile, faced a hostile press from the start. He was portrayed as 'Mr Corbean' and a 'Court Jezter' who was 'red and buried' and represented the 'looney left'. One evaluation concluded that he 'was represented unfairly by the British press through a process of vilification that went well beyond the normal limits of fair debate and disagreement in a democracy'.[43] Winning an election would therefore always be difficult, and there is a case to be made that he faced an unfair playing field.

A STATECRAFT APPROACH

To provide answers to these questions, a clear framework is necessary. One way of providing an assessment is to evaluate Labour leaders on whether or not they were successful at achieving *statecraft*, which is the art of winning elections and maintaining power.[44]

No doubt, many leaders will want to achieve more than this. They may be concerned about their legacy and how they will be viewed by future generations or be driven by a desire to implement policies that they think will improve the good of their party and the people. However, none of this is possible without achieving office first. Without office, they may not remain as party leader long because of the cut-throat nature of politics. General election defeats inevitably come with leadership challenges and expectations of resignation.

So, how can we assess Labour leaders' successes in winning office? The simplest approach would be to count the number of elections that they fought, the number they won and the number they lost (see Chapter 3). This is an

---

43 Nick Couldry and Bart Cammaerts, 'Journalistic Representations of Jeremy Corbyn in the British Press: From Watchdog to Attack dog', Media@LSE report, July 2016.

44 The approach was first developed by Jim Bulpitt in his paper, 'The Discipline of the New Democracy: Mrs Thatcher's Domestic Statecraft', *Political Studies*, 34(1), 1986, pp. 19–39. We adapted the approach for the purposes of assessing political leadership in Jim Buller and Toby S. James, 'Statecraft and the Assessment of National Political Leaders: The Case of New Labour and Tony Blair', *British Journal of Politics & International Relations*, 14(4), 2012, pp. 534–55. See the bibliography for further reading on statecraft theory.

important step but only takes us so far. A more detailed approach is to look at what political leaders need to achieve in order to accomplish this goal and then evaluate them by each of these things. The statecraft approach argues that leaders need to achieve five tasks, and each of these is outlined in the next section.

Yet as has already been alluded to, some leaders are gifted more fortunate circumstances than others when trying to win elections for their party. We have argued elsewhere that the context in which leaders find themselves must be factored into our assessments of them. This is not an easy task either, however. Can we realistically say, for example, that Clynes's circumstances were twice as easy as, say, Lansbury's? Or Corbyn's twice as hard as Attlee's? Given that leaders operate in different historical moments, which are *qualitatively* different in kind, quantitative measurement is difficult. The circumstances that leaders face are also different for each individual. A Labour leader who had already been Chancellor, like Brown, will always have a very different experience of trying to establish governing competence on the economy to one who has not held such a position.[45] Nonetheless, to aid discussion, Table 2.1 lists some of the contextual factors that might come into play. These will be unpacked under each statecraft task considered next.

TABLE 2.1: CONTEXTUAL FACTORS TO BE CONSIDERED WHEN ASSESSING LEADERS.

Statecraft task	Contextual factors
Winning electoral strategy	• party resources and campaign infrastructure • unfavourable electoral laws (constituencies, electoral administration, electoral system, party finances) • partisan alignment of the press • ability to call election when polls are favourable
Governing competence	• party reputation • conditions for successful economic growth • foreign policy disputes • time in office

45 For an extended discussion, see Buller and James, op. cit., 2012, pp. 534–55; Buller and James, op. cit., 2015.

Statecraft task	Contextual factors
Party management	• presence of credible rival leaders • rules for dethroning • levels of party unity • available mechanisms for party discipline • time in office
Political argument hegemony	• ideological developments at the international level • alignment of the press and digital platforms • available policy ideas • developments in the party system • time in office
Constitutional management	• presence of policy triggers or favourable conditions to enact (or prevent) change

Winning electoral strategy

Firstly, leaders need to develop a winning electoral strategy by crafting an image and policy package that will help the party achieve crucial impetus in the lead-up to the polls. Opinion polls, and to some extent local and European election results, give a very good indication of how a party is faring in the development of a winning strategy and allow a party leader's fortunes to charted over time, although this information is not as readily available for the earlier Labour leaders, when polling was more infrequent or did not take place at all.

In developing a winning strategy, the leader will need to pay close attention to the interests of key segments of the population, whose votes might be important in gaining a majority. Leaders may need to respond to transformations in the electoral franchise, demography or the class structure of society and build new constituencies of support when necessary. These changes can often be advantageous to the leader. The extensions of the franchise in the Representation of the People Act 1918, for example, tripled the electorate to include more working-class voters. This had the potential to turn electoral politics upside down in Labour's favour.

It is not just a matter of getting more votes than the opposition, however, because the distribution of votes is just as important. Labour's high-water mark of votes came under Attlee in the 1951 general election, but the party ironically lost power to the Conservatives in that election, who had recorded fewer votes. The February 1974 general election saw Harold Wilson win fewer votes than his opponent, Edward Heath, but more seats. The 2024 general election was a huge electoral success for Labour, partly due to tactical voting and a divided right. A winning electoral strategy therefore takes this into consideration.

This point highlights how electoral laws can make it easier or more difficult for leaders to win power. While Attlee may have felt cheated in 1951, the first-past-the-post electoral system is usually an advantage for the Labour Party in the post-war period. It has reduced the chances of new parties entering the political system and has given them and the Conservatives a disproportionately high share of seats in the House of Commons for their share of the popular vote, as Figure 1.1, in the previous chapter, illustrates. The way in which the constituency boundaries are drawn have given a systematic advantage to Labour over the Conservatives at times.

The laws on party funding and electoral administration will also directly affect a leader's chances of winning an election. Having money to spend does not guarantee success, but it helps. To some extent, leaders can build electoral resources by developing electoral momentum and credibility and courting appropriate prospective funders. However, party resources and electoral war chests will also depend on other factors such as the historic relationships between the party and business and the party and the unions. Electoral administration can matter too. The procedures used to compile the electoral register and voter identification laws can affect some parties more than others.[46]

During the life of the Labour Party, the media has become increasingly important, with the rising distribution of newspapers, radio and TV – and then social media. The media, however, is rarely neutral. Although broadcast television has remained relatively neutral in Britain, newspapers are typically

46 Toby S. James, 'Electoral Administration and Voter Turnout: Towards an International Public Policy Continuum', *Representation*, 45(4), 2010, pp. 369–89; Edward Fieldhouse, Ralph Scott, Christopher Prosser, Jack Bailey and Jonathan Mellon, 'Who lacks voter identification? The electoral implications of the Elections Act 2022', *Parliamentary Affairs*, December 2024.

openly hostile towards leaders. Some broadcasters will be particularly influential, and this will benefit some leaders and disadvantage others.[47] The impact of social media algorithms on political attitudes and voting behaviour is still being explored – but could be a source of advantage for some leaders.[48] In addition, the longer a government is in office, the harder it might be to achieve a winning electoral strategy. Criticisms may accumulate, and governments that appeal to the electorate on platforms of 'renewal' or 'modernisation', for example, may see the efficacy of this appeal wane over time.

The rules and traditions of an election campaign can advantage or disadvantage statecraft strategies. TV debates are known to affect electoral outcomes, so if a TV debate takes place, candidates with better communication skills will be favoured. The contexts in which leaders try to communicate can be critical in determining how effective they have been.

When the incumbent leader can decide the time of an election due to the absence of fixed parliamentary terms, they may have some advantage. Leaders do not always get this right, though. Harold Wilson's Labour Party overtook the Conservative opposition in the opinion polls for the first time in three years in May 1970 and called a snap election. Support for Labour quickly collapsed again and the Conservatives won the election.[49] The act of timing an election has therefore been called 'the most important single decision taken by a British Prime Minister'.[50]

Governing competence

Secondly, a leader must cultivate a reputation for governing competence, especially in the area of economic policy. Many have argued that leaders can be 'too far to the left' or 'too far to the right' and that this might adversely

---

47 John Street, *Mass Media, Politics and Democracy*, London, Bloomsbury, 2021.

48 Andrew M. Guess et al., 'How do social media feed algorithms affect attitudes and behaviour in an election campaign?', *Science*, 381(6656), 2023, pp. 398–404.

49 Alistair Smith, 'Election Timing in Majoritarian Parliaments', *British Journal of Political Science*, 33(3), 2003, pp. 397–418, p. 399.

50 Kenneth Newton, 'Caring and Competence: The Long, Long Campaign', in Anthony King ed., *Britain at the Polls 1992*, Chatham, NJ: Chatham House, 1993.

affect their chances of being re-elected. Many psephologists think, however, that what matters more is whether a leader is perceived to be competent on a problem that the public consider to be pressing.[51] The problem that is usually most pressing is, in the words of Bill Clinton's campaign strategist, 'the economy, stupid'. Or, as Harold Wilson suggested: 'All political history shows that the standing of the government and its ability to hold the confidence of the electorate at the general election depends on the success of its economic policy.'[52] Being seen to be the party that will bring jobs, prosperity and economic growth is a vote-winner. On issues like the economy, there is less disagreement that this is what voters want. The paramount question for them is which leader and which party will deliver them.

Understood in this way, the fortunes of many leaders may be the result of their ability to generate a perception of being competent in managing the economy. It is perception, rather than reality, that is important. John Major was initially successful in statecraft terms, insofar as he won the 1992 general election even though the economy had suffered from the greatest recession since the 1930s. Yet, paradoxically, Major lost in 1997 when economic growth was strong and unemployment and inflation were falling. The Conservatives' long-term lead over the Labour Party on economic management was lost following 'Black Wednesday' on 16 September 1992, when sterling suffered a serious crisis, interest rates soared and Britain exited the European Exchange Rate Mechanism (ERM). An economic recovery followed, but there was no similar recovery of confidence among the electorate in the Conservatives' ability to manage the economy.[53]

A leader's ability to achieve governing competence is hindered or helped by numerous factors. Political leaders take office with a number of historical

---

51 Harold D. Clarke, David Sanders, Marianne C. Stewart and Paul Whiteley, *Political Choice in Britain*, Oxford and New York, Oxford University Press, 2004); Harold D. Clarke, David Sanders, Marianne C. Stewart and Paul Whiteley, *Performance Politics and the British Voter*, Cambridge, Cambridge University Press, 2009.

52 Neil T. Gavin and David Sanders, 'The economy and voting', *Parliamentary Affairs*, 50(4), 1997, pp. 631–40.

53 Ibid.

legacies. Their parties might be associated with being 'strong' or 'weak' on the economy. Once in office, the ability of a leader to develop a reputation for competence is strongly influenced by the state of the economy. They may inherit an economy with a balance-of-payments deficit, sluggish growth and a high public deficit. Responsibility for slow growth can sometimes be shifted to predecessors or other factors; however, this might not be a successful long-term strategy. Sometimes politically difficult decisions are required, such as making budget cuts or raising taxes to invest in new industries and infrastructure to establish new growth.

In the domain of foreign policy, some leaders may inherit pressing international crises such as an ongoing war or a diplomatic conflict with a potential aggressor. The international political system is also increasingly interlinked, with the divide between 'domestic' and 'foreign' policy disappearing, especially for members of the EU. This integration of the internal and external realms may, in itself, present opportunities and constraints. There may be times when political leaders utilise international institutions to help them manage or solve national problems – or use them as scapegoats for their own mistakes.

Party management

Thirdly, leaders need to successfully manage their party. Party leaders do not always fall from office at election time. Margaret Thatcher was ejected by members of her own Cabinet. Leaders therefore have to ensure that members of the (shadow) Cabinet, parliamentary party, party management and grassroots are content enough with their performance to allow them to continue. This does not mean the relationship between leaders and their party need always be harmonious. Leaders might deliberately cultivate an antagonistic relationship with any of these elements in order to prove to the wider public that they are different. They will, however, need to fend off any potential leadership challenges and ensure sufficient coalescence so as not to threaten their credibility for being able to deliver legislation and appear competent in office.

Party management will also be more difficult for some leaders than others.

Some leaders will face credible rivals equipped with the political skill and courage to challenge them, and some will not. In some circumstances, the rules for dethroning a leader will make a challenge from a rival relatively cost-free and easy; in others, less so. It is in no party's interest to undertake a long and protracted internal leadership battle because this may affect the party's electoral interests. A failed attempt to oust a leader can also have negative consequences for the careers of the instigators. If a rival needs a significant amount of the parliamentary party to trigger a contest, many will be deterred.[54] In recent times, Conservative MPs were able to oust Theresa May, Boris Johnson and Liz Truss, as well as Iain Duncan Smith previously. By contrast, Labour MPs failed to remove Jeremy Corbyn on a number of occasions.

Party dissent can undermine the authority of a leader and lead to such leadership challenges. The ability to resolve this dissent can be influenced by the sanctions available to the leader to discipline errant party members, the degree to which there is greater homogeneity of preferences within the party, whether there are strong traditions of party loyalty and whether there are specialist committee systems and established spokespeople on particular issues.

It is also worth noting that the longer a government is in office, the greater opportunity there is for restlessness among backbenchers to occur and leadership challengers to arise. A honeymoon period of party discipline may appear and disappear.

Winning the battle of ideas

Fourthly, leaders will need to win 'the battle of ideas', so that the party's arguments about policy solutions and the general stance of government become generally accepted among the elite and perhaps even the general public. In more grand terms, this has been termed 'political argument hegemony'. A

54 Tim Heppell, *Choosing the Labour Leader*, London, I.B. Tauris, 2010; Thomas Quinn, *Electing and Ejecting Party Leaders in Britain*, Basingstoke, Palgrave, 2012.

party leader who is successful at this might find that political opponents come to adopt their policies as manifesto commitments in the run-up to an election or that they become the hallmark of government policy in future years.

Winning 'the battle of ideas' might involve victories in particular policy issues, such as health care, nuclear disarmament, home rule or immigration. It might also involve victories over more deep-rooted questions, such as the role of government in society. It is often thought, for example, that Margaret Thatcher was successful in generating a new discourse during the 1980s, which moved the electorate towards the right and helped her to win three consecutive elections. There is some evidence that Thatcher was less successful in achieving political argument hegemony among the public than was widely thought,[55] but subsequent Labour Party politicians certainly came to accept many of her Conservative government's policies during the 1990s, suggesting some success at the elite level.[56] Tony Blair could be argued to have been successful in winning debates about civil liberties, devolution and constitutional change while in office.

External factors may make winning the battle of ideas more or less difficult for leaders. There have been major ideological changes across all western democracies since the formation of the Labour Party. Industrial societies, political scientist Ronald Inglehart has argued, have undergone a *cultural shift* since the 1970s. New post-material issues like the environment and human rights have arisen and the old left/right politics are no longer applicable.[57] However, it is also thought that there has subsequently been a *cultural backlash* to these changes, causing the rise of authoritarian populist values in many countries.[58] Opposing individuals, leaders and political figures can

---

55 Ivor Crewe, 'Has the Electorate Become Thatcherite?' in Robert Skidelsky ed., *Thatcherism*, Oxford, Blackwell, 1988, pp. 25–49.

56 Buller and James, op. cit., 2012.

57 Ronald Inglehart, *Culture Shift in Advanced Industrial Society*, Princeton, NJ, Princeton University Press, 1990.

58 Pippa Norris and Ronald Inglehart, *Cultural Backlash: The Rise of Authoritarianism-Populism*, New York, Cambridge University Press, 2019.

also be important. Nigel Farage had an unmistakable influence on political debate from outside of Westminster.[59]

The evolution of digital media has also arguably reshaped how political ideas and ideologies are produced, received and shared.[60] Digital media has enabled new ideological entrepreneurs to use the platform to share their ideas. This has encouraged, argues Alan Finlayson, particular styles of rhetoric and communication, which are often positioned as being against the mainstream. Online political influencers such as Tommy Robinson, Carl Benjamin (aka Sargon of Akkad), Paul Joseph Watson and Katie Hopkins have amassed enormous numbers of followers.[61] Exposure to online political influencers has been linked to the rise of extremist views.[62]

Leaders will be better able to win the battle of ideas if they are given a credible set of policy ideas. They may be reliant on think tanks or their party to develop a new narrative and win over political support. Time in office, events and the partisan bias of the media are all important for this statecraft task too.

Constitutional management

Lastly, leaders may need to maintain or change the constitutional rules of the game to make winning elections easier.[63] As noted earlier, electoral laws can benefit or disadvantage a party. It is not just laws that might matter, however, as other aspects of the constitution can be important too. For example, a House of Lords that is packed with opposition peers can make it difficult for a government to pass legislation. This legislation might be essential for developing a winning electoral strategy or achieving governing competence.

---

59 Andrew Crines and Tim Heppell, 'Rhetorical style and issue emphasis within the conference speeches of UKIP's Nigel Farage 2010–2014', *British Politics*, Vol. 12, 2017, pp. 231–49.

60 Alan Finlayson, 'YouTube and Political Ideologies: Technology, Populism and Rhetorical Form', *Political Studies*, 70(1), 2020, pp. 62–80.

61 Hope Not Hate, *State of Hate 2024: Pessimism, Decline and the Rising Radical Right*, accessed 23 July 2025 (https://hopenothate.org.uk/wp-content/uploads/2024/03/state-of-hate-2024-v15.pdf).

62 Rachel Gibson, Esmeralda Bon, Philipp Darius and Peter Smyth, 'Are Online Political Influencers Accelerating Democratic Deconsolidation?', *Media and Communication*, 11(3), 2023, pp. 175–86.

63 Toby S. James, *Elite Statecraft and Election Administration: Bending the Rules of the Game*, Basingstoke, Palgrave Macmillan, 2012.

Maintaining any constitutional rules that advantage the party, and reforming those that do not, therefore equates to good statecraft.

Leaders might want to adopt other strategies. They might want to back reforms, if they are popular with the public, to win over voters. They might also promise reforms to other parties, in order to entice them to form coalitions in legislation or government formation. David Cameron's promise to Nick Clegg to hold a referendum on electoral system reform was probably good, albeit risky, statecraft. Even though a reformed electoral system might have disadvantaged the Conservatives at future elections, it was a 'deal-breaker' in forming the coalition and bringing Cameron to power.

Some constitutional management could be praised as 'good statecraft' because it helps leaders to maintain power – but should undoubtedly be criticised from a normative perspective. There has been an increase in the number of leaders around the world who have undertaken constitutional reforms to entrench their power through acts of democratic backsliding.[64] There has been evidence of these acts in the UK too, with leaders threatening to remove constitutional rights, reduce the right to protest and abusing their power of office.[65] In an ideal world, these transgressions against democratic norms should be punished at the ballot box by voters. However, the fragility of democracy and the rise of populism means that this cannot be guaranteed.

CONCLUSION

Assessing political leaders is difficult. The statecraft framework, however, offers one way in which we can assess party leaders. It suggests that we ask:

64 Nancy Bermeo, 'On Democratic Backsliding', *Journal of Democracy*, 27(1), 2016, pp. 5–19; Fabio Angiolillo, Martin Lundstedt, Marina Nord and Staffan I. Lindberg, 'State of the World 2023: Democracy Winning and Losing at the Ballot', *Democratization*, 31(8), 2024, pp. 1597–621.

65 Toby S. James, *UK Democracy Under Strain: Democratic Backsliding and Strengthening 2019–2023*, Unlock Democracy, London 2023.

- Whether the leader moved their party towards the goal of winning and maintaining office or not?
- How did the leader fare in achieving the five tasks necessary for statecraft?
- What challenges did each leader face in trying to achieve statecraft?

We should 'reward' in our assessment those who do well in achieving the statecraft functions and criticise those who do not. But we should also bear in mind that achieving these tasks is much easier for some than it is for others. This means that we should also 'reward' those leaders who did well in difficult circumstances and 'punish' those who did not in more favourable times. We can differentiate between statecraft that accepts and operates within the boundaries of democracy and that which transgresses democratic principles for power maximisation. Transgressing democracy should not be 'rewarded'.

The statecraft approach does not produce unambiguous answers. Assessing each of the leaders by the five statecraft functions described here requires the analyst to exercise some interpretation and judgement as they look at each leader. No one context will be the same for each leader, and there might be disagreement on whether, for example, a leader has won the battle of ideas (political argument hegemony) or not. However, the statecraft approach does provide a clear framework for structuring the comparison of leaders and hopefully furthers rather than hinders discussion.

CHAPTER 3

MEASURING THE SUCCESS OR FAILURE OF LABOUR LEADERS: THE GENERAL ELECTION TEST

CHARLES CLARKE

In this chapter, Charles Clarke examines whether or not the success or failure of leaders can be measured, particularly by their general election results. He provides tables that show the increase or decrease in the number of seats in Parliament, in Labour's share of the vote and the number of votes cast for Labour, all of which are objective measures of performance outcomes. On this basis, he develops a 'league table' of Labour leaders and demonstrates that, as far as Labour prime ministers are concerned, there is a good correlation with the more subjective assessments that have been made. On this basis, he draws some conclusions about the reasons for their relative successes and failures.

• • •

The premise of this book is that the quality of political leadership is important. History is not driven solely by inevitable forces, important though they are. The decisions and actions of political leaders make a difference and can change outcomes, with big consequences for people's lives.

That said, the mechanism of leadership is difficult to describe and even more difficult to measure. The effectiveness of potential Labour leaders, in, for example, a leadership election, is very difficult to predict. This chapter offers one means of measuring the success or failure of Labour leaders over time.

One complication should be addressed immediately, which is that the office of leader was only established in 1922, after the general election of that year. The previous 'leaders' cited in this book (Keir Hardie, Arthur Henderson, George Nicoll Barnes, William Adamson and John Robert Clynes) were all in fact the elected 'chairman' of the Parliamentary Labour Party (PLP) – a role that entailed somewhat different responsibilities to those of 'leader'.

Leadership of political parties is not the same as leadership of countries or governments, though they do overlap, of course. Just seven of the nineteen Labour leaders since Hardie have been Prime Minister (compared with twenty out of twenty-four Tory leaders), and so only seven have had the opportunity for their leadership of government to be held to account at a general election. Of those, five (Ramsay MacDonald, Clement Attlee, Harold Wilson, Tony Blair and Keir Starmer) were in a position to set the terms of their own premiership, while two (James Callaghan and Gordon Brown) faced the difficulty of having to try to define their own leadership, of both government and party, following a fairly lengthy period of a dominant predecessor in government office.

Moreover, wider circumstances, notably economic ones but also recently the Brexit debate, create tight constraints within which leaders have to operate. As Toby James and Jim Buller set out in Chapter 2, maintaining a sense of governing competence among the electorate is an important criterion against which leadership will be tested. Economic competence is central to that and has been a traditional weak spot for Labour. Labour governments have faced a constant battle to demonstrate their economic competence in office. Following the stock market crash (1931, MacDonald), devaluation (1949, Attlee and 1967, Wilson) and the 'winter of discontent' (1978–79, Callaghan), only the Blair government succeeded in gaining the economic confidence of the electorate – at least until the global financial crisis (2008, Brown).

Despite such constraints, there is value in considering how well different leaders have performed given the hands with which they were dealt. It is more than just a party game to wonder how Labour fortunes would have differed had Clynes defeated MacDonald (1922), Herbert Morrison defeated Attlee

(1935), Nye Bevan defeated Hugh Gaitskell (1955), Denis Healey defeated Michael Foot (1980), Roy Hattersley defeated Neil Kinnock (1983), David Miliband defeated his brother Ed (2010) or Corbyn failed to achieve the necessary thirty-five MPs' nominations (he got thirty-six) in 2015.

There are a number of possible numerical measures of success in leadership. These include changes in the number of party members, opinion-poll ratings and performances in other votes, for example in local government or European Parliament elections. A number of more subjective assessments of performance (KPIs in modern management jargon) could be developed. Occasional comparisons of prime ministers have been generated in this way, though so far not of party leaders.

However, in a parliamentary democracy, the most authoritative measure must surely be performance in general elections. This is, in truth, what drives both political parties and their leaders. It is not always the definitive determinant of behaviour – political leaders, particularly in government, will sometimes take actions that they believe to be in the national interest, even if such actions don't favour their party support. However, no political leader will ever forget their party interest. They will always take into account the impact of their actions upon their party's performance at the forthcoming general election.

One possibly important exception to this general rule is economic policy, where Labour leaders have faced the squeeze between economic 'responsibility' in office and the impact upon their party performance at the next general election. The most acute example is the behaviour of MacDonald in 1930–31. His economic decisions in government split the Labour Party and led to his personal excoriation for decades. In a rather similar way, many Labour politicians saw UK membership of the European Union in the 1970s and 2010s as a central national interest which overrode issues of party electoral interest and so pursued this issue above all other concerns.

So, this chapter consists principally of a simple statistical measurement of the general election performance of Labour leaders since Keir Hardie, in the form of an overall 'league table' of those who have contested general elections.

For these, there are three reasonably objective measures of success – the number of parliamentary seats won or lost in a general election, the increase or decrease in the share of the vote and the change in the number of votes gained, though the last is of less interest than the first two. Other general election performance measures – such as the change in the proportion of the electorate or the swings between Labour and other main parties – could also have been chosen, but the simplest measure seems most appropriate.

Despite its weaknesses, general election performance does provide a useful basis to compare the performances of Labour leaders and is certainly of more value than the entirely subjective measurements that are discussed below.

This election performance measure does mean that two important Labour leaders, George Lansbury and John Smith, do not appear, since they didn't lead the party into a general election. George Lansbury, a Christian pacifist, was generally regarded as a good leader, but he took up the leadership at the age of seventy-two and suffered from ill health. He fell out of step with his party in the increasingly threatening international climate and so resigned shortly before the 1935 general election. John Smith, sadly, died young before he could contest – and probably win – the 1997 general election.

There is a definitional issue, too. The 1931 destruction of Labour was the consequence of MacDonald's leadership, even though Henderson had become leader again after MacDonald, just two months before polling day – a week after the National Government had been formed. My tables attribute the results to MacDonald, even though Henderson was technically leader at the time. This seems to me a fair allocation of responsibility, particularly when considering political leadership qualities.

The overall results for Labour are shown in the following tables. Tables 3.1 and 3.2 set out Labour's election performances in relation to the changes in parliamentary seats, vote share and number of votes cast from election to election. Tables 3.3 to 3.5 rank these results by election and then Tables 3.6 to 3.8 rank the leaders by their cumulative overall results. Table 3.9 creates a 'league table' for Labour leaders on this basis and Table 3.10 looks at the specific performances of Labour leaders of the opposition and compares them.

The figures are drawn from Colin Rallings and Michael Thrasher's *British Electoral Facts 1832–2012*[66] and after that the House of Commons Library summary.[67]

TABLE 3.1: LABOUR PERFORMANCES IN EACH OF THE THIRTY-TWO GENERAL ELECTIONS 1906–2024.

Year	Leader	Seat change	Vote percentage change	Net seat gain/loss	Net vote percentage gain/loss	Term of office
2024	Starmer	+211	+1.6	+211	+1.6	Unfinished
2019	Corbyn	-60	-7.9	-30	+1.7	4yr, 6m
2017	Corbyn	+30	+9.6			
2015	Miliband	-26	+1.4	-26	+1.4	4yr, 7m
2010	Brown	-97	-6.2	-97	-6.2	2yr, 11m
2005	Blair	-57	-5.5	+84	+0.8	12yr, 11m
2001	Blair	-6	-2.5			
1997	Blair	+147	+8.8			
1992	Kinnock	+42	+3.6	+62	+6.8	8yr, 9m
1987	Kinnock	+20	+3.2			
1983	Foot	-60	-9.3	-60	-9.3	2yr, 11m
1979	Callaghan	-50	-2.4	-50	-2.4	4yr, 7m
1974 Oct	Wilson	+18	+2.1	+61	-4.5	13yr, 2m
1974 Feb	Wilson	+13	-5.9			
1970	Wilson	-76	-4.9			
1966	Wilson	+47	+3.9			
1964	Wilson	+59	+0.3			
1959	Gaitskell	-19	-2.6	-19	-2.6	7yr, 1m

66 Colin Rallings and Michael Thrasher, *British Electoral Facts 1832–2012*, London, Biteback, 2012, tables 2.01 and 2.03.

67 Richard Cracknell and Carl Baker, 'General Election 2024: Results and Analysis', House of Commons Library, 24 September 2024, accessed 24 July 2025 (https://researchbriefings.files.parliament.uk/documents/CBP-10009/CBP-10009.pdf).

Year	Leader	Seat change	Vote percentage change	Net seat gain/loss	Net vote percentage gain/loss	Term of office
1955	Attlee	-18	-2.4	+225	+12.9	20yr, 2m
1951	Attlee	-20	+2.7			
1950	Attlee	-78	-1.9			
1945	Attlee	+239	+10.0			
1935	Attlee	+102	+7.1			
1931	MacDonald	-235	-6.2	-90	+1.2	8yr, 9m
1929	MacDonald	+136	+3.8			
1924	MacDonald	-40	+2.6			
1923	MacDonald	+49	+1.0			
1922	Clynes	+85	+8.9	+85	+8.9	1yr, 9m
1918	Adamson	+15	+14.4	+15	+14.4	3yr, 3m
1910 Dec	Barnes	+2	-0.6	+2	-0.6	1yr, 0m
1910 Jan	Henderson	+11	+2.2	+11	+2.2	6yr, 4m
1906	Hardie	+27	+3.5	+27	+3.5	1yr, 11m

Table 3.1 simply shows the number of seats and share of vote gained or lost at every general election from 1906 to 2024, together with the Labour leader for that election (note the previous point about 1931). The three right-hand columns show, against their final general election, the cumulative totals for each leader and the length of time served as leader.

TABLE 3.2: LABOUR PERFORMANCES IN TERMS OF VOTES GAINED OR LOST IN EACH OF THE THIRTY-TWO GENERAL ELECTIONS 1906–2024.

Year	Leader	Votes	Overall
2024	Starmer	-560,335	-560,335
2019	Corbyn	-2,608,867	+921,727
2017	Corbyn	+3,530,594	

Year	Leader	Votes	Overall
2015	Miliband	+740,787	+740,787
2010	Brown	-945,919	-945,919
2005	Blair	-1,172,517	-2,008,048
2001	Blair	-2,793,214	
1997	Blair	+1,957,683	
1992	Kinnock	+1,530,677	+3,103,550
1987	Kinnock	+1,572,873	
1983	Foot	-3,075,284	-3,075,284
1979	Callaghan	+75,139	+75,139
1974 Oct	Wilson	-188,537	-759,093
1974 Feb	Wilson	-563,142	
1970	Wilson	-887,871	
1966	Wilson	+890,821	
1964	Wilson	-10,364	
1959	Gaitskell	-189,082	-189,082
1955	Attlee	-1,543,629	+5,755,624
1951	Attlee	+682,707	
1950	Attlee	+1,298,430	
1945	Attlee	+3,642,255	
1935	Attlee	+1,675,861	
1931	MacDonald	-1,720,787	+2,412,281
1929	MacDonald	+2,881,330	
1924	MacDonald	+1,049,307	
1923	MacDonald	+202,431	
1922	Clynes	+1,991,572	+1,991,572
1918	Adamson	+1,873,975	+1,873,975
1910 Dec	Barnes	-133,855	-133,855
1910 Jan	Henderson	+183,994	+183,994
1906	Hardie	+258,965	+258,965

Table 3.2 shows the changes in the number of votes cast for Labour in each

election. In both 1918 and 1929, the franchise increased substantially as a result of women voting for the first time.[68] In 1918, 5,551,580 more votes were cast than in 1910 – more than double, despite the battlefield slaughter of the First World War. In 1929, 6,008,096 more votes were cast than in 1924 – an increase of more than a third.

TABLE 3.3: LABOUR PERFORMANCES IN EACH OF THE THIRTY-TWO GENERAL ELECTIONS 1906–2024, RANKED BY SEATS GAINED OR LOST.

Year	Leader	Seat change	Vote percentage change
1945	Attlee	+239	+10.0
2024	Starmer	+209	+1.6
1997	Blair	+147	+8.8
1929	MacDonald	+136	+3.8
1935	Attlee	+102	+7.1
1922	Clynes	+85	+8.9
1964	Wilson	+59	+0.3
1923	MacDonald	+49	+1.0
1966	Wilson	+47	+3.9
1992	Kinnock	+42	+3.6
2017	Corbyn	+30	+9.6
1906	Hardie	+27	+3.5
1987	Kinnock	+20	+3.2
1974 Oct	Wilson	+18	+2.1
1918	Adamson	+15	+14.4
1974 Feb	Wilson	+13	-5.9

68 A detailed account of the changes in the electorate can be found in Neil Johnston, 'The History of the Parliamentary Franchise', House of Commons Library, last updated 1 March 2013, accessed 24 July 2025 (https://commonslibrary.parliament.uk/research-briefings/rp13-14/). The franchise changed considerably over the period from 1835 to the present day, and so the numbers voting are not strictly comparable year by year. After 1832, the Reform Acts of 1867/68 and 1884 increased the electorate significantly, so that 1,478,395 more people voted in 1868 than in 1865, and in 1885, 1,278,819 more people voted than in 1880. In both 1918 and 1929, the franchise increased substantially – mainly because women voted for the first time.

Year	Leader	Seat change	Vote percentage change
1910 Feb	Henderson	+11	+2.2
1910 Dec	Barnes	+2	-0.6
2001	Blair	-6	-2.5
1955	Attlee	-18	-2.4
1959	Gaitskell	-19	-2.6
1951	Attlee	-20	+2.7
2015	Miliband	-26	+1.5
1924	MacDonald	-40	+2.6
1979	Callaghan	-50	-2.4
2005	Blair	-57	-5.5
2019	Corbyn	-60	-7.9
1983	Foot	-60	-9.3
1970	Wilson	-76	-4.9
1950	Attlee	-78	-1.9
2010	Brown	-97	-6.2
1931	MacDonald	-235	-6.2

Table 3.3 shows the same information as Table 3.1 but puts the results in order of seats gained or lost by Labour.

TABLE 3.4: LABOUR PERFORMANCES IN EACH OF THE THIRTY-TWO GENERAL ELECTIONS 1906–2024, RANKED BY SHARE OF VOTE GAINED OR LOST.

Year	Leader	Seat change	Vote percentage change
1918	Adamson	+15	+14.4
1945	Attlee	+239	+10.0
2017	Corbyn	+30	+9.6
1922	Clynes	+85	+8.9
1997	Blair	+147	+8.8
1935	Attlee	+102	+7.1

Year	Leader	Seat change	Vote percentage change
1966	Wilson	+47	+3.9
1929	MacDonald	+136	+3.8
1992	Kinnock	+42	+3.6
1906	Hardie	+27	+3.5
1987	Kinnock	+20	+3.2
1951	Attlee	-20	+2.7
1924	MacDonald	-40	+2.6
1910 Feb	Henderson	+11	+2.2
1974 Oct	Wilson	+18	+2.1
2024	Starmer	+209	+1.6
2015	Miliband	-26	+1.5
1923	MacDonald	+49	+1.0
1964	Wilson	+59	+0.3
1910 Dec	Barnes	+2	-0.6
1950	Attlee	-78	-1.9
1955	Attlee	-18	-2.4
1979	Callaghan	-50	-2.4
2001	Blair	-6	-2.5
1959	Gaitskell	-19	-2.6
1970	Wilson	-76	-4.9
2005	Blair	-57	-5.5
1974 Feb	Wilson	+13	-5.9
2010	Brown	-97	-6.2
1931	MacDonald	-235	-6.2
2019	Corbyn	-60	-7.9
1983	Foot	-60	-9.3

Table 3.4 shows the same information as Table 3.1 but puts the results in order of share of vote gained or lost by Labour.

TABLE 3.5: LABOUR PERFORMANCES IN EACH OF THE THIRTY-TWO GENERAL ELECTIONS 1906–2024, RANKED BY VOTES GAINED OR LOST.

Year	Leader	Vote change
1945	Attlee	+3,642,255
2017	Corbyn	+3,530,594
1929	MacDonald	+2,881,330*
1922	Clynes	+1,991,572
1997	Blair	+1,957,683
1918	Adamson	+1,873,975*
1935	Attlee	+1,675,861
1987	Kinnock	+1,572,873
1992	Kinnock	+1,530,677
1950	Attlee	+1,298,430
1924	MacDonald	+1,049,307
1966	Wilson	+890,821
2015	Miliband	+740,787
1951	Attlee	+682,707
1906	Hardie	+258,965
1923	MacDonald	+202,431
1910 Jan	Henderson	+183,994
1979	Callaghan	+75,139
1964	Wilson	-10,364
1910 Dec	Barnes	-133,855
1974 Oct	Wilson	-188,537
1959	Gaitskell	-189,082
2024	Starmer	-560,335
1974 Feb	Wilson	-563,142
1970	Wilson	-887,871
2010	Brown	-945,919
2005	Blair	-1,172,517

Year	Leader	Vote change
1955	Attlee	-1,543,629
1931	MacDonald	-1,720,787
2019	Corbyn	-2,608,867
2001	Blair	-2,793,214
1983	Foot	-3,075,284

*In both 1918 and 1929, there was a substantial increase in the franchise.

TABLE 3.6: OVERALL CUMULATIVE LABOUR LEADERS' PERFORMANCES IN THE THIRTY-TWO GENERAL ELECTIONS 1906–2024, RANKED BY SEATS GAINED OR LOST.

Number of elections	General elections	Leader	Seats	Vote percentage change	Term
5	1935, 1945, 1950, 1951, 1955	Attlee	+225	+12.9	20yr, 2m
1	2024	Starmer	+209	+1.6	Unfinished
1	1922	Clynes	+85	+8.9	1yr, 9m
3	1997, 2001, 2005	Blair	+84	+0.8	12yr, 11m
2	1987, 1992	Kinnock	+62	+6.8	8yr, 9m
5	1964, 1966, 1970, 1974 Feb, 1974 Oct	Wilson	+61	-4.5	13yr, 2m
1	1906	Hardie	+27	+3.5	1yr, 11m
1	1918	Adamson	+15	+14.4	3yr, 3m
1	1910 Feb	Henderson	+11	+2.2	6yr, 4m
1	1910 Dec	Barnes	+2	-0.6	1yr, 0m
1	1959	Gaitskell	-19	-2.6	7yr, 1m
1	2015	Miliband	-26	+1.4	4yr, 7m
2	2017, 2019	Corbyn	-30	+1.7	4yr, 6m
1	1979	Callaghan	-50	-2.4	4yr, 7m
1	1983	Foot	-60	-9.3	2yr, 11m
4	1923, 1924, 1929, 1931	MacDonald	-90	+1.2	8yr, 9m
1	2010	Brown	-97	-6.2	2yr, 11m

Table 3.6 shows the cumulative performance of each Labour leader over the total number of general elections for which they were leader. These are

then ordered by total number of seats gained or lost over their period of leadership.

TABLE 3.7: OVERALL CUMULATIVE LABOUR LEADERS' PERFORMANCES IN THE THIRTY-TWO GENERAL ELECTIONS 1906–2024, RANKED BY SHARE OF VOTE GAINED OR LOST.

Number of elections	General election	Leader	Seats	Vote percentage	Term
1	1918	Adamson	+15	+14.4	3yr, 3m
5	1935, 1945, 1950, 1951, 1955	Attlee	+225	+12.9	20yr, 2m
1	1922	Clynes	+85	+8.9	1yr, 9m
2	1987, 1992	Kinnock	+62	+6.8	8yr, 9m
1	1906	Hardie	+27	+3.5	1yr, 11m
1	1910 Feb	Henderson	+11	+2.2	6yr, 4m
2	2017, 2019	Corbyn	-30	+1.7	4yr, 6m
1	2024	Starmer	+209	+1.6	Unfinished
1	2015	Miliband	-26	+1.4	4yr, 7m
4	1923, 1924, 1929, 1931	MacDonald	-90	+1.2	8yr, 9m
3	1997, 2001, 2005	Blair	+84	+0.8	12yr, 11m
1	1910 Dec	Barnes	+2	-0.6	1yr, 0m
1	1979	Callaghan	-50	-2.4	4yr, 7m
1	1959	Gaitskell	-19	-2.6	7yr, 1m
5	1964, 1966, 1970, 1974 Feb, 1974 Oct	Wilson	+61	-4.5	13yr, 2m
1	2010	Brown	-97	-6.2	2yr, 11m
1	1983	Foot	-60	-9.3	2yr, 11m

Table 3.7 shows the cumulative performance of each Labour leader over the total number of general elections for which they were leader. These are then ordered by the total share of vote gained or lost over their period of leadership.

TABLE 3.8: OVERALL CUMULATIVE LABOUR LEADERS' PERFORMANCES IN THE THIRTY-TWO GENERAL ELECTIONS 1906–2024, RANKED BY VOTES GAINED OR LOST.

Leader	Cumulative vote change
Attlee	+5,755,624
Kinnock	+3,103,550
MacDonald	+2,412,281
Clynes	+1,991,572
Adamson	+1,873,975
Corbyn	+921,727
Miliband	+740,787
Hardie	+258,965
Henderson	+183,994
Callaghan	+75,139
Barnes	-133,855
Gaitskell	-189,082
Starmer	-560,335
Wilson	-759,093
Brown	-945,919
Blair	-2,008,048
Foot	-3,075,284

Table 3.8 shows the cumulative performance of each Labour leader over all the general elections for which they were leader. These are then ordered by the total number of votes gained or lost over their period of leadership. It is important to recall that both MacDonald's and Adamson's increases are not properly comparable with the others, as there was a very large increase in the number of votes cast in both 1918 and 1929.

TABLE 3.9: LABOUR LEADERS' 'LEAGUE TABLE', RANKED BY SEATS GAINED OR LOST.

Ranking by seats gained or lost	Leader	Ranking by share of vote	Prime Minister?
1	Attlee	2	Yes
2	Starmer	8	Yes
3	Clynes	3	No
4	Blair	11	Yes
5	Kinnock	4	No
6	Wilson	15	Yes
7	Hardie	5	No
8	Adamson	1	No
9	Henderson	6	No
10	Barnes	12	No
11	Gaitskell	14	No
12	Miliband	9	No
13	Corbyn	7	No
14	Callaghan	13	Yes
15	Foot	17	No
16	MacDonald	10	Yes
17	Brown	16	Yes

Table 3.9 is a reworking of Table 3.6 as a summary 'league table'. It orders the Labour leaders by the number of seats won or lost. The figure in the third column is their position in the 'share of vote' league table. The final column indicates which Labour leaders became Prime Minister.

• • •

A number of observations can be made about these tables (and about Labour leadership in general), particularly 3.6 and 3.7, the overall rankings of the seventeen leaders by seats and vote share gained or lost.

First, they demonstrate the importance of major contextual issues. For example, the extraordinary successes of Adamson in 1918 and Attlee in 1945 are undoubtedly primarily due to the social and industrial transformation of the country through both world wars – a change that was, of course, common to many countries.

Second, as mentioned earlier, the performances of Callaghan and Brown, following, as they both did, successful predecessors, show the difficulties of succeeding to political leadership late in the term of a governing political party. John Major and Rishi Sunak's experiences were largely the same.[69]

Third, it helps you do well if your opposition is weak. For example, Blair was faced with William Hague, Iain Duncan Smith and Michael Howard – the only Tory leaders (along with Austen Chamberlain) since 1832 who never became Prime Minister. And Starmer faced a weakened Sunak, who then ran a dreadful campaign. That said, the political strategy of leaders can play quite a role in determining the identity of the leadership of their opponents! Blair also benefited from the widespread sense that 1992 was the 'wrong' result, which needed to be put right in 1997.

Fourth, there are significant variations between the performances of the ten Labour leaders (in fifteen elections) who contested a general election as the formal Leader of the Opposition,[70] rather than as Prime Minister or as leader of a minor party. This can be seen in Table 3.10, which is a sub-section of Table 3.6 above.

• • •

TABLE 3.10: PERFORMANCES OF LABOUR LEADERS OF THE OPPOSITION.

Year	Leader	Seat change	Vote percentage change
1945	Attlee	+239	+10.0
2024	Starmer	+209	+1.6
1997	Blair	+147	+8.8

69 Benjamin Worthy, 'Ending in failure? The performance of "takeover" Prime Ministers 1916–2016', *Political Quarterly*, 87(4), 2016, pp. 509–17.

70 The role developed through the late nineteenth century and was effectively consolidated following the 1911 Parliament Act.

Year	Leader	Seat change	Vote percentage change
1929	MacDonald	+136	+3.8
1935	Attlee	+102	+7.1
1964	Wilson	+59	+0.3
1923	MacDonald	+49	+1.0
1992	Kinnock	+42	+3.6
2017	Corbyn	+30	+9.6
1987	Kinnock	+20	+3.2
1974 Feb	Wilson	+13	-5.9
1955	Attlee	-18	-2.4
1959	Gaitskell	-19	-2.6
2015	Miliband	-26	+1.5
2019	Corbyn	-60	-7.9
1983	Foot	-60	-9.3

The enormous variation in performance highlights the particularly bad results in 1955, 1959, 1983, 2015 and 2019, when Labour actually lost seats while challenging from opposition. In none of these years could their Conservative prime ministerial opponents be thought to have been highly successful and utterly dominant. Gains for the opposition should have been possible, and failure to achieve at least some progress should raise serious questions about the quality of the leadership of the opposition in those five cases. Might a different leader have led to a significantly better result for Labour, with enormous political implications for the country? This discussion is more than a parlour game.

Fifth, these tables suggest that those who did better were more successful at another of Toby James and Jim Buller's criteria: 'devising a winning electoral strategy'. Attlee, Starmer, Clynes, Blair, Kinnock, Wilson and Hardie were all significantly more effective at doing this than Gaitskell, Miliband, Callaghan, Foot, MacDonald, Corbyn and Brown. Similarly, 'party management', another of Toby James and Jim Buller's criteria, was better handled by Attlee, Blair, Kinnock, Wilson and Starmer than it was by Gaitskell, Foot, MacDonald, Corbyn and Brown.

Sixth, there are some striking divergences between the change in the share of vote and the change in the number of seats, due to the nature of the British electoral system. Increasing seats and not just vote share must therefore be a key dimension of a leader's electoral strategy. The most notable is the difference between Starmer's 2024 landslide in terms of seats and his small increase in vote share, which was principally due to tactical voting because of the immensely strong desire to remove the Tories. Similarly, Labour's result in the general elections of 1924 (MacDonald), 1951 (Attlee) and 2015 (Miliband) showed an increase in Labour's share of the vote combined with a decrease in the number of seats held. In February 1974 (Wilson), the reverse happened – an increase in seats, despite a substantial fall in the share of the vote. In addition, Labour's massive increase in the share of the vote in 1918 (Adamson) was not reflected in an equivalent increase in seats, which took some years to work through, and Corbyn's very large increase in vote share in 2017 reaped only a relatively minor increase in the number of seats gained, mainly because his votes were being piled up in seats that were already Labour.

The variances between performance in share of the vote and seats should give rise to more consideration of electoral strategy leading up to any modern general election.

Perhaps as a result of these factors, the cumulative results for MacDonald, Wilson, Blair and Starmer show a significant divergence between their performances in winning seats and in increasing the share of the vote. MacDonald and Corbyn in 2019 did significantly worse on seats than vote share, while Wilson, Blair and Starmer were much more successful at winning seats than increasing Labour's share. Wilson and Blair also did relatively poorly in terms of the number of votes lost over the course of the elections they fought – Blair particularly so. Surprisingly, Wilson lost popular votes in 1964 compared with 1959, as indeed he did in four of the five elections he contested.

The main reason for these divergences is either the performance of third parties or the existence of deep divisions within Labour. The impact of either of these is exaggerated by the vagaries of the British voting system.

At an individual level, few will be surprised by Attlee's towering result.

However, he was a lot more than simply the beneficiary of a major social shift. His leadership successes in bolstering Labour's position, particularly during the war, are increasingly well understood.[71]

Both Clynes and Kinnock turn out to perform significantly better than most people would expect. Conversely, the relatively good performances of both Blair and Wilson will not surprise many, contesting, as they did, eight general elections between them – and seven successfully.

Labour's steady advance in its early years, from 1906 to 1918, is reflected in the performance of its leaders (all chairmen of the PLP) over that period: Hardie, Henderson, Barnes and Adamson. Labour was a steadily growing opposition, which did not have to deal with the responsibilities of power until 1923 and then, disastrously, 1929.

At the bottom end of the table, the performances of Callaghan and Brown reflect the difficulty of coming in at the end of a fairly lengthy period of Labour dominance, while the poor performances of Gaitskell (which will surprise many), Miliband, Corbyn and Foot reflect the difficulty of evolving a genuine, winning strategy and minimising party disunity in opposition – and the failure of these leaders to do so.

MacDonald's poor showing is, of course, the direct outcome of the disastrous Labour split following 1931, though it is striking that, even after the split, his period of leadership still saw an increase in Labour's share of the vote.

Some corroboration of the rankings in this Labour leaders' league table comes from various subjective assessments of prime ministers done in recent years, though none of these have any objective basis. A number of exercises have been carried out in what Kevin Theakston, in Chapter 17 of his book *British Prime Ministers, Politics and Political Leadership in Number 10*, calls 'a veritable cottage industry of Prime Ministerial evaluation'. As these analyses are all of Prime Ministers, they cover only just over a third (seven out of

71 See, for example, Robert Crowcroft, *Attlee's War: World War II and the Making of a Labour Leader*, London, I.B. Tauris, 2011.

nineteen) of Labour leaders and look at their prime ministerial, rather than party leadership, qualities. They are nevertheless of interest.

Theakston points to three categories of subjective assessments: historically informed qualitative judgements, mass public opinion surveys and targeted group surveys of, for example, academics or MPs.

Table 3.11 lists the exercises that have taken place, with their ranked order of Labour prime ministers (and one ranking of leaders of the opposition). Obviously, none of these exercises include Keir Starmer, whom it is too early to judge.

TABLE 3.11: LABOUR LEADERS IN SUBJECTIVE RANKINGS OF BRITISH PRIME MINISTERS.

Date	Evaluation	Ranking
Historically informed qualitative judgements		
1999	BBC Radio 4, based on twenty historians[72]	Attlee, Wilson, Callaghan, MacDonald
2000	BBC Politics Group, from twenty-two academics[73]	Attlee, Wilson, MacDonald, Callaghan
2001	Peter Hennessy in *The Prime Minister: The Office and its Holders since 1945*[74]	Attlee, Blair, Callaghan, Wilson
2006	Francis Beckett in *BBC History Magazine*[75]	Attlee, Blair, Wilson, Callaghan, MacDonald
2010	Phil Collins, Ben Macintyre, Matthew Parris, William Rees-Mogg, Peter Riddell and Phil Webster in *The Times*	Attlee, Blair, Wilson, Callaghan, MacDonald, Brown
2015	Danny Finkelstein, Lucy Fisher, Oliver Kamm, Patrick Kidd, Damian McBride, Tim Montgomerie, Jenni Russell, Rachel Sylvester, Phil Webster and Giles Whittell in *The Times*	Attlee, Blair, Wilson, MacDonald, Callaghan, Brown
2020	Iain Dale, with contributors, in his book *The Prime Ministers*[76]	Attlee, Blair, Wilson, MacDonald, Brown, Callaghan

72 'Churchill "greatest PM of 20th century"', BBC News, last updated 4 January 2000, accessed 25 July 2025 (http://news.bbc.co.uk/1/hi/uk_politics/575219.stm).

73 Ibid.

74 See Chapter 19 of Hennessy's book.

75 'Thatcher and Attlee top PM list', BBC News, last updated 29 August 2006, accessed 19 February 2015 (http://news.bbc.co.uk/1/hi/uk_politics/5294024.stm).

76 Iain Dale, 'Ranking Our 55 Prime Ministers - An Impossible Task, But a Fascinating One', IainDale.com, last updated 12 November 2020, accessed 25 July 2025 (https://www.iaindale.com/articles/ranking-our-55-prime-ministers-an-impossible-task-but-a-fascinating-one).

Date	Evaluation	Ranking
2022	Anthony Seldon in *The Impossible Office? The History of the British Prime Minister*[77]	Attlee, Wilson, Blair, MacDonald, Callaghan, Brown
Surveys of opinion		
2004	Theakston/Gill, Leeds University, with 139 academics[78]	Attlee, Blair, Wilson, Callaghan
2008	BBC *Newsnight* poll, 27,000 respondents[79]	Attlee, Wilson, Blair, Callaghan, Brown
2010	Theakston/Gill, Leeds University, with 106 academics[80]	Attlee, Blair, Wilson, Callaghan, Brown
2014	Royal Holloway Group PR3710, 158 MPs' assessment of Prime Ministers[81]	Attlee, Blair, Wilson, Callaghan, Brown
2016	Theakston, Leeds University, with eighty-two academics[82]	Attlee, Blair, Wilson, Callaghan, Brown
2016	YouGov poll of 1,692 people[83]	Blair, Brown (who were the only Labour options in the poll)
2021	Theakston/Gill, Leeds University, with ninety-three academics[84]	Attlee, Blair, Wilson, Brown, Callaghan
2022	Ipsos UK poll of 1,111 people[85]	Blair, Wilson, Brown, Attlee, Callaghan

77 See Chapter 10 of Seldon's book.

78 Kevin Theakston and Mark Gill, 'Ranking Twentieth-Century British Prime Ministers', *British Journal of Politics and International Relations*, Vol. 8, 2006, pp. 193–213.

79 'Churchill tops PM choice', BBC Newsnight, last updated 1 October 2008, accessed 19 February 2015 (http://news.bbc.co.uk/1/hi/programmes/newsnight/7647383.stm).

80 Kevin Theakston and Mark Gill, 'The Post-War Premiership League', *Political Quarterly*, 82(1), 2011, pp. 67–80.

81 Royal Holloway Group PR3710, 'British MPs on British PMs: Parliamentary Evaluations of Prime Ministerial Success', Politics, 35(2), pp. 111–27.

82 Kevin Theakston, 'Academics rate David Cameron among worst post-war prime ministers', The Conversation, last updated 13 October 2016, accessed 25 July 2025 (https://theconversation.com/academics-rate-david-cameron-among-worst-post-war-prime-ministers-66780).

83 Matthew Smith, 'David Cameron was the best Prime Minister since Thatcher', YouGov, last updated 10 August 2016, accessed 25 July 2025 (https://yougov.co.uk/politics/articles/16170-cameron-best-prime-minister-since-thatcher).

84 Kevin Theakston and Mark Gill, 'Theresa May joint worst post-war prime minister, say historians and politics professors in new survey', The Conversation, last updated 6 July 2021, accessed 25 July 2025 (https://theconversation.com/theresa-may-joint-worst-post-war-prime-minister-say-historians-and-politics-professors-in-new-survey-163912).

85 'Ipsos UK Political Pulse Past PMs', Ipsos UK, last updated August 2022, accessed 25 July 2025 (https://www.ipsos.com/sites/default/files/ct/news/documents/2022-08/ipsos-political-pulse-polling-past-prime-ministers-august-2022.pdf).

Date	Evaluation	Ranking
2024	Royal Holloway Group PR3710, sixty-seven MPs' assessments of Prime Ministers[86]	Attlee, Blair, Wilson, Brown, Callaghan
Rating as Leader of the Opposition		
2021	Theakston/Gill, Leeds University, with eighty-five academics[87]	Blair, Wilson, Smith, Gaitskell, Kinnock, Attlee, Miliband, Callaghan, Corbyn, Foot

One of these assessments is on their tenures as Leader of the Opposition, a different role from Prime Minister and rather nearer that of party leader. The academics' assessment of the leaders of the opposition does correlate fairly well with the actual election outcomes, with the major exception of Hugh Gaitskell, where the academic judgement is significantly more positive than his election performance.

• • •

In 2010, Stephen Bray, for Iain Dale's Diary, produced an amalgamation of most of these judgements, which suggested that the ranking of Labour prime ministers was Attlee, Wilson, Blair, Callaghan, MacDonald and Brown.[88]

Clearly, the criteria for all of these assessments vary: they are about prime ministerial and governmental leadership rather than party leadership, they use different measures and timescales for the assessments and they involve greatly different techniques to come to their judgements. None of them have any objective validity. Moreover, some of these assessment have considered wider questions, such as the correlation between the length in office as leader within the rankings, and have also included comparisons with economic

86 Royal Holloway Group PR3710, 'The Good, the Not so Good, and Liz Truss: MPs' Evaluations of Postwar Prime Ministers', *Political Quarterly,* last updated 21 March 2024, accessed 25 July 2025 (https://politicalquarterly.org.uk/blog/the-good-the-not-so-good-and-liz-truss-mps-evaluations-of-postwar-prime-ministers-2/).

87 Mark Gill and Kevin Theakston, 'The league table of post-war leaders of the opposition according to academics', LSE, last updated 13 July 2021, accessed 25 July 2025 (https://blogs.lse.ac.uk/politicsandpolicy/post-war-leaders-of-the-opposition/).

88 Stephen Bray, 'Guest Post: The Greatest Prime Ministers of All Time', Iain Dale's Diary, last updated 5 August 2010, accessed 19 February 2015 (http://iaindale.blogspot.co.uk/2010/08/guest-post-greatest-prime-ministers-of.html).

indicators such as unemployment, growth or inflation. Such data can provoke interesting conversations but do not really provide clear guidance.

Nevertheless, what is striking about these assessments, subjective though they are, is that they mainly grade Attlee as clearly the best Labour leader, with Blair and Wilson second and third (in one order or the other) and Callaghan, MacDonald and Brown fourth, fifth and sixth, usually in that order. This is the same ranking generated by the general election result methodology of this chapter.

This correlation should not be overstated. For example, the same general election result methodology for the Conservatives and Liberals shows Churchill and Gladstone doing pretty badly, though, obviously, both do well in the more subjective assessments.

Nevertheless, it does imply that a rating based upon electoral performance does have some value and, from the point of view of party leadership, could be extended to leaders who did not become Prime Minister. This is more important for Labour than it is for the Conservatives, almost all of whom became Prime Minister.

Nor should the figures reported in this chapter be treated as some form of comprehensive and authoritative statement on the quality of Labour's successive leaders. The outcome of general elections is not the sole determinant of the success or failure of leaders. However, electoral performances should perhaps be considered as a contributory factor when assessing how Labour leaders have done, and there are a number of leaders, particularly Clynes and Kinnock, who deserve a rather more positive historical assessment than they sometimes receive.

Perhaps most importantly, when considering potential candidates for leadership, it might be worth including a judgement about how they are expected to perform in their next general election, and their prospective ability to fulfil Toby James and Jim Buller's 'statecraft' criteria ought perhaps to be taken into account.

CHAPTER 4

ASSESSING THE POLICY AND SOCIETAL IMPACT OF LABOUR LEADERS

TOBY S. JAMES

Leaders promise change in their manifesto commitments. But what type of change can they deliver? This chapter argues that, in addition to the political and electoral changes set out in Chapters 2 and 3, change can occur in any of four connected areas: societal structure, political institutions, policy areas and the international dimension. We should examine the effects of leaders across all of these areas in order to see the full and 'hidden' impacts of leaders, in addition to their headline statecraft successes and failures.

• • •

Standing outside 10 Downing Street, Keir Starmer said in his first speech as Prime Minister: 'Changing a country is not like flicking a switch … This will take a while. But have no doubt that the work of change begins – immediately.'[89] Walking up the spiral stairs of 10 Downing Street for the first time, with black and white portraits of their predecessors overlooking them, new prime ministers no doubt wonder whether history will remember them – and how. All prime ministers probably hope to leave office having

89 '"Work of change begins" – Keir Starmer's No 10 speech in full', BBC News, last updated 5 July 2024, accessed 25 July 2025 (https://www.bbc.co.uk/news/articles/crgewjwqqq4o).

brought about transformational change for their country and party. Like the portraits of former headmasters and headmistresses peering over Dumbledore and Harry Potter in the halls of Hogwarts, former leaders will have plenty to say about the difficulty of achieving change.

What, after all, does transformational change look like? Where can it be seen? If a leader could be said to have had a transformational impact, how would we know? What would it look like? Victory in a war? A new health service? Immigration flows changed? A new political culture? And how quickly can change occur? Some leaders around the world have overseen transformational change during their tenure. Nelson Mandela brought through the end of apartheid and established a new political order in South Africa in the 1990s.[90] Deng Xiaoping introduced market reforms into China (alongside authoritarian crackdowns) as part of the policy of 'reform and opening up' between 1978 and 1989.[91] Estonian Prime Minister Mart Laar was a an advocate for Estonia's rapid digital transformation, making the country a global leader in e-government.[92]

Transformational change is difficult, however. Prime ministers are, after all, only one person amid a web of other powerful people and organisations. The reality of the world is that given the huge complexity of social life and the multiple forces for continuity and change, a single governmental office is always likely to have a limited impact. Change can sometimes only occur at the right time.

Chapter 2 of this volume introduced the statecraft framework as a method for evaluating leaders *politically*. The framework examined the extent to which they were successful in winning and maintaining office. However,

---

90 Nelson Mandela, *Long Walk to Freedom: The Autobiography of Nelson Mandela*, London, Hachette UK, 2008.

91 Barry Naughton, 'Deng Xiaoping: The Economist,' *The China Quarterly* 135 (1993): 491–514.

92 Mathis Bitton, 'The Estonian Miracle: E-Estonia and the Future of Digital Infrastructure', VR/AR Association, last updated 11 November 2022, accessed 31 July 2025 (https://www.thevrara.com/news2/2022/11/11/the-estonian-miracle-e-estonia-and-the-future-of-digital-infrastructure).

political leaders will often want to achieve more than this. They may be concerned about addressing a specific policy issue, want to bring about broader social change or have their legacy in mind. Even if leaders are simply power-maximising office seekers, they will have a broader impact on the rest of the world.

This chapter therefore provides a further framework by considering the nature of change that can be achieved. It firstly considers the different areas of UK society where change might occur as a result of the leader. It then sets out some reasons why change is difficult and some different types of change, before considering some broad changes that have occurred across the long durée of time considered in this volume. This sets up the remainder of the volume to examine the changes that specific leaders introduced – and the extent to which they should or should not be attributed to them.

WHERE DOES CHANGE OCCUR?

Leaders who reach power can have an impact beyond the 'Westminster bubble'. I suggest here that there are four broadly connected areas of change that leaders can effect (Figure 4.1).[93] Each of these are introduced here to serve as yardsticks that can be used to consider the changes that leaders made.

93 Toby S. James, 'Assessing the Policy Effects of Political Leaders: a Layered Framework', *Policy Studies*, 42(5–6), 2021, pp. 437–54.

FIGURE 4.1: THE LAYERED FRAMEWORK FOR UNDERSTANDING POLICY CHANGE.

Policy and policy problems	
Economic policy	Environmental policy
Welfare policy	Foreign policy
Housing policy	LGBTQ+ policy

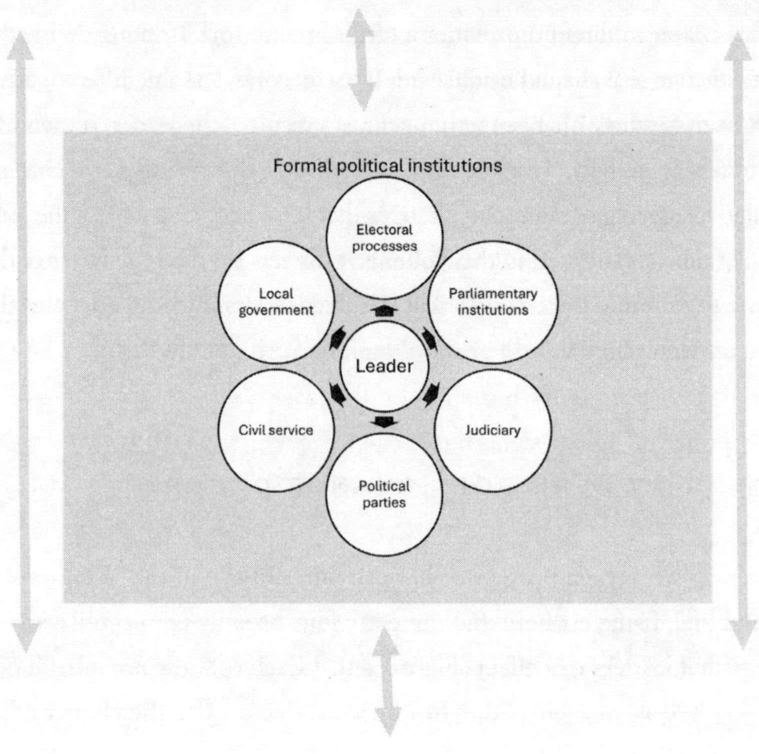

1. Societal structure

At the broadest possible level, at the base of the diagram in Figure 4.1, is the societal structure. These are deep-rooted economic, political, demographic, ideational or social relationships and institutionalised patterns of behaviour in society. The basic socio-economic structure for nearly all societies around the world today is capitalism. This was not the case for much of the twentieth century, which Eric Hobsbawm termed the *Age of Extremes*, in which fascism and communism competed with liberal capitalism.[94] But not all models of capitalism are the same. The laissez-faire model allows the economy to be led by free markets, while the coordinated market economy model gives the state power to direct the economy and a greater role for trade unions.[95]

Societies are also shaped by the extent to which they are a democracy. The long march of history has been towards the advancement of democracy worldwide, but there has been recent evidence of democratic backsliding, even within so-called 'established' democracies. 'Democracy' itself, meanwhile, has different meanings. Barebones definitions focus on the provision of elections in which the result is accepted by the loser.[96] A broader definition focuses on the extent to which all individuals are empowered to live their lives to the fullest.[97] This requires elections in which every adult has the right to vote and constitutionally protected human rights but also other measures which affect people's daily lives, such as access to health and education and a reasonable standard of living.

Societies can be structured into cleavages based on material antagonistic relations and/or the consolidation of political values into opposed groups. It has been long thought that societies tend to be divided along one of the following dimensions: left and right, church and state, urban and rural, centre and periphery.[98]

---

94 Eric Hobsbawm, *The Age of Extremes: The Short Twentieth Century 1914–1991*, London, Michael Joseph, 1994.

95 David W. Soskice and Peter A. Hall, *Varieties of Capitalism: The Institutional Foundations of Comparative Advantage*, Oxford: Oxford University Press, 2001.

96 Adam Przeworski, *Democracy and the Market: Political and Economic Reform in Eastern Europe and Latin America*, Cambridge and New York, Cambridge University Press, 1991.

97 Toby S. James, 'Real Democracy: A Critical Realist Approach to Democracy and Democratic Theory', *New Political Science*, 46(3), 2024, pp. 228–58.

98 Seymour M. Lipset and Stein Rokkan, *Party Systems and Voter Alignments: Cross-National Perspectives*, Vol. 7, New York, Free Press, 1967.

2. *Formal political institutions*

Formal political institutions are the sites where politics and power play out, which provide a direct steer in setting policy. Alongside the executive, they include the legislature, judiciary and bureaucracy of the state. Each plays a central role in deliberating, bargaining, setting and adjudicating policies and contain balances of power within them. A key formal institution is the practice of elections, which provide citizens with a way of shaping policy by choosing their representatives. Political parties provide the mechanism for leaders and candidates to contest elections.

The formal political institutions in the UK have been long described as the 'Westminster Model'. The model was underpinned by the idea of 'parliamentary sovereignty' – there was no higher authority in the land than Parliament. Power resided amid the iconic green benches of the House of Commons – and in the hands of the Prime Minister who could command a majority across them. There would be no codified constitution, judicial power or devolved bodies to constrain the power of the leader. This would come to be changed, in part, as New Labour introduced constitutional reforms between 1997 and 2010.[99]

3. *Policy and policy problems*

The third domain is what we might conventionally call policies and policy problems. These include the economy, housing and welfare (see Figure 4.1). It is often held that 'it's the economy, stupid' and that economic issues dominate the media and shape the outcomes of electoral events. However, there are a multitude of areas of importance.

4. *Internationalisation*

Leaders can have profound effects outside of national borders. This is

99 Jack Straw, 'New Labour, Constitutional Change and Representative Democracy', *Parliamentary Affairs*, 63(2), 2010, pp. 356–68. Patrick Dunleavy, Alice Park and Ros Taylor, 2018, *The UK's Changing Democracy: The 2018 Democratic Audit*, London, LSE Press, 2018.

especially the case when the leader is the head of state of a global superpower. The UK is no longer a superpower, but it is an important global actor. *Domestic policies* may have a profound impact outside of national borders. The effect might be direct. Changes made to the corporate tax rate, for example, might lead companies to relocate from other places. Should a state lower corporation tax, other countries may respond in competition – but also because a norm has been set about the acceptability of such a change. Leaders may also shape their states' *international policies*, such as whether to have trade agreements with other states and whether to commit to military involvement. *Speech and rhetoric* can also have important causal effects, by signalling, for example, the value of democracy and human rights.

Interconnectivity

Examining these four areas provides a way of identifying the different effects that leaders have had, but they are all closely and interactively connected. Policy problems occur as a result of the nature of the societal structure. Capitalism can breed inequality. Societal structures can also produce what comes to be seen as a policy problem. Policies passed by political institutions can resolve policy problems but also affect the nature of the societal structure. There is therefore an endless web of interactions. Changes caused by the leader are therefore only one of the causal forces in the policy process, but they are an important one.

THE CHANGE CHALLENGE

Change that has taken place in Britain over time can easily be attributed to particular leaders or parties. Leaders will make campaign promises about certain changes to try to win office, and if these changes occur, the leader could easily be attributed as the cause of change. Newspaper infographic timelines often have markers for when a political leader came into office – and this gives the visual impression that they should receive credit for what is to follow. Above all, leaders like to claim credit for 'changing Britain' or their party during their time in office.

Change is difficult, however. To begin with, leaders have limited tools to operate with.[100] The available mechanisms include trying to communicate with the public, their party and parliamentarians – but there is no certainty that their message will be understood or listened to. They can try to pass new laws to change society, but proposed bills take time to reach the statute book and even longer to be implemented. Some more direct policy interventions may require careful political negotiation. They can reshuffle their Cabinet and appoint ministers – but they have to manage the balance between competing factions and personalities.

A broader issue is that the changes leaders make take place in a complex world. Prime ministers do not have a series of switches and buttons that they can press to control society like a factory machine controller or a biologist in a hermetically sealed lab. Leaders are not powerless, but their steering of the ship takes place in an ocean of other currents. There are four central change challenges, which we will discuss in the following pages.

1. Prevailing forces

There are prevailing causal forces and currents within political systems. These might include longer-term trends towards an ageing society, rising house prices, rising economic inequality or climate change. They might also include changing social attitudes resulting from technological change. The trade tariffs announced by US President Donald Trump were forecast to have

100 For different perspectives on the powers available to leaders, see Christopher Byrne and Kevin Theakston, 'Understanding the power of the prime minister: structure and agency in models of prime ministerial power', *British Politics*, Vol. 14, 2019, pp. 329–46; Keith Dowding, 'Prime-ministerial power institutional and personal factors', in Paul Strangio, Paul 't Hart, James Walter eds, *Understanding Prime-Ministerial Performance: Comparative Perspectives*, Oxford, Oxford University Press, 2013, pp. 57–78; Richard Heffernan, 'Prime Ministerial Predominance? Core Executive Politics in the UK', *British Journal of Politics and International Relations*, 5(3), 2003, pp. 347–72.

negative aggregate effects on the global economy by the IMF.[101] Decisions announced in the Chancellor's Budget would therefore be mediated by these external factors. Immigration into the UK, meanwhile, is shaped by 'push' factors and 'pull' factors such as humanitarian crises, wars, economic crises and climate crisies. Changes to migration policy are therefore mediated by this. There are also global shifts in values and choices of political leader – including the current global rise in authoritarian populism.[102] Attempts to shape values in British society by party leaders are therefore mediated by this too.

2. *Complexity*

The butterfly effect is a concept in chaos theory that suggests small changes or events in a system can lead to significant and unpredictable outcomes over time. It is often illustrated with the metaphor that the flap of a butterfly's wings in one part of the world can eventually influence the formation of a tornado elsewhere. For example, a Tunisian street vendor, Mohamed Bouazizi, set himself on fire in protest against government corruption in December 2010. A single video spread rapidly on social media platforms, leading to widespread protests, and contributed to the eventual overthrow of various regimes as part of the Arab Spring. Meanwhile, subprime mortgage defaults in the US set in chain a series of economic events that led to the collapse of major financial institutions like Lehman Brothers, sparking a global economic crisis – and eventually the global financial crisis. Political change is therefore often described as partially random or a fluke.[103]

The concept of the butterfly effect overestimates the randomness of change, however. Sparks from the Arab Spring generated flames because of existing tensions and grievances in several countries. The global financial crisis was possible because of the housing bubble and the deregulated international

---

101 Lukas Boer and Malte Rieth, 'The Macroeconomic Consequences of Import Tariffs and Trade Policy Uncertainty', International Monetary Fund, IMF Working Papers, 19 January 2024.

102 Pippa Norris and Ronald Inglehart, *Cultural Backlash: The Rise of Authoritarianism-Populism*, New York, Cambridge University Press, 2019.

103 Brian Klass, *Fluke: Chance, Chaos, and Why Everything We Do Matters*, London, John Murray, 2024.

system. However, political systems are closely connected. This means that a war or conflict such as the Russo-Ukraine War, which occurred following the Russian invasion of Ukraine, can have ripple effects far and wide.[104] Attempts by leaders to make change can be derailed by any of these effects.

3. Visibility

When change occurs in a science experiment, it is much easier to observe and attribute change. Molecules can be measured, quantities adjusted and the experiment repeated to make sure that the outcome was not a fluke. Change in the social world is not like this. There are huge volumes of movements of people, ideas, goods and resources around the world, which cannot be accounted for in economic models. Some things are also not observable. For example, we cannot know whether Brexit was a contributing cause of Vladimir Putin's decision to invade Ukraine in 2022. It has been argued that Brexit may have contributed towards a perception of a divided and weakened Europe and divisions in EU–UK relations and in NATO/the Western alliance. We do not have access to Putin's war room, however, so any attempt to establish causation is probably only ever going to be speculative. Uncertainty about cause and effect enables politicians to make all kinds of claims about the different effects of certain policies. Jacob Rees-Mogg, for example, has claimed that Brexit stopped the invasion of Ukraine from succeeding.[105]

4. Time lags

Change also takes time, and the effects are not immediately obvious in econometric models – or in the minds of the public. The Brexit process illustrates

---

104 Pierre Bocquillon, Suzanne Doyle, Toby S. James, Ra Mason, Soul Park and Matilde Rosina, 'The effects of wars: lessons from the war in Ukraine', *Policy Studies*, 45(3–4), 2024, pp. 261–81.

105 'Brexit stopped Ukraine invasion from succeeding, Jacob Rees-Mogg says', Sky News, last updated 14 May 2023, accessed 17 July 2025 (https://news.sky.com/story/brexit-stopped-ukraine-invasion-from-succeeding-jacob-rees-mogg-says-12880590).

this perfectly.[106] The UK public voted for Brexit in the EU Referendum on 23 June 2016. Prime Minister Theresa May formally invoked Article 50 to kick-start a two-year countdown to the UK formally leaving the EU on 29 March 2017. An extension request was submitted in March 2019 to continue membership until June 2019. Another was submitted in April 2019 to extend membership until October 2019. And another in October 2019. Only on 31 January 2020, nearly four years after the referendum, did the UK leave. And only on 31 December 2020 did the transition period end and the UK leave the EU single market and customs union.

Analysis from the Office for Budget Responsibility in May 2024 argued that the post-Brexit UK–EU trading relationship will reduce long-run productivity by 4 per cent relative to remaining in the EU.[107] Exports and imports will be around 15 per cent lower in the long run than if the UK had remained in the EU. Some economic effects arguably took place immediately. Brexit created uncertainty which affected investment decisions. But many effects will be longer term and were muddied by other factors such as the Covid pandemic. In the meantime, Britain has undergone a major parliamentary pantomime preparing and passing the legislation. The connection between the vote in 2016 and prosperity of the UK economy in the future will hardly be clear for the public.

TYPES OF CHANGE

Given that leaders enter political systems where there are already rivers of causation flowing, the critical question is to what extent are leaders

106 Nigel Walker, 'Brexit timeline: events leading to the UK's exit from the European Union', House of Commons Library, last updated 6 January 2021, accessed 28 July 2025 (https://commonslibrary.parliament.uk/research-briefings/cbp-7960/).

107 Office for Budget Responsibility, 'Brexit analysis', last updated 1 February 2025, accessed 28 July 2025 (https://obr.uk/forecasts-in-depth/the-economy-forecast/brexit-analysis/). See also Jun Du, Emine Beyza Satoglu and Oleksandr Shepotylo, 'How Did Brexit Affect UK Trade?', *Contemporary Social Science*, 18(2), 2023, pp. 266–83.

responsible for changing these causal forces or introducing new forces? What would the world have looked like if they had not acted? It is suggested here that we might initially envisage six possible types of change:[108]

- Birth: they might create new forces which previously did not exist.
- Accelerate: they might accentuate, strengthen and thicken existing forces.
- Slow: they might reduce the power of causal forces.
- Stop: they might entirely cease existing causal forces.
- Reconfigure: they might qualitatively change the nature of causal forces.
- Redirection: they might make a minor adjustment to the nature of causal forces.

Some of these forms of change are more important than others. In the interests of simplicity, it may be possible to further streamline this and consider whether, for each event, a leader has instigated:

- No change.
- Minor change: acceleration or slowing of existing forces of causation.
- Major change: a change in the path and direction of causation.
- Seismic change: the construction of new causal forces.

108 Toby S. James, 'The effects of Donald Trump', *Policy Studies*, 42(5–6), 2021, pp. 755–69.

LONGUE DURÉE CHANGE IN BRITAIN

There has undoubtedly been change in the UK over the period covered in this volume. Summarising such change is deeply difficult, but one approach is descriptive detail. In 1901, the population of the UK was 38.3 million, life expectancy was forty-five years for males and forty-nine for females, and the average family size was 3.5 children.[109] By 2023, the population had reached 68.3 million,[110] life expectancy had reached 78.6 years for males and 82.6 years for females,[111] and the average number of children per family was 1.74.[112] The climate was 1.5°C cooler in the period 1850–1900, before the effects of climate change were felt.[113]

This descriptive detail is helpful because all aspects of social life are important – and are part of the framework set out above. However, there is also value in an oversimplified story, which enable the 'bigger picture' to be seen. Seeing the 'big picture' matters as it allows overall trends and transformations to be seen – in other words, the forests rather than just the trees. This also provides a narrative that leaders can construct to set directions for society.

One way to examine the bigger picture is to scrutinise the successful

109 Joe Hicks and Grahame Allen, 'A Century of Change: Trends in UK Statistics Since 1900', House of Commons Library, 22 December 1999.

110 'Population estimates for the UK, England, Wales, Scotland and Northern Ireland: mid-2023', Office for National Statistics, last updated 8 October 2024, accessed 28 July 2025 (https://www.ons.gov.uk/peoplepopulationandcommunity/populationandmigration/populationestimates/bulletins/annualmidyearpopulationestimates/mid2023).

111 'National life tables – life expectancy in the UK: 2020 to 2022', Office for National Statistics, last updated 11 January 2024, accessed 28 July 2025 (https://www.ons.gov.uk/peoplepopulationandcommunity/birthsdeathsandmarriages/lifeexpectancies/bulletins/nationallifetablesunitedkingdom/2020to2022).

112 'Average number of dependent children per family, England and Wales, 2019, 2022 and 2023', Office for National Statistics, last updated 12 July 2024, accessed 28 July 2025 (https://www.ons.gov.uk/peoplepopulationandcommunity/birthsdeathsandmarriages/families/adhocs/2189averagenumberofdependentchildrenperfamilyenglandandwales20192022and2023).

113 Grahame Madge, '2024: record-breaking watershed year for global climate', Met Office, last updated 10 January 2025, accessed 28 July 2025 (https://www.metoffice.gov.uk/about-us/news-and-media/media-centre/weather-and-climate-news/2025/2024-record-breaking-watershed-year-for-global-climate).

'regimes of accumulation' that have existed in Britain.[114] Regimes of accumulation are brief periods of sustained economic growth. They include a mode of accumulation – the way in which the economy is structured, what is produced, by whom and how wages and profit are assigned. They also include a mode of regulation – which are the political systems, norms and ideas that sustain the regime. Regimes of accumulation are temporary. After a period of stability, they run into problems, which can create pressures for political and economic change.

There were arguably regimes of accumulation in Britain during the early periods covered by this book. During a time of imperial capitalism, the British Empire was used to extract resources from overseas peoples and a system of imperial preference on trade tariffs allowed the export of goods. The aristocratic landowning elite held power, but then saw their power decline. The widening of the franchise led to the development of new political parties, notably the Labour Party. The state remained small, although it expanded to play a pivotal role in education and poor relief.

There are two more distinct periods in the time covered by this book.[115] The Keynesian welfare state, in place from 1945 to the 1980s, was Keynesian in that full employment was a primary goal of economic policy and the state would intervene to boost the economy if needed. Collective bargaining with trade unions was undertaken to determine wages. The national state was the primary entity promoting economic affairs. A welfare state was established to provide a safety net for citizens, including universal health care and education.

A globalised neo-liberalism approach was in place from the 1970s and 1980s, when the Keynesian welfare state was said to have been in crisis. The state was rolled back, the power of trade unions was reduced and a free market was encouraged. Tackling inflation became the primary target of government policy. The economy transitioned towards being service-based and

114 Michel Aglietta, *A Theory of Capitalist Regulation: The US Experience*, London, Verso, 1979; Bob Jessop, *The Future of the Capitalist State*, Cambridge, Polity Press, 2002.

115 Bob Jessop, *The State: Past, Present and Future*, Cambridge, Polity Press, 2015; Bob Jessop, 'The Organic Crisis of the British State: Putting Brexit in its Place', *Globalizations*, 41(1), 2016, pp. 133–41.

'knowledge-based.' The economic dividends of globalisation were sought, with manufacturing products being imported from overseas. Immigration and membership of the EU was a key component to growth and the provision of a national workforce. Personal debt played an important role in maintaining expenditure in the economy.

The coherence of this approach has been unravelling as a result of a series of societal shifts, caused or illustrated by:

- Perpetual sluggish economic growth and real-wage stagnation.
- Economic inequality and an underlying economic 'precariat' – especially in former industrial areas.
- A political backlash to immigration and globalism.
- An ageing population and shrinking pool of younger workers.
- Technological changes such as AI threatening white-collar jobs.
- Intergenerational wealth and opportunity gaps for younger people.
- Populist backlashes to equality, diversity and inclusion policies.
- Environmental crises arising from global warming.
- Global power shifts, including BRICS countries becoming more aggressive on the world stage.

It is not entirely clear what the next regime of accumulation will be – and this may only be apparent to future historians, who have the benefit of hindsight. In the US, Donald Trump has looked set to break with the existing American model of combining liberal democratic politics and Reaganite free-market economics.[116] He has set the US on a path towards authoritarianism, in which a leader is demolishing the state and reconstructing it with partisan, loyal supporters. This is accompanied by anti-migrant rhetoric and a war on diversity and inclusion. The US has ripped up the existing soft-power approach to world politics and replaced it with aggressive transactional nationalism.

One alternative pathway is the focus on a 'Green New Deal'. This would involve a collective approach to addressing climate change, while also creating new jobs, promoting economic growth and reducing economic inequality.[117] The case has also been made for universal basic income, embracing the benefits of technology and automation in a more egalitarian way.[118] Or leaders may double-down on neo-liberalism and continue to reduce the size of the state.

There is no clear approach yet in the UK. The Boris Johnson government reversed some globalism with Brexit, bringing decision-making back to the UK from Europe. A focus on 'levelling up' could involve heavier public spending and the addressing of social inequalities. In office, Keir Starmer has promised to slash government size and maintain low taxes. UK political leaders after the New Labour years have increasingly used anti-immigrant rhetoric – even if immigration numbers continue to rise. The approach is therefore closer to the renewed neo-liberal model than any other.

CONCLUSION

All leaders want to deliver change of some sort. Supporters or critics of prime ministers will tend to rush to make the case that leaders have birthed major or seismic change. A key claim of this book is that leadership matters and this is possible. However, we should also recognise the value

116 Steven Levitsky, 'The New Authoritarianism', *The Atlantic*, last updated 10 February 2025, accessed 28 July 2025 (https://www.theatlantic.com/ideas/archive/2025/02/trump-competitive-authoritarian/681609/).

117 Joseph E. Stiglitz, *The Road to Freedom: Economics and the Good Society*, New York, Norton and Company, 2024; Ann Pettifor, *The Case for the Green New Deal*, London and New York, Verso, 2020.

118 Nick Srnicek and Alex Williams, *Inventing the Future: Postcapitalism and a World Without Work*, London and New York, Verso, 2015.

of leadership that can slow or reconfigure societal problems in the face of major challenges. This may involve resetting public expectations of what is possible during the life of one parliament.

Political change can come in multiple forms. Chapters 2 and 3 have focused on the political and electoral change that leaders can bring. This chapter has sought to bring the other dimensions of change into focus before the book departs to examine specific leaders in detail.

PART II

ASSESSMENTS OF LABOUR LEADERS

CHAPTER 5

KEIR HARDIE

KENNETH O. MORGAN

Keir Hardie, a coal miner from the age of ten, went on to become the first Labour Member of Parliament in 1892. He later represented Merthyr Tydfil from 1900 until his death in 1915. In 1906, he was elected to lead twenty-eight other Labour Party MPs in the Commons, but resigned within two years as internal rivalries developed. Yet Kenneth O. Morgan argues that Hardie contributed more to the rise of Labour as a political force than any other man. For all his passionate crusading, he was a pragmatic strategist who concentrated his political efforts on increasing Labour representation in Parliament, which in turn laid the road to power. He knew how and when to use industrial protest and popular protest to good effect. It was also Hardie who provided many of the policy platforms – unemployment and poverty, women's and racial equality, decolonisation, devolution and internationalism – on which Labour would contest elections for many subsequent generations. More than any other Labour leader, he became a legend, greatly revered.

• • •

Keir Hardie was a founder not a leader. Like the Independent Labour Party (ILP) in general, his democratic instincts rebelled against the very idea of leadership. This view swayed the Labour Party in its early years. Not until 1922 did it confer the title of 'leader' (rather than solely 'chairman') onto one of its members – significantly, it was Ramsay MacDonald who first received this accolade. Hardie was a crusader, an evangelist and an idealist, who disliked the compromises of parliamentary leadership and the business details that went with it. Thus, the Liberal journalist A. G. Gardiner wrote in somewhat exaggerated terms in 1908 that Hardie 'was the one man in the PLP who was unqualified to lead it'.[119] Hardie's intimate colleague John Bruce Glasier wrote that being the first chairman of the party in 1906–7 was 'a seat of misery' for his friend.[120] Glasier, indeed, did not want him to be the chairman at all, but rather wanted him to reserve himself as an inspirational force in promoting socialism. But Hardie, however reluctantly, felt it was his duty to stand, since otherwise the party would be led by a non-socialist trade unionist like David Shackleton. In the end, Hardie defeated Shackleton by fifteen to fourteen on a second vote. The first vote had been a tie – fourteen all – and it seems to have been MacDonald, who abstained the first time, who cast the decisive vote.[121]

Hardie gave up the chairmanship with much relief at the end of 1907, during a lengthy tour around the world that took him to Canada, Japan, the Straits Settlements, India and South Africa – far removed from the parliamentary pressures of Westminster. In India, in particular, he was greeted by massive crowds and, in Madras especially, as a Christ-like prophet: 'I honestly believe that I am being worshipped in certain quarters.' It was all a far cry from the fractious pressures of London politics.[122]

His period of leadership had seen the party achieve some notable victories in the Commons, principally the passage of the Trade Disputes Act of 1906 to reverse the Taff Vale verdict. This act was in fact the Labour Party's own, substituted for the government's more limited bill, and was sponsored by Shackleton and backed by Hardie, among others. It safeguarded trade union funds by giving the unions complete financial immunity in the event

119 Alfred George Gardiner, *Prophets, Priests and Kings*, London, Rivers, 1908, p. 86.

120 Bruce Glasier, *J. Keir Hardie MP: A Memorial*, Manchester, National Labour Press, 1915, p. 50.

121 Ramsay MacDonald to Bruce Glasier, 21 July 1906 (Independent Labour Party Archive, London School of Economics Library).

122 Keir Hardie to Bruce Glasier, 8 October 1907 (Independent Labour Party Archive, London School of Economics Library).

of industrial disputes and strike action; it was hailed as 'the Magna Carta of Labour'.

But, in general, his period as party chairman was an unhappy and unproductive time for Hardie. It led to much criticism from MacDonald, Henderson and others for his seemingly wayward and unbusinesslike methods. He came under fire for his gestures of support towards Victor Grayson, an erratic loose cannon of far-left views and demagogic style, who actually won a sensational by-election victory at Colne Valley in 1907, much to the Labour Party's embarrassment. Grayson soon proved to be an impossible colleague in the Commons.

Hardie's involvement with the suffragettes also led to much criticism of him at the 1907 annual party conference, which provoked his dramatic, perhaps melodramatic, threat that he would resign as party chairman. There was also disagreement with Hardie's decision to go abroad on his lengthy world tour, leaving his colleagues to labour on as best they could in his absence. MacDonald saw it as a form of vanity on Hardie's part – though of course he himself was a political prima donna par excellence. To his own relief, Hardie's decision to resign as chairman took effect while he was abroad, and he was succeeded in January 1908 by the far more organised figure of Arthur Henderson.

After all this, John Burns, an undistinguished Cabinet minister, was to claim, with much exaggeration, that Hardie, who had never run anything greater than the Auchinleck school board, had no practical achievements to his name. The title he deserved, claimed Burns sourly, was 'Barren Cumnock in the Duchy of Doctrinaire'.[123] Of course, Burns ignored the skills required for the founding of the Labour Party, to which he himself had been strongly opposed.

But it was certainly the case that Hardie was temperamentally disinclined to focus on the need to communicate with other parties and groups or to follow the path of strategic compromise. In addition, the minutiae of day-to-day

123 John Burns's diary, 26 September 1915 (British Library, Add.MSS. 46,337).

parliamentary business were not something to which he naturally put his mind. He differed from both MacDonald and Henderson in this respect. Hardie as leader was an agitator, not an operator.

As a parliamentary colleague, Hardie, like others in the distinctly unfraternal early Labour Party (Henderson and Philip Snowden, for instance, and MacDonald especially), could pose difficulties, sometimes creating problems for party discipline. He was a temperamental, often moody Lowlander, whose relations with that other prickly Scot, the Highlander Ramsay MacDonald, were often volatile. Mavericks in the ranks, such as George Lansbury, who resigned his seat to fight a losing by-election at Bow & Bromley, or even the rebellious Victor Grayson, would often turn to Hardie for some moral support.

Hardie was, in any case, a very private, complex man, inclined on occasions to complain about how he found political agitation (for which he had a unique gift) to be a torment and a burden. Like others in the early party, such as Frank Smith, he was prone to dabble in spiritualism.[124] His marriage was an unhappy one and his relations with young female socialists were complicated and often ambiguous. Sylvia Pankhurst, with whom his relationship was physical, was only the most celebrated and intense of his various attachments.[125]

And yet Hardie was, by any standards, a great man in politics – an astonishing pioneer whose career transformed the face of British politics for ever. By contemporaries, he was variously compared with Christ and (by MacDonald himself) Moses, leading the children of Labour out of the wilderness and towards the Promised Land. Hardie's suffering in 1915, during the horrors of the First World War, led to comparison[126] with the sufferings of Christ at Gethsemane.

In his own fashion, therefore, Hardie was a kind of saint, and, as with Gandhi or Mandela, saints can often be difficult. He was a very shrewd saint, with

124 Kenneth O. Morgan, *Keir Hardie: Radical and Socialist*, London, Weidenfeld & Nicolson, 1975, p. 46.

125 Caroline Benn, *Keir Hardie*, London, Hutchinson, 1992, pp. 236–9.

126 Wil Jon Edwards, *From the Valley I Came*, London, Angus & Robertson, 1956, pp. 120–21.

extraordinary persuasive and inspirational powers. He was also a highly practical saint: witness him telling the young Fenner Brockway that his speech at party conference was very good – although it was essentially an ILP speech, not a Labour Party one.[127]

Despite his distaste for leadership and his personal idiosyncrasies, Keir Hardie, as orator, editor and crusader, contributed more to the rise of Labour as a political force than any other man. He was a unique moral force. In this sense, he was the greatest leader of them all.

Hardie's career was remarkable both for his intuitive grasp of strategy and his judgement on policy. On party strategy, he showed extraordinary insight. A self-taught man who left school at the age of ten to go down the Ayrshire pits, he proved to be more perceptive and far-sighted in many key respects than the middle-class, self-proclaimed intellectuals of the Fabian Society.

First and foremost, he created the Labour Alliance. He saw that, in order to flourish, democratic socialists should make common cause with the growing ranks of the trade unions. They not only represented the direct popular voice of the industrial working class – as no other body could – but the unions were also changing their character and composition, as the relatively small ranks of Lib–Lab skilled craftsmen (often termed, not always in a complimentary way, the 'aristocracy of labour') were hugely swollen by the unionisation of vast numbers of unskilled and general workers: the so-called 'New Unionism'. Trade unionists, too, had been newly radicalised by a series of judicial verdicts in the later 1890s that seemed to show the judges siding with capitalist employers and imperilling the basic right to withdraw labour. The alliance between the socialists of the ILP and the (less important) Marxist Social Democratic Federation (SDF) and trade unions was the essential foundation for the new party, and it was Hardie who was mainly responsible.

Hardie was a passionate man, but he was also a pragmatist. He insisted that the essential objective should be to win Labour representation in Parliament, rather than pursue any particular ideological programme. Shrewdly, he

---

127 Private interview with the late Lord Brockway, 19 March 1974.

worked at first on the labour movement in his native Scotland, establishing key contacts with the Scottish Trade Union Congress (TUC), formed only as recently as 1897 – its chairman, Bob Smillie, was an old ILP comrade of Hardie's from the western Scottish coalfield. In April 1899, a formal special conference of the Scottish TUC at Dundee carried a motion in favour of a new initiative for Labour representation. Critics of his attacked Hardie for 'nobbling' the conference. He was said to have hardly been off the platform at all, whether in moving motions or in even proposing votes of thanks to the musicians.[128] But it was a decisive episode in Labour politics. It led to the British TUC conference at Plymouth in September 1899, where a motion calling for a special conference of working-class organisations to promote greater parliamentary representation was carried by 546,000 to 434,000. The motion was moved by an ILP associate of Hardie's – a member of the hitherto cautious Amalgamated Society of Railway Servants (AMRS).

The meeting at the Memorial Hall, Farringdon Street, London, the following February took a similar view and the Labour Representation Committee (LRC) was founded. From the start, the trade unions were central to its operations, along with the shock and anger stirred by the Taff Vale verdict in 1901, which implied the imposition of financial penalties on the right to strike. It was Hardie's strategic vision that brought the new body into being.

At the same time, Hardie was clear that the new party – which, in effect, it had become – should be much more than a trade union or working-class party. It should look beyond the narrow confines of 'economism' and embody a wider, distinctly socialist thrust, too. Hence the vital need that the trade union mass membership should work in partnership with middle-class professionals and intellectuals, as the ILP had made a point of doing ever since its foundation in Bradford in 1893.

On this basis, he welcomed the way that Eugene Debs's Socialist Party of America had found support from intellectuals, social workers and journalists in the Progressive Movement. Labour in Britain needed the stimulus of new,

---

128 Miss W.H. Irwin to Ramsay MacDonald, 4 May 1899 (National Archives, MacDonald Papers, 5/6).

radical ideas. In Hardie's terms, Labour 'should blend the classes into one human family'. The outstanding quality of the ILP, he wrote, was its 'broad, tolerant catholicity'.[129] The Labour Party that came into formal existence in 1906 should be broad based; indeed, the term 'broad church' was highly appropriate for this movement that had grown out of the popular religion of the Nonconformist chapels in areas such as the West Riding, the Lancashire textile communities and the south Welsh mining valleys. The concept was that the party should lapse into neither sterile 'economism' nor the faddism of doctrinaire intellectuals – it should flourish because all its varied components interacted and each played an essential part.

Second, Hardie insisted that Labour should be an independent party, although it should collaborate tactically with other parties too, of course – notably the radicals in the post-Gladstonian Liberal Party. Hardie thus gave his somewhat reluctant blessing to the secret 'entente' that MacDonald negotiated with the Liberal Chief Whip Herbert Gladstone in 1903, which guaranteed Labour a free run against the Conservatives in about thirty seats at the following election. In two-member seats, LRC candidates ran in double harness with Liberals, as Hardie himself did in Merthyr Tydfil in 1900, and as MacDonald did in Leicester and Philip Snowden did in Blackburn in 1906. During the later stages, Hardie even flirted with the notion of a new radical force consisting of Labour and 'pro-Boer' Liberals such as Lloyd George; he even contemplated the socially conservative John Morley as its possible leader, but the idea was, fortunately, soon dropped.[130] Otherwise, Hardie was strong and consistent in emphasising the need for independence in structure, priorities and (thanks to the unions) finance.

There were many other scenarios against which Hardie had to contend. There were the Lib–Labs, strong in the older craft unions and also in the miners' unions, who wanted no change, and chose to see themselves as a pivotal pressure group within a broad Liberal coalition. There were the Fabians,

---

129 Keir Hardie, *The ILP and All About It*, London, Independent Labour Party, 1909, pp. 6, 11–12; *My Confession of Faith in the Labour Alliance*, London, Independent Labour Party, 1909, p. 12.

130 *Labour Leader*, 3 February, 16 June 1900.

notably the Webbs, who did not favour a Labour Party at all at first, and preferred to see socialists as a leaven within the political world, working with allies, radical Liberals on the London county council and even, perhaps, Conservatives such as Balfour on educational reform.

The Fabians tended to keep aloof at this early stage. On trade policy, they were sympathetic to tariff reform, while Hardie and the ILP were traditional free traders, hostile to monopoly. In external policy, the Webbs endorsed the principles of empire, and were friendly with Liberal imperialists like Rosebery and Haldane, whereas Hardie and his friends passionately supported those fighting for colonial self-government, Hardie also steered clear of the Marxists of the SDF. For an old stable country like Britain, revolutionary dogma was a wholly misconceived option. In Marx himself as a pioneer, Hardie naturally found much to praise. He tried to claim that Marx's socialism was basically evolutionary – fully compatible with parliamentary politics. But too many of his supposed followers proclaimed an ideology that was rigid and intransigent. Socialists, wrote Hardie, should 'make war upon a system not a class'.[131] Hardie had thus to define a strategy that transcended the negativism of the Lib–Labs, the intellectual detachment of the Fabians and the revolutionary programme of the Marxists. It is part of his great contribution to Labour thereafter that he was successful in so doing.

Third, Hardie also consistently emphasised the priority to be given to constitutional action. During the fierce ideological debates of 1910–14 – when doctrines of industrial unionism or syndicalism, as preached in France and the USA, had much impact in areas such as south Wales – Hardie urged restraint. He saw a kind of dangerous nihilism in the upsurge of such doctrines. Labour, he proclaimed, should *use* the state, not destroy it.[132] The social liberation of the worker could only be achieved thus.

At the same time, Hardie was anxious to claim that industrial and political protest should proceed side by side. He took fierce issue with Philip

---

131 *Labour Leader*, 2 September 1904.

132 *The Metropolitan*, New York, June 1912, pp. 13–14 (copy in Tamiment Library, New York City).

Snowden's view in the pages of the *Labour Leader* that strike action was damaging to labour and should be largely abandoned.[133] On the contrary, Hardie had seen the harsh experiences of exploited working men in Wales, ranging from the rural slate workers of the Penrhyn quarries – denied the right to form unions at all – to the miners of the Welsh steam-coal valleys – prevented from receiving fair wages due to their being employed in 'abnormal places' at the coal face. These men were confronted with determined employers calling in violent police forces, like the dreaded 'Glamorgans' used at Tonypandy, and the Home Office even deployed the armed forces, who patrolled the Rhondda with fixed bayonets in 1910 and shot down six workers during a rail strike in Llanelli in 1911.

For Hardie, industrial power was an essential weapon as well. It was, after all, workers' pressure in the pits, dockyards and factories that led to the miners' minimum wage becoming a parliamentary priority. In Ireland, Hardie was strongly sympathetic to the strike action pursued by followers of 'Larkinism' among the Dublin tramway workers, whose support for their union led to violent and indiscriminate reprisals by the police. His analysis was often far from being a model of clarity, and it was often inconsistent. But he did sense that the injustices of labour were not only there to be debated in the parliamentary arena – they stemmed from fundamental inequalities emerging from the very essence of capitalism itself, which called for the mobilisation of workers' power. Hardie was a democratic socialist who saw both the democracy and the socialism of that creed as vital for the crusade.

His final strategic insight was that Labour should, above all, pay due regard to British traditions of popular protest. He located the antecedents of the labour movement in many places, not only in the Peasants' Revolt, Chartism or reactions to early industrialism, but also in a vibrant radical tradition shown during the American and French revolutionary wars, the anti-war campaigns of Cobden and Bright, the New Liberalism championed by Lloyd George in his own day, and the 'liberty tree' cherished by the common people

133 *Labour Leader*, 2 October, 23 October 1913.

through the ages. Hardie always showed respect for history. He had done so as a young socialist in Scotland, when he read deeply on the uprising of William Wallace in 1297 and 'The Ballad of Chevy Chase'. He was to do so again as a Welsh MP, cherishing the cultural antecedents of the Welsh people, as in the National Eisteddfod.

One model for him there was Jean Jaures of the French socialist movement, thus linking the social conflicts of Hardie's own day with the revolutionary traditions of 1789, 1848 and 1871. Hardie also noted approvingly how Jaures worked closely with French radicals in fighting the injustices of the Dreyfus affair as Jacobins would have done 100 years before. He believed a successful Labour Party should be inspired by its radical and national predecessors. It should not sulk in its own ideological tent or threaten non-cooperation with the rest of the political world. It should encourage and associate itself with contemporary New Liberal movements of social reform. Lloyd George's 'People's Budget' of 1909 aroused Hardie's enthusiasm. With some exaggeration, Hardie thought it partly socialist in intent. He was broadly content with the progressive alliance with the Liberals up to the First World War, and lent his support to Liberal causes such as educational reform, temperance and the disestablishment of the Church in Wales.

One principle on which he was very firm was to ensure that Labour, unlike the Socialists in France, or the Geman Social Democrats, should not be an anti-clerical party. On the contrary, he himself had grown into socialism through a dissenting Protestant church in the west of Scotland, and his speeches were full of Biblical imagery, hailing the kingdom of Christ on earth. The ILP's appeal, *Clarion* vans and all, was revivalist. Thus it was that, in strongly Nonconformist communities in the mining villages of West Yorkshire, Durham and Northumberland, the Lancashire textile towns, and, increasingly, the valleys of south Wales (all of them invincibly Liberal since the Third Reform Act of 1884), the new party found its most zealous support. Several leading Nonconformist ministers and a few important Anglican clergymen actually joined Labour, as did some theologians who championed R. J. Campbell's 'new theology'. Hardie understood Britain to be a land with deep roots in radicalism and populism, much of it of Christian origin. In many ways, he responded to the country's injustices less as a politician than as a mystic, or perhaps a *fin-de-siècle* artist or poet – albeit an often sentimental one. While not versed in the minutiae of British history, he had the wisdom to see that it suggested essential keys to social progress. Like Nye Bevan, Hardie argued that you could only know where you were going if you understood where you had come from. Hardie spent much time denouncing tawdry Edwardian doctrines of national and imperial greatness, and was denounced as an unpatriotic extremist for it – as was Bevan years later for the phrase 'lower than vermin'.

Hardie condemned an international arms race. He was a republican, and poured contempt on the royal family for becoming the mouthpiece of jingoism and for its links with the repressive Tsar of Russia. He was rebuked by the Speaker for making a highly personal attack on the King in the Commons, and was, for a period, excluded from royal garden parties as a punishment – events it is inconceivable Hardie would ever have wished to attend anyway. The King is said to have remarked: 'We don't want any bloody agitators here.'[134] And yet, in his gut instincts for what British Labour was and could be, Hardie like Bevan was fundamentally a patriot and a history man.

The other area in which Hardie's influence was centrally important was policy. This is frequently under-estimated. Hardie is too often seen as a sentimental romantic, focusing on simple values such as the joys of nature or the rural symbolism of May Day – 'A thing of joy and beauty … a day with sport, sunshine and green fields, with the singing birds and the flowers … a sacred day devoted to the cause of Labour and humanity.' But he was far more constructive than that, and impressed his views on the party in several key areas, even if some of them emerged as centrally important only in the longer-term future.

From his 'cloth-capped' (actually 'deer-stalkered') entry into Parliament as MP for West Ham South in 1892, Hardie put an emphasis, hitherto unknown

134 Bruce Glasier's diary, 7 May 1910 (University of Liverpool Library).

in the House of Commons, on working-class issues. He championed many causes that remain of much relevance to Labour at the present time – a minimum wage, the ending of child poverty and slum housing, the rights of immigrant workers and of women in 'sweated trades'. He spoke, in general terms, of the desirability of a national health service, financed from progressive redistributive taxation, not a poll tax like the 1911 National Insurance Act of Lloyd George. They should 'tax wealth not poverty'.

Most strikingly, Hardie took up in the 1890s, and again after 1903, when trade declined, the great theme of unemployment. It was an unfamiliar concept to the early Victorians, as their economy grew and overseas competition appeared less than threatening. The very word 'unemployment' only first emerged in public discourse in the 1880s, around the time of the violent unemployed riots in Trafalgar Square in 1887. Hardie made several of his most notable speeches in Parliament on this issue, and received the proud accolade of being 'the member for the unemployed'. He spoke on the topic with more passion than precision, His knowledge of economics was sketchy to the extreme – 'Socialism is much more than either a political creed or an economic dogma,' he once wrote[135] – and his specific proposals, such as labour colonies for the unemployed along the lines of the 'home colonies' started at Hollesley Bay, Mayland and Laindon, would hardly have dealt convincingly with the problem. The sums Hardie proposed to assist those out of work would make only a small impression on an unemployed total he claimed to be as high as six million.

Nevertheless, Hardie gave the issue a new public prominence, while working with leftish philanthropists like the American millionaire Joseph Fels on practical schemes of outdoor relief.[136] In 1905, he caused something of a sensation when, alone among Labour members and publicists, he gave support to the Unionist government's Unemployed Workmen Bill, since, for all its shortcomings, it did affirm that the community should provide work for all

135 Keir Hardie, *From Serfdom to Socialism*, London, 1907, pp. 25–6.

136 Arthur Power Dudden, *Joseph Fels and the Single-Tax Movement*, Philadelphia, Temple University Press, 1971, pp. 65–6; Mary Fels, *Joseph Fels: His Life Work*, New York, B. W. Huebsch, 1920.

those thrown out of work through the vagaries of trade. It also laid down that the cost of this should be a charge on public funds and, also, most importantly, that those receiving assistance should not suffer in their voting rights or public eligibility in general. His attitude led to fierce attacks on Hardie by his old enemy John Burns, whose own efforts to deal with unemployment at the Local Government Board under the succeeding Liberal government proved to be highly inept. But it gave the Labour Party a transcendent social cause by which it was to be uniquely identified until well after the general election of 1945, perhaps even until the inflationary fears of the 1970s. The 'member for the unemployed' had helped ensure that his new creation was, and would for decades remain, 'the party for the unemployed'.

On other issues, Hardie's legacy was to emerge most powerfully long after his death. Thus he became a courageous champion of the women's suffrage cause, as indeed did MacDonald, Snowden and other socialists. Hardie was friendly with the Pankhurst family and worked closely with prominent suffragettes, including his private secretary and virtual housekeeper, Margaret Travers Symons. He was to be embarrassed in 1908 when she interrupted a debate in the Commons with cries of 'Votes for women!' and was banned from the House for two years by the Speaker. After that, there is a sign that Hardie withdrew somewhat from his close connections with the Women's Social and Political Union, fearing that their militancy might lead them to become, for the women's movement generally, 'what the SDF had been to socialism'[137] – a small, disruptive, doctrinaire rump.

Nevertheless, Hardie's distinctive prominence in the women's cause henceforth linked Labour to feminism. As chairman in 1906–7, when he challenged the authority of the party conference on the adult suffrage issue, there were many who feared that, under him, there was a danger that the emancipation of women might become Labour's dominant cause. 'The women's suffragists have run away with him,' wrote Glasier.[138] Hardie devoted much thought to

137 Keir Hardie to Bruce Glasier, 7/8 January 1908 (Glasier Papers).

138 Bruce Glasier's diary, 30 November 1906, 19 January 1907.

the women's cause in all its aspects, assisted by his close personal involvement with the youngest of the Pankhursts, Sylvia, who became his lover. Hardie and Sylvia both saw beyond the question of the ballot when reflecting on the liberation of women: civic emancipation would lead on to social and cultural emancipation, bearing on the status of women not just as voters, but as taxpayers, workers, wives and mothers. However, the political dividend for Labour was long delayed, as the enfranchised women after 1918 invariably threw their votes behind right-wing parties. Labour, to many, seemed a macho, male party. But, in the longer term, the women's cause became central to Labour's identity. Again, Hardie should take much of the credit. We can speculate that egalitarian proposals such as all-women shortlists for parliamentary candidatures would have had his enthusiastic support.

Ethnic as well as gender questions were among Hardie's priorities. He always strongly identified Labour with racial equality. He spoke out on behalf of Jewish and other immigrant refugees at the turn of the century – victims of Russian anti-Semitic pogroms, stigmatised in Britain as 'aliens' – and he similarly defended the Jew, Alfred Dreyfus, in France. Overseas, his was a staunch voice for colonial liberation. He championed the Boer cause strongly during the South African War. More unusually, he spoke out on behalf of the African majority, oppressed by the Boers on racial grounds, and was one of the very few MPs to criticise the South African self-government measure of 1910, as it would diminish the human rights of black Africans in Cape Colony and Natal, who would be dragged to the same level of near-servitude as their brethren in Transvaal and the Orange Free State.[139] His meeting in Johannesburg in October 1907 ended in uproar and he narrowly escaped with his life. He returned to South African affairs in 1913 and 1914, condemning the policy of the South African government to use troops to intimidate striking black and 'coloured' workers in the mines of the Rand, and to sanction the widespread use of emergency measures and martial law – again, an area largely neglected by other British MPs.

---

139 *Labour Leader*, 17 April 1908.

In India, which Hardie visited just before travelling to southern Africa, he spoke out passionately on behalf of the country being governed by Indian people: the same principles should apply to India as to Ireland, whose self-government the Liberal Party had endorsed for many years. He took the same line when meeting Egyptian socialists in 1909. He worked closely with Indian nationalists such as B. G. Tilak and the Congress movement, and, as has been mentioned, was greeted with passionate enthusiasm in Madras and elsewhere as a Christ-like saviour figure. Here again, Hardie was taking a prophetic, if unpopular, line. In India, the transfer of power in 1947, for all the communal atrocities that accompanied it, was always associated specifically with the Labour Party. When James Callaghan visited India as Prime Minister in 1977, it was a badge of honour for him that he had been a minister in Attlee's liberating government.[140] In South Africa later on, the ending of apartheid and the release of Nelson Mandela in the early 1990s may reasonably be seen as the culmination of a century-old humanitarian, libertarian crusade against racial injustice, within which Hardie had ensured Labour a special role. An insular late-Victorian party, dedicated to democratic socialism in one country, had been imperishably linked with colonial freedom and racial equality. In the Caribbean, in central Africa, on the Indian subcontinent and in south-east Asia, young nationalist leaders, from Grantley Adams in Barbados to Lee Kuan Yew in Singapore, drew their basic political philosophy from principles set down long ago by the Edwardian Labour Party.

In the United Kingdom, Hardie's influence on Labour's policy was also important. He endorsed a pluralist form of socialism. He argued, as did the ILP, with its emphasis on local government, that socialism should be decentralised and devolved, with power located in the grass-roots and local communities. He wrote extensively in local newspapers such as the *Merthyr Pioneer*. He argued fiercely against the bureaucratic, centralised system of socialism favoured by the German Social Democrats.[141] Here, the logic

---

140 Conversations with Lord Callaghan in the 1990s.

141 Morgan, op. cit., 1975, p. 209.

of Hardie's argument was less than clear. He could hardly deny that national development programmes to protect the 'right to work', or welfare proposals on behalf of the 'national minimum' and living wage, would entail massive steps towards collectivism. But he hoped that a state-run economy could and would evolve into a form of 'free communism', based on each according to his own needs. The detail for an institutional framework of socialism was not Keir Hardie's strong point – no more than it was Marx's. But one crucial marker that he did lay down was on behalf of devolution, which he strongly supported for both Scotland and Wales. He had been a Scottish home ruler in his early years in Scotland – as had Ramsay MacDonald – and as MP for Merthyr Tydfil he had identified warmly with the national and cultural aspirations of Wales. He learned to sing the Welsh national anthem. He praised the National Eisteddfod as (he claimed) a medieval organisation to protect native Welsh bards against literary blacklegs! And he upheld Welsh home rule:

> *Y Ddraig Goch ar Faner Goch*, the Red Dragon and the red flag. The nationalist party I have in mind is the people of Wales fighting to recover possession of the land of Wales … that is the kind of nationalism that will be emblazoned on the red flag of socialism.[142]

The Labour government of 1997, as it tried to fight free of the corporate unionism of 1945, could thus find its legitimate ancestry in Keir Hardie. But so, too, perhaps, could Plaid Cymru.

Hardie's policy decisions thus had a profound, long-term impact on Labour's programmes in government, years after his death. In one other area, however, he failed – as indeed did the working-class movement in all countries. Hardie felt himself to be an internationalist, a citizen of the world. He associated enthusiastically at the Socialist International (SI) with great leaders like Jean Jaures, August Bebel and Victor Adler. He had frequent

142 Keir Hardie, *The Red Dragon and the Red Flag*, Merthyr, Independent Labour Party, 1912.

personal contact, too, with the Socialist Party leader Eugene Debs, and Sam Gompers of the American Federation of Labor in the United States. Hardie visited America three times.[143]

Along with other Labour leaders, Hardie worked closely with socialists in Germany and elsewhere to try to defuse international crises such as the Anglo-German naval confrontation of 1909. The corollary, Hardie argued, was that the workers should lead the international quest for a permanent peace. He criticised the building up of the Triple Entente and the Triple Alliance, which threatened to plunge a thriving world, in which the workers were gaining affluence and political power, into a maelstrom of carnage. With his close friend, the French socialist Edouard Vaillant, he attempted to persuade the SI to campaign for a worldwide strike against war.[144]

In August 1914, it was painfully evident that he had not succeeded. The British labour movement, like its corresponding factions in all other belligerent countries, flocked to the 'patriotic' cause, and workers volunteered to join the army in their hundreds of thousands. Even four years later, after so much slaughter, the bulk of working-class opinion remained committed to fighting the war. Hardie himself became a political outcast, like MacDonald and others in the ILP, reviled for his anti-war views.

He died, psychologically shattered, in September 1915 – a tragic, very old man of fifty-nine. The anti-war views of Hardie became more acceptable as post-war revulsion set in; another courageous dissenter, MacDonald, became Labour's symbol of the brave new world, and served as Prime Minister on two occasions. Hardie, like Labour in general from the Great War in 1914 to the invasion of Iraq in 2003, found a country at war very hard to reconcile with socialist principles. Bernard Shaw spoke poignantly and eloquently of Hardie's fate after his death. 'What else could Keir Hardie do but die?' But Shaw added: 'Like John Brown's body, his soul goes marching on.'

---

143 Morgan, op. cit., 1975, pp. 185–7.

144 Edouard Vaillant to Keir Hardie, 1 August 1912 (Independent Labour Party Archive).

Sylvia Pankhurst wrote her own touching, highly personal tribute: 'He has been the greatest human being of our time.'[145]

Hardie, then, was a commanding non-leader. In strategy and in policy, his influence over the nascent, struggling Labour Party was immense. He was to be Labour's undisputed folk hero down the generations. His character and style embodied his message even more than his policies. A Welsh admirer, Wil Jon Edwards, wrote that 'the man and his gospel were indivisible'[146] – as we have seen, Biblical analogies came naturally to those reflecting on Hardie's career.

Hugh Dalton was one middle-class undergraduate converted on the spot to socialism after seeing Hardie, in 1907, confronting a rowdy and violent audience of wealthy bullies at Cambridge in the mould of Oxford's Bullingdon Club. Dalton was deeply moved by Hardie's sublime courage, 'his simplicity of speech and thought and faith'.[147] Clement Attlee, employed as a social worker in the slums of the East End, was another such convert.

Through example, persuasion and evangelism, Hardie made socialists by the tens of thousands. For all his limitations of intellect and temperament, he embodied the ethic of democratic socialism as few others have done.

There was one electrifying moment at the 1914 ILP annual conference (the twenty-first), held appropriately at St George's Hall, Bradford (like the first, in 1893), with Hardie presiding. On the last day, he spoke to an audience of children. He told them to aim for a life of generosity and comradeship. They should love their fellow men and hate injustice, cruelty and war. 'If these were my last words, lads and lasses, I would say them to you: "Live for that better day."'[148] This complicated anti-leader was a unique moral force in leading the country there.

---

145 *Merthyr Pioneer*, 9 October 1915; *Workers' Dreadnought*, 16 October 1915 (material in Sylvia Pankhurst archive B/12, Institute of Social History, Amsterdam).

146 Wil Jon Edwards, op. cit., p. 111.

147 Hardie, op. cit., 1912.

148 Keir Hardie to Rose Davies, 1914 (Glamorgan Record Office, Cardiff, D/Dxik,30/27).

CHAPTER 6

GEORGE NICOLL BARNES AND WILLIAM ADAMSON

WILLIAM W. J. KNOX

George Nicoll Barnes and William Adamson were just two of several chairmen of the PLP prior to 1922, but are significant as they both fought general elections. Barnes took up the position in 1910. He stayed in office for only a year, though long enough to fight two general elections, before resigning due to ill health in the context of party indiscipline. Adamson's tenure, meanwhile, lasted from 1917 to 1921 following the chairmanships of MacDonald and Henderson (which will be considered in subsequent chapters), and fought the 1918 general election. William W. J. Knox argues that Barnes and Adamson became leaders due to fortunate circumstances rather than their own leadership abilities, and produced relatively unremarkable legacies for the party. Although they made modest parliamentary gains at their respective elections, more was expected of them given the size of the party's base.

• • •

In Shakespeare's *Twelfth Night*, Malvolio, in a moment of self-delusion, remarks: 'Some are born great, some achieve greatness, and some have greatness thrust upon them.'[149] In the case of George Barnes and William Adamson, it is tempting to amend the quotation to read: 'Some are born mediocre, some achieve mediocrity, and some have mediocrity thrust upon them.' Both men became chairmen of the PLP by default rather than for any obvious,

---

149 For a similar adaption of Shakespeare, see Joseph Heller's *Catch-22*.

particular talent for party politics or any ability to inspire those around them. Their rise to prominence could only have occurred in a political party in which the concept of leadership was barely developed. Yet this verdict may be a little hasty and unfair. Barnes served with distinction in the coalition government of Lloyd George, was a signatory to the 1919 Versailles Peace Treaty, and used his influence to get an agreement among all parties at the talks to set up a commission for world labour – this evolved into the International Labour Office (ILO). Adamson served as leader for nearly four years – longer than any other trade unionist – and was the first Labour Leader of the Opposition in Parliament. As leader of the Fife miners, he held out against the challenge of the Communist Party throughout the 1920s, and was Secretary of State for Scotland on two occasions. Thus, while distinctly uncharismatic politicians, their durability suggests that they were perhaps more politically astute than they have been given credit for. Moreover, their lack of education and the tough circumstances in which they grew up, only serve to remind us how remarkable their achievements were.

Barnes was the older of the two men by four years. He was born in Lochee, near Dundee, in 1859 – the son of a skilled engineer and mill manager from England, who had strong religious convictions and was a Tory. When Barnes was eight, the family moved to England, finally settling down in Middlesex, where George attended Enfield Highway Church School for four years, walking 2 miles to get there. In spite of his petit bourgeois background, George was sent out to labour at the age of eleven in a factory. From there, he found work as a clerk for 7s. a week, but, as the job had no promise of anything better, Barnes was apprenticed, like his father, to the engineering trade. His father was a seminal influence and Barnes's religious convictions, although, ultimately, not his politics, were shaped by him. As he recalled in his autobiography, his father would be 'arguing theology one night and hammering Gladstone the next'.[150]

There was very little in his early life to suggest he would reach Cabinet

150 George Nicoll Barnes, *From Workshop to War Cabinet*, London, Herbert Jenkins, 1923, p. 10.

rank in the wartime coalition government. He said that during his apprenticeship he did not do 'study[ing] of any kind', however, he did read 'a lot' ('without method or guidance') and showed an interest in 'public affairs'.[151] It seems as if his interest in politics was sparked by attending hustings during the 1874 general election, as he listened to one of the Liberal candidates make a speech in Dundee that left him 'in open-eyed wonder'.[152] Having moved from firm to firm, district to district, during his apprenticeship years, Barnes found work in Barrow-in-Furness for two years, before moving to London – a move that was to leave an indelible mark on his political outlook.

Barnes found himself without a job during the slump in 1879, 'facing the winter as one of London's unemployed'.[153] After ten weeks out of work in a pre-welfare society, he found poorly paid employment in an engineering shop in Shoreditch before moving to the Isle of Dogs and, then, finally settling in Fulham, where he got married and began to take an active interest in trade unionism. The question of unemployment was something he continued to take an interest in, arguing that it was essentially the consequence of under-consumption and could only be remedied when the 'great mass of the people ... had longer wages, shorter hours of work, and were in a position to buy back some of those goods they were constantly producing in ever-increasing quantities'.[154]

Adamson, on the other hand, was from a decidedly working-class background. His father was a miner and he was brought up in a little mining village, Halbeath, near Dunfermline, Fife. Like Barnes, he received an elementary education in a Dame school run by a mining engineer's wife. At the age of eleven, Adamson's father died, and, due to family poverty, he was forced to enter the mines as a pit-boy. At school, he had only picked up the 'rudiments' of literacy; however, he extended this by reading in his

---

151 Barnes, op. cit., p.16.

152 Ibid., p.18

153 Ibid., p.24

154 *The Scotsman*, 2 May 1910.

spare time, sometimes well into the early hours of the morning. His desire for self-improvement was mirrored in the homes of hundreds of young artisans in Scotland in the second half of the nineteenth century. As a young miner, Adamson was a member of the village Mutual Improvement Society, where he came under the influence of religion, temperance and the poetry of Robert Burns. These early formative religious, moral and literary influences remained with him all his life: he was deeply proud of his Baptist Church connection; a total abstainer, who in later years founded the Dunfermline Temperance Council; and, as an ardent student and admirer of Scotland's national bard, he was much sought-after for Burns festival orations.[155]

Barnes's formative steps into public life were through the trade union movement. Barnes had become an active member of the Amalgamated Society of Engineers (ASE), as well as the cooperative movement, and was a founder member of the ILP in 1893. He was associated with figures on the left in London and had a reputation as a 'militant and energetic "new" unionist'.[156] Although in later life he played down his early left-wing activism, claiming himself at the time to have been a moderate, he was involved in the unsuccessful campaign to elect Tom Mann of the Marxist SDF in 1891 as general secretary of the ASE. Furthermore, in 1910, Barnes wrote a pamphlet for the ILP on Marxism, stating that much of the progress of the labour movement in Britain towards unity was 'due largely to Karl Marx'.[157] However, as far as he was concerned, New Unionism was not intended to foment revolution, but rather for 'gingering up the old unionism' for 'parliamentary purposes'.[158]

His moderateness reflected the craft mentality of the engineers who elected him, at the age of thirty-seven, general secretary of the ASE in 1896, after four years as assistant secretary. The society was the most powerful and wealthy trade union in Britain at the time, but barely was the appointment of Barnes

155 William W. J. Knox, *Scottish Labour Leaders 1918–1939: A Biographical Dictionary*, Edinburgh, Mainstream, 1984, p. 58.

156 James B. Jeffreys, *The Story of the Engineers*, London, Lawrence & Wishart, 1945, p. 41.

157 George Nicoll Barnes, *Karl Marx*, London, The Labour Party, 1910, p. 21.

158 Barnes, op. cit., pp. 38–9.

ratified when it was plunged into turmoil by the great lockout of 1897 – an event that threatened the union's very survival. On the surface, the dispute with the employers was over demands for an eight-hour day, but, as Barnes himself recognised, it was 'really the question of machines and workshop management'.[159] The key factor in the dispute was the rights and prerogatives of management to manage.

The experience of the lockout was a particularly bruising one for Barnes, and it was to have a lasting influence on his views on industrial relations. He became convinced of the Liberal concept of essential harmony between capital and labour and, as such, advocated closer ties between bosses and workers through shop-floor representation on boards of directors. At the same time, he condemned sectional 'internecine strikes', the ability of a minority of 'woolly headed and truculent' workers 'to foment trouble', and the greed of some employers.[160] He saw greater scope for the state to intervene in industrial disputes and to introduce legislation that would eliminate strikes altogether, saying: 'We need not strike at all, except through the ballot box.'[161]

This shift to the centre ground was perhaps a reflection of the difficulties Barnes faced in running the ASE during a period in which employers had the upper hand. The defeat in 1897 had allowed capital to impose a humiliating and highly restrictive set of terms on the ASE. In honouring them, the NEC came into conflict with the rank and file over such issues as the premium bonus system. Matters came to a head in the north-east of England in 1908 over the refusal of the local branches to accept the executive's policies and call off their strike. Failing to convince or bully the district officials into compliance saw Barnes resign as general secretary. In his resignation statement, he said that 'there had been the development of an undemocratic feeling in the trade unions which worked out in the direction of mistrust of officials'.

Adamson's introduction to trade unionism was equally traumatic. In the

159 Ibid., p.48.

160 Ibid., pp. 50–51.

161 *Engineering*, 5 November 1897.

early 1870s, there was an upsurge in mining trade unionism in Scotland after many years of inactivity. In June 1870, the eight-hour day was won by Fife miners and, nearly a year later, in February 1871, the Fife, Clackmannan and Kinross Miners' Association (FCKMA) was formed. The employers hit back after a fourteen-week lockout in 1877 ended in victory for the miners. By 1880, nearly all the county and local mining unions had collapsed or been driven underground. Adamson went through these stirring and difficult times as a young man in his twenties and, as with Barnes, they had a lasting impact on his attitudes towards employer–employee relations.

He rose through the mining ranks, from Halbeath delegate to vice-president in 1894, then, in 1908, to general secretary of the FCKMA. Adamson was the epitome of the Labourist miner: a firm, unyielding trade unionist, favouring conciliation and arbitration, and seeing strikes as a last resort, 'only after contracts had been duly fulfilled'. As with Barnes, he was also a strong advocate of using parliamentary democracy to improve the living standards of mining communities, as well as conditions of work.

Although both had their political baptism as Liberals, their stories provide for the construction of a political narrative of disillusionment, which was articulated in the journey of the organised working class from the party of Gladstone to independent Labour representation. It was felt that the Liberals, when in office, had turned against their core Lib–Lab support. The engineering lockout of 1897, the failure to introduce an eight-hour day for miners, the unwillingness to put up working men as parliamentary candidates through social snobbery, and the legal assaults on the new unions during the 1890s all alienated the organised working class. But this did not denote an ideological break with Gladstonian Liberalism. When Barnes was invited to stand for Labour in Dundee in 1902, he declared that 'he was prepared to accept only on the condition that he was adopted by the Liberals. If there was a Liberal in the field he would not stand.'[162] One central tenet of Gladstonian Liberalism

162 I. G. C. Hutchinson, *A Political History of Scotland 1832–1924: Parties, Elections and Issues*, Edinburgh, John Donald Short Run Press, 1986, p. 261.

– anti-landlordism – was deeply embedded in Barnes's political philosophy, with him describing the hereditary House of Lords as 'an absolutely ridiculous thing, an insult to the intelligence of the people of this country'.[163]

The continuing influence of Liberal radicalism was reflected in the general election campaigns of the 1900s. During the 1906 general election, the pact agreed between Labour secretary, Ramsay MacDonald, and the Liberal Chief Whip, Herbert Gladstone, did not operate in Scotland, owing to the political hegemony of the Liberals north of the border. The LRC put up four candidates, of whom two were successful: Barnes in Glasgow Blackfriars (Gorbals from 1918) and Alex Wilkie, of the Shipwrights Association, in Dundee. The Scottish Workers' Parliamentary Election Committee put up a further five candidates, but they were all defeated. Throughout his campaign, Wilkie emphasised his Liberal sympathies and, in his election manifesto, also managed to avoid using the word 'Labour'. [164] When Adamson stood as Labour candidate for West Fife in 1910, the local Liberal newspaper praised him as a 'fine upholder of Liberal principles'.[165]

It was clear that the Labour Party was, prior to 1918, little more than a trade union pressure group in parliament.[166] It was also manifestly far from being a socialist party. As the party's historian G. D. H. Cole stated: 'Right up to 1914, the Labour Party neither stood, nor professed to stand, for socialism. There were … socialists in its ranks … But [also] in its ranks were quite a number who neither were, nor called themselves, socialists; and behind these men were the trade unions.'[167]

Indeed, the vast majority of the Labour MPs elected in 1906 were trade union leaders, who combined their union work with their parliamentary

163 *The Scotsman*, 22 January 1907.

164 W. H. Fraser, 'The Labour Party in Scotland', in K. D. Brown ed., *The First Labour Party*, London, Croom Helm, 1985, p.46.

165 *West Fife Echo*, 2 February 1910, quoted in Hutchinson, op. cit., p.261.

166 Ross McKibbin, *The Evolution of the Labour Party, 1910–1924*, London and New York, Oxford University Press, 1983, p. 1.

167 G. D. H. Cole, *A History of the Labour Party from 1914*, London, Routledge & K. Pau, 1948, p. 3.

duties – some had to, since MPs did not receive a salary until 1911. Adamson carried on into the 1930s, while Barnes was convinced that if 'Labour representation is to be effective, Labour representatives should give up trade union work and devote themselves to Parliament entirely'.[168]

The fact that most of the Labour MPs were not wholly dependent on politics for their livelihoods or careers allowed a great deal of scope for independent thought and action. Indeed, local constituency parties had little control over the views of candidates, and they could select whomever they chose, as long as he had the financial backing of an affiliated organisation.[169] Barnes recognised this problem, saying that we 'were loose in our discipline ... and pretty difficult to manage and pretty evenly divided ... this weakened us as a team'.[170] When he became chairman of the PLP in February 1910, through the rotational system then in place and MacDonald's unavailability for personal reasons, the issue of party discipline came to the fore.

MacDonald, who had cultivated the Liberal Party and had engineered the pact that brought a measure of electoral success in 1906, was keen that nothing should be done to endanger that relationship. The evidence that cooperation with the Liberal Party was crucial to success was overwhelming. Where there was a straight fight between a Labour and Liberal candidate, the former was normally defeated. In 1906, in twenty-four constituencies in which there was a straight contest, Labour lost – and, in four of them, Labour came bottom of the poll. It was clear that if any headway were to be made, the Liberals had to be kept onside.

However, shortly after the first general election of January 1910, a by-election was called at Swansea, which, under the terms of the electoral pact, should have meant that Labour step aside and give the Liberals a free run at the Tories. However, Ben Tillett, leader of the dockers' union and author

---

168 Barnes, op cit., pp. 59–60.

169 Duncan. Tanner, *Political Change and the Labour Party, 1900–1918*, Cambridge and New York, Cambridge University Press, 1990, p. 89.

170 Barnes, op. cit., p. 83.

of a pamphlet highly critical of Labour in Parliament,[171] threw his hat into the ring as an independent socialist candidate with the support of local ILP branches. Although Tillett had little chance of winning the seat, the fear was that he would split the vote and allow the Tories in. As it turned out, he came third, while the Labour leadership urged the Swansea voters to elect the Liberal candidate.

It was this kind of ill discipline that had caused Barnes to resign as general secretary of the ASE in 1908, but he continued as chairman of the PLP through the general elections of 1910. The performance of the party was hardly inspiring. It put up seventy-eight candidates in the January election and won forty seats. In December, spreading resources in a more concentrated manner, it fielded fifty-six candidates, but only increased the number of MPs to forty-two; indeed, the party's share of the vote had decreased by 0.2 per cent. This was highly disappointing, particularly as trade union membership stood at 2,565,000 in 1910.[172]

As reflected in Tillett's intervention at Swansea in 1910, there was a growing unease among some of the more left-wing members of the party over the party's direction. Criticism had come from within the ASE over the performance of the Labour MPs elected in 1906. One member wrote that 'the list of what George Barnes and Charles Duncan had done in the House since 1906 could be inscribed on the side of a threepenny piece'.[173] That criticism became louder when one of the party heavyweights, David Shackleton MP, at the invitation of Winston Churchill, left in 1910 to join the civil service as a special advisor to the Liberal government on labour issues. Many members were asking the question: what did the party stand for and whom did it represent?

By February 1911, Barnes had had enough and, on the grounds of ill health, resigned as chairman to be replaced by Ramsay MacDonald. However, the split within the party intensified during the First World War.

---

171 Ben Tillett, *Is the Parliamentary Labour Party a Failure?*, London, Twentieth-Century Press, 1908.

172 McKibbin, op. cit., 1983, p. 86.

173 Jeffreys, op. cit., pp. 161–2.

In the 1890s, Barnes had been a member of the International Crusade of Peace and had said at one of its meetings that 'most wars … could have been avoided if there had been … enlightened public opinion and a smaller number of men trained in the art of war'.[174] However, when Britain and her Allies declared war on Germany in August 1914, Barnes, as well as Adamson, was as jingoistic as Ben Tillett or H. M. Hyndman in their opposition to what they saw as Prussian militarism. Such was Barnes's enthusiasm for war that, before the introduction of conscription, he took part in recruiting drives. In his autobiography, he recalled speaking from a cart with the Marquis of Bath in the west of England and on large platforms in Scotland with Lord Curzon.[175]

With the fall of Asquith in 1916, Barnes was invited, along with other Labour leaders including Arthur Henderson, to join Lloyd George's coalition as Minister of Pensions. Barnes had a distinguished record in fighting for the introduction of old-age pensions in 1908; indeed, his crusade led to the saying that Barnes and pensions were inseparable.[176] While in wartime government, he improved 'both the level and system of administration of service pensions'.[177] His big moment came in 1917, when Arthur Henderson resigned and Barnes replaced him in the War Cabinet as Minister without Portfolio.

In accepting the ministerial role and becoming embedded in the coalition government, Barnes was increasingly the subject of criticism from inside a party that was beginning to move away from uncritical support for the war effort. By 1917, it was claimed in Scotland that: 'The strength of hostility to militarism … may be gathered from the fact that the war party is a discredited minority in nearly all the trades and labour councils north of the Tweed.'[178] The change in mood was also reflected in the party's dissatisfaction with the speed and direction of the government in reaching a peace settlement with

---

174 *The Times*, 16 February 1899.

175 Barnes, op. cit., p. 112.

176 Jeffreys, op. cit., p. 133.

177 Alastair Reid, 'Barnes, George Nicoll (1859–1940)', *Oxford Dictionary of National Biography*, Oxford and New York, Oxford University Press, 2004.

178 *Scottish Review*, spring 1917.

Germany.[179] In 1917, the Labour Party held a conference to discuss whether it should participate with other socialists of various national and political backgrounds, including the German Social Democrats, in a peace conference to be held in Stockholm to bring an end to hostilities and show the way to permanent world peace. Barnes opposed the idea of a negotiated peace, saying: 'I believe that the only way of ending this war is the way in which our brave boys at the front are trying to end it.'[180] Government hostility to the proposed conference ensured that it came to nothing, but the Labour delegates endorsed it in spite of Barnes's opposition. However, his opposition to the peace conference may also have been influenced by personal factors. Barnes's son, a second lieutenant in the Seaforth Highlanders, was killed in action in October 1915, aged twenty-five.[181]

It was increasingly obvious that Barnes was completely at odds with the mood of the Labour Party, but he repeatedly rejected calls to resign from the coalition, dismissing his critics as 'simple and excitable adherents and camp followers'.[182] As far as he was concerned, he had been mandated to serve as Labour's representative in the Cabinet until a peace treaty was signed. He was determined to see it through, even resigning from the party and fighting the 1918 general election as one of four coalition Labour candidates, comfortably defeating the official Labour candidate for Glasgow Gorbals – the Marxist school teacher and anti-war protestor John McLean, who Barnes described as an 'agent for Russian Soviet power' and someone who 'shared the … Soviet hatred of our parliamentary institutions'.[183] His patriotism was rewarded, and in 1920 he was made a member of the Order of Companions of Honour.[184] The order was founded in 1917 by George V and consists of the monarch plus sixty-five ordinary members.

179 Reid, op. cit.

180 Mary Agnes Hamilton, *Arthur Henderson: A Biography*, London, W. Heinemann, 1938, p. 153.

181 *The Scotsman*, 4 October 1915.

182 Barnes, op. cit., p. 196.

183 Ibid., p. 203.

184 *The Scotsman*, 3 January 1939.

Recognition by the establishment pushed Barnes further to the right of the Labour Party and his views on the class struggle were clearly unwelcome on Red Clydeside, the centre of the more radical ILP. According to Barnes, 'class war, direct action, revolutionary propaganda' were clearly unnecessary in a country 'in which the humble and haughty have equal right of speech and vote'.[185] In spite of returning to the party fold after Versailles, the local Gorbals Labour Party refused to endorse his candidacy for the 1922 general election. Indeed, such was the opposition to Barnes in Glasgow that, when he was about to receive the freedom of the city, cries of 'traitor' rang out from some of the audience.[186]

After this rejection, he retired from public life in Britain, devoting himself to the ILO[187] – which he, as British Labour's only representative, had fought for at the 1919 Paris peace talks – and the League of Nations – whose first assembly, in 1920, he had attended as one of three British delegates. His one major regret, he claimed, was that he 'wish[ed] we had done more to have brought the Kaiser and other chief warmongers to trial, and if found guilty to have hanged them out of hand'.[188]

Adamson had a much lower profile during the war years. He was as implacably opposed to Prussianism as Barnes and was 'heart and soul for a vigorous prosecution of the war, less an inconclusive peace occur and leave the power and menace of the Prussian military caste intact'.[189] However, he did not succumb to the win-at-all-costs mentality of Barnes, voting against the second reading of the Military Service Bill in January 1916,[190] which sought to introduce conscription. Like Barnes, he too had lost a son in the conflict.

In spite of his pro-war stance, Adamson did not share in the general

185 Barnes, op. cit., p. 290.

186 *The Times*, 29 November 1922.

187 George Nicoll Barnes, *History of the International Labour Office*, London, William & Norgate Ltd, 1926.

188 Barnes, op. cit., p. 264.

189 *Glasgow Herald*, 24 February 1936.

190 David Howell, 'Adamson, William (1863–1936)', *Oxford Dictionary of National Biography*, Oxford and New York, Oxford University Press, 2004.

opprobrium of those Labour politicians who had supported Lloyd George's coalition government. After the 1918 general election, Labour became the official opposition in Parliament, and Adamson was unanimously elected as party leader – a move that had the support of the press. *The Times* said of him: 'In training and outlook he is the antithesis of his predecessor, Mr Asquith. Mr Adamson has little scholarship, and no dialectic, but he is as shrewd as he is sincere.'[191] The party itself was less enthusiastic. As Beatrice Webb said of him: 'He is most decidedly not a leader, not even like [Arthur] Henderson, a manager of men.'[192] Later, Labour MP for Jarrow, Ellen Wilkinson, criticised him as being 'unfit' for the post of Scottish Secretary, and 'useless' in the House of Commons.[193] Although his obvious working-class origins, his awkwardness in manners, and his slowness and deliberateness in speech were calculated to arouse, in intellectuals like the Webbs, a sense of derision, Adamson's term of leadership was far from disastrous for the future of the party: his leadership was competent if rather uninspiring and undynamic. He was a safe pair of hands – a man unlikely to upset his colleagues or country. Emanuel Shinwell said of his selection as leader that it 'was motivated by a desire to have a chairman who would create the minimum of trouble, so the movement got the results it deserved'.[194]

The 1918 general election saw Labour put up 361 candidates, but the outcome was below expectation, as only sixty-one (including four Labour MPs who stood as coalition candidates) were returned to Westminster. The main reason for Labour's lack of success was that the election was fought on the old restricted franchise; it would take until 1922 for the electoral reforms of 1918 to massively impact upon the size of the electorate, doubling the number of voters from 10,434,000 to 20,874,000. It also faced the daunting task of challenging the charismatic wartime premier Lloyd George, whose slogans

191 *The Times*, 8 January 1919.

192 Beatrice Webb, *Diaries 1912–1924*, London and New York, Longman, 1952, p. 142.

193 David Torrance, *The Scottish Secretaries*, Edinburgh, Birlinn, 2006, p. 106.

194 Emanuel Shinwell, *The Labour Story*, London, McDonald, 1963, pp. 111–12

of 'hang the Kaiser' and 'a land fit for heroes' powerfully resonated with the public imagination. In spite of these political difficulties, Labour increased its share of the total vote from 7.1 per cent in 1910 to 21.5 per cent in 1918 – an increase of 14.4 per cent. The party now had the support of nearly 2,250,000 voters – an outcome that made Adamson, if measured by election results, the most successful leader in the history of the Labour Party.[195] However, as it stood, Labour remained a mainly northern trade union pressure group in Parliament. Twenty-five of the newly elected MPs were from the Miners' Federation alone, and 'all but eight of the remainder were union nominees'.[196] Added to this, most of Labour's political heavyweights had lost their seats in the election, including Henderson, Frederick Jowett and MacDonald.

The expansion of the electorate was in proportion to Labour's ambition for a share of real power. But to achieve this, it was obvious that a more dynamic and charismatic leader in the age of communication was needed. Thus, a short illness in 1921 was the pretext for Adamson to step down from leadership to be replaced in the immediate term by another trade unionist, J. R. Clynes, who led the party into the 1922 election. The outcome saw Labour win 142 seats to the Liberal Party's sixty-two, and a whole raft of new of faces sat on the cross benches, many of them non-trade unionists. Ramsay MacDonald's election as leader reflected the new social composition of the PLP and, under his leadership, Labour began to prepare for government.

In some ways, his loss of leadership of the party was fortuitous for Adamson as it allowed him space to concentrate on trade union affairs. The FCKMA in the early 1920s was in a state of disarray, and conflict and tension continued throughout the decade and for most of the 1930s. The main reason why the tense situation developed was the fact that the old conservative mining leaders, like Adamson, had become increasingly detached from a rank-and-file that had been radicalised during the war years and was moving in a left-wing direction. The lengthy struggle between the radical and communist left and

195 See Charles Clarke's analysis in Chapter 3. The second most successful was Clement Attlee, who increased the party's share by 10 per cent in 1945.

196 McKibbin, op. cit., 1983, p.111

the old guard for control was a tortuous one and is told in all its byzantine detail elsewhere,[197] however, his involvement did major damage to his reputation both at the time and since. He was shown to be high-handed, duplicitous and undemocratic.

While Adamson had been involved throughout the '20s in the power struggles within the FCKMA, two minority Labour governments had taken office, and in both he served as Secretary of State for Scotland. His time at the Scottish Office was undistinguished, Adamson preferring to concentrate on the civic side of the post (attending freedom ceremonies and social occasions) rather than engaging with the business of policy formation, which he left to his under-secretary, the very able Tom Johnston.[198] However, he came out in favour of Scottish devolution. In 1924, when Labour MP George Buchanan introduced a private members' bill to establish a single-chamber assembly for dealing exclusively with Scottish issues, Adamson expressed his approval of the idea of Scottish self-government within a federal UK.[199] Although Buchanan's bill was talked out by the Tories at its second reading, Adamson's intervention showed that he was clearly proud of his Scottish ancestry. On behalf of the Scottish Home Rule Association, he had delivered an oration on the anniversary of the birth of the medieval Scottish patriot William Wallace at Elderslie, Renfrewshire, in 1924, in which he said that he looked 'forward with confidence to the time when Scottish legislation [will] be enacted by Scotsmen in a Scottish Assembly'.[200]

His second stint as Secretary of State for Scotland was a more traumatic experience. In December 1929, Adamson was knocked down by a bus crossing Southampton Row but, in spite of the fact that he suffered cuts and bruises

---

197 Robert Page Arnot, *A History of the Scottish Miners*, London, Allen & Unwin, 1955; Alan Campbell, *The Scottish Miners, 1874–1939: Trade Unions and Politics, Vol.* 2, Aldershot, Ashgate, 2000; Abe Moffat, *My Life with the Miners*, London, Lawrence & Wishart, 1965; Roderick Martin, *Communism and the British Trade Unions, 1924–1933*, Oxford, Clarendon Press, 1969.

198 Torrance, op. cit., p. 106.

199 Hansard, 9 May 1924.

200 *The Scotsman*, 25 August 1924.

and his clothes were torn to shreds, he was still able to take his place in the Commons that afternoon.[201] The experience proved minor compared to the economic storm that was brewing in the western world.

Mass unemployment and economic depression following the Wall Street Crash in 1929 blew the minority Labour government off course and created a fiscal crisis. MacDonald's reaction was to form the National Government with the Liberals and the Tories, committed to swingeing cuts in public expenditure. The decision split the Labour Party. Adamson, along with the majority of Labour MPs, opposed the cuts, saying: 'I've never voted against the poor yet and I can't now.'[202] The fall of the Labour government in 1931 was followed by a general election in which Adamson lost his West Fife seat to the Unionist candidate, but only through the intervention of the communist candidate Willie Gallacher, who polled 7,000 votes. He was defeated again four years later by the 'Rids' (Reds), when Gallacher narrowly triumphed by 593 votes after a bitterly fought election. The defeat was evidence of the strong feelings against him in the mining communities of Fife. Adamson died shortly after this, followed four years later by Barnes.

Adamson and Barnes were primarily in the mould of late nineteenth-century conservative trade union leaders; indeed, as one political commentator said of the former, 'He has little of the revolutionary in his nature'[203] – a judgement endorsed by his Tory Lord Advocate, who said he 'found him far from revolutionary. He was a real canny Scot.'[204] Their political and industrial attitudes were formed during the high-water mark of Gladstonian Liberalism and this exercised a lasting impact on them, although they ultimately rejected the Liberal Party.

However, their rejection was organisationally motivated rather than ideologically. They remained committed to an older set of values, based on

---

201 Torrance, op. cit., p. 107.

202 Quoted in Torrance, op. cit., p. 108.

203 Anon, *The Scottish Socialists*, 1931, p. 119.

204 Lord Macmillan, *A Man of Law's Tale*, 1953, p. 90, quoted in Torrance, op. cit., p. 103.

notions of respectability, which included self-help, sobriety and thrift. They were the living embodiment of the iconic figure of nineteenth-century Scottish literature: the 'lad o' pairts'. Barnes said that his purpose in writing his autobiography was 'to give encouragement to some who, born like men in humble circumstances, aspire to step a little aside from the beaten track'.[205] These values were quickly seen as outdated in the socially polarised decades of the '20s and '30s, and served to alienate them from their union members and constituents. Unfortunately for these former frock-coated Labour aristocrats, the masses had become classes.

However, to men like Adamson and Barnes, progress was not measured by the level of class consciousness achieved by the working class – indeed, they tended to speak out against class-based politics – rather it was to be found in the improving material conditions of life and thus the creation of the basis for the possibility of triumphing over adversity. As Barnes put it:

> I have seen freedom broadening down to the class in which I was born … and which I have tried to serve. When I was young, working people were uneducated and unenfranchised. They were poor and dependent and their working days were banded by age and want without concern by the state, which their labour had enriched. Now they have at least a modicum of education, they are politically, as well as industrially, organised and, although there is still unemployment and … fear of want, these grim problems are being tackled with greater knowledge and more humane feeling than ever before.[206]

As political leaders, they were unsuccessful in the tests of leadership: their performances at general elections were not particularly impressive; they were uninspiring; they failed to manage their party; and they were leaders purely by default.

---

205 Barnes, op. cit., p. xi.

206 Barnes, op. cit., p. 295.

CHAPTER 7

JOHN ROBERT CLYNES

PHIL WOOLAS

John Clynes was leader of the Labour Party from February 1921 to November 1922. He was, therefore, at the helm when the party made a great breakthrough at the 1922 general election, increasing parliamentary representation from fifty-two to 142 seats. Clynes went on to serve as Lord Privy Seal and Deputy Leader of the House in the first Labour government, and then as Home Secretary in the second. He remained in Parliament for a total of thirty-five years. In spite of this, Phil Woolas notes that Clynes is one of the lesser-known figures within the Labour Party's history, but argues that he deserves much credit. Clynes led the Labour Party to become the main party of opposition, deposing the Liberals and laying the pathway for the first Labour government. He also contributed to the growth of unionism, to the socialist movement in Britain (intellectually, by rejecting Bolshevism) and to party unity, by not challenging his successor Ramsay MacDonald.

• • •

If this book were a quest to establish not just who the most successful leader of the Labour Party has been, but who was its bravest, John Robert Clynes would win without contest. His life was remarkable. His childhood, upbringing and experiences shaped not just his life and career, but the political philosophy of the British Labour Party, and, in turn, laid the foundations of modern Britain.

Astonishingly, given his profound influence on the Labour Party's birth and political and ideological development, he remains the least known of the party's leaders. Indeed, the PLP chair in 2006, Tony Lloyd MP, had to argue for Clynes's inclusion in the pamphlet celebrating Labour's centenary.[207] As a successor in the same north Manchester constituency, Lloyd was aware of his predecessor's incredible career, but depressed by the ignorance among his contemporaries of John Robert's existence, let alone monumental service.[208]

Perhaps this is because Clynes is the only leader in Labour's history to have been involuntarily deposed.[209] Cruelly, he had the opportunity of being Prime Minister snatched away from him by a handful of impatient new-intake MPs – ironically elected on the wave of Clynes's successful electoral strategy – and the ambition of Ramsay MacDonald. It is breathtaking but futile to speculate on how Britain's history would have been different but for the five votes by which he lost on that day in November 1922.

A more likely explanation, however, than that of the victor writing history, is Clynes's simple lack of ego and profound commitment to solidarity, both as a philosophical axiom and as an electoral necessity. The selfless political ego is rare in our times, yet for Clynes it was an obvious prerequisite to leadership. If millions of impoverished Britons were to be liberated from their servitude, they needed power, and power to Clynes required sacrifice by leadership. The self-educated mill-boy had rationalism at his very core; it was the central tenet of his political consciousness. To him, socialism was not just the morally right course of action to adopt, but the only coherently intellectual one. Not without a sense of humour – sometimes dry, sometimes cutting – he genuinely believed that political power for the working class required its leaders to be selfless rationalists. Respect from colleagues, opponents, the King and the people were reward enough, if unsought-for by him and his wife Mary. Starting work as an eight-year-old on the 5 a.m. shift was, if nothing else, character-forming.

207 Alan Haworth and Dianne Hayter, *Men Who Made Labour: The Parliamentary Labour Party of 1906 – The Personalities and the Politics*, London, Routledge, 2006.

208 Private correspondence, Tony Lloyd MP to author.

209 The position at the time was known as chairman of the parliamentary party. The name change took place on MacDonald's succession to Clynes.

Such was his self-control, born of this background, that he seems almost to have chosen his own personality.

Yet this wonderful and optimistic aspect of his demeanour explains both why he was a hugely successful leader and why he allowed power to be snatched from him. The story is humbling. Comparisons to modern, TV-age, 'here today, gone tomorrow' politicians are depressing, as those politicians, when aware, are the first to confess.

Notwithstanding his incredible life story, his role in the founding of general trade unionism and the Labour Party, his fifty-year political career, and his contribution to the intellectual creation of the architecture of British socialism (even if just for his brief sojourn as chairman of the party – as the position was called then), his place on the podium of successful leaders would be secure. Of all Labour's leaders, only Clement Attlee achieved greater electoral success, and Clynes beats Blair when you look at the raw electoral arithmetic.[210]

The case for Clynes, however, is not just that he was the second most successful leader in terms of his electoral legacy. However influential a leader is in taking his or her party from A to B, it surely must be recognised that this influence must take into account the slings and arrows of political fortune. Clynes was able to lead Labour to electoral success in 1922 because of his lifelong strategic approach to politics, the electorate's respect that reaped, and the shaping of events to his will, rather than the will of his formidable opponents. On this measure alone, as we will see, he is on the winners' podium. Labour's fortunes before the First World War were really that of a fringe pressure group. After it, under Clynes's leadership – itself based, in the public mind, on his service, policies and dignity throughout the war, and especially on his attitude and reaction at the October 1918 Special Conference – Labour replaced the Liberal Party as the main opposition, and subsequently as the party of government.

To this historic and epoch-changing success must be added his long-term influence in shaping British politics to the advantage of his party and to the

---

210 See Chapter 3.

lives of those it represented. My contention is that he, more than anyone else in the twentieth century, was responsible for ensuring the improved social mobility and well-being of more of our citizens than any other person. A bold claim – especially of a man who history has ignored. So, who was he?

FROM THE FLOOR OF THE WORKHOUSE TO THE FLOOR OF THE HOUSE OF COMMONS

John Robert Clynes was born in Oldham, in what is now Greater Manchester, on 27 March 1869. He died on 23 October 1949 in Putney, south London. Within a few weeks, his wife of fifty-six years, a former card-room girl in the cotton mills and his lifelong companion, also passed away.

Born to an Irish immigrant father who worked for the parks department in Oldham, variously digging graves and labouring on the creation of the famously beautiful Alexandra Park, John Robert, or Jack as he was known by the family,[211] was the eldest of seven (surviving) children. He was born in a cramped terraced house on the site of what is now Tommyfield Market in central Oldham. He shared a bed with his brother, attended elementary school for a mere five years and started work in the Dowry cotton mill in Lees, walking the 3 miles there to start his shift at 5 a.m., aged ten. From the age of twelve he worked full time as a 'little piecer', picking cotton threads from underneath the life-threatening machinery.

Imagine a ten-year-old child with bare feet in a smoke-stacked mill – a human anthill of 2,000 souls – working in the dark from before dawn. Death by accident was common, as the children slipped on the oily shop floor. Personal accounts[212] tell us it was the noise that dominated the working environment. The little piecers were essential to the production process, as

211 Interestingly, he was known by his colleagues as 'Jimmy' but by his family as 'Jack'. Mary, his wife, was called 'Polly' by her family and friends in Oldham, but remained Mary when in London.

212 See, for example, Brian R. Law, *Oldham Brave Oldham: An Illustrated History of Oldham, 1849–1999*, Oldham, Oldham Council, 1999.

they were the only ones small enough to dip under the machinery to keep the line going. The little girls, aged ten, were urged, but not compelled, to wear hairnets. The awful reality was not just that they were frequently scalped by getting their hair caught in the machines, but that the noise of the mill was so great that their fellow workers could not hear their screams. This was the childhood of the future occupant of No. 11 Downing Street.

Clynes's journey out of his situation was through a self-taught education. Earning pennies by reading the newspapers to the blind in the cooperative reading rooms in Oldham, he bought second-hand books to teach himself Shakespeare, Carlyle and Mill, among others, while his siblings slept. According to his only biographer, the young Clynes learned the *Oxford English Dictionary* by rote.[213]

By the age of eighteen, Clynes was an accomplished public speaker and debater and ready to take on the world. Perhaps inevitably, he became a trade union organiser, recruited to the General and Municipal Workers Union (GMWU) by Will Thorne, on the strength of Thorne hearing him address a workers' rally. Clynes always thought that trade unionism without political representation was not the answer to the working class's problems. He helped found the ILP and the LRC, and threw himself into building the labour movement. After three unsuccessful attempts to be elected as a councillor in Oldham, he became one of the first Labour Members of Parliament, elected in the 1906 general election for the constituency of Manchester North East. He served as an MP thereafter, until 1945, with just a four-year break. In the First World War, he joined the coalition government as one of the first Labour Party members to hold ministerial office. He was deputy to the Minister for Food Control, Lord Rhondda, and, on Rhondda's early death, Clynes took over the office.

In the post-war election of 1918, Labour returned fifty-seven MPs and was clearly on an upward trajectory. By then, Clynes was already held in high regard. *The Observer*, in an editorial at the end of the First World War in June

213 Edward George, *From Mill-boy to Minister: The Life of John Robert Clynes*, London, T. F. Unwin, 1918.

1918, predicted: 'Within ten years, the Labour Party will form the government and John Robert Clynes will be the Prime Minister.'[214]

He was seen by many as the natural choice for deputy leader in 1918,[215] his skills as an orator complemented his ministerial and trade union experience. Never a flamboyant speaker, he relied on cold facts and rational argument to wrong-foot his opponents. He inspired support through his grasp of the real-world hardships of voters and through his unbreakable logic, politely delivered. Never a tub-thumper, he was nonetheless called for when the chips were down.

He became the leader of the Labour Party in 1921 and served for a brief twenty-one months. On losing the post, he immediately took the office of deputy leader, and served loyally for ten years – one of only two people to serve as deputy after being leader. He went on to hold high office as Lord Privy Seal and Deputy Leader of the House in the first Labour government, then Home Secretary in the second. In the first, he was effectively the Deputy Prime Minister, and in the second, with Ramsay MacDonald holding the posts of both Prime Minister and Foreign Secretary, Clynes was effectively in charge of domestic policy.

Clynes's remarkable achievement in rising up the social ladder is therefore unsurpassed. Even Keir Hardie and MacDonald cannot compete, although admittedly Henderson would have a claim. No leader since comes close.

CLYNES AS LABOUR PARTY LEADER

In February 1921, Clynes replaced William Adamson as party leader. Adamson, while respected, had been largely absent due to illness, and was seen by many as not up to the job. Manny Shinwell, for one, described him as 'a dour and phlegmatic Scottish miners' leader, very much out of his depth in

214 *The Observer*, 30 June 1918.

215 Vice-chairman of the PLP.

the Commons'.[216] The former food controller, and, by now, trade union president, was the obvious choice as successor. According to Philip Snowden:

> Clynes had considerable qualifications for parliamentary leadership. He was an exceptionally able speaker, a keen and incisive debater, had wide experience of industrial questions, and a good knowledge of general political issues. In the Labour Party conferences, when the platform got into difficulties with the delegates, Mr Clynes was usually put up to calm the storm.[217]

It is worth noting that John Robert Clynes was the first English person to lead Labour, and it is not fanciful to suggest that this was an electoral asset to the party. While politics in those times was conducted without electronic media, and the public was largely ignorant of its leaders' accents, Clynes's affinity with the working class reached at least as far as the conurbations by reputation, if not through the many thousands of public meetings he attended.

As a measure of his modesty and subjugation to political rather than personal advantage, it is also worth quoting his reaction on being elected leader. In his memoirs, written fifteen years after, he recalled: 'Now I, as an ex-millhand, was within measurable distance, so people said, of becoming the first Labour Prime Minister, not so much through efforts of my own to seek distinction, as because of the unflinching loyalty and courage of the Labour rank and file.'[218]

This modesty, which appears throughout his life, was undoubtedly a vote-winner – if only indirectly – not least through the loyalty and confidence it instilled in his shadow Cabinet and among the wider PLP.

So, by the time of the 1922 election, Clynes as leader was unchallenged within the Labour Party, and bestrode a united party organisation. The goal

---

216 Emanuel Shinwell, *The Labour Story*, London, McDonald, 1963.

217 Philip Snowden, *An Autobiography, Vol. 2*, London, I. Nicholson & Watson Ltd, 1934, p. 531.

218 John Robert Clynes, *Memoirs Vol. 1*, London, Hutchinson, 1937.

was to replace the Liberals (both parties) as the agent for social reform and as the opposition to the Tory Party. By now, the Irish question, in what would become the Irish Free State, was being resolved, at least in terms of parliamentary arithmetic. The tide was with him. The extension of suffrage to all men over twenty-one and to property-owning women had to be exploited to the benefit of Labour rather than the Liberals. This was achieved through a pragmatic, step-by-step approach to policy.

The electoral threat to Labour came from abroad. The Russian revolution had support within the trade unions and from some in the nascent Labour Party. From 1918 onwards, the right in British politics were always able to play the 'reds under the beds' tactic. While adopting a conciliatory foreign policy within the framework of unflinching support for the British monarchy, Clynes's patriotism was unquestionable. Central to this was his abhorrence of revolution. His experience of harsh working conditions and the slaughter of the First World War, his internationalism and his self-taught study of history all informed his view that revolutions did not liberate the working class, but rather led to their butchering and starvation. He was not a timid socialist, far from it – and indeed nobody ever accused him of being one – but he did think that a Bolshevik revolution would harm not the rich, but the poor. In any event, despite the horrors of deprivation, Britain could at least claim a democratic system, subject to the rule of law. As leader, he made these views clear, and reassured the populace that he and Labour had the people's interests at heart.

A further obstacle to electoral success was psychological. This is a British phenomenon that beleaguers the party to this day. Above all else, Clynes and the other members of the 'Big Five'[219] knew that they had to prove to a class-ridden British society, creeping its way towards democracy, that ordinary working people were competent to govern. This had been Clynes's guiding strategy throughout the war. While his primary goal had been to do what

219 The 'Big Five', as they became known, were: John Clynes, Philip Snowden, Arthur Henderson, Ramsay MacDonald and J. H. Thomas. Although at this stage MacDonald was outside Parliament, the wider strategy was discussed among this core group throughout the 1920s.

was best from the point of view of the alleviation of poverty and the advancement of social justice, he matched this concern with his firmly held view from childhood that *the* pre-requisite for the election of organised Labour into Parliament – and socialists into democratic government, having rejected the revolutionary road – was the demonstration of competence. It is hard, perhaps, for the post-Second World War generation, who accept meritocracy as the conventional wisdom, to grasp the height of the political mountain that Clynes and his team had to climb. Having successfully served as War Minister, however, Clynes's credentials for competence were strengthened.

Armed with this political advantage, a solid practical programme of social advancement and the opportunity to build on the sacrifice and slaughter in northern France, Clynes led the party to huge progression in 1922. In the general election of that year, under Clynes's stewardship, Labour's representation increased in Parliament from fifty-seven MPs, elected in 1918, to 142. The vote saw a swing to Labour of 9 per cent. This meant, in brutal terms of power, that Labour were the second party. The forward march of socialism had started. Clynes had succeeded in supplanting the Liberal Party as the opposition – a position from which they have never recovered. He paved the way for the first Labour government, which occurred barely a year after his triumph. Above all, he broke the class-ridden, centuries-old yoke that dictated in the minds of the British working class that ordinary people were incapable of governing. While his true triumph would not be seen until 1945, when the party he had midwifed to power took a majority in Parliament, his contribution as leader to the 1922 result and his influence in building the Labour Party throughout his career are unsurmounted.

So, electorally, his case is strong. Apart from the arithmetic quirk of 1906 – when, by definition, the LRC's numbers increased infinitely from zero to twenty-nine, among whom, of course, was Clynes – and the aberration of 1935 – following the National Government and the betrayal by Clynes's vanquisher, MacDonald, when he was re-elected into the House – no other leader has increased the Labour share of the vote by more. Tony Blair did increase the proportion of Labour MPs by a slightly greater margin, but, measured by increase in the share of the vote, Clynes is the winner. In these terms, even Attlee did not match his success.

The question mark over Clynes's success as a leader is, of course, the fact that he was deposed. The challenge by MacDonald was not out of the blue. MacDonald's absence from the political firmament, based on his undoubtedly principled opposition to Britain's participation in the First World War, led, in the eyes of his supporters, to a hero's return. So, how did Clynes let this happen? Did he take his eye off the ball and become complacent, simply failing to see the plot unfolding? Or did his selfless commitment to the party he had done so much to build outweigh his personal ambition? His memoirs give us a clue to his state of mind:

> I hope that nothing I may say further on the subject will cause anyone to conclude that I harbour the slightest personal feeling against MacDonald because he eventually replaced me. Indeed, when I was beaten by a few votes, I felt that he had rid me of a burden rather than robbed me of any ambition to become the first Labour Prime Minister.[220]

The simple fact is that Clynes did not see the challenge coming. Perhaps he was incapable of reading the motives of those less honourable than himself. Perhaps he was over-confident and simply got his numbers wrong. More likely, Clynes had a statesman's view. He had spent his life building the party and devoting himself to it. His lack of ego simply prevented him from grubbing around the corridors for votes. Either they wanted him, or they didn't. Whatever they chose, he was happy to serve, and his loyalty to MacDonald as his deputy was remarkable. Yet this loyalty did not diminish him in the eyes of his contemporaries. Rather, it enhanced his reputation as the father figure of the British labour movement. To someone who had started work in the mills at ten years old, what was important was not who held high office, but whether Labour won. He knew also from

220 Clynes, op. cit. (1).

decades of struggle that disunity was Labour's enemy. Maybe he should have done more to project himself, but it is difficult to conceive that those discontented with his gradualism would have remained as loyal to him as he did to them.

A further claim for Clynes's greatness is that he shaped democratic socialism and ensured that revolutionary socialism (and indeed its counterpart, fascism) took no hold in Britain, as it was doing elsewhere. As he told George V when receiving his seals of office in the first Labour government: 'Constitutional monarchy has nothing to fear from organised Labour as long as constitutional monarchy recognises the will of the people.' He was, indeed, the critical political figure in convincing King George that Labour could form a government without threat from those who had murdered his cousin, Tsar Nicholas.

Perhaps his best claim to the mantle of greatest leader of the Labour Party is this: having lost the power he had done so much to gain, Clynes ensured that Labour survived and prospered. His architecture of an alliance between the trade unions, the Labour Party and the intellectual middle classes has stood the test of time. The victories of 1945, 1964 and 1997 were built upon it. He showed that a mill-boy could govern, which was a necessary pre-requisite for the introduction of democracy, and the basis of post-war prosperity. His politics is best expressed by a quote from his speech to the victorious Labour activists in 1924, repeated by David Miliband in his valedictory speech to the Labour conference in Manchester in 2010: 'Labour enters Parliament not to win the class war, but to end it.'

As well as laying out the party's organisational and political ideology for 100 years to come, Clynes led by the example of unity. At five critical junctures in the party and country's history, Clynes, by his actions, held the movement together, and thereby, some claimed, parliamentary democracy itself:

- The conduct of the First World War, through his stance that Labour must be part of the national effort to defeat the enemy, and, with it, his acceptance of office as Minister for Food Rationing.

- The unifying of the party, when he accepted the majority position of the 1918 conference to leave the Lloyd George coalition.
- The clear rejection of communism following the October revolution.
- The unifying of the party at the time of the MacDonald-led breakaway.
- The rejection of the leadership offer in 1935.

These acts, and others, provided the practical implementation of the sloganeering of the left. They showed that the idealism of socialists was indeed relevant to the daily hardship of working-class people; that it was not hot air, nor was it dangerous. Indeed, Clynes's leadership while in office – as formal leader of the party and in other roles where he was a leading embodiment of its values – demonstrated the necessity of changing the world order. It had taken just eighteen years from birth to government, and, within thirty-nine years, his more electorally successful heir, Clement Attlee, would reap the harvest.

It is often claimed that the first two Labour governments achieved little in the way of social progress and economic egalitarianism. And, to be fair, neither of those two governments had anything close to a majority in the House. But this misses the point. The great advancements of the period – universal suffrage, the introduction of pensions, public education, the working week, industrial conditions and wage increases – have all been credited, by the Liberal interpreters of our history, to the Liberal Party. But the Liberals were swept out of office and replaced by Labour as the radical party, due to the millions of working-class voters who were inspired by the policies advocated by Labour. And those policies and that advocacy, through writings, pamphlets, speeches and mostly political organisation, were crafted and implemented at that crucial juncture, not by MacDonald, but by Clynes. Time after time – at conferences, in the PLP, as president of the GMWU, as minister in the

First World War, as president of the TUC, as leader and deputy leader and as elder statesman – it was Clynes who was called upon when difficult decisions arose. And he never shirked them – often to his own loss.

On the night MacDonald beat Clynes to become the new leader, only a few days after the general election that saw Labour's greatest success to date (at that point), MacDonald failed to turn up to the victory rally at the Kingsway Hall in Holborn. It was Clynes, installed as the deputy leader only hours before and stripped of leadership by the narrowest of margins (sixty-one votes to fifty-six), who turned up to give the speech. It was, of course, already prepared, and outlined the forthcoming successful path to power. Only just more than a year later, the Labour Party, which Clynes had helped to form only eighteen years previously, would form the government.

It is often said that victory has a thousand fathers, and it is certainly the case that the MacDonald version of history took hold rapidly. With no rebuttal from the Clynes side of the story, the truth has been lost. It is worth looking at the conventional wisdom at the time, though, perhaps best expounded by H. Hessell Tiltman. Published in 1929, Tiltman's sycophantic and premature biography of MacDonald[221] gives an insight into the writing-out of history of Clynes. In 350 pages of text, covering MacDonald's life through to the advent of his second premiership in 1929, and despite his having worked and fought alongside Clynes for thirty-five years in building the labour movement, including seven hard years with Clynes as his loyal and effective deputy, John Robert warrants but three mentions in the book. Remember, also, that Clynes was more than just the deputy leader of the party. In MacDonald's first term, he held the office of Foreign Secretary as well as Prime Minister – the empire being the focus of major governmental decisions. Domestic policy was, by and large, left to Clynes. He lived at No. 11 and held office as Lord Privy Seal and Deputy Leader of the House (the PM being nominal Leader of the House). Yet, despite these formidable powers and positions, Clynes features as a minor figure in this and other accounts of MacDonald's time.

221 H. Hessell Tiltman, *Ramsay MacDonald, Labour's Man of Destiny*, London, Jarrolds, 1929.

Of course, by the time of the great betrayal in 1931, it was, with awful irony, Clynes who lost his constituency seat as a result.

The reason for this great act of redaction was Clynes's own personality. He simply saw the political cause as being greater than his status within it. It is this unshakeable adhesion to the greater good, the power of reason and the overwhelming necessity to hold together – the lifelong proof of the GMWU's 'unity is strength' call to arms – that caused this wonderful leader to be airbrushed out of political history. To this day, we read a Liberal version of our history. For example, in Andrew Marr's brilliant account of the rise of democracy in his bestselling book *The Making of Modern Britain*[222] (and in the vast majority of accounts of the period), no mention is made of the role of Clynes's statecraft in engineering the replacement of Liberalism with Labour socialism as the opposition to the Conservatives.

Yet, Tiltman does give service in his account of MacDonald's victory over Clynes. His side of the story is wholly through the prism of his returning hero and helps explain how it was that Clynes came to lose:

> When once the pendulum begins to move, it does not pause midway in its swing. The man who was ready to serve in the rank and file was, within a week of his re-election to Parliament, and to the surprise of even some members of his own party, elected leader of the PLP in place of J. R. Clynes.[223]

The usurping of Clynes, when mentioned in our history books at all, follows this narrative. Seen as a stepping stone in the career of MacDonald, the true significance has been lost. Tiltman inadvertently gives the game away: 'It is worthy of note that MacDonald owed his election to the votes of the more advanced block in the party, who expected from him a "fighting lead", which they felt was lacking under Mr Clynes.'[224]

---

222 Andrew Marr, *The Making of Modern Britain*, London, Pan, 2010.

223 Tiltman, op. cit.

224 Ibid.

The so-called 'advanced block' – that is, the newly elected and impatient – would swallow its naivety in bucketloads just nine years later, in 1931. Yet Clynes's very loyalty was his downfall. The PLP, following the election in 1922, numbered 142. His defeat to MacDonald, by a mere five votes, was a surprise to all. Yet the numbers show that twenty-five Labour MPs simply failed to turn up to vote. Most of these were trade union officials and representatives still engaged in their industrial work, surprised by their election success. There's little doubt that these men were Clynes's supporters. The usurpers, including the 'Red Clydesiders', paid no heed to Clynes's success in leading them to that point, but instead, in their ambition, plumped for the man they saw as the more flamboyant, exciting and closer to their hearts than their heads.

Perhaps, though, Clynes's lasting achievement was that of forging, explaining and leading the ideological creation of the party. By melding the 'Labourism' of the trade unions and the intellectualism of the Fabian wing, he, along with Henderson, shaped Labour's brand of democratic socialism. It is a balance that is dangerously out of kilter today, but so far it has served well. The rise in the fortunes of the mill-boy John Robert Clynes to the chambers of power in Whitehall was shadowed by the emergence of the people from Victorian squalor to prosperous democratic society – a rise made possible by Clynes himself.

CHAPTER 8

RAMSAY MACDONALD

DAVID HOWELL

Ramsay MacDonald was the first ever Labour leader to become Prime Minister. When the Conservatives lost a vote of confidence in January 1924, King George V asked MacDonald to form a government with support from the Liberals. That government was short-lived. It lasted only nine months before being defeated at the 1924 general election. MacDonald became Prime Minister once again in 1929, however, forming the second Labour administration, after becoming the largest party in the House of Commons. Yet MacDonald was to be vilified by his own party when he decided to push ahead with cuts in unemployment benefits, against the will of the majority of the Labour government, and formed the National Government, with himself as Prime Minister, until 1935. David Howell argues that the party owed much to MacDonald, who patiently built coalitions between trade unionists, socialists and, when prudent, the Liberals in the early years of the party. As Prime Minister, MacDonald also faced debilitating challenges during the second government, with a worldwide economic recession and relatively few policy options at hand. MacDonald may claim to have acted in the national interest in implementing economic orthodoxy during times of national crisis, Howell argues, but the reality was that he implemented regressive social policies, and the impact on the Labour Party's electoral fortunes was disastrous.

• • •

When politicians dispersed for their summer holidays at the end of July 1931, Ramsay MacDonald's position as head of the second Labour government and leader of the Labour Party seemed secure. Although his minority administration faced a deteriorating economy and by-elections offered sombre evidence of eroding support, adversity seemingly strengthened appeals for Labour solidarity. The government's survival depended on an understanding with a sizeable section of an increasingly fissiparous Liberal Party, and, at the beginning of the summer recess, the auguries looked auspicious.

Within a month, this agenda lay in ruins. A financial and budgetary crisis was complemented rapidly by a political earthquake. By the last week in August, the Labour government had disintegrated and MacDonald headed the National Government, accompanied by a handful of Labour colleagues. His new administration was backed by the Conservatives and almost all Liberals, but opposed by the Labour Party. What was proclaimed as a temporary expedient to deal with a crisis rapidly became a durable reshaping of the party system. Conservative pressure for an election proved irresistible; supporters of the National Government could obscure their differences under the assertion that the Labour Party was economically incompetent and therefore anti-patriotic. The result was Labour's near obliteration as a parliamentary presence. The 287 MPs elected in May 1929 went down to just fifty-two in 1931 – six of whom had not even stood as official candidates.

MacDonald was thereafter demonised in Labour folk memory as the ultimate renegade, who succumbed to the aristocratic embrace, abandoning and then waging a devastating war on the party he had led. The party responded by anticipating, by a quarter of a century, a process of de-Stalinisation: MacDonald's portrait disappeared from party premises and trade union banners.

Attlee's effectiveness as leader depended significantly on the certainty that he would not be mistaken for a second MacDonald. The idea of the leader as a flamboyant personification of the party gave way to that of the discreet and dutiful team player. Yet any casting of MacDonald as the traitorous destroyer of the party has to reckon with his earlier achievements as party architect.

MacDonald's Labour Party has parallels with a Chekhov play: understanding is inexorably coloured by the observer's knowledge of what is to come.[225]

Labour politics in the 1920s must be understood on its own terms and not seen as the prelude to an inescapable 1931. Yet the connections between the optimism and uncertainties of that earlier world and Labour's great disaster must also be explored – only then can the complexities of MacDonald's leadership and of the context within which he operated be appreciated. Labour's political leadership in the 1920s remained very much the preserve of the generation that had entered the Commons in 1906 and 1910. MacDonald, Arthur Henderson, Philip Snowden and J. R. Clynes had all been born in the 1860s, Jimmy Thomas in the subsequent decade. Through their diverse political identities they personified the alliance between the ILP and the trade unions. Personal relationships were rarely close, but, post-war, they all agreed on Labour's political strategy. MacDonald, however, made a distinctive and arguably crucial contribution to this collegiate enterprise.[226]

As secretary of the LRC, and subsequently of the Labour Party from 1900 to 1912, he had patiently constructed an alliance between socialists and trade unionists that he hoped would combine enthusiasm with organisational resources. This statement of independence was complemented by the negotiation of a limited and secret electoral pact with the Liberals. This deal proved decisive in the election of thirty Labour MPs in the 1906 election, including MacDonald himself as MP for Leicester. From 1910, the imperative of parliamentary arithmetic brought Labour closer to the Liberal

225 The outstanding biography is David Marquand, *Ramsay MacDonald*, London, Jonathan Cape, 1977; see also the new introduction to the second edition, published in 1997, and Marquand's entry in *Oxford Dictionary of National Biography* Vol. 35, Oxford, Oxford University Press, 2004, pp. 268–83. For an earlier assessment, see C. L. Mowat, 'Ramsay MacDonald and the Labour Party', in Asa Briggs and John Saville eds, *Essays in Labour History 1886–1923*, Hamden CT, Archon Books, 1971, pp. 129–51. Lord Elton followed MacDonald's lead in 1931: his first and only volume of a projected biography, published in 1939, ends in 1919. Some sense of his interpretation of MacDonald's later career can be found in his obituary in Labour's *Newsletter*, 20 November 1937. For an analysis by a supporter of MacDonald in 1931, see Reginald Bassett, *Nineteen Thirty-One: Political Crisis*, London, Macmillan/New York, St Martin's Press, 1958.

226 For Labour politics under MacDonald's leadership, see: David Howell, *MacDonald's Party: Labour Identities and Crisis 1922–1931*, Oxford, Oxford University Press, 2002; Neil Riddell, *Labour in Crisis: The Second Labour Government 1929–1931*, Manchester, Manchester University Press, 1999.

government – how this de facto alliance of progressives would have developed in the absence of a major European war remains a perennial subject for counter-factual history.[227]

MacDonald's response to the war was cloaked in ambiguity. Neither a pacifist nor the pro-German vilified by the jingo press, he evinced the sentiments of a high-minded Liberal or ethical socialist. He opposed British entry into a European war, fearing illiberal consequences; subsequently, he argued for a negotiated settlement and campaigned against the encroaching authoritarianism of the British state. Predictably, he was heavily defeated in Leicester in the 1918 election, but as disillusion grew with the Versailles settlement, and more broadly with the economic failings of post-war society, MacDonald's wartime position seemed to some both principled and prescient.

The Labour Party entered the 1918 election with enhanced ambitions; in terms of seats, its rewards were meagre. In the November 1922 election, the party advanced significantly and MacDonald re-entered the Commons as MP for Aberavon. At the first meeting of the PLP, he was narrowly elected chairman and, in effect, Labour's first national leader. One highly supportive newspaper predicted that he would 'infallibly become the symbol and personification of the party'. Egon Ranshofen-Wertheimer, the perceptive London correspondent of the German Socialist newspaper *Vorwaerts*, observed MacDonald's years of dominance; he characterised MacDonald as 'the personification of all that thousands of downtrodden men and women hope and dream and desire ... he is the focus of the mute hopes of an entire class'. Wertheimer's specific parallel with Lenin could jar, but the claim illuminated the personalised carnivals that were MacDonald's election tours. Beatrice Webb, austere and acerbic, suggested that MacDonald was a 'magnificent substitute for a leader'.[228]

---

227 For the disintegration of the Progressive Alliance and its consequences, see Ross McKibbin, *Parties and People: England 1914–1951*, Oxford and New York, Oxford University Press, 2010, Chapters 1–2.

228 *New Leader*, 24 November 1922; Egon Ranshofen-Wertheimer, *Portrait of the Labour Party*, London, G. P. Putnam's Sons, 1929, pp. 174–5; Margaret Cole ed., *Beatrice Webb's Diaries 1924–32*, London, Longman, 1956, p. 112, entry for 2 August 1926.

Substitute or not, MacDonald returned to King's Cross from his new Seaham constituency in May 1929 as leader of the largest party in the Commons. Since November 1922, Labour had doubled its representation. Labour had just won eighty-one seats for the first time. Given that electoral success is a prime criterion for assessing party leadership, MacDonald could claim a signal achievement. Yet placing performance in context is crucial; this period was distinctive in its partisan complexities and volatilities. By 1918, Britain could claim to be a formal electoral democracy for men; a decade later, with the equalisation of the franchise for women (an issue of both age and class), any qualification became redundant. Expansion of the franchise on a vast scale destroyed the apparent stabilities of Edwardian politics; this loss of signposts was compounded by the partisan legacies of war. The Progressive Alliance of Liberal and Labour, to which MacDonald had made a major contribution, was dead. The Liberal Party was incoherently, if venomously, divided into partisans of Asquith or Lloyd George, plus those who wished the destructive feuding would end. Labour's response under MacDonald was to attempt a reconstruction of the Progressive Alliance, under the hopefully extensive and attractive umbrella of the Labour Party.

The success of Sinn Féin across most of nationalist Ireland in 1918, and the subsequent creation of the Irish Free State, decisively changed the Westminster arithmetic. A major obstacle to a Conservative majority had vanished. Yet the interplay between complex party competition and the electoral system meant that elections had the potential to produce unpredictable outcomes, in which the relationship between votes cast and seats won would be disproportionate. The consequence was the prospect of minority government and subsequent bargaining. Much of party politics during the period of MacDonald's Labour leadership can be understood as a series of attempts to construct a viable and durable anti-Labour majority. The post-war Lloyd George coalition was seen by some adherents as the basis for a new centre party that could respond to the rise of Labour. This aspiration foundered on the reefs of Tory and Liberal tribalism. In 1924, a Conservative combination of Baldwin's mannered moderation and anti-socialist hyperbole produced a majority inflated by the support of anxious Liberals. This majority proved vulnerable to a Liberal revival in 1929. As yet, the conundrum remained.[229]

Amid these complexities and uncertainties, Labour made progress. Within the 142 seats won in November 1922, Labour enjoyed absolute majorities in eighty-five and was unopposed in four more. This achievement suggested that the party had a base of seats that it was likely to retain in most circumstances. Typically, these strongholds rested on the electoral strength of specific and well-unionised occupational groups. Coal-mining seats became more solid for Labour as, for many miners, post-war optimism was destroyed by industrial defeats, wage cuts, short-term working and unemployment. Sections of heavy industry developed strong Labour loyalties – for example, Sheffield steel workers. Railway trade unionists often provided the nucleus for local party organisation, not least in small towns and rural areas. Within this advance, MacDonald was a powerful – and, on occasions, inspirational – presence. When Oswald Mosley successfully contested Smethwick in 1926, thousands gathered to hear MacDonald one December evening. But for all of MacDonald's rhetoric denying Labour was a class party, and his encouragement of well-heeled candidates such as Mosley, the reality remained throughout the '20s that Labour's electoral base was not just working class, but heavily dependent upon specific occupational groups. MacDonald's ambition to construct Labour as the post-war Progressive Alliance was unrealised.[230]

Such a limitation was obscured by the fact that the party was advantaged due to the combination of a first-past-the-post electoral system, and unstable and ambiguous relations between the parties.

---

229 See: McKibbin, op. cit., 2010, Chapter 2; Maurice Cowling, *The Impact of Labour 1918–1924*, Cambridge, Cambridge University Press, 1971; Philip Williamson, *National Crisis and National Government: British Politics, the Economy and Empire 1926–1932*, Cambridge and New York, Cambridge University Press, 1992.

230 Howell, op. cit., 2002, Chapter 19.

TABLE 8.1: LABOUR PARTY PERFORMANCE IN GENERAL ELECTIONS, 1922–29.

Year	Total vote	Percentage of all votes cast	Candidates	MPs
1922	4,237,349	29.9	414	142
1923	4,439,780	31.0	427	191
1924	5,489,087	34.0	514	151
1929	8,370,417	37.8	569	287

Source: Author, compiled from Rallings and Thrasher, *British Electoral Facts 1832–2006* (Aldershot, Ashgate, 2007), pp. 23–8.

Given that one priority of Labour strategy in the 1920s was to eliminate the Liberals as a credible party, achievement of this objective, at least in the short term, would damage Labour. The party's unexpected arrival in office in January 1924 was the consequence of the Liberal advance into Tory territory, resulting from Baldwin's calling of an election on the Liberal's iconic issue – free trade. The subsequent decline in Liberal candidacies in 1923–24, from 457 to 339, was one cause of the decisive Conservative victory in the latter election. Equally, the Liberal expansion back to 507 candidates in 1929 damaged the Conservatives and thereby helped Labour. By the mid-'20s, the Baldwin-led Conservative Party was proving more effective than Labour in attracting former Liberal voters. The irony for Labour's strategy was that its long-term objective – a secure position in a two-party system – would mean a worsening of the party's electoral terms of trade, without any guarantee of subsequent improvement.

TABLE 8.2: LABOUR PARTY PERFORMANCE IN GENERAL ELECTIONS, 1931–35.

Year	Total vote	Percentage of all votes cast	Candidates	MPs
1931	6,640,220	31.1	515	52
1935	8,325,491	38.6	551	154

Source: Author, compiled from Rallings and Thrasher (2007), pp 28–32.

The 1931 contest could hardly have occurred under worse circumstances for Labour, yet the contrast with 1923 – an election that was genuinely a three-way contest – is nevertheless telling. Virtually the same share of the vote saw 139 fewer Labour MPs returned. The 1935 result demonstrated the basic problem: Labour's share of the vote returned to its 1929 level, but its number of seats was cut by almost half.

An electoral achievement that was impressive yet brittle inevitably posed problems of party management, particularly in 1924 and 1929–31. Compromises in office could generate resentment by both high-minded socialists, sensitive to betrayals of principle, and to pragmatic trade unionists, seeking specific improvements. Yet throughout his leadership, MacDonald's position was never seriously questioned. Tensions between individuals, not least those at the top of the party, were inevitable; so were the complaints of those who did not obtain ministerial office.

None of this mattered. Notably, despite the mounting economic difficulties after 1929, MacDonald remained effectively unchallenged – a contrast with the torrent of criticism unleashed on Baldwin in opposition, and with the shambles that was the Liberal Party. MacDonald was backed by firm majorities across Labour's key institutions: the PLP was dominated by loyalists who would support him in any critical vote.

Under the second Labour government, trade unionist concerns typically focused on unemployment benefits – both levels and conditions. They strongly opposed the ostentatious revolts that they associated with the left-moving ILP, believing these to be both self-indulgent and counter-productive. Discretion mattered in terms of propriety and effectiveness. Similarly, within Labour's national executive committee (NEC), criticism could be marginalised. The development of a new policy document in 1927–28 was settled very much on MacDonald's terms, despite the presence of articulate critics who demanded greater precision in policy proposals. The resulting *Labour and the Nation* was overwhelmingly approved at the 1928 party conference. Critics were marginalised – the whole affair given a suitably ethical tone by George Lansbury's chairmanship. In October 1930, MacDonald spoke at what would be his last party conference. An emotional socialist appeal disarmed many of those who were increasingly critical about the Labour government's seeming inability to address mounting unemployment. An observer noted that MacDonald concluded with 'a purple peroration, which could have done duty at any Labour conference in the last twenty years'.[231]

Across all these arenas, MacDonald's position was protected by Arthur Henderson, who, from June 1929, showed a great capacity to alternate between the roles of Foreign Secretary and party secretary. If MacDonald was the elegant artist, Henderson, in football terms, was the ball-winner, indulging in the dark arts to allow the star turn to display his talents. Mosley, having quit the government in May 1930 over the unemployment crisis, took his case to a PLP meeting; MacDonald and the minister responsible, Jimmy Thomas, responded unconvincingly to Mosley's case. Henderson, however, provided a masterclass in party management. He transformed the issue from the merits or otherwise of Mosley's agenda on unemployment to an issue of proper procedure and trust in colleagues, allowing Mosley to be portrayed as the unreasonable outsider. The crisis for the party, if not for the unemployed, was defused. Similarly, Henderson's influence produced an ethos of sweet reasonableness on the NEC, even as the government was about to fragment in August 1931. At conference, he was an omnipresent influence – the dutiful administrator, effectively shepherding delegates in pursuit of a conference that allowed a managed diversity.[232]

The marginalisation of dissent under MacDonald and Henderson suggested that Labour had become a less tolerant party. The range of permitted identities had narrowed. Communists had been purged from conference and local parties. The lengthy process reflected the desire of MacDonald's close

231 For MacDonald's dominance, see Howell, op. cit., 2002, Chapter 4; for the comment, see *Manchester Guardian,* 6 October 1930.

232 For Henderson, see: Mary Agnes Hamilton, *Arthur Henderson*, London, W. Heinemann, 1938; Ross McKibbin, 'Arthur Henderson as Labour leader', *International Review of Social History*, Vol. 23, 1978, pp. 79–101; Fred Leventhal, *Arthur Henderson*, Manchester, Manchester University Press, 1989; Christopher Wrigley, *Arthur Henderson*, Cardiff, GPC Books, 1990. The PLP meeting in May 1930 is discussed in Robert Skidelsky, *Politicians and the Slump: The Labour Government of 1929–1931*, London and Melbourne, Macmillan, 1967, pp. 184–9.

allies and trade union leaders, who, after the defeat of the general strike and the long agony of the miners' lockout (with its subsequent recriminations), turned their anger on the left. Space for independent activities by women inside the party withered. Women were increasingly defined in terms of economic and social citizenship; women supporters of MacDonald, most notably Margaret Bondfield, opposed any emphasis on gender issues as divisive. More broadly, dissent was portrayed as uncomradely, and identified increasingly with an ILP left, viewed widely as unrealistic and self-advertising. These developments harmonised with the dominant desire among the unions. A Labour government was a necessity. In pursuing this objective, trade unionists chloroformed their doubts about Labour politicians and their sometimes minimal links with, and understanding of, the union movement. Such self-abnegation deepened intolerance of those who engaged in public criticism.

This trade union loyalism underpinned MacDonald's dominance of party institutions and of successive Labour Cabinets. Senior members of MacDonald's administrations had entered politics as trade unionists. Many retained close ties with their own unions or with the wider trade union world. There lay a potential challenge to MacDonald's dominance. During the 1920s, the Labour Party and the Trades Union Congress (TUC), starting from an expectation of close cooperation, had developed distinct priorities and institutional cultures. Political and industrial issues were dealt with by the appropriate organisation, but problems arose when issues could not be thus contained. Labour politicians were uncomfortable about the political implications of the general strike. Trade union leaders felt slighted by many ministers during the brief 1924 government and resolved that a second Labour government must be different. In turn, Labour ministers were sensitive to claims by opponents that trade unions were afforded special privileges; many believed that ministers, not least socialist ones, needed to look beyond sectional interests. Within the TUC, a rising and increasingly self-confident figure, the Transport and General Workers' Union (TGWU) leader Ernest Bevin, prioritised industrial concerns, and had a visceral suspicion of politicians. Here was a world of labour where party and ministerial considerations were not pre-eminent, and MacDonald's writ did not operate. Were significant figures in this world to oppose a Labour government on a major issue, the impact on the party institutions could be dramatic.[233]

The minority status of both of MacDonald's Labour governments inevitably limited expectations, and provided a convenient alibi for failings. No one within the leadership group, and few within the PLP, thought that a minority government should propose a bold socialist programme in the Commons, and, after the inevitable defeat, campaign on the programme in the subsequent election. Only extreme optimists could believe that such a profession of faith would be successful. Instead, Labour needed to use its time in government to demonstrate its competence. From the very beginning, Labour MPs had seen Parliament as an institution that could be used constructively, not as a theatre for disruptive scenes. MacDonald's dismay in June 1923, when some of the ILP left staged a dramatic defiance of the Speaker, was evident.[234] In his desire to be constructive, he was joined by the bulk of Labour MPs who had served on local councils or were familiar with established systems of collective bargaining. The 1924 government demonstrated that Labour ministers would respect constitutional practices, and endorse, with varying degrees of enthusiasm, the accompanying etiquette. Within their various offices, they demonstrated the varieties of ingenuity and inadequacy characteristic of any government. To demonstrate competence was an achievement that would resonate with working-class voters, who could take pride in the very existence of the government. Yet office alone would never be enough. Even minority Labour governments were expected to not just demonstrate competence in administration; they were expected to make a difference politically. Such expectations faced the difficulty that verdicts of competence concerned not just administrative effectiveness, but also the substance of policy.

Labour governments experienced relatively few problems on foreign affairs.

233 For early disquiet, including ministerial suggestion of trade union dictatorship, during the second Labour government, see 'Discussion at TUC general council on relations with Labour government', 26 June 1929 (TUC Archive MS 292 750 1/10).

234 The scenes and suspensions can be followed in HC Deb., 5th ser., vol. 165, 27 June 1923.

Liberal opinion had reacted against the Versailles settlement, and, more broadly, scepticism about military solutions to international problems left its mark on popular culture, not least in R. C. Sherriff's 1928 play set on the Western Front, *Journey's End*. In 1924, MacDonald doubled up as Foreign Secretary – that a critic of British intervention, with the exception of the Soviet Treaty, attracted little criticism illuminated the consensus on pacification. Similarly, Henderson, at the Foreign Office from 1929, was considered an effective advocate of that consensus on foreign policy. Perhaps critically for his and the party's future, Henderson's tenure distanced him from the government's growing domestic difficulties.

By contrast, Labour governments were faced with a much more challenging prospect on economic problems. The quest for the pacification of Europe was central to an economic orthodoxy that saw such normalisation as integral to an export-based revival of the British economy. Public works were viewed sceptically as a diversion of funds from private investment; the return to the gold standard of 1925, at a punitive exchange rate with the dollar, was accepted as an inescapable constraint. That a party of the left largely endorsed such doctrines was testament to the party's radical Liberal roots, most obvious in Labour's support for free trade – an attachment that was as much moral as economic. MacDonald embraced a dominant sentiment that socialism would emerge, not from a crisis of capitalism, but from its flourishing. Philip Snowden, his Chancellor, preached these doctrines with the rigid fervour of his Nonconformist, West Riding roots – a socialist evangelist turned Chancellor, at one with the urbane pronouncements of Treasury officials.[235]

Snowden's austerity, and its endorsement by most Labour politicians, demonstrated a naive readiness to defer to the economic views of the highly educated and self-confident, both in Whitehall and the City. Increasingly, from mid-1929, it was thought such orthodox responses to deepening depression might assuage respectable opinion, but this conditional respectability

---

235 Oswald Mosley's scepticism on the return to gold was expressed in his 1925 pamphlet 'Revolution by Reason'.

was bought at the cost of the disillusionment of party members and Labour voters. One response was to demonstrate competence in areas that could be protected, to some extent, from the core economic difficulties. When Henderson addressed the need for an attractive agenda at the 1930 party conference, he repeated an innovation from the previous year. Fresh from electoral victory, Snowden as Chancellor and Thomas as Minister for Employment had addressed delegates. A year later, Thomas, his credibility destroyed, had moved to the Dominions Office, and another instalment of Snowden's patronising economic lectures seemed unattractive. Instead, party managers turned to Arthur Greenwood, Herbert Morrison and Christopher Addison. Their records in housing, transport and agriculture, they hoped, would indicate ministerial competence to uneasy party delegates and perhaps to a wider public.

MacDonald's party offered little ideological challenge to prevailing economic orthodoxies. Socialist rhetoric provided, at best, a fig leaf for conformity. Such vacuity doubtless helped to inspire John Maynard Keynes's comment in December 1930: 'So long as party organisation and personal loyalties cut across the fundamental differences of opinion, the public life of this country will continue to suffer from a creeping paralysis.' This assessment has resonances in some later historiography; Labour's emergence as a major party and its mixture of economic orthodoxy and socialist utopianism has been seen as blocking the possibility of a meaningful challenge on economic questions from the centre left. This seems a simplistic representation of a complex problem.[236] Whatever Labour's limitations, the Liberals lacked credibility as partners for a progressive economic option. They campaigned in the 1929 election on a programme of public works, yet the response of

236 Keynes's comment is in his 'Sir Oswald Mosley's manifesto', *The Nation and Athenaeum*, 13 December 1930. For the debate about feasibility of alternative policies, see: Skidelsky, op. cit., 1967; Ross McKibbin, 'The Economic Policy of the Second Labour Government', *Past and Present*, Vol. 65, 1975, pp. 95–123; Duncan Tanner, 'Political leadership, intellectual debate and economic policy during the second Labour government 1929–1931' in E. H. H. Green and Duncan Tanner eds, *Political Leaders, Moral Values and the Reception of Economic Debate*, Cambridge, Cambridge University Press, 2007, pp. 113–50, McKibbin, op. cit., 2010, pp. 69–86.

almost all Liberals to the 1931 crisis was to embrace orthodoxy, spiced by anti-Labour rhetoric. The basis for a Progressive Alliance majority in Parliament on economic issues did not exist. Similarly, a variety of alternative programmes emerged within the labour movement: the ILP's living wage doctrine; the proposals by Oswald Mosley for public works, protection and a streamlined executive; the work of the TUC research department under Walter Milne-Bailey.[237] But such agendas easily aroused opposition on factional or personal grounds. There was, in 1929–31, no parliamentary majority for a radical alternative. An election was soon to demonstrate that, in a crisis, the electorate would decisively endorse conservatism.

Whether a coherent alternative policy was available is debateable; that the constraints on the government were severe is evident. Yet the administration's orthodoxy was subject to one significant qualification. The TUC leadership might have felt disappointed by the government's lack of achievement, and slighted by ministerial distance; nevertheless, TUC pressure restrained the impact of austerity on unemployment benefit. Such incremental gains mattered to trade union leaders who could justify, not least to themselves, continuing support for a Labour government. They also mattered to the guardians of orthodoxy, who saw in such concession and procrastination compelling evidence that a Labour government, despite Philip Snowden, could never be accepted as 'sound' on the economy.

Such an exercise in procrastination provided one tributary of the terminal crisis. In February 1931, the government had secured Liberal support in a crucial parliamentary vote through a proposal to set up a committee to review national expenditure under the chairmanship of Sir George May of the Prudential assurance company. The May Report was published at the end of July; the minority recommendations by the Labour committee members were subsequently ignored. The majority report opposed increased taxation as inimical to economic recovery. Instead, the projected deficit necessitated

237 Howell, op. cit., 2002, pp. 264–78; Robert Skidelsky, *Oswald Mosley*, London and Holt, Rhinehart & Winston, 1975, pp. 199–233. For Milne-Bailey, see TUC research department memorandum, 17 August 1931 (TUC Archive MS 292/420/2).

extensive expenditure cuts – the majority coming from a proposed cut of 20 per cent in unemployment benefit. Hope of a response in the autumn would have involved negotiations with sympathetic Liberals and discussions with, among others, the TUC. This strategic agenda disintegrated in the face of a financial crisis. With most politicians on holiday, a Cabinet sub-committee explored possible responses; their deliberations were followed by discussions in full Cabinet. Yet a meeting with Conservative and Liberal leaders on 20 August suggested that any hope of a Progressive Alliance option was giving way to Conservative–Liberal agreement on further economies, hopefully with a compliant Labour government forced to harvest the subsequent unpopularity. Later the same day, two meetings with the TUC general council dramatically transformed the government's predicament. Bevin and the TUC general secretary Walter Citrine attacked the ministerial case – one forcefully, the other with an administrator's distaste for lack of both substance and respect. MacDonald's dismissive response demonstrated a distaste that went beyond the immediate crisis: 'It was practically a declaration of war … The TUC undoubtedly voice the feeling of the mass of workers. They do not know and their minds are rigid and think only of superficial appearances and so grasping at the shadow lose the bone.'[238]

This confrontation proved crucial; the consequential waves were evident around the Cabinet table. A small number of ministers – Lansbury, Greenwood and Addison – were already unhappy about proposed cuts. After 20 August, they were joined by Henderson – always sensitive to trade union opinion – and where he went, others followed. The final Cabinet vote on a proposed 10 per cent cut in unemployment benefit three days later was symbolic and decisive. In an almost evenly divided Cabinet, Henderson was the most senior figure in the dissenting minority. The division fitted no pattern; trade unionists, ex-Liberals, and first- and second-generation Labour figures were on both sides. The subsequent resignation of the government was

238 See: Marquand, op. cit., Chapters 25–6; the minutes of the joint meeting of the Labour Party NEC and the general council of the TUC, 3 p.m., 20 August 1931; the minutes of a ministerial meeting with representatives of the general council, 9.30 p.m.; MacDonald's comment in his diary, 21 August 1931.

expected to be the final chapter. The party would go into opposition. Economies would be implemented by others, followed by an election. Whether MacDonald was expected to remain as party leader was obscure; one possibility for him was to resign and support the economies from the back benches.

Instead, he announced to his Labour colleagues the formation of the National Government, with himself as Prime Minister. He was joined in the Cabinet by three of his former colleagues and by senior Conservatives and Liberals. The initiative was presented as a short-term arrangement to implement economy measures; there would then be an election and a return to partisan alignments. Labour ex-ministers and backbenchers were astounded. Such a possibility had never been discussed within the Labour Party – a contrast with the prelude to the party's participation in the wartime coalitions. With the strong backing of the TUC, many Labour MPs reacted vigorously to the transformation. When the PLP met on 28 August, MacDonald's son Malcolm spoke, as did John Sankey, who had continued as Lord Chancellor. Otherwise, the field was left to those firmly committed to opposing the National Government, and thereby inexorably drawn to criticise MacDonald and his few Labour allies.

Such solidarity brought out Sankey's prejudices. Having experienced the wrath of the PLP, he expostulated in the privacy of his diary: 'Very hostile as all the trade unionists were there … Feelings bitter … They have gone mad and talk about the class war.'[239] Yet many present had mixed emotions – anger and confusion jostled with pain. Some reacted dismissively to those longstanding critics of MacDonald who claimed wisdom before the event. Public passions were complemented by private ambivalence. Some wrote to MacDonald. Jack Lawson epitomised the moderate and respectable Durham miners' leadership. He told of 'deep respect … rooted in an undying affection', and suggested the breach could well be temporary. Will Lunn, a Yorkshire miner, drew the line at the proposed cut in unemployment benefit: 'I think we have been let down by the two men whom I have loved and revered

239 Sankey's diary (Sankey Papers c285).

more than any men I have ever known in public life.' Gordon Macdonald, from the Lancashire coalfield, seemed less torn in his reaction. He wrote of his lifelong friends among the unemployed, and contrasted their poverty with the 'full display of immense wealth'.[240] The kaleidoscope of responses was underlain by a shared memory. Several could recall the decisions taken by individual unions and by the party conference in November 1918 that Labour should quit the Lloyd George coalition. Sankey might conjure up madness, bitterness and class war, but, in fact, the positions taken in 1918 and 1931 were consistent with the sentiments that had informed the foundation of the LRC in 1900 – a commitment to independence and a focus on what were understood as labour interests.

MacDonald's talents and choices had been central to Labour's development over three decades. Yet in 1931, he went against the cultural and organisational identity that had secured Labour solidarity. One explanation, offered not least by him, suggested that he deliberately placed the claims of the nation before those of his party. This characterisation begged the question as to how national needs were understood. For MacDonald in 1931, saving the nation meant endorsing an agenda that was economically regressive and led to a regime that, throughout the '30s, effectively sought an alliance of those with something to lose – however little – against the workless and the poor. As Labour leader, MacDonald, the personification of the Victorian virtues of thrift and industry, showed little empathy towards the unemployed; he was susceptible to sensational press reports about affluent life on the dole. His attitude to trade unions had always been ambivalent, too. He recognised them as central to the party, but was prone to place their sectionalism in opposition to his vision of socialism. Pre-war syndicalism, wartime trade union patriotism, the miners' leader A. J. Cook's oratory – all aroused MacDonald's contempt as fatally as the events of 20 August 1931. He discovered that the party he had led was not a new form of progressivism garnished with socialist rhetoric,

240 Jack Lawson to Ramsay MacDonald, 1 September. 1931; Will Lunn to Ramsay MacDonald, 30 August 1931; Gordon Macdonald to Ramsay MacDonald, 29 August 1931 (all in MacDonald Papers 1315).

but a party whose advances since 1918 had been based on strongly unionised communities. Such supporters were typically not the left critics MacDonald derided; they were men and women who wanted fair treatment from employers and government. When MacDonald made his choice in August 1931, he effectively denied the identity of the party he had led into office.

The National Government did not conform to its initial prospectus. Further financial pressure led to the abandonment of the gold standard – the preservation of which had been a key objective of the new administration. What should have been an embarrassment was spun into a great economic and political opportunity. The only threat was the possibility of a Labour government. Conservative pressure for an election grew; here was a chance to destroy Labour for the most patriotic of reasons.

MacDonald was expelled from the Labour Party at the end of September. After much bargaining and agonising, he led the National Government into a vicious election campaign that achieved its objective. Any residual sympathy for him within the Labour Party died. MacDonald unexpectedly held Seaham, but he seemed bemused by the overall outcome, with a massive Conservative majority won under National Government auspices: 'Once again, I record that no honest man should trust in too gentlemanly a way the Conservative wire-pullers.'[241] MacDonald had always been naive about the inequalities of power he faced as a Labour leader, and about the determination of the privileged to retain what they had. In this, he was at one with the party he led.

241 MacDonald's diary, 29 October 1931.

CHAPTER 9

ARTHUR HENDERSON

CHRIS WRIGLEY

Arthur Henderson, who began his political career as an agent to a Liberal MP, came to play an important role in the development of the Labour Party. He is given credit by historians for building the party's organisation by linking the industrial and political factions. Henderson was also, in effect, leader no fewer than three times. He was chairman of the party twice (1908–10 and 1914–17) and then leader for thirteen months, from September 1931. Henderson, therefore, took Labour into the general election of that year, which was to become one of the greatest defeats in the party's history, with Henderson losing his own seat. Chris Wrigley argues, however, that Henderson could not be blamed for that result, coming, as it did, after MacDonald and Snowden had split with the Labour Party and formed the National Government with the parliamentary opposition. In fact, it could have been a worse defeat, were it not for Henderson's appointment as leader. Henderson was a good but not outstanding speaker, nor was he notably innovative in developing policy, but he provided moderate and experienced, if not charismatic, leadership during a time of great turmoil for the party.

• • •

Arthur Henderson (1863–1935) was leader of the Labour Party in 1931–32, fighting the disastrous 1931 general election. He was also chairman of the PLP twice, in the period before the formal post of leader existed. He became the second chairman of the PLP in 1908 and was in that position at the time of the January 1910 general election. He was again chairman of the PLP in 1914–17, taking over after James Ramsay MacDonald resigned following the outbreak of the Great War. In 1917–18, Henderson played a major role in revitalising the Labour Party through a new and socialist constitution, reorganising it as an electoral machine and, building on wartime social changes, assisting it in formulating a full range of policies to offer the post-war electorate. He saw himself, rightly, as the Labour Party's great organiser. In 1931, he told the Webbs that he had hoped to continue as Foreign Secretary in the Lords and 'devote himself to the party machine', adding that he 'had never wished to be leader, but only the manager of the party'.[242]

Henderson was unique among Labour Party leaders in having been a professional political organiser before being elected to Parliament. Henderson had been the agent of the Liberal MP, Sir Joseph Pease, for the Barnard Castle constituency in County Durham from December 1895 until early 1903. At the third LRC conference, held in Newcastle upon Tyne in February 1903, Henderson moved a successful amendment to increase the trade union levy from 1d to 4d per member. In so doing, he drew on his expertise as an agent, observing: 'If they were going to do something more than simply play a game, they must not be satisfied to go on, for instance, depending upon a register that was made up by the other parties.' He had been engaged for the past seven years in connection with registration work, and happened to know what expense was associated with that work: 'If they were going to build up a perfect machinery of organisation and registration they could not do it on a 1d contribution.'[243]

Although still a paid Liberal agent, Henderson's union, the Friendly Society of Iron Founders, sent him to assist Will Crooks in the Woolwich by-election of March 1903, which Crooks won easily for the LRC.[244] Arthur Henderson was elected in a by-election for Barnard Castle in July 1903. Henderson went on

---

242 Cole, op. cit., p. 287, entry for 20 September 1931.

243 Labour Representation Committee, 'Report of the Third Annual Conference of the Labour Representation Committee', 21 February 1903, p. 34.

244 Wrigley, op. cit., 1990, p. 26; Paul Tyler, *Labour's Lost Leader: The Life and Politics of Will Crooks*, London, I.B. Tauris, 2007, p. 114.

to be the Labour Party's major organiser. When he was the party's treasurer (1903–12), he and Ramsay MacDonald, the Secretary 1900-12, dominated the organisation of the party on behalf of its NEC. Henderson took over as party secretary in 1912 – his 'succession gave organisation much more energetic direction', in Ross McKibbin's view – and he held on to the post (with breaks in 1924 and 1929) until 1934. He had been acting secretary from August 1906 until January 1907, and then from September to December 1909. He enjoyed having his hands on the levers of the party machine. As McKibbin has commented, 'Henderson had a tendency to accumulate responsibilities, but a disinclination to shed them.'[245] He saw himself more as an organisation person than as being at the front of the political stage as leader, and he played key organisational roles in the 1918–24 general elections. He also liked the power behind the scenes of the parliamentary party that came with being Chief Whip – a post he held from 1906 to 1908, from January to August 1914, from 1920 to 1924, and from 1925 to 1927.

In the early years, Henderson's position owed a lot to his experience as a political organiser. He gave the party much of its electoral advice. At the 1907 Labour Party conference, he spoke up for the appointment of an election agent.[246] This matter was referred back to the NEC and, in the following year, a sub-committee reported on the matter. At the 1908 conference, Henderson again supported this appointment, saying: 'The head office was constantly receiving communications asking for explanations and definitions of difficult points of election law and of registration law.' Most of those communications were handed over to him to explain, and he thought it was too much to expect that a man like himself, engaged in so many other things, should be called upon to give all these explanations.[247] The burden of giving detailed electoral advice was lifted from Henderson with the appointment of Arthur Peters as national agent (1908–18).

245 McKibbin, op. cit., 1983, pp. 72 and 125. He even became secretary and treasurer from 1930.

246 The Labour Party, 'Report of the Seventh Annual Conference of the Labour Party', 24 January 1907, pp. 47–8.

247 The Labour Party, 'Report of the Eighth Annual Conference of the Labour Party', 20 January 1908, p. 55.

Henderson's status in the early Labour Party also owed a great deal to his position as a representative of a major trade union – the fourth largest to affiliate with the LRC in its first year.[248] The trade unions provided funds and organisation, and were vigilant as to expenditure on political administration. Henderson had been apprenticed at twelve as an iron-moulder in Newcastle upon Tyne. In 1892, he had become the union's district delegate for the Newcastle area. The following year, he left his trade and instead worked for the *Newcastle Evening News*, while still working for the union. He made a national reputation for himself when acting for his union during the great iron-founders' dispute of 1894. When, in 1902, Henderson's union balloted for someone to be parliamentary candidate and general organiser until elected, Henderson topped the poll of six nominees.[249]

His union's support for the independent labour politics of the LRC was decisive in moving Henderson from Lib–Lab to Labour politics. His change of allegiance had nothing to do with him having any form of socialist beliefs. The trade union–socialist alliance of the LRC was sensitive to 'the various attempts that have been made to initiate a Labour representation movement as an adjunct to trade unionism', as the first annual report put it when giving a brief history.[250] Henderson had been an offshoot of such moves. When he stood in a Newcastle council by-election in November 1892, he was backed by the Tyneside National Labour Association and secured the seamen's leader – Middlesbrough MP, Joseph Havelock Wilson – to speak for him. Later, Havelock Wilson recalled that Henderson had 'made a brilliant speech' in support of the distinguished Gladstonian Liberal MP, John Morley, 'with the result that he was immediately regarded as the coming man of politics'.[251] Henderson advocated a mix of trade unionist and radical policies; in this, he

---

248 It affiliated with 18,357 members (5.2 per cent of the trade union total in 1900–01).

249 Friendly Society of Iron Founders, 'Monthly Report', January 1903.

250 Labour Representation Committee, 'Report of the First Annual Conference of the Labour Representation Committee', 1 February 1901, pp. 7–8.

251 J. Havelock Wilson, *My Stormy Voyage Through Life*, London, Cooperative Printing Society, 1929, p. 266.

was somewhat similar to John Burns and the London Progressives. But he was also very much a product of north-east England politics – as McKibbin put it: there, 'advanced radicalism, temperance, class harmony and Methodism were characteristic'.[252]

Henderson was a committed Methodist, having been converted by Gypsy Smith at a Salvation Army street meeting in 1879 or 1880,[253] and, in the 1890s, he spoke widely at North of England Temperance League meetings. Apart from the centrality of trade unionism to his politics, his Nonconformist background and the venues for the development of his speaking skills were similar to the background of many radical Liberals, including his contemporary David Lloyd George. Like Lloyd George, he had grown up as an admirer of Gladstone, and Henderson's politics certainly owed more to him than to Marx or Robert Owen.

HENDERSON AS PARTY CHAIRMAN

He came to be chairman of the PLP in 1908 because he was the most able of the early trade unionist MPs – or at least the most able available after David Shackleton declined to be chairman, even though Shackleton had acted in that capacity when Keir Hardie was ill and abroad for much of 1907. Henderson remained on his union's executive committee after becoming an MP, and he became its president in 1910. Like J.R. Clynes, he remained very much in touch with his trade union roots. Henderson, in early 1908, was forty-four, full of confidence – stemming from his major role in a skilled union and his nonconformity – and an able speaker. His abilities in this respect have been undervalued by several historians. Henderson did not match up to the rhetoric – sometimes flowery and not filled with meaning, but often outstanding – of an orator such as MacDonald.

---

252 McKibbin, op. cit., 1978, pp. 79–101.

253 There is no consensus on the exact date, nor does the biography of Gypsy Smith help on this.

He had no wish to emulate the socialist equivalents of the 'Come to Jesus' rhetoric of several of the early ILP 'prophets'. Clynes wrote of him that he had 'qualities of exposition', useful on the shop floor.[254] Alan Taylor, who heard him speak in Preston in the 1920s, recalled that he was 'a good speaker – very effectively making his points' and, while he was something of the stolid trade unionist, the fact 'that he had been a Methodist preacher came through very clearly'.[255]

He was not the only able trade unionist of the first three decades of the Labour Party – others such as Jimmy Clynes, Willie Adamson and George Barnes also took on leading roles – but he was probably the weightiest politically, before Ernest Bevin in the 1940s. Like Bevin, he became a domineering figure in the party, but not as brutal as Bevin could be in his treatment of others. He gained the nickname 'Uncle Arthur' from Peter Curran MP when shepherding to a train a Labour delegation in Germany, 1912.[256] 'Uncle Arthur' did not have the sinister connotations that became attached to 'Uncle Joe' for Stalin, but it did involve bossiness. One person who worked with Henderson when he was Foreign Secretary (1929–31) recalled: 'He was genial by nature but was apt to get irritable and shout at people.'[257] One former Labour MP, Lord Snell, recalled:

> Robust in expression, a little prone to carry any disputed point by verbal assault, he was quickly roused to wrath, but was even more quickly composed. He was always approachable, always reliable, and considerate in

254 On class unity and brotherhood, including in skilled unions, see, for instance: Mary Ann Clawson, *Constructing Brotherhood: Class, Gender and Fraternalism*, Princeton NJ, Princeton University Press, 1989, pp. 256–9. John Robert Clynes, *Memoirs, Vol.* 2, London, Hutchinson, 1937, p. 210.

255 Talking with the author, 30 July 1984; Chris Wrigley, *A. J. P. Taylor: Radical Historian of Europe*, London and New York, I.B. Tauris, 2006, p. 29.

256 Edwin A. Jenkins, *From Foundry to Foreign Office: The Romantic Life-Story of the Rt Hon. Arthur Henderson, MP*, London, Grayson & Grayson, 1933, p. 36.

257 Major A. C. Temperley, *The Whispering Gallery of Europe*, London, Collins, 1938, p. 163.

> his judgements, sometimes a little more 'Uncle Mussolini' than the 'Uncle Arthur', who was a revered friend of us all.[258]

Henderson felt deeply the many slights that MacDonald inflicted on him. Although their Labour politics were very similar, and Henderson went out of his way to support MacDonald, Kenneth O. Morgan was perceptive in observing: 'In many ways they were two prima donnas locked in combat.'[259] The relationship lasted so long because Henderson's priority was party organisation, not being leader.

Before the First World War, Labour's electoral strategy was the responsibility of the NEC. Henderson, along with MacDonald, was a key figure as party treasurer. Being chairman of the parliamentary party at the time of the January 1910 election added to this.[260] As Neal Blewett has argued, in 1910 much depended on constituency-level organisation – sometimes controlled by dominant unions such as the miners, sometimes by trades councils, and occasionally by working men's clubs. In other places, the Labour candidates benefited from the Liberal organisations.[261]

The Labour Party owed much of its 1906 parliamentary success to the secret 1903 Gladstone–MacDonald electoral pact, which gave the party a run against Conservative candidates, without Liberal intervention, in many seats. More than this, the pre-First World War Labour Party was the beneficiary of electoral swings against the Conservatives and Liberal Unionists in 1902–7, but did poorly when there were electoral swings against the Liberals, as in 1911–14. In the run-up to the January 1910 general election, the electoral

---

258 Lord Snell, *Men, Movements and Myself*, London, Dent, 1936, p. 233.

259 Kenneth O. Morgan, *Labour People: Leaders and Lieutenants: Hardie to Kinnock*, Oxford and New York, Oxford University Press, 1987, p. 78.

260 He stood down on 15 February 1910.

261 Neal Blewett, *The Peers, the Parties and the People: General Election of 1910*, London, Macmillan, 1972, pp. 283–6; McKibbin, op. cit., 1983, pp. 16–19.

strategy was to focus Labour's attack on the House of Lords and on Labour's social proposals, with Henderson also speaking out against tariffs.[262]

The PLP did try to differentiate its approach to the House of Lords from that of the Liberals, though. Some wished to move an amendment to Asquith's resolution – which declared the House of Lords's rejection of a financial measure to be a breach of the constitution – that would demand the abolition of the House of Lords. Instead, they agreed that Henderson should not move an amendment but instead should reiterate Labour's policy of the abolition of the Lords, as expressed in a motion he had moved in June 1907.[263]

The party's election address began with, and devoted nearly half the space to, the issue of the House of Lords. After denouncing it for having 'mutilated or destroyed' many important bills passed by the House of Commons, it observed: 'Not content with this, they now claim the right to decide what taxes shall be paid, upon whom they will be levied, and for what purpose they will be spent.' It concluded: 'The Lords must go.' The other half of the manifesto listed some of the party's 1906 pledges that had been fulfilled. It also promised to achieve: the Right to Work; the break-up of the Poor Law; the abolition of poverty; the extension of non-contributory old-age pensions; and the full extension of the franchise to men and women. It used the slogan: 'The land for the people. The wealth for the wealth producers.' Roy Douglas may well have been right when he argued: 'Most of the pre-1914 Labour MPs, like a very large section of contemporary Liberals, were probably stirred more by the land question than by any other.'[264]

Henderson was a leading figure in the general election campaign of December 1909 and the first half of January 1910 – at least, the press saw him as such. Henderson's speeches were reported by *The Times* as being by the chairman of the Labour Party, with only Keir Hardie getting anywhere near as much

262 *The Times*, 4 January 1910.

263 'Political Notes', *The Times*, 2 December 1909; Jenkins, op. cit., pp. 28–30.

264 Roy Douglas, 'Labour and the Constitutional Crisis' in Brown, op. cit., p. 221; Roy Douglas, *Land, People and Politics: A History of the Land Question in the United Kingdom, 1878–1952*, London, Alison & Busby, 1976.

coverage. Yet Henderson's role in the January 1910 election was much less high-profile than that of Labour leaders after the Second World War.

Labour's election strategy was hobbled both by the central issues of the House of Lords and the Budget, and by widespread suspicions that, in practice, the Labour Party was not as independent as its constitution proclaimed. Not only was Labour committed to the abolition of the House of Lords, but it also fully supported the 'People's Budget', believing many aspects of it to have been taken from Labour policies. Hence, it was difficult not to appear to be in the Liberal slipstream. The sudden calling of the election caught Labour out, in that many potential candidates had not been endorsed, and many constituencies' electoral organisations were not ready. With potential Labour candidates withdrawing, the Tory press and Labour left, as well as other socialist groups, were both quick to accuse the Labour leadership of dirty deals with the Liberals. Yet, as Neal Blewett has observed, for Labour's right wing, especially some miners, there were not enough deals with the Liberals.[265] Henderson, a devout Methodist, cannot have been comfortable making denials of a Liberal–Labour deal – even if there was no fresh, detailed pact (like that of 1903), there was probably at least a general understanding and some local arrangements. At Canning Town, on 10 December, he said: 'There had been no alliance. It would be against the constitution of the Labour Party. It was quite true that candidates had been withdrawn, and others might be withdrawn ... They had withdrawn candidates to oblige nobody, but only to suit themselves.'[266] Henderson himself may have been a beneficiary, as it was believed he would lose in 1910 in a three-way contest, and there was serious talk of an independent Liberal standing in January.[267]

Henderson was most probably intending to stand down from the chair of the parliamentary party in 1910 anyway. But it seems very likely that he was confirmed in doing so by a major crisis in trade union relations with

265 Blewett, op. cit., p. 237.

266 *The Times*, 11 December 1909.

267 *The Times*, 10 January and 12 January 1910.

the Labour Party – one that would affect him even after the public payment of MPs. This was the Osborne Judgment, delivered on 21 December 1909, which undercut the rights trade unions believed they had to fund political parties. Henderson withdrew from being the main speaker at an election meeting in Stockport on 30 December in order to attend a meeting of Labour representatives in London that day and the next, trying to find ways around the judgment.[268] Henderson and his colleagues devoted much time in 1910 to adjusting Labour's policies to achieve a partial reversal of the Osborne Judgment with the Trade Union Act, 1913.[269]

Henderson's second period as chairman of the PLP came in early August 1914, when MacDonald resigned after the outbreak of war. Henderson supported the war effort, condemning Prussian militarism and believing that Germany had 'prepared for and fought a war of aggression, not of defence'.[270] Henderson's three sons fought, and David Henderson was killed on the Somme on 15 September 1916. In the preface to his small book, *The Aims of Labour*, Henderson wrote that he intended any profits from the sale of the book to go to:

> The fund the Labour Party is promoting with a view to erecting a suitable and lasting memorial to the honour of those who have fallen on the field of battle in furtherance of the ideals and aims that inspire British democracy and on behalf of which British Labour has sacrificed so much and so freely.[271]

He was the Labour Party's first Cabinet minister, serving under H. H. Asquith – as president of the board of education from May 1915 until August

---

268 Barnes, the deputy chairman, spoke in his place. *The Times*, 31 December 1909.

269 Henry Pelling, 'The Politics of the Osborne Judgment', *Historical Journal*, Vol. 25, 1982, pp. 889–909; Chris Wrigley, 'Labour and the Trade Unions' in K. D. Brown, op .cit., pp. 129–57.

270 Arthur Henderson, 'Prussian Militarism' (an interview with Arthur Draper of the *New York Tribune*) in *British Finance and Prussian Militarism*, London and New York, Hodder & Stoughton, 1917, p. 17.

271 Arthur Henderson, *The Aims of Labour*, New York, Headley Bros, 1918, p. 5. The preface is dated 22 December 1917.

1916, when he became Paymaster General – and under David Lloyd George – as a member of the small War Cabinet and as Minister without Portfolio from December 1916, until he resigned on 11 August 1917 over his desire for the Labour Party to be represented at an international socialist conference in Stockholm. He had hoped that attendance at this conference would strengthen the Kerensky government in Russia and keep that ally in the war. Throughout his time in these posts, his main government task was being the major industrial relations advisor, and he formally became Labour advisor to the Ministry of Munitions, with George Roberts, Labour MP for Norwich, as his deputy, in August 1916, before having a more prestigious overview as a member of Lloyd George's War Cabinet.[272] In the sphere of industrial relations, he exhibited competence, even if many trade unionists pressing for better pay and conditions in wartime Britain were highly critical of him for taking on the role. For Henderson, however, it was a natural concomitant to supporting the drive for victory, just as, in 1940–45, Bevin took on manpower issues.

On 24 October 1917, Henderson stood down as chairman after three years. In large part, his motivation again was to do work that he believed was more valuable for the party. Henderson's biggest electoral contribution to the Labour Party came after his second period as chairman of the parliamentary party, and before the 1918 general election. With Sidney Webb and Ramsay MacDonald, Henderson was responsible for producing revised internal and external policies for Labour in the post-war world, and a new, socialist constitution. Henderson was the main force behind the reorganisation of the Labour Party, making it more effective as a national electoral organisation, and this included creating a press and publicity department.[273] He was blunt as to the crucial importance of party reorganisation in January 1918 at the annual conference:

---

272 On Henderson's substantial role as an industrial trouble-shooter for Asquith and Lloyd George, see 'Oiling the War Machine' in Wrigley, op. cit., 1990, Chapter 5.

273 J. M. Winter, *Socialism and the Challenge of War: Ideas and Politics in Britain, 1912–1918*, Routledge & Kegan Paul, 1974, pp. 259–63; Laura Beers, *Your Britain: Media and the Making of the Labour Party*, Harvard University Press, 2010, pp. 34, 38–9.

> It was no use the executive issuing anything in the nature of the programme; it was no use talking about building a new social order or reconstructing society, until they had taken into very careful consideration their present position as an organised political force. They had done so, and come to the unanimous conclusion that Labour, as politically organised in the existing circumstances, was altogether inadequate to the great task that lay immediately before it. They had never, in the proper sense, claimed to be a national political party.[274]

ARTHUR HENDERSON AS LEADER

When Henderson became leader in 1931 his role was very much that of damage limitation. The 1931 general election was Labour's worst electoral disaster, but it would be very wrong to blame Henderson's leadership for this dismal result. Indeed, it might be better to ask whether it could have been even worse had not a respected Labour figure of great experience been willing to take over after the departure of Ramsay MacDonald, Philip Snowden, J. H. Thomas and others. Henderson's contribution in 1931 was to provide experienced and moderate leadership, but it was not dynamic or very effective during the 1931 general election. However, that was an election that could not be salvaged by a party that had just divided. Although politics was very different in 1846, the Conservative Party had a bad experience in shedding its leaders then – although not too bad when emerging from an unpopular coalition government in 1922. In 1931, it was a far more damaging split than in 1922, and was in the midst of an international economic crisis.

Henderson had a wealth of experience in both the labour movement and in Whitehall. As well as his earlier roles, he had been a lacklustre Home Secretary in the first MacDonald Labour government of 1924. He had a more

---

274 Speaking on the New Constitution, 23 January 1918; The Labour Party, 'Report of the Annual Conference of the Labour Party', 1918, p. 19.

distinguished record as Foreign Secretary in MacDonald's second Labour government of 1929–31, where he did impress with his initiatives. Unlike MacDonald as Foreign Secretary in 1924 and as Prime Minister in 1929–35, Henderson did not give the impression of being embarrassed by Labour Party policies. Indeed, when resisting a unilateral disarmament motion, he told the 1930 Labour Party conference that he 'was trying religiously to stick by *Labour and the Nation*'.[275] Foreign policy was the area of government activity where most election promises (other than disarmament) were fulfilled. In spite of friction between Henderson and MacDonald over foreign policy, the Prime Minister used the loyal and hard-working Henderson as, in effect, deputy Prime Minister when he was away in March 1931.

Henderson declined to be involved in plans to replace MacDonald, either in 1924 or twice during the second Labour government. Indeed, he kept the door open for MacDonald's return during the First World War and tried to do so even after the 1931 split, being the sole voter against MacDonald's expulsion at the Labour Party's NEC on 28 September. In the situation after MacDonald's defection in 1931, Henderson had major assets: he had immense experience in the party organisation and in Parliament; he was usually in tune with the Labour Party's membership; and, especially important, he represented the solid trade union base of the party. Within the parliamentary party and among most trade union leaders on Labour–trade union joint bodies and meetings, Henderson was able to carry support for policies in a way that MacDonald and Snowden could not. In the Cabinet crisis over cuts, he predictably went with the view of the trade union movement, finding additional cuts unacceptable beyond the initial package of £56 million. With MacDonald, Snowden and Thomas gone, Henderson was the near inevitable replacement.[276] Near – as Clynes, who was deputy leader, and who, like Henderson, had kept close to the trade unions, might have

275 The Labour Party, 'Report of the Thirtieth Annual Conference', 8 October 1930, p. 240.

276 As Dalton observed in his diary, 24 August 1931. Quoted in Leventhal, op. cit., p. 193.

taken on the leadership, although he declined and later observed that 'others deserved the position'.[277]

Henderson sensibly had doubts that he should take on the leadership, not least because he had been a member of the Cabinet economy committee and had supported the first tranche of £56 million in cuts. He also would have been sensible to give up either his Labour Party posts or his League of Nations work; instead, as was his weakness, he added another huge task to his already big workload. He did, however, have two deputy leaders, in Clynes and Willie Graham, not just one.

Henderson had to promote Labour in spite of the glaring contradictions in its policies. A TUC-dominated trade union and Labour Party committee produced a policy document approved on 27 August that rejected all the cuts, especially in unemployment benefits, and proposed various taxes on wealth. In September, Henderson and other prominent Labour figures moved away from denouncing all the cuts. However, he was embarrassed by having accepted £56 million of cuts (subject to cooperation by the Conservatives and the Liberals) under MacDonald, which he acknowledged in the Commons on 7 September, and by being in a Cabinet that had accepted a revenue tariff, thereby proving willing to break with free trade.[278] Yet these were concessions intended to avoid or lessen cuts to unemployment benefit.

Later in September, Henderson greatly disappointed his parliamentary colleagues by not vigorously condemning the government when it abandoned the gold standard – its defence being the ostensible reason for forming the National Government. As Andrew Thorpe has argued, this may have been due to Henderson's desire to try to avoid an early general election and to appear patriotic over the retreat from gold.[279] However, his troops greatly needed lifting and encouraging in their struggle with MacDonald and the

---

277 Clynes, op. cit., (2), p. 198.

278 Andrew Thorpe, *The British General Election of 1931*, Oxford, Clarendon Press, 1991, pp. 133, 136–7 (see also the same author's 'Arthur Henderson and the British Political Crisis of 1931', *Historical Journal*, 31(1), 1988, pp. 117–39).

279 Thorpe, ibid., pp. 146–8. For a harsher view, see Williamson, op. cit., pp. 429–31.

National Government. Henderson, faced with the disdain of many, offered to resign. He was successfully urged to continue. Henderson, as usual, would have preferred an organisational role. As Dalton said: 'He must look after the organisation in view of an early election.'[280]

Henderson had no new ideas on economic policy. He had relied on Snowden and, with Snowden gone, he relied much on Willie Graham, who had been president of the board of trade. Graham had been an admirer, even an acolyte, of Snowden, following in his free-trade and balanced-budget footsteps.[281] Ernest Bevin had an alternative economic policy but, when electors still in employment feared for their jobs and savings, Henderson would have been ill advised to have gone for a mix of deficit finance and tariffs alongside the agreed abandonment of the gold standard.[282] In his Burnley constituency on 25 September, Henderson outlined what were to be Labour's main election policies: the public control of the banks; the reconstruction of industry; support for agriculture; and the scrapping of the Economy Bill. In the 1931 general election, Henderson presided over Labour's worst defeat, losing his own seat again (as in the 1918, 1922 and 1923 elections).

Henderson was one of the many links between the working-class Liberal politics of late-Victorian Britain and the socialist politics of the Labour Party from 1918. In many respects, he was at the radical end of the Nonconformist and Temperance supporters of Gladstone. This is so with regard to the Ottoman Empire and Ireland. In 1917, Henderson commented to an American newspaper reporter: 'Though Armenian atrocities are not much talked about here, they have undoubtedly made a deep impression on the minds of the working population who, I think, are determined that never again shall

---

280 Dalton's diary, 24 August 1931.

281 Thomas N. Graham, *Willie Graham*, London and New York, Hutchinson, 1948, pp. 184–7.

282 For a recent reappraisal of Bevin's economic arguments, see Chris Wrigley, 'Labour dealing with Labour: aspects of economic policy' in John Shepherd, Jonathan Davis and Chris Wrigley ed., *Britain's Second Labour Government, 1929–31: A Reappraisal*, Manchester, Manchester University Press, 2011, pp. 37–54. For an excellent broader discussion of economic policy, see Peter Clarke, *The Keynesian Revolution in the Making 1924–1936*, Oxford, Clarendon Press, 1988.

a Christian nation be under the yoke of the Turk.'[283] As for Ireland, Henderson was long a supporter of the Irish Nationalist Party. By early 1920, he recognised the widespread desire in Ireland, outside of Ulster, for Britain to 'clear out', but, until autumn 1920, he wanted Ireland to remain within the British Commonwealth. However, as he put it in a motion of censure on Lloyd George's coalition government, 25 October 1920, he was appalled by 'reprisals on the part of those whose duty is the maintenance of law and order'. When Labour's call for an independent investigation was defeated in the House of Commons, Henderson headed Labour's own investigation, which visited southern Ireland for just over two weeks in November to December 1920. He followed his Irish trip with a series of public meetings in 1921, at which, he believed, the 'moral fervour and the deep indignation' of earlier times was displayed. Labour's Irish investigation marked the end of Lib–Lab Irish policy as much as the new Labour Party constitution and organisation of January 1918 marked the end of the pre-1914 style of Labour Party politics.[284]

ASSESSING HENDERSON

Henderson's first period as chairman of the PLP was in a different phase of Labour Party politics to his period as leader (1931–32). Henderson's leadership in 1908–10 was criticised by the ILP wing of the party. This was partly due to his failure to insist sufficiently on the Labour Party's independence. Keir Hardie complained that his successor as chairman of the parliamentary party was 'reactionary and timid'.[285] However, Henderson's was a different style of politics to that of the self-proclaimed prophets or apostles of socialism, such as Keir Hardie, Philip Snowden or Glasier.

283 Henderson, op. cit., 1917, p. 21.

284 The Labour Party, 'Report of the Labour Commission to Ireland', December 1920; Wrigley, op. cit., 1990, pp. 135–7.

285 Lawrence Thompson, *The Enthusiasts*, London, Victor Gollancz, 1971, p.156.

Henderson, as a former Lib–Lab local politician, simply did not deem the Liberals to be as bad as the Conservatives and Liberal Unionists. Glasier complained of Henderson's 'eternal appearances on Temperance and Methodist platforms', his deeply held religious views ('a canting humbug on religion') and his 'seeming camaraderie with the Liberals'. Henderson's sober worthiness connected well with many hitherto Liberal-supporting working people. Yet Glasier held kindred views to Henderson's when it came to gambling – joining with Henderson in June 1913 in opposition to removing an embargo on betting on a *Daily Citizen* sports page – and he echoed Henderson when he said that he 'regarded betting as a more degrading slavery than landlordism and capitalism'.[286] Even on independence, there is a case for seeing Henderson as a realist, given his immense desirability for Labour to avoid as many three-way contests as possible. Even Keir Hardie went in for secret talks with south Wales Liberals; as Kenneth Morgan has commented: 'It was far from being crystal-clear what distinguished his approach from the Lib–Labism of Shackleton or Henderson, which he so often criticised.'[287] As for MacDonald, it is probable that Henderson threw cold water on his aspirations to take office in a Liberal Cabinet in 1910–14, being mindful of his own public denials of deals being done and of the iron-founders' views.[288]

As for his alleged timidity, it was the case that he did not give charismatic leadership, either in the Commons or in the country. This was partly due to how he interpreted the role of chairman of the parliamentary party. He saw it as being the spokesperson for the Labour group. It was also partly due to Henderson not seeing the need on the current big issues to be abrasive. He was impressed by Lloyd George's radicalism and, in 1909–10, was pleased with the 'People's Budget' and the confrontation with the House of Lords, even if he was committed to ending not mending it. His record as chairman

286 Morgan, op. cit., 1975, p. 220; Thompson, ibid., p. 186.

287 Morgan, ibid., p. 229.

288 Marquand, op. cit., pp. 142–3, 150–51, 159–63; Leventhal, op. cit., p. 40; Wrigley, op. cit., 1990, pp. 66–7.

of the PLP was not strong, but it was arguably no worse, and probably better, than Keir Hardie's before and Barnes's after him – Keir Hardie being a non-team player, even when team leader, and Barnes being impetuous and deemed by many as not adequately representing Labour's views.

By 1931, the post of leader was very significantly different from that of the earlier chairman of the PLP. It involved being the face of the Labour Party in an era of radio and newsreels, as well as popular newspapers.[289] Henderson, as he well knew, lacked the charisma and oratory skills of MacDonald. He also lacked the inclination for virulent attacks on colleagues of three decades – in this, he was markedly unlike Philip Snowden. Henderson's successes in Whitehall had been in industrial relations and in foreign policy. In the 1931 general election, the Conservatives and Liberal Nationals nearly ignored foreign policy and barely mentioned Henderson's big issue: the forthcoming world disarmament conference.[290] Probably no Labour leader, even with greater time before a general election, could have moved the national political debate away from the economic crisis to more favourable areas, especially not when nearly all the media poured vitriol on to the Labour Party. Part of his timidity in autumn 1931 came from his electoral organisational experience, with him tactically, desperately desiring to defer a general election.

Henderson was a mediocre leader in 1931–32, but in taking on the leadership at that time, he did the Labour Party, and the labour movement as a whole, a major service. The trade union movement would have been highly reluctant to have a non-trade unionist as leader after the defection of MacDonald and Snowden (both of whom had so often in the past voiced their distaste for the trade unions). Henderson had wide appeal to the 'respectable working class', which, other than in the conditions of 1931, would have been a notable asset. One working-class woman later recalled: 'He was a man of integrity who showed how an ordinary working man could achieve a lot in

289 On this see Beers, op. cit., pp. 129, 141–2.

290 Thorpe, op. cit., p. 249.

public. People liked to look up to such figures. They showed what working people could aspire to.'[291]

Being leader in the 1931 general election was his last major service to the party. He had long been in touch with the mood of the mass of the party. Now he was fast losing touch. During and after the general election, Henderson tried to return Labour to being the party of the 1920s, while the bulk of the labour movement was moving on after the defections and the bitter general election to policies of greater state intervention, as acted on by Attlee's 1945–51 majority Labour governments.[292] It was very much time for him to give up being leader when he stood down in 1932.

291 Monica Walsh recalling Henderson in Burnley (in conversation with the author, 5 July 1987).

292 See, for example, Daniel Ritschel, *The Politics of Planning: The Debate on Economic Planning in the 1930s*, Oxford, Clarendon Press, 1977.

CHAPTER 10

GEORGE LANSBURY

JOHN SHEPHERD

The pacifist George Lansbury was Labour Party leader from 1932 to 1935, coming to power in the aftermath of the disastrous 1931 general election to face Ramsay MacDonald and the massed ranks of the National Government at Westminster. John Shepherd argues that Lansbury was a much-beloved politician, highly effective at organising a depleted parliamentary party of only forty-six Labour MPs, as well as restoring the morale of the wider labour movement. In his three years at the helm, during which time party organisation was strengthened, Labour gained ten seats in by-elections, and eventually returned 154 MPs at the 1935 general election. However, though Lansbury did much to preserve party unity, he had been unable to prevent the ILP's disaffiliation. He is often described as having been driven from leadership, following a brutal attack by the trade union leader Ernie Bevin at the party conference in 1935. Shepherd, however, contends that George Lansbury had already considered resigning, since his absolute Christian pacifism was irreconcilable with Labour foreign policy in the face of international fascism.

• • •

The Christian socialist and pacifist George Lansbury (1859–1940), who led the Labour Party from 1932 to 1935, was described by A. J. P. Taylor as 'the most lovable figure in modern politics'.[293] In 1965, Taylor's memorable portrayal of this socialist pioneer evoked memories of Lansbury's

293 A. J. P. Taylor, *English History 1914–1945*, Oxford, Clarendon Press, 1965, p. 142, n. 3.

immense personal popularity and his exceptional ability to connect with ordinary people, which always characterised his politics. Lansbury spent most of his political life in the Labour Party. He campaigned for social justice for working people and the unemployed, women's suffrage, world disarmament and the abolition of imperialism. Imprisoned twice for his political beliefs, he was often the party rebel *par excellence*, and a thorn in the side of Ramsay MacDonald, Labour's first Prime Minister. However, Lansbury was never seen as a candidate for party leadership, nor did he aspire to the position.[294]

Yet, unexpectedly, George Lansbury was destined to take on the party leadership with Labour fortunes at their nadir after the second Labour government's downfall and the party's rout at the 1931 general election.[295] In 1931, Lansbury was elected unanimously as chairman of the PLP at Westminster. He formed a short-lived dual leadership with the party leader, Arthur Henderson, who was out of Parliament after losing his seat. In October 1932, on Henderson's resignation, Lansbury succeeded him as party leader, combining both roles until his own resignation in 1935.

A year before, at the 1934 Labour Party conference at Southport, George Lansbury spoke openly about the party leadership and his possible resignation with considerable honesty:

> I never dreamed in my wildest imagining that I would ever be called upon to act as the [party] spokesman. I have never considered myself the leader – but as spokesman of my colleagues in the House of Commons, I have been proud to be one of that little band. I am proud to have been chosen to speak for them whenever it was necessary for me to speak on behalf of the party … It was an accident that put me there – the accident of the last

---

294 For modern studies of George Lansbury, see Raymond Postgate, *The Life of George Lansbury*, London, Longmans, Green & Co., 1951; Jonathan Schneer, *George Lansbury*, Manchester, Manchester University Press, 1991; John Shepherd, *George Lansbury : At the Heart of Old Labour*, Oxford, Oxford University Press, 2004. See also: Andrew Thorpe, 'George Lansbury 1931–1935' in Jefferys, op. cit., pp. 61–79; Peter Shore, *Leading the Left*, London, Weidenfeld & Nicolson, 1993, pp. 17–34.

295 The position of leader of the Labour Party was created in 1922. Ramsay MacDonald defeated J. R. Clynes narrowly in the first leadership contest. Previously, the chairman of the PLP led the party – a position that MacDonald himself, among others, had held.

> general election – I am only there as long as my colleagues think it wise for me to be there. When they think change is needed, then I shall go.[296]

This chapter examines the circumstances in which George Lansbury, seemingly as poacher turned gamekeeper, became leader of the Labour Party, at seventy-two, during a worldwide economic crisis, the rise of international fascism and major political realignment in Britain. It assesses the qualities and skills of a politician who never fought a general election as party leader and was regarded by many as merely an elderly stop-gap between the major figures of Ramsay MacDonald and Clement Attlee in the Labour pantheon. Finally, the chapter reviews Lansbury's resignation as party leader after his celebrated clash with the trade union boss, Ernie Bevin, as hailstones thundered down on the Dome at the 1935 Brighton party conference.

POLITICAL CAREER: FROM LIBERALISM TO LABOUR

As a committed Christian socialist, George Lansbury's political trajectory was often tempestuous, from his early days as a Gladstonian Liberal Party agent to his leadership of the British Labour Party during the Depression years of the 1930s.[297]

Like many Labour pioneers, George Lansbury's early political loyalties were with Gladstonian Liberalism. In the late 1880s, Lansbury earned a significant reputation as the local Liberal Party agent with unflagging energy and political acuity, who had secured three Liberal election triumphs, including Jane Cobden's successful campaign to be returned to the newly founded London county council. As a young labourer (from the age of sixteen to eighteen), Lansbury had been a regular spectator in the Strangers' Gallery at Westminster, witnessing the parliamentary debates between Gladstone

296 The Labour Party, 'Report of the Annual Conference', 1934, p. 146.

297 John Shepherd, 'A Life on the Left: George Lansbury (1859–1940): A Case Study in Recent Labour Biography', *Labour History: A Journal of Labour and Social History*, No. 87, November 2004, p. 147.

and Disraeli. As a young Christian radical, he was drawn to the individual liberty, freedom for subject peoples and community of interest of different social classes that characterised Gladstonian Liberalism. A highly traumatic emigration to Australia in 1884–85, with his wife Bessie and their young family, launched Lansbury into British politics on their return.

However, by the early 1890s, after declining Liberal patronage to pursue a parliamentary career, a disenchanted Lansbury had switched to socialism. He left the Liberals to form the Bow & Bromley branch of the Marxist SDF. He had increasingly realised that democracy, political reform and increased Labour representation would not be achieved in the late-Victorian party. He later observed: 'Liberalism would progress just so far as the capitalist money bags would allow it to progress, and so I took the plunge and joined the SDF.'[298]

Lansbury's long political career comprised nearly a lifetime of selfless public service to ordinary people, during which he held every elective office: local councillor; county councillor; Poor Law guardian for over thirty years; and, from 1910 to 1912, and 1922 to 1940, MP for Bow & Bromley.

In the SDF, he was elected as a Poor Law guardian – an office he held continuously until its abolition in 1928. In 1895, he became the SDF's national organiser, touring Britain as a propagandist for socialism. According to SDF leader Henry M. Hyndman, Lansbury was 'the best organiser the federation had ever had'. In the 1890s, George Lansbury temporarily lost his Christian faith, and with his wife and family joined the East London Ethical Society. However, Lansbury eventually became a leading figure in the Church Socialist League.[299] Lansbury also stood unsuccessfully for Parliament for the SDF twice in 1895, with further election defeats in 1900, 1906, January 1910, and the 1912 by-election.

By around 1904, Lansbury had joined the ranks of Labour via the ILP, as well as being associated with the Fabian Society. Lansbury's reforming work

298 George Lansbury, 'How I Became a Socialist', *Labour Leader*, 17 May 1912.

299 Shepherd, op. cit., 2004, pp. 40–41, 97.

as a Poor Law guardian led to his membership of the Royal Commission on the Poor Laws and Relief of Distress 1905–19. He was a co-signatory of the famous Minority Report with Beatrice Webb, which demonstrated Lansbury's public standing as a working-class representative on the Victorian Poor Law.

In 1906, Lansbury finished bottom of the poll at Middlesbrough (the only time he was a parliamentary candidate outside London), where his election agent Marion Coates Hansen – a member of the local ILP and a feminist – encouraged him to include 'votes for women' in his election manifesto. Lansbury entered Parliament on his fifth attempt, in December 1910, but, disenchanted with Ramsay MacDonald's parliamentary leadership, resigned his seat to force a by-election over 'votes for women' in 1912 – the only occasion an MP has resigned over women's rights. For Lansbury, a popular champion of the women's cause, gender superseded social class in his political advocacy.[300]

Previously, the Speaker had suspended him from Parliament for his outburst of rage in the House against the Liberal Prime Minister H. H. Asquith over the forcible feeding of imprisoned suffragettes. While Lansbury and members of his family had been highly visible in the women's suffrage movement, the resignation of his seat also reflected his growing disenchantment with the Labour leader Ramsay MacDonald's close association with the Liberals. Lansbury lost the 'suffragettes' by-election' and did not return to Parliament until 1922. In 1913, Lansbury's fervent speech at the Albert Hall, defending suffragette militancy, resulted in his prosecution and imprisonment.

Clement Attlee called GL (as Lansbury was often affectionately known) 'Lansbury of London', owing to his close identification with the East End, which shaped his political identity.[301] As a local politician and MP for Bow & Bromley, his family home, based in his impoverished constituency, became a haven of political activity. He travelled by public transport, particularly as a

---

300 Ibid., Chapter 7.

301 See Clement Attlee's review in *The Observer* (30 December 1951) of Raymond Postgate, *The Life of George Lansbury*, London and New York, Longmans, 1951, in Frank Field, *Attlee's Great Contemporaries: The Politics of Character*, London, Continuum, 2009, pp. 1–3. For important glimpses of family life, see Edgar Lansbury, *George Lansbury, My Father*, London, Sampson Low, Marston & Co., 1934.

Cabinet minister and Leader of the Opposition. The charismatic Lansbury cut a distinctive figure: a large-framed man with a kind face, embellished by mutton-chop whiskers, who carried a booming voice. At first he preached the merits of socialism on street corners (and in nearby Victoria Park), but, by the First World War and beyond, his reputation as a politician on the left commanded large audiences, such as at the Albert Hall rallies.

Out of Parliament for ten years, Lansbury embarked on a new career as editor-proprietor of the newly founded socialist *Daily Herald*, which became the newspaper of the movement – more important than the Labour Party's relatively short-lived *Daily Citizen*. Lansbury showed astute business acumen in running his paper, employing a galaxy of writers and intellectuals, including the brilliant Australian political cartoonist Will Dyson. The *Daily Herald* survived regular financial crises and its columns were open to a wide spectrum of dissenting groups. During the First World War, the paper was published as a pacifist weekly. In 1922, Lansbury arranged for the paper to be taken over by the Labour Party/TUC, and it eventually survived as a commercial daily until 1964.

In 1919, Labour won control of Poplar council for the first time, with George Lansbury, aged sixty, elected as the first Labour mayor in one of the poorest parts of London. As a significant municipal employer, the councillors were determined to tackle unemployment and improve working conditions through an extensive programme of social reforms, including equal pay for women workers and a minimum £4 weekly wage for council employees.

In 1921, Lansbury took the leading role in the 'Poplar Rates Revolt', infamously known to opponents as 'Poplarism'. It was a defining episode in the political life of George Lansbury and his family. Thirty Poplar councillors, including Lansbury's son Edgar and daughter-in-law Minnie, willingly went to prison with him to defend their poor East End constituents in defiance of the government, the courts and the leadership of the Labour Party. The Poplar councillors, who were mainly local manual workers, aimed to end the unreformed rating system that favoured the wealthier west London boroughs to the disadvantage of the poorer East End. It was a battle that included dramatic scenes of public support on the street, as the councillors marched to the High Court, and their eventual conviction, resulting in six weeks in prison.[302]

Ramsay MacDonald always remembered the class warrior and republican George Lansbury as 'the brawling vestryman from Poplar', for his role in the Rates Revolt. Also, members of the Lansbury family were members of, or associated with, the British Communist Party. Though not a member of the Communist Party in Britain, Lansbury himself had visited Russia and met Lenin and other prominent Bolsheviks.[303] When MacDonald formed his minority 1924 government, partly in deference to King George V, there was no Cabinet place for the popular Lansbury.[304] According to the Fabian socialist Sidney Webb, it was 'the most glaring omission'.

After the left's disappointment with the 1924 Labour government, George Lansbury was nominated by the ILP to stand against MacDonald for the PLP chairmanship, but Lansbury refused to allow his nomination to go forward. While he demonstrated no ambition for the party leadership, Lansbury's personal popularity saw him elected top of the PLP executive with sixty-seven votes, compared to Arthur Henderson's relatively poor showing in eleventh place with thirty-eight votes.[305] The idealist Lansbury was also a pragmatist, needing the Labour Party as much as the party needed him. In his autobiography, he criticised the Labour leadership and the power of the party machine, but, as chairman of the 1928 Labour Party conference, he appealed for party unity and backed *Labour and the Nation* – Labour's policy for the next election.[306]

In 1929, MacDonald brought Lansbury into his second Labour Cabinet as First Commissioner of Works – traditionally a minor office concerned

---

302 For 'Poplarism', see: Noreen Branson, *Poplarism, 1919–1925: George Lansbury and the Councillors' Revolt*, London, Lawrence & Wishart, 1979; Shepherd, op. cit., 2004, Chapter 11.

303 For the Lansbury family and British communism, see Kevin Morgan, *Labour Legends and Russian Gold*, London, Lawrence & Wishart, 2006, Chapter 4.

304 John Shepherd and Keith Laybourn, *Britain's First Labour Government,* Basingstoke and New York: Palgrave Macmillan, 2006, pp. 62-64.

305 Howell, op. cit., 2002, pp. 33–4.

306 Shepherd, op. cit., 2004, pp. 222, 248–51.

with historical monuments and with little scope for public expenditure. The energetic Lansbury distinguished himself by fundraising to promote a popular programme of recreational activities for the Royal Parks, including 'Lansbury's Lido' on the Serpentine in Hyde Park, which A. J. P. Taylor later described as the minority administration's only memorable achievement. Lansbury was also given a limited role under the ineffective J. H. Thomas, along with Oswald Mosley and Tom Johnston, advising on strategies for dealing with mass unemployment following the Wall Street Crash of 1929. In 1931, the second Labour government resigned following the financial and political crisis of 19–24 August, when a substantial minority of the Cabinet (nine votes to eleven) refused to accept the 10 per cent reduction in unemployment benefits. Lansbury had been one of the first ministers to oppose this proposal. As events developed daily, Lansbury's Whitehall office became the meeting place for Cabinet ministers opposed to the expenditure cuts. The crisis of 1931 resulted in the controversial formation of the National Government, led by Ramsay MacDonald, and the realignment of political parties, which placed George Lansbury unexpectedly in the role of Labour leader.

LABOUR LEADER

The general election of 1931 marked the all-time low of Labour electoral fortunes, and was by far Labour's greatest defeat of the twentieth century. The National Government had secured a landslide victory, winning a gargantuan total of 554 out of the 615 seats in the new Parliament, as well as 67 per cent of the total votes cast. Labour's parliamentary representation was virtually annihilated, reduced to only forty-six MPs, plus six unendorsed ILP members, from the 267 MPs they had when the election was called.

In addition, the 1931 election caused a major reversal in the party hierarchy. The old order of Labour leaders, who did not accompany MacDonald into the National Government ranks, had been devastated in the electoral avalanche.[307] In this unprecedented parliamentary rout, a total of fourteen Labour Cabinet members and twenty-one other members and party whips had been defeated at the hands of the electors. Arthur Henderson, who was out of Parliament after losing Burnley by 8,200 votes, was re-elected unopposed as party leader.

On 3 November 1931, the septuagenarian George Lansbury was unanimously elected as chairman of the PLP – there appeared to be literally no other choice. George Lansbury was the only former Cabinet member (on the Labour side) among His Majesty's Opposition to salvage his parliamentary seat, albeit he held Bow & Bromley with a largely reduced majority of 4,664 after an 11.1 per cent swing to his Tory opponent – his narrowest winning margin in the five elections of the inter-war years.[308]

With Clement Attlee and Stafford Cripps, George Lansbury formed a socialist triumvirate that played an important role in running the PLP. The former Solicitor General, Stafford Cripps, had been the only Labour member returned in the west of England (Bristol East). Clement Attlee, the ex-Postmaster General, only just hung on at Stepney (by 551 votes). Attlee later recalled: 'On going to the first party meeting after the election, I had a message from Arthur Henderson that George Lansbury would be proposed as leader and myself as deputy. These nominations went through without opposition.'[309]

As PLP chairman, Lansbury led the opposition to the National Government at Westminister. However, for eleven months, Henderson –without a seat in Parliament – was the Labour Party leader as well as party secretary and part-time party treasurer. Aged sixty-seven, Henderson was obviously in continuingly poor health. A great part of his time was devoted to presiding over the World Disarmament Conference in Geneva, where it was feared 'he might die in the chair'. However, he steadfastly continued with this new role, for which he received the Nobel Peace Prize in 1934. Henderson played, at

307 Ben Pimlott, *Labour and the Left in the 1930s*, London, Allen & Unwin, 1986, pp. 15–17, 21.

308 Shepherd, op. cit., 2004, pp. 282–3.

309 Clement Attlee, *As It Happened*, London, Heinemann, 1954, p. 75.

most, a nominal role as Labour leader, and found himself increasingly out of touch with the leftward direction of this party. After being shouted down at the party conference in October 1932, Henderson resigned on 18 October. Lansbury was elected unopposed as party leader in his place.[310]

With Henderson's prolonged absences abroad, George Lansbury had increasingly taken over many of his leadership duties, including giving keynote speeches on Britain and the world situation. Addressing the annual conference of Labour women, Lansbury declared: 'Few movements could have stood the desertion of some of its chief leaders … in spite of unparalleled difficulties, the Labour organisation remained intact.'[311] On India, he pronounced: 'There could be no peace in India without the Congress. Conferences without Gandhi were like the play without Hamlet.'[312] On the Far East, Lansbury looked to the League of Nations 'to settle the dispute [between China and Japan] peacefully and amicably'.[313] George Lansbury also undertook morale-raising visits to constituencies throughout Britain, using the oratorical skills he had first honed as an itinerant socialist propagandist for the SDF over thirty years before.

It is difficult today to imagine the anger and disillusionment experienced by rank-and-file Labour members following Ramsay MacDonald's decision to break with his colleagues and form the National Government, not to mention the impact of the 1931 election catastrophe. For many, MacDonald – Britain's first Labour Prime Minister, with his handsome aura and socialist oratory about the New Jerusalem – had been an iconic leader, and one of the architects of the Labour Party. But, in 1931, odium was heaped on him, with accusations of treachery and betrayal for collaboration with the party's political opponents in order to form the National Government, which held power in the Depression years of the 1930s. Vi Willis, from a working-class Labour family

---

310 Leventhal, op. cit., pp. 200–201; Wrigley, op. cit., 1990, pp. 179–82.

311 *The Times*, 16 June 1932.

312 Ibid., 11 January 1932.

313 Ibid., 1 February, 4 February 1932.

in Ilford, recalled her father's fury as he destroyed the portrait of MacDonald that hung in the hallway. He was no longer her father's idol as he had 'killed the Labour Party'.[314] There was deep distrust of intellectuals within the labour movement, including among trade union bosses, such as Ernest Bevin.

In leading HM Opposition, George Lansbury cut a different political figure to MacDonald, whom he faced across the despatch box after the so-called 1931 'Great Betrayal'. Lansbury provided a sharp contrast to MacDonald's Olympian style of leadership. 'If George Lansbury had left us, I should have doubted Christ himself,' was how miners' leader and parliamentary secretary to the Ministry of Labour (1929–31), Jack Lawson, underlined their new leader's value to the Labour Party.[315]

Lansbury embraced long-held ideas of working-class participation in a political democracy. He declared: 'Leaders may be necessary, but the best kind of leader is one who leads from the centre of those he speaks for; in fact, it is not possible for me to imagine the need for leadership in a educated democracy.'

In 1931, George Lansbury brought an encouragingly defiant tone about the party's future. Sir Charles Trevelyan had written despairingly to Lansbury from his Northumberland estate: 'A puzzled, deceived and rather frightened nation has played for safety. I am afraid it will have a bitter period to repent in.' But the former Labour Secretary of State for Education also added: 'My fine friend, this later work of yours, which seems to have been thrust upon you, may be the greatest you ever had to do.'[316]

Lansbury later confided to Trevelyan: 'As a matter of fact … I honestly believe the movement is going to be purer and stronger for the very defeat we have sustained.'[317] In public, Lansbury remained unwavering in the face of the massive National Government victory at the polls. He replied to the press:

---

314 Vi Willis, quoted in Daniel Weinbren, *Generating Socialism: Recollections of Life in the Labour Party*, Stroud, Sutton, 1997, p. 86.

315 'George Lansbury by Jack Lawson' typescript, May 1940 (Lawson Papers, Box 5).

316 Charles Trevelyan to George Lansbury, 29 October 1931 (Lansbury Papers, Vol. 8, fos 172–3).

317 George Lansbury to Charles Trevelyan, 5 January 1932 (Trevelyan Papers, CPT 145).

> Most emphatically I do not believe that this means the smashing of the labour movement. I have lived through too many terrible defeats of Labour to despair. After the election of 1906, the Tories were reduced, I think, to 130 members, but they soon revived again. So will it be with us.[318]

Hugh Dalton, whose leadership ambitions had been dashed by his defeat in the 1931 catastrophe, gave his description of the Lansbury–Attlee–Cripps triumvirate:

> The parliamentary party is a poor little affair, isolated from the national executive [committee], whose only MP is Lansbury. Attlee is the deputy leader of the parliamentary party – a purely accidental position as someone puts it – and he and Cripps, who are in close touch with [G. D. H.] Cole, sit in Lansbury's room at the House [of Commons] all day and all night and continually influence the old man. With none of these are Henderson's relations close or cordial.[319]

Though often held in great esteem, George Lansbury was not without other critics. 'His bleedy heart has run away with his bloody head,' was one common criticism. 'No bloody brains to speak of,' was Beatrice Webb's acidic verdict, though the intellectual Marxist Harold Laski admired him.[320] Also, as party leader, Lansbury could appear muddle-headed, particularly when he seemed to publicly support the hated means test imposed by the National Government. It was a fatal error, which the champion of the unemployed and marginalised constantly had to defend during his leadership.[321]

However, Attlee provided a very different perspective. He wrote to his brother Tom:

318 *Manchester Guardian*, 29 October 1931.

319 Ben Pimlott, *Hugh Dalton*, London: Papermac, 1985, pp. 203–5. See also: diary entry, 8 October 1932 (Dalton Papers); Ben Pimlott ed., *The Political Diary of Hugh Dalton 1918–40, 1945–60*, London, Jonathan Cape (in association with the London School of Economics and Political Science), 1986, p. 169.

320 Harold Joseph Laski, 'Why I am a Marxist', *Nation*, 14 January 1931, p. 59.

321 For more detail, see Shepherd, op. cit., 2004, pp. 300-2.

> I had a very strenuous time during the session, having to speak on something or other every day almost. GL makes an excellent leader. He has far more idea of teamwork than JRM ever had. We are quite a happy family. GL, Cripps and I inhabit the Leader of the Opposition's room and get on excellently.[322]

MacDonald's leadership had been criticised for him being, at times, moody and aloof, which often distanced him from his backbenchers. Under Lansbury's leadership, there were at least weekly meetings of the PLP, and its executive met daily to plan parliamentary strategy. In addition, Lansbury, Attlee and Cripps worked closely, often changing schedules, to ensure one of them was always on duty on the front bench.

Even so, at Westminster, Lansbury faced the challenge of leading a PLP that was greatly reduced in numbers and quality of personnel. At the outset, Lansbury had despatched a personal appeal to every member of the PLP to keep up attendances, votes, questions and speeches on behalf of the constituents who had returned them to Westminster in 1931, so that, in his words, 'as sure as the sun rises, victory, full and complete, will in the near future come to the cause we represent'.[323]

Half of the PLP were trade union-sponsored MPs, mainly older miners from the Welsh and Yorkshire coalfields, who played relatively little part in parliamentary business at Westminster. As Attlee reflected, they 'could not contribute much beyond their votes'. A great deal of the work, especially for the debates on national and international policy, rested squarely on the shoulders of Lansbury, Attlee and Cripps. In February 1932, Attlee confided to his brother Tom: 'We have been having a very strenuous time in the House. I have to spend hours on the bench. The government are very cheap in their arguments.'[324]

---

322 Clement Attlee to Tom Attlee, 18 December 1931 (Attlee Papers, fo. 45).

323 *Daily Herald*, 9 November 1931.

324 Clement Attlee to Tom Attlee, 29 February 1932 (Attlee Papers, fo.46).

In the Commons, the leadership could draw on active support from only around thirty of the forty-six PLP members as effective parliamentary performers, including the charismatic Nye Bevan. He had entered Parliament in 1929 and, for a while, was Lansbury's personal private secretary.[325] There were examples of significant initiatives by the opposition against incredible odds. The press calculated that the hard-working Tom Williams, Labour spokesman on agriculture, in 1932 'filled no fewer than 274 columns of Hansard … asked 607 oral questions and sixty-seven written ones'. [326] At the same time, Attlee maintained his high regard for Lansbury's collective leadership, observing:

> Our fellows have done extraordinarily well, especially our miners, George Hall, Tom Williams and David Grenfell. The last two, especially, promoted to the front bench have risen to the occasion and made themselves conversant with all kinds of subjects … GL has been splendid all through and Stafford Cripps a tower of strength.[327]

In these circumstances, Lansbury repeatedly proved to be an effective and revered leader, especially in bolstering the morale of his small parliamentary band. His son-in-law and first biographer observed Lansbury's 'brilliantly successful' technique of organising the small PLP like a propaganda meeting from his SDF days in the 1890s. Singing of 'The Red Flag' often rang out in the parliamentary lobbies, and, for those speaking in the Commons but lacking in parliamentary oratory, Lansbury was invariably beside them, whispering guidance in his characteristic booming voice (which could often be heard in the press gallery).[328]

During the 1931–35 parliament, though the greatly diminished Labour

---

325 Andrew Thorpe, 'George Lansbury 1932–1935' in Jefferys, op. cit., pp. 65–6.

326 C. R. Attlee's 'Foreword' in Lord (Thomas) Williams of Barnburgh, *Digging for Britain*, London, Hutchinson, 1965, pp. 7–8.

327 Clement Attlee to Tom Attlee, 15 July 1931 (Attlee Papers, fo.46).

328 Raymond Postgate, *The Life of George Lansbury*, London: Longmans, 1951, p. 279.

opposition had no prospect of defeating the National Government outright, the PLP maintained a robust and disciplined scrutiny of considerable amounts of government legislation and business, such as the expenditure cuts on public services in 1931, the taxation of cooperative profits in 1933 and the Unemployment Bill of 1934.[329]

Lansbury's main task in rebuilding the party for the future was to keep Labour united, avoiding further departures following the earlier defections of Oswald Mosley, Ramsay MacDonald and their supporters.[330] An immediate problem was the worsening relationship with the ILP, which had developed well before Lansbury took over the party helm. In 1931, in a swift but unproductive move, Lansbury invited the ILP leader, the charismatic James Maxton, to take his seat alongside Lansbury on the Labour front bench. Before 1914, Lansbury had been a leading ILP figure, and also associated, in the 1920s, with Maxton and the ILP Clydesiders in their criticism of MacDonald's moderate gradualist policies. During the second Labour government, the disenchanted left wing of the ILP had been in open revolt over party discipline and the observation of PLP standing orders, which did not permit an individual MP to vote against the party line.

Despite intensive negotiations and a special meeting with his former friend Fenner Brockway (the new ILP leader) at his Bow home, George Lansbury could do nothing to resolve the injurious conflict between the two parties.[331] Lansbury had confided to Trevelyan: 'I want very much unity with the ILP, and especially unity in the House – but I am now convinced that this is hopeless.'[332] Twenty years before, Lansbury had clashed with his party's leadership over his independent stand on women's suffrage. As Labour leader, Lansbury now

329 Andrew Thorpe, 'George Lansbury 1932–35' in Jefferys, op. cit., pp. 65–6.; Shepherd, op. cit., 2004, p. 295–6.

330 Lansbury publicly ruled out an electoral pact with the Lloyd George Liberals, despite former Labour Cabinet colleague Christopher Addison's attempts as an intermediary. Kenneth O. Morgan and Jane Morgan, *Portrait of a Progressive: The Political Career of Christopher, Viscount Addison*, Oxford, Oxford University Press, 1980, pp. 215–17.

331 Fenner Brockway, *Inside the Left: Thirty Years of Platform, Press, Prison and Parliament*, London, 1942, p. 238.

332 George Lansbury to Charles Trevelyan, 5 January 1932 (Trevelyan Papers, CPT 145).

firmly believed that the ILP had become 'a party within a party'. In the end, this widening gulf led to the controversial and momentous decision by the ILP, the largest socialist grouping, to disaffiliate from the Labour Party at its special conference in July 1932 in Bradford – its birthplace in 1893.[333]

During these years, his commitments as leader of the PLP curtailed George Lansbury's attendance of NEC meetings, where he was the only MP. He was present at fifteen out of twenty-four meetings in 1931–32, and fifteen out of twenty-two in 1932–33, while his serious illness after his accident in December 1933 meant he attended only ten NEC meetings that year. However, on his return to the party leadership in 1934–35, Lansbury missed only seven out of the twenty-seven NEC meetings.[334]

Lansbury's leadership must also be considered in the context of a significant power struggle between different groupings over Labour policy and political strategy. As Ben Pimlott has written, a new and younger generation gained control in the Labour Party following the changes brought about by the 1931 election. In reality, during Lansbury's years as leader, there were two separate centres of power, often in conflict over policy: one at Transport House, dominated by the NEC; and the other the PLP and its executive at Westminster. There was also an evolving alliance between moderates in the political and industrial wings of the labour movement, as seen in the revived National Joint Council (later renamed the National Council of Labour).

Outside Parliament, the NEC, with Hugh Dalton and Herbert Morrison dominant, established a new policy committee and sub-committees, which brought together politicians like them with trade union leaders, including Ernest Bevin and Walter Citrine. In 1932, the founding of the Socialist League attracted leading left-wing intellectuals among a membership of 3,000, and had some influence at party conferences.[335]

Politically, the leadership of Lansbury, Attlee and Cripps was therefore

---

333 For an excellent account, see Keith Laybourn, '"Suicide During a Fit of Insanity" or the Defence of Socialism?', *The Bradford Antiquary*, 3rd ser., No. 5, 1991 , pp. 41–53.

334 See Thorpe in Jefferys, op. cit., p. 67.

335 Pimlott, op. cit., 1986, pp. 17–20.

well to the left of the NEC, and far more sympathetic with party activists in the wider movement. The 1932 party conference at Leicester witnessed successful resolutions on the public ownership of the Bank of England, including the joint stock banks, and workers' control of the nationalised industries. In 1933, at Hastings, conference passed Trevelyan's resolution, binding a future Labour government to advance 'definite socialist legislation'.

As party leader, George Lansbury – by working with differing personalities across the political spectrum, as well as by lifting the spirits of the wider movement – held his party together for a future return to office. During this time, no one directly challenged his position. In March 1932, the NEC quickly quelled press speculation about a change in leadership before Arthur Greenwood's victory at the Wakefield by-election that same month. The strain of leadership at times took its toll, with an exhausted Lansbury confessing to Cripps that he had 'felt like joining the communists'. However, he took inspiration from his socialist faith in seeking a Christian solution to contemporary social and economic difficulties.[336]

As party leader, George Lansbury suffered ill health and family bereavements – devastating blows that were to seriously affect him personally, as well as the management of the Labour opposition. On 23 March 1933, his wife Bessie died at the age of seventy-two. The importance of their marriage to the Labour leader cannot be stressed enough. For over fifty years, Bessie Lansbury – also a strong socialist and internationalist – had supported her husband through every vicissitude of political life, including his imprisonments and the constant pressures of being Leader of the Opposition. Attlee informed his brother Tom: 'Lloyd George had never known such a wave of sympathy in the House and the country' – an indication of the public standing of the Lansburys in national life. In May 1935, George Lansbury's son Edgar predeceased him after a serious illness.[337]

---

336 Interview with Michael Foot, 7 August 1999; Morgan, op. cit., 1987, pp. 97–8; Pimlott, op. cit., 1985, Chapter 14.

337 Clement Attlee to Tom Attlee, 3 April 1933 (Attlee Papers, fo. 58). For an excellent study of the interrelationship between illness and political life by a physician and senior politician, see David Owen, *In Sickness and In Power: Illness In Heads of Government During The Last 100 Years*, London, Methuen, 2008.

In December 1933, the major injury of a broken leg, sustained at a Labour Party gathering at Gainsborough, had taken Lansbury out of front-line politics for seven months, and the hard-working Attlee took over his role. In the main, historians have tended to disregard Lansbury's absence from the party leadership – in some cases, not mentioning it. Though his accident had brought him close to death, he had no doubts about continuing as party leader on his recovery. While he remained in touch with Labour politics, his enforced stay in hospital was a turning point in George Lansbury's life. He produced a new Christian socialist manifesto for the British people, published in the *Clarion*, with his book *My England* based on these articles. Above all, his religious faith was reaffirmed and he returned determined to secure the abolition of fascism, imperialism and war. At the same time, the serious deterioration in the international situation had important implications for Labour Party foreign policy.[338]

LEADERSHIP CRISIS AND RESIGNATION

As party leader, George Lansbury is probably remembered most for the manner of his departure from the leadership, following his clash with the general secretary of the TGWU, Ernie Bevin – the most powerful union leader in Britain – in the longest and most highly charged two-day debate at the 1935 party conference. In a memorable encounter in British politics, the pugnacious Ernie Bevin attacked the pacifist George Lansbury with a brutal speech, sharpened by accusations of betrayal of party loyalty, which reduced Virginia Woolf, in the audience at the Dome, to tears.[339] A week later, Lansbury met the PLP to resign. Leonard Woolf commented that Bevin had 'battered the poor man to political death'.[340] According to

338 Shepherd, op. cit., 2004, pp. 298–9.

339 Anne Olivier Bell and Andrew McNellie ed., *The Diary of Virginia Woolf*, Harmondsworth, Penguin, 1982,.p. 345 (entry for 2 October 1935).

340 Leonard Woolf, *Downhill All the Way: An Autobiography of the Years 1919–1939*, New York, Harcourt, Brace & World, 1967, p. 244–5.

Professor McKenzie, it was 'the only clear-cut instance of a Labour leader being driven from office'.[341]

However, the circumstances surrounding Lansbury's resignation are more complex. Far from being driven out of office, relinquishing the party leadership was very much Lansbury's decision alone. He had been an out-and-out pacifist throughout his political life, and his pacifism was well known when he was elected Labour leader. He willingly admitted: 'In 1931, when I became leader of the Labour Party, I was up against the difficulty of squaring my pacifist principles with the policy of my party.'[342]

Moreover, Lansbury realised his pacifism was increasingly distancing him from the party he led. In the weeks before the 1935 conference, Lansbury made a number of public statements at speaking engagements in Britain. In Ipswich, he addressed an audience of over 3,000 as part of a 'Victory for socialism' campaign: 'If I had my way, I would stand up before the world unarmed. But that, I am told and I know, is not the result of a show of force, but because of the spirit of good behaviour, which is in the heart of everyone.'[343]

On 19 August, he had written to *The Times* calling on the Pope and the Archbishops to convene a convocation of all religions in the Holy Land. Campaigning in the Dumfries by-election in September, he gave a press interview:

> During the whole period I have been serving as leader of the Labour Party, I have made it quite clear that under no circumstances could I support the use of armed force, either by the League of Nations or by individual nations. However anomalous the position may appear to be, it has been accepted by the parliamentary party and by the national executive [committee] of the Labour Party.[344]

341 Robert Trelford McKenzie, *The British Political Parties: The Distribution of Power within the Conservative and Labour Parties*, London, Heinemann, 1964, p. 378.

342 George Lansbury, *My Quest for Peace*, London, Michael Joseph, 1938, p. 16.

343 *Daily Herald*, 6 April 1935.

344 *Manchester Guardian*, 9 September 1935.

Lansbury came under increasing pressure when, before the Brighton conference, the pacifist Arthur Ponsonby resigned his Labour leadership in the Lords, and Stafford Cripps resigned from the NEC. Lansbury took the opportunity at the NEC meeting on 19 September to raise his own position, but was informed this was a matter for the PLP – although, 'in the opinion of the NEC, there is no reason why he should tender his resignation'.

On a number of occasions, his desire and willingness to resign was made clear. Shortly before the 1935 party conference, Lansbury wrote privately to the new party secretary Jim Middleton:

> This note is to say the position at conferences and meetings … is quite impossible … the question of possible war and preparations for war cannot be dodged or avoided and so we are forced to contradict each other in a friendly though painful way. Someone should break the circle. Everyone publicly and … privately urges me to continue. My own mind never wavers. I should resign … cannot they [the NEC] pass a friendly resolution saying the situation is one that must be resolved? The party cannot go into a general election with a leader who disagrees with them on so fundamental a question of policy. I should take action myself, were it not for the request at meetings and from my colleagues to remain.[345]

On 30 September 1935, delegates gathered for the Labour Party conference against the background of the international tensions surrounding the Italy–Abyssinia dispute, and Hugh Dalton moved the NEC five-paragraph resolution, which called on the British government and other nations 'to use necessary measures provided by the covenant [of the League of Nations] to prevent Italy's unjust and rapacious attack upon the territory of a fellow member of the League'.[346]

Lansbury's impassioned speech on his dilemma as a Christian pacifist

---

345 George Lansbury to Jim Middleton, September 1935 (Middleton Papers, MID 54).

346 The Labour Party, 'Report of the Thirty-Fifth Annual Conference', 1935.

and the leader of the Labour Party was greeted at the outset with loud and prolonged applause, accompanied by the singing of 'For He's a Jolly Good Fellow'.

Bevin, who had been sitting with his trade union delegation in the main body of the conference hall, replied angrily to Lansbury's conflict of loyalties between personal conscience and political party, with accusations of betrayal. Bevin argued that Lansbury had participated in the collective discussions on socialism and peace and could not go back on a decision he had not voted against. According to the official party conference report, Bevin added: 'It is placing the executive and the movement in an absolutely wrong position to be taking your conscience round from body to body asking to be told what you ought to do with it.' Bevin's sneer has often been seen as the spark that ignited Lansbury's resignation, particularly as some present in the Dome recalled pugilistic Bevin accusing Christian, pacifist Lansbury of 'hawking your conscience'. If so, in Bevin's abrasive and odious language, 'hawking' meant 'selling for money' – and, in Lansbury's case, nothing was further from the truth. At the end of Bevin's speech, Lansbury was unable to reply and was reduced to calling out a few points when the microphones had been switched off. The journalist Trevor Evans recalled that Lansbury stood nearby, wringing his hands in disbelief and anguish over 'hawking his conscience'.[347] The thirty-year-old Socialist League delegate Lionel Elvin, who had also spoken at the 1935 conference, was adamant that Bevin had used this taunt.[348] An unapologetic Bevin commented: 'Lansbury's been dressed in saint's clothes for years, waiting for martyrdom. All I did was set fire to the faggots.'[349]

A week later, George Lansbury attended the PLP meeting he had summoned before the conference, and, after explaining his position for an hour,

347 T. Evans, 'Peace Issue at the 1935 Labour Conference', BBC Sound Archives. I am grateful to the late Ivan Howlett (BBC Radio 4) for a copy of this recording.

348 Interview: Professor Lionel Elvin, 30 May 2001. For more on the Lansbury–Bevin confrontation, see Shepherd, op. cit., 2004, pp. 320–28.

349 Francis Williams, *Nothing So Strange: An Autobiography*, London, Cassell, 1970, p. 139.

resigned the party leadership and withdrew from the room. Remarkably, on Lansbury's return, the PLP, by thirty-eight votes to seven (with five abstentions), asked him to continue as their leader, though Lansbury then insisted on resigning. After his resignation, George Lansbury wrote: 'No single one of my colleagues who had urged me to remain, or anyone else, said a word in my defence.' Far from being driven from the leadership, George Lansbury is probably the only Labour leader in the party's history whose colleagues would not let him leave the fray. Within two weeks, Stanley Baldwin, who had replaced Ramsay MacDonald, called the 1935 general election. Though Labour had gained ten seats in by-elections under Lansbury's leadership – and there was an improved performance at the polls, with 154 Labour MPs returned – the National Government still had a large and commanding majority of 429 MPs.

However, George Lansbury was re-elected as the pacifist MP for Bow & Bromley. In his final years, until his death in 1940, he undertook a tireless international peace crusade throughout the United States, Canada and Europe, including visits to Hitler and Mussolini in an attempt to prevent the advent of the Second World War.[350]

George Lansbury's unforeseen stint as party leader against seemingly impossible odds still echoes today in Labour's circles. In 2013, in rediscovering the party's lost traditions, Jon Cruddas MP, shadow Cabinet member and head of Labour's Policy Review, proclaimed the East End socialist as 'the greatest Labour Leader of the Opposition'. For future party leaders in the post-war years, George Lansbury's unique legacy was 'to leave a party for them to inherit and subsequently lead'.[351]

---

350 George Lansbury, 'A Page of History' (Lansbury Papers, fo. 214); for Lansbury's peace journeys, see D. Lukowitz, 'George Lansbury's Peace Missions to Hitler and Mussolini in 1937', *Canadian Journal of History*, 15, 1980, pp. 67–82.

351 Jon Cruddas, 'George Lansbury Memorial Lecture', *New Statesman*, 7 November 2013, accessed 31 May 2015.

CHAPTER 11

CLEMENT ATTLEE

NICKLAUS THOMAS-SYMONDS

Clement Attlee served as leader of the Labour Party from 1935 to 1955. He fought four general elections as leader, winning a landslide in 1945, a narrow majority in 1950, and then losing in 1951 and 1955. He was the first party leader to have a majority in the House of Commons. Nicklaus Thomas-Symonds argues that Attlee was the greatest Labour leader of all. Not only was his electoral record hugely impressive, but his governments followed through on their election promises and delivered long-lasting change in Britain. It was under Attlee that the modern welfare state and the National Health Service were created, and the architecture of post-war foreign policy was established. This set the contours of British politics for the decades to come. Attlee's leadership style was collegial, and this approach helped him get the most from his Cabinet. But the absence of leadership on issues such as the devaluation crisis of 1949, and his naive approach to the electoral boundaries, undermined his statecraft.

• • •

Clement Attlee has a strong claim to not only be the Labour Party's best leader, but the greatest post-war Prime Minister of them all. Some thirty-seven years after his death, in 2004, a University of Leeds/ Ipsos MORI poll of university academics rated Attlee the twentieth-century's top Prime Minister, with an average mark of 8.34 out of 10.[352] The Labour

352 Theakston and Gill, op. cit., 2006, pp. 193–213.

Party's greatest achievements are the Attlee governments' achievements. From 1945 to 1951, the governments set about fulfilling their manifesto commitments, with the creation of the modern welfare state and the founding of the British institution that is the National Health Service, establishing the principle of free health care at the point of delivery. The Attlee government also set the course of post-war British foreign policy, decolonising large parts of the British Empire, including India, and forging an enduring relationship with the United States.

The Attlee governments established the so-called 'post-war consensus', with both major political parties, Labour and the Conservatives, working within a policy framework of a mixed economy, and maintained high levels of employment. Only two other peacetime twentieth-century British governments can claim to have shifted the political centre of gravity: the Liberal governments of 1905 to 1915, which provided the foundations of the welfare state upon which the Attlee governments built; and Margaret Thatcher's Conservative governments of 1979–90, with their emphasis on free markets, privatisation and the curtailing of trade union power.

In his groundbreaking studies of leaders, the Pulitzer Prize-winner James MacGregor Burns proposed a theory of 'transformational leadership'. It does not have to effect 'total change, which is impossible in human life', rather its consequence should be that 'new culture and value systems take the place of the old'.[353] MacGregor Burns counts Clement Attlee alongside Winston Churchill in his 'age of the titans', but, equally, points out that 'the rise and fall of luminaries' serves to illustrate 'the relation [sic] between leaders' character and qualities and the social and political context in which they operated, and the role of each in change'.[354]

Attlee, one of eight children, was born on 3 January 1883 into a professional middle-class background. His father Henry Attlee was an eminent solicitor who became the president of the Law Society. His mother Ellen had a background

353 James MacGregor Burns, *Transforming Leadership: A New Pursuit of Happiness*, New York, Grove Press/Atlantic Monthly Press, 2004, pp. 24–5.

354 Ibid., p. 25.

in medicine and art. Her father Thomas, a descendant of doctors, had been educated at Cambridge and became secretary of an art union. Attlee had a strict Anglican, Victorian childhood. It left him with an enduring sense of Christian morality: he was honest and straightforward, without a whiff of scandal in his personal life. He was not, however, left with a belief in God: he remarked that he believed in the ethics of Christianity, but not the 'mumbo jumbo'. He was a passionate monarchist, deeply attached to the British crown; one of his earliest memories was Queen Victoria's Golden Jubilee in 1887.

In the Easter term of 1896, Attlee passed his entrance examinations for Haileybury College – a public school proud of its tradition of training civil servants for India, which Attlee was to grant independence from Britain as Prime Minister in 1947. In October 1901, he went up to University College, Oxford, where he read history. Too shy to speak in Oxford Union debates, Attlee won a half-blue in billiards. He graduated with a second-class degree, ruling out a career as an academic, and fell back upon his father's influence to start training as a barrister. However, he was unenthusiastic about a legal career, and his life was changed in October 1905, when, as he put it, 'an event occurred that was destined to alter the whole course of my life'.[355]

The occasion was a visit with his brother Laurence to Haileybury's Stepney boys' club in London. Set up to support poor boys in the East End, it showed Attlee, at first hand, the effect of the harsh Victorian attitude to poverty – one that blamed the poor themselves. Attlee realised why the Poor Law was so hated, and became a socialist, recognising the effect of the social and political system on income distribution. He joined the Fabian Society and the ILP. In 1907, he became manager of the Stepney boys' club, supplementing his income with lecturing at the London School of Economics from 1912. When the First World War broke out in August 1914, Attlee's patriotism found expression, as he volunteered to fight long before conscription was introduced. In 1915, he served at Gallipoli, where the appalling living conditions led to him contracting dysentery and passing out. He was

355 Attlee, op. cit., p. 18.

withdrawn from front-line service and placed on a hospital ship, where he was given the choice of returning home or being dropped off at Malta. Deeply committed to the cause, Attlee chose Malta, in order to return quickly to Gallipoli. He later served in Mesopotamia, where he was hit by shrapnel, and twice in France, where he was struck by falling wood. As a result, when the armistice was signed on 11 November 1918, Attlee was in Wandsworth Hospital. A short distance away, in Wandsworth Prison, was his brother Tom, who had been a conscientious objector. That Attlee did not hold this against him is not only an indication of his deep affection for his brother, it is also an indication that he could compartmentalise his life: deal with one issue; put it at the back of his mind; move on to the next. This is a vital quality for any successful Prime Minister.

After the war, Attlee threw himself into political activity in London's East End, and moved into a flat in Limehouse. In November 1919, with Attlee having written the election addresses, Labour won forty-three of the sixty seats on Stepney borough council. After the election, at the age of thirty-six, Attlee was co-opted as mayor of Stepney. It was valuable experience, seeing the London boroughs struggle with the rising cost of unemployment benefit. It also gave him a platform from which to launch his parliamentary career, as he won the Limehouse constituency within Stepney borough in the general election of 15 November 1922, defeating his sole opponent, a Liberal (Sir William Pearce), by 9,688 votes to 7,789. This was a period of change for Attlee. In the summer of 1921, he met his future wife Violet Millar, whom he married in January of the following year. He was to have a long, happy marriage and four children.

As a new MP, Attlee was appointed as one of the parliamentary private secretaries to the then Labour leader Ramsay MacDonald. When MacDonald became Prime Minister of the first Labour government in January 1924, Attlee was appointed under-secretary of state for war. As a minority government, this Labour administration was always likely to be short-lived, and, after a defeat on a vote of censure, the Conservatives were re-elected on 29 October 1924. In November 1927, as an opposition MP, Attlee was appointed to the

Indian Statutory Commission under Sir John Simon, tasked with considering the future governance of India, before serving in the second (minority) Labour government of 1929 to 1931, first as Chancellor of the Duchy of Lancaster (from May 1930) and then as Postmaster General (from March 1931). In August 1931, in the midst of the Great Depression, the Labour Cabinet failed to agree on the cut in unemployment benefit required to preserve the government's credit. MacDonald resigned as Prime Minister, but formed the National Government on 24 August 1931.

Labour's defeat in the subsequent general election, held on 27 October 1931, was catastrophic, leaving it with a mere fifty-two parliamentary seats. Yet, ironically, this afforded a great opportunity for Attlee to gain prominence. He hung on in Limehouse by only 551 votes, and was one of only three government ministers to retain their seats – the others being the former First Commissioner of Works, George Lansbury, and former Solicitor General, Stafford Cripps. When the parliamentary party met after the election, the titular leader, Arthur Henderson – now without a parliamentary seat – sent a message for Lansbury to be elected party leader, and Attlee his deputy. In the parliament of 1931–35, Attlee, Cripps and Lansbury shared the duties of the Leader of the Opposition. Lansbury was even away ill for eight months from December 1933, giving Attlee the opportunity to stand in for him as party leader. When Lansbury's pacifism incurred the wrath of then TGWU general secretary Ernest Bevin at the 1935 party conference, Lansbury relinquished the leadership on 8 October, leaving Attlee as the acting leader for the 1935 general election (at which the National Government took over 50 per cent of the popular vote and 432 Commons seats, though Labour did gain over 100 seats, moving them to 154).

After the 1935 election, Attlee stood for the leadership against Arthur Greenwood and Herbert Morrison. Both Greenwood and Morrison had lost their seats in 1931, and, while Greenwood had returned via a by-election in 1932, Morrison had had to wait until the 1935 general election itself to return. Attlee presented the result as follows: in the first ballot, Attlee took fifty-eight votes, Morrison forty-four, and Greenwood thirty-two. Greenwood then dropped out, and the final result was Attlee eighty-eight, Morrison forty-four.[356] Attlee's prominence among the MPs who had sat in the 1931–35 parliament was undoubtedly crucial. The cull of leadership rivals in 1931, combined with the demise of Lansbury and the drift to the left of Cripps – who was to be expelled from the party in 1939 – left Attlee in the leading position to seize the leadership at a time when Labour were not expected to be forming a government any point soon.

Attlee's leadership of the Labour Party lasted twenty years, from 1935 to 1955. No other leader of a major political party in twentieth-century Britain held the reins for so long. Timing was a key factor in this. Without the Second World War, Labour would most likely have lost a general election in 1939 or 1940, and Attlee would probably have lost the leadership. In addition, Attlee's two main rivals for the leadership – Ernest Bevin and Herbert Morrison – were bitter political enemies. Bevin, orphaned as a child, rose through the trade unions to become the first general secretary of the TGWU. He was then the wartime Minister of Labour from 1940, and Foreign Secretary under Attlee after 1945. Morrison, also self-made and from a working-class background, was the son of a policeman, and forged his career in local government, rising to become leader of the Labour group on the London county council in the 1930s. He was the wartime Home Secretary from 1942 and Attlee's deputy after 1945, before a brief period as Attlee's Foreign Secretary.

Attlee was not a particularly successful Leader of the Opposition in the years before the Second World War. He had to tread a very careful line as fascism spread across Europe. On the one hand, he had to avoid charges of pacifism; on the other, he had to oppose the accretion of arms in the hands of the (capitalist) British government. His uninspiring compromise position was that re-armament was necessary so as to be 'consistent with our country's responsibilities [of collective security] in the League of Nations'.[357] The issue of confidence in Attlee's leadership first arose in early June 1939, when

356 Ibid., p. 81.

357 The Labour Party, 'Report of the Thirty-Sixth Annual Conference', 1936, p. 206.

Attlee was absent from a Labour Party NEC meeting directly after the party conference, as he was having a prostate operation. In the event, only Ellen Wilkinson, a supporter of Morrison, abstained from supporting Attlee on the confidence motion, but it was a portent of things to come.

In May 1940, when Churchill replaced Neville Chamberlain as Prime Minister, Attlee joined the War Cabinet as Lord Privy Seal. He became a highly effective but unobtrusive member of the wartime coalition. After the fall of the Singapore naval base in February 1942, Attlee became Deputy Prime Minister and Dominions Secretary. In September 1943, Attlee, remaining Deputy Prime Minister, relinquished the Dominions Office to become Lord President of the Council. His new role gave him a greater coordinating role in government – the Lord President's Committee (which he now chaired) being the principal forum for considering legislation on the domestic front. He also chaired the Cabinet during Churchill's frequent travels abroad to conferences. Attlee was extraordinarily efficient in the conduct of government business, never willing to waste time. In early 1945, he even chided Churchill for his failure to read the conclusions of Cabinet committees prior to War Cabinet meetings.[358]

Yet Churchill did not see Attlee as a threat to him in the post-war general election of 1945. On polling day, 5 July, *The Times* found the Prime Minister to be in a 'supremely confident mood'.[359] The results were not declared until 26 July, owing to the logistics of collecting votes from service personnel still abroad. The forces had overwhelmingly backed the Labour Party, which won a Commons majority for the first time, taking nearly 12,000,000 votes (47.8 per cent) and winning 393 seats. The Conservatives won 213 seats on just under 10,000,000 votes (39.8 per cent) and the Liberals fell to only twelve seats, on fewer than 2,300,000 votes (just 9 per cent). Attlee may not have been responsible for the surge of left-wing feeling brought about by the

358 The letter Attlee sent to Churchill on 19 January 1945 is set out in Kenneth Harris, *Attlee*, London, Weidenfeld & Nicolson, 1984, pp. 241–3.

359 *The Times*, 5 July 1945.

war, but he had handled Churchill well in the election campaign itself. The Prime Minister had declared that Labour 'would have to fall back on some kind of Gestapo, no doubt very humanely directed in the first instance'.[360] The next day, Attlee responded quietly but firmly: 'He wanted electors to understand how great was the difference between Winston Churchill, the great leader in war of a united nation, and Mr Churchill, the party leader of the Conservatives.'[361]

Yet, so close to being appointed Prime Minister, Attlee's leadership came under threat. Days prior to the declaration of the results, on 24 July, Morrison penned a letter to Attlee indicating that, if he was re-elected to Parliament, he would 'accept nomination to the leadership of the party'.[362] There was a precedent: J. R. Clynes had led the party during the 1922 general election campaign, only for the new parliamentary party to elect Ramsay MacDonald as its leader afterwards. On the afternoon of 26 July, in Labour Party headquarters at Transport House, party secretary Morgan Phillips, Bevin and Morrison met Attlee. With Morrison out of the room, Bevin told Attlee: 'Clem, you go to the Palace straight away.'[363] Bevin had strong views on the kind of leader he felt the party needed. He was suspicious of intensely personal leadership, like that of MacDonald, and saw the Edwardian Liberal Prime Minister Sir Henry Campbell-Bannerman as a more useful precedent, with 'his gift of holding a team of clever men together'.[364]

Bevin's loyalty was also crucial in the final leadership crisis of Attlee's reign, in 1947. The pound-to-dollar 'convertibility clause' in the $3.75 billion American loan agreement of November 1945 was to prove a major problem when it came into effect on 15 July 1947: it produced a drain on sterling that

360 David Cannadine ed., *The Speeches of Winston Churchill*, London, Penguin, 1990, p. 274.

361 Clement Richard Attlee Papers (Bodleian Library, Oxford, MS Attlee, dep. 18, correspondence and papers 18 May 1945 to 13 August 1945).

362 Ibid.

363 Alan Bullock, *The Life & Times of Ernest Bevin: Vol. 2: Minister of Labour 1940–1945*, London, Heinemann, 1967, pp.392–3. Bullock footnotes that both Morgan Phillips and Attlee gave accounts to him.

364 Hugh Dalton, *The Fateful Years: Memoirs, 1931–45*, London, Muller, 1957, p. 467.

precipitated an economic crisis and the eventual suspension of convertibility. Cripps, then president of the board of trade, conceived a plan that he, with Chancellor Hugh Dalton and Morrison, should go together to ask Attlee to resign in favour of Bevin, ostensibly to provide firmer leadership. However, Morrison would never have agreed to topple Attlee in favour of anyone but himself.[365] When Cripps did visit Attlee to put forward the proposition on 9 September, it was alone. He suggested the idea of Bevin becoming Prime Minister and Minister of Production, Attlee Chancellor, and Dalton Foreign Secretary.[366] But Attlee was sure of Bevin's loyalty. He rang Bevin and asked if he wanted to change jobs; Bevin confirmed that he did not.[367] Later, Attlee said that if you had a good dog like Ernest Bevin, there was no point in barking yourself.

The PLP was very united under Attlee's premiership. Attlee, conscious of the distance backbenchers had come to feel from MacDonald during the second Labour government of 1929–31, established links between government ministers and other Labour MPs, including specific parliamentary party subject groups and a liaison committee.[368] As a gesture of goodwill, standing orders were suspended, which allowed party discipline to be voluntary rather than formally enforced. Relations with the trade unions were similarly cordial. On 28 July 1945, two days after Attlee was appointed Prime Minister, he received a letter from TUC general secretary Walter Citrine, which set the tone.[369] Citrine asked for 'closest cooperation' between the trade unions and the government to avoid the bad feeling that had existed between the TUC and previous Labour governments. Attlee duly adopted a consultative approach, and his government did not face any sustained

365 Hugh Dalton, *High Tide and After: Memoirs 1945–60*, London, Muller, 1962, p. 242.

366 Ibid., p. 245.

367 K. Harris, op. cit., p. 349.

368 Clement Richard Attlee Papers (Bodleian Library, Oxford, MS Attlee, dep. 19, correspondence and papers 14–17 August 1945).

369 Clement Richard Attlee Papers (Bodleian Library, Oxford, MS Attlee, dep. 18, correspondence and papers 18 May 1945 to 13 August 1945).

period of industrial unrest. When there were strikes, he acted decisively. Within days of taking office, military labour was used to break the 'go slow' protest on wages at the Surrey Commercial Docks. In other dockers' disputes in June 1948 and May to July 1949, Attlee used troops. What was far less favourable towards the Attlee governments was the attitude of the press, which was, on the whole, hostile. Attlee responded with a steely determination to get the job done, despite critical comments. In 1947, he remarked: 'We are not, I think – despite some prognostications in the newspapers – yet halfway through this parliament. We intend to complete our programme.'[370]

Any Prime Minister of any government coming to power in 1945 after the Second World War was going to have a unique opportunity to affect post-war history. The war had not only provided the catalyst for radical political change, it had provided practical options, too, with the publication, in November 1942, of Sir William Beveridge's 'Social Insurance and Allied Services' report. That said, the ending of the war also presented enormous challenges. Demobilisation had to be carefully managed (which it was) so as not to create large-scale unemployment. There was also a demand for hundreds of thousands of homes every year, against a background of a raw materials shortage, but satisfying this demand for housing proved more difficult. On 21 August 1945, the American government ended Lend-Lease, which, in return for military bases, had provided Britain with aid. Keynes said that Britain now faced a 'financial Dunkirk'. In response, the Attlee government negotiated the American loan, and also received around $3 billion in Marshall aid from the United States between April 1948 and December 1951.

On taking office in 1945, the Attlee government set to work quickly and efficiently. As Foreign Secretary, Bevin was kept away from Morrison (Lord President of the Council and Attlee's deputy), who was dominant on the domestic front. This was to ensure that their rivalry did not undermine the government as a whole. Morrison skilfully piloted large-scale measures of nationalisation through Parliament. The Bank of England was subjected

370 The Labour Party, 'Report of the Forty-Sixth Annual Conference', 1947, p. 119.

to public control. Coal, civil aviation and the Cable and Wireless telecommunications company were quickly brought into public ownership, as were utilities such as electricity, gas, and rail transportation. The government also created the modern welfare state, with comprehensive sickness and unemployment cover introduced in the 1946 National Insurance Act. Attlee brought the creative best out of Aneurin Bevan, who had been a vocal critic of the wartime coalition, by appointing him Minister for Health and Housing. Bevan painstakingly negotiated with the British Medical Association, and the National Health Service was introduced in July 1948.

Attlee's role in this frenzy of political activity from 1945 to 1948 was to make the government work most effectively. His role was to find the consensus position in his Cabinet with little fuss: 'The essential quality of the PM is that he should be a good chairman, able to get others to work … The decision that he must take is not that a certain course should be followed but that a decision must be come to.'[371] Attlee's leadership was intolerant of idle chatter. Discussion had to be purposeful: 'Democracy means government by discussion, but it is only effective if you can stop people talking.'[372] Attlee did not see the Prime Minister as an active contributor to government policy; he might need to be the final arbitrator between different policies, but, in general, the departmental ministers should get on with their jobs.

Attlee's 'hands-off' approach had its drawbacks, such as failing to mitigate the damaging coal shortage in the winter of 1946–47, when he left matters in the hands of the Minister of Fuel and Power, Manny Shinwell, for too long. The government adopted 'austerity' policies under the chancellorship of Stafford Cripps from November 1947 onwards, and Attlee offered no firm leadership during major economic challenges, particularly the devaluation crisis of 1949, when he delegated matters (Cripps and Bevin were sent to

---

371 Attlee produced a memorandum on the organisation of government (reproduced in K. Harris, op. cit., Appendix III, pp. 589–95), which was with his autobiographical notes. It was written in the 1930s, though it was with a note dated 1948. This quotation is at p. 591.

372 Speech at Oxford, 14 June 1957, as quoted in Anthony Jay ed., *The Oxford Dictionary of Political Quotations*, Oxford, Oxford University Press, 1996, p. 20.

America to negotiate a solution). The government's failure to find any sort of solution to the Palestine question before surrendering the mandate to the United Nations in 1948 can be attributed, at least in part, to Attlee's failure to understand the importance of the issue of a Jewish homeland to American President Harry S. Truman. Attlee refused Truman's request to allow 100,000 Jews into Palestine upon taking office in 1945; granting that request would have at least engaged the American President at an early stage. Attlee largely left the conduct of foreign affairs to Bevin, though. When he visited Truman, for the first time since 1945, to discuss the Korean War in December 1950, it was only because Bevin was too ill to travel.

This raises an important question as to the extent to which the successes of the Attlee government can be credited to Attlee's leadership style. The answer is that Attlee is entitled to as much credit for the successes as he is criticism for the failures. Until his final months in office, Attlee managed his team of Cabinet ministers highly effectively. They quarrelled, but, until Bevan's resignation six months before the government left office, not to an extent that undermined the government. Greatness need not be about an individual's own deeds; it can also be about getting the best out of other great men. This Attlee did. The government's 'Big Five' all made enormous contributions.[373] Also, Attlee was willing to take on a greater responsibility in certain policy areas he saw as particularly important: for example, the development of Britain's nuclear weapons, which he undertook via a Cabinet committee, secret from even the full Cabinet; and independence for India, where he changed the Viceroy, dismissing Lord Wavell and replacing him with Lord Mountbatten. Attlee personally deserves great credit for navigating his way towards independence for India on 15 August 1947.[374]

---

373 Dalton did resign as Chancellor after leaking Budget details to John Carvel, lobby correspondent of the *Daily Star*, on his way to give the Budget speech of 12 November 1947. The details were published in a newspaper scoop. However, Dalton did then return to Cabinet six months later, on 31 May 1948, as Chancellor of the Duchy of Lancaster.

374 However, the haste with which Attlee left India came at a human cost – the holding over of the partition lines with the new Muslim states caused what would be today called 'ethnic cleansing' in villages near the new borders.

Attlee's 1945 government dominated the battle of ideas in British politics. He was able to declare at the 1947 Labour party conference: 'Today there is no coherent alternative policy to Labour's in this country. Our opponents are bankrupt of ideas.'[375] The tactic of the Conservatives to return to power in 1951 was to simply accept many of the Labour changes. R. A. Butler reputedly said: 'If they [the people] want that sort of life [welfare and high public spending] they can have it, but under our auspices.'[376] The Conservatives only reversed two of the Attlee nationalisations, both of which had obvious flaws in any event. The first – road haulage – could not solve the practical challenges of controlling all commercial movement of goods by road. The second – iron and steel – had caused great controversy within the Attlee government itself, and had been difficult to justify on anything other than ideological grounds. However, Attlee also had to accept the inevitable. Britain's financial dependence on the United States, from the loan in 1945, determined the general direction of its foreign policy: the 'special relationship' across the Atlantic, and the formation of the North Atlantic Treaty Organisation (NATO) in 1949.

The success of the 1945–48 period brought its own problems. The 'completion of Labour's mission' (to use Richard Crossman's words) in these years opened up a debate as to the direction the party should now go in.[377] The widespread nationalisation meant there were few industries left to be taken into state control. In the general election of February 1950, which Labour won with a narrow majority of only five seats, the only firm Labour promises on nationalisation were in the beet-sugar manufacturing, sugar refinement, and cement industries. Disagreement on future direction was to find expression in the dispute that erupted between the new Chancellor Hugh Gaitskell, who succeeded Cripps at the Treasury in October 1950, and Aneurin Bevan, who was moved sideways to become Minister of Labour in January 1951.

---

375 The Labour Party, 'Report of the Forty-Sixth Annual Conference', 1947, p. 119.

376 As quoted in Dennis Kavanagh, *Thatcherism and British Politics*, Oxford, Oxford University Press, 1987, p. 191. Kavanagh footnotes that it is based on 'private information'.

377 Crossman's phrase is in Janet Morgan ed., *The Back-bench Diaries of Richard Crossman*, London, Hamish Hamilton /Jonathan Cape, 1981, p. 400.

The division was about much more than personal rivalry. The Korean War broke out on 25 June 1950, when North Korean troops, with Soviet military hardware, crossed the 38th parallel, the latitude line forming the border with South Korea. The United States pushed Britain to increase its defence spending in response. In 1951, for the next three years, Gaitskell allocated basic sums of £500 million, then £880 million, then £1,000 million to an increased defence programme.[378] Bevan attacked this re-armament programme on practical and political grounds: he did not think it possible to spend such large sums in the time envisaged (on which he was proved correct), and was deeply concerned about, what he perceived to be, the move to aggressive militarism in American foreign policy, beyond simply repelling the North Korean invaders. The increased defence spending also had the effect of requiring cuts elsewhere. In the event, the charges Gaitskell introduced were on teeth and spectacles in the National Health Service, which were estimated to bring in £13 million. Bevan was outraged that such a small sum was being saved in a Budget of over £4,000 million, and at the price of the principle of health care free at the point of delivery.[379] However, his regular requests for further money for the NHS had tried the patience of many of his Cabinet colleagues. Attlee was in hospital with a duodenal ulcer for a key part of the dispute, and his absence was particularly noticed on 9 April, when there were two Cabinet meetings held to try to thrash out a compromise. However, the key participants did visit his bedside. Crucially, Attlee failed to work harder on persuading Hugh Gaitskell to find an alternative in relation to what was an insignificant amount of money. It had far-reaching consequences. Bevan's resignation from the government on 23 April 1951 was the first public symbol of disagreement at the top of the Labour Party on its future direction in the post-war era.

With a tiny majority, the timing of the next general election was a test of Attlee's judgement. In this immediate post-war period, the two main parties,

---

378 Public Records: National Archives, Cabinet Papers: CAB 128/19, CM (51) 4, 25 January 1951.

379 Public Records: National Archives, Cabinet Papers: CAB 128/19, CM (51) 25-6, 9 April 1951.

the Conservatives and Labour, regularly took over 90 per cent of the popular vote between them. The issue in the next election, to use Attlee's words, would be the 'way the liberal cat jumps'.[380] With one election quickly following another, the cash-strapped Liberals would not be able to run a large number of candidates, hence what their voters did in the absence of a Liberal candidate was crucial. In the end, the Liberals ran only 109 candidates, having run 475 in 1950. Attlee's view was that 'the Liberals tended in most areas to give two or three votes to the Conservatives for every one they gave to Labour'.[381] Against this political background, the key factor in Attlee's decision to call the election for 25 October 1951, twenty months after the 1950 election, was the wish of King George VI. Attlee's deep respect for the crown was at play here. The King wanted the parliamentary position dealt with before he went on a trip to Australia, though in the event he was too ill to travel anyway. In Attlee's defence, he also took into account the welfare of his MPs. With a tiny majority, there was a frequent need to bring in elderly and infirm MPs to vote in the Commons. He later remarked: 'The strain on our Members [of Parliament], some of whom were in indifferent health, was very great.'[382] However, Attlee's failure to wait a further few months, in order to give the Liberals less time to find the money for more candidates, deprived Labour of the opportunity to take some credit when austerity measures such as rationing were lifted.

A further factor against the interests of the Labour Party in the 1950 and 1951 elections was the 1948 Representation of the People Act, which changed the electoral boundaries for Westminster, creating new constituencies favourable to the Conservatives. Attlee's failure to manipulate the situation to his party's advantage was an example of his personal integrity, but also naivety. Knowing the problem was an over-representation of predominantly Conservative rural areas at the expense of predominantly Labour urban areas, the Cabinet

---

380 C. R. Attlee Papers (Bodleian Library, Oxford): letters to Tom, 21 October 1951.

381 Attlee, op. cit., p. 208.

382 Ibid., p. 206.

did agree to the creation of seventeen extra urban seats on 8 March 1948.[383] However, there was little beyond this to mitigate the favouring of rural areas in the act, which was of great benefit to the Conservatives. The electoral system certainly worked to the benefit of the Conservatives after that. At the 1951 general election, Labour lost twenty seats, leaving the party with 295 MPs, while the Conservatives gained twenty-two, giving the party 321 MPs and an overall majority of seventeen. Yet Labour won most votes – over 13,900,000 (48.8 per cent) – while the Conservatives won just over 13,700,000 votes (48 per cent). Numerically, the Labour vote actually rose during the years of the Attlee governments, from just under 12,000,000 in 1945, to just over 13,200,000 in 1950, and then to the 1951 total.

Back in opposition in his final four years as party leader, Attlee had to deal with the dispute between the Bevanites and the Gaitskellites. In March 1952, Bevan and fifty-six other Labour MPs defied the party whip on the issue of re-armament, and, later that year, the atmosphere at the party conference in Morecambe was extraordinarily bad-tempered. The Bevanites became angered by the ideologically aggressive anti-communist policy of John Foster Dulles, who became US Secretary of State in 1953. Attlee tried to maintain a sense of balance throughout this difficult period, with his ultimate aim of keeping the party together. In 1955, he played a key role in preventing Aneurin Bevan from being expelled from the party: his personal opposition to the expulsion was a key factor in keeping Bevan within the party.[384] Labour may have lost the general election of May 1955, but, with the party having gone through such internal turmoil, a loss of only eighteen seats was not a discreditable achievement.

Attlee has a strong claim to be the greatest Labour leader on statistical grounds: not only in terms of longevity (political survival being a measure of success in itself), but also in the fact that the tiny parliamentary party he

---

383 Hansard, HC 1947–8, vol. 449, col. 162, 6–23 April 1948.

384 'Another decisive factor – which, alone, probably turned the table – was Attlee's opposition to expulsion' – Eric Shaw, *Discipline and Discord in the Labour Party: The Politics of Managerial Control in the Labour Party, 1951–87*, Manchester, Manchester University Press, 1988, p. 43.

inherited as caretaker leader in 1935 – the fifty-two seats won in 1931 had been increased only by a handful of by-election victories – had increased to 277 members by the time he resigned the leadership in 1955. There was also the landslide general election victory of 1945, and the fact that the number of voters Labour gained in the 1951 general election has still not been surpassed. But such analysis alone ignores circumstances. Attlee's strongest claim to be Labour's most successful leader lies in what the government he led achieved: the way it changed the lives of ordinary people; the way it produced, in the words of James MacGregor Burns, a change of culture and values for the post-war era. Attlee was not a 'celebrity' as we understand the term today. He was quintessentially British: brisk, unfussy, reserved and proud of his country. His obituary in *The Times* stated that 'much of what he did was memorable; very little that he said'.[385] That is exactly how Attlee would have wanted to be remembered.

385 *The Times*, 9 October 1967.

CHAPTER 12

HUGH GAITSKELL

BRIAN BRIVATI

Hugh Gaitskell was leader of the Labour Party from 1955, after just ten years in Parliament. He fought the 1955 general election but was defeated by Harold Macmillan's Conservatives by a margin of 49.7 to 46.4 per cent of the popular vote. Labour was expected to have won that election, and Gaitskell faced criticism afterwards. This culminated in two leadership challenges, but he defeated both Harold Wilson in 1960 (by 166 votes to eighty-one) and Anthony Greenwood in 1961 (by 171 votes to fifty-nine). Gaitskell died suddenly in 1963, aged fifty-six. Brian Brivati argues that assessing Gaitskell against the statecraft criteria would leave him judged as a failure. However, this overlooks the other ways in which he provided leadership. This chapter argues that Gaitskell, like Blair, was a bold party reformer who sought to change the party's position on Clause IV, nuclear disarmament, and membership of the European Economic Community (EEC). He was a leader who sought to teach and lead the electorate with his political philosophy, rather than treating the Labour Party as a vote-maximising machine. The challenges he faced in doing so mirror the challenges more contemporary party leaders have faced, too.

• • •

The purpose of this volume is to assess leadership. Who was the best leader of the Labour Party in its history? The model presented in the introduction asks for an assessment of leaders across perfectly defensible variables of winning electoral strategy, governing competence, party management, political argument hegemony, and bending the rules of the game. Gaitskell comprehensively lost the only election he fought as leader, so he never governed the country, though he governed the party in such a way as to ensure that, for most of his leadership, a large faction of it fought against his every idea and proposal, purely because they came from him. He lost the argument on revising Clause IV and was heavily defeated at conference on unilateral nuclear disarmament. He never held the state, so he never got to change the constitution. On any rational model of leadership of the Labour Party, he was a failure, and should thus appear towards the bottom end of the league tables so beloved by political scientists, who like to see the world through their regression analysis. But this conclusion depends, in part, on what you mean by 'the Labour Party' and what you really mean by 'leadership'. Before considering Gaitskell in the light of these two ideas, we need to look at the major moments in Gaitskell's leadership of the Labour Party, and what relevance, if any, his leadership personality and political philosophy have for judging the leaderships of the Labour Party today.

Hugh Gaitskell chose the Labour Party; he was not born into it. He was also widely considered to be an unlikely leader of it. Gaitskell was born at Campden Hill in Kensington, and later lived in Onslow Gardens, South Kensington – which, even in those days, were considered prestigious addresses. His father had joined the Indian Civil Service straight from Oxford and served his career in Burma, where Hugh, the youngest of three children, spent time, until he was sent back to the UK to start school. His father died, however, when Hugh was nine, and his mother remarried and returned to Burma. Thereafter, the young Hugh Gaitskell, who was known as Sam, passed most school holidays with his older brother Arthur, or with other relatives.

His preparatory school was Lynams, also known as the Dragon School, in Oxford. It mostly took the sons of professional people and Oxford dons, and was remarkable for its liberal approach to learning, and what we might today call 'life skills'. The head (the 'Skipper') dressed like a merchant seaman, wore a red tie, and was an early socialist who had broadened the school's roll to include the sons of Oxford tradesmen.[386]

The atmosphere at Lynams was free and easy; dress was unconventional; games were not compulsory – though Sam loved learning to box and play tennis and rugby.[387] The boys were also allowed the freedom to travel into town on their bicycles. It was even the case that girls were brought in to teach 'courtesy' and manners to the very young men the school was educating.

It is often claimed that Gaitskell's socialism was a product of the general strike in 1926, but his friend, the poet John Betjeman, once wrote that Gaitskell's views took shape during his time at the Dragon School. 'This is where I first became a socialist,' Gaitskell said one day, many years later, as he was passing a small parade of shops where the boys had bought their sweets. It was in an area of Oxford that contrasted starkly with the affluent, detached, Gothic Revival houses elsewhere in the city, and, for the first time, he was made aware that some people were not as well-off as others.[388] In spite of this, Betjeman did not consider Gaitskell a politically minded person until much later in his life.

After Lynams, Gaitskell attended Winchester School and then New College, Oxford, to study the recently established Honours degree – philosophy, politics and economics (PPE). Winchester was critical in shaping Gaitskell's character, but Oxford made more of an impact in terms of his politics. To be a Wykehamist was to have 'a blend of intellectual arrogance and conventional good manners'.[389] But it was at Oxford, in the winter of 1924–25, where Gaitskell met Maurice Bowra, then dean of Wadham. According to Bowra, Gaitskell had a lively taste for food, drink and uninhibited conversation, and was on affectionate terms with a wide circle of friends, including

---

386 John Betjeman in William Rodgers ed., *Hugh Gaitskell 1906–1963*, Thames & Hudson, London, 1964, p. 15.

387 Brian Brivati, *Hugh Gaitskell*, London, Richard Cohen Books, 1996, p. 6.

388 Rodgers, op. cit., p. 16.

389 Brivati, op. cit., p. 8.

'some highly attractive and intelligent girls',[390] and another undergraduate – W. H. Auden. 'I was surprised that I had not heard more,' Bowra wrote after Gaitskell's death. 'He was eighteen years old, slim, curly haired and fresh-coloured, and had not yet developed any of the prominent features that were to delight caricaturists in his later years.'

At this stage, however, Gaitskell was 'no more remarkable' as a student than many of his clever contemporaries.[391] He had very little interest in the philosophy element of PPE, but was extremely engaged and challenging when it came to politics and economics.

For most of this period, Stanley Baldwin was Prime Minister. Britain was a highly divided society and seemed likely to remain so. The peace in 1918 had produced unemployment, overcrowding, the dole and the Poor Law. Gaitskell was repelled by Baldwin and his complacency, and outraged by the poor social conditions of the post-war years. He read Marx, going through a very brief Marxist phase in 1931,[392] but, by 1934, he did not consider it a solution ('too mechanical to be right and too inhuman to deserve any devotion'),[393] and was certainly not a Christian socialist. Indeed, Gaitskell had abandoned Christianity at school, finding its ethics too vague and too subjective to lead to practical political outcomes.

Gaitskell's main political guidance came from G. D. H. Cole, an early Fabian who arrived at Oxford as a reader in economics in 1924. Cole's socialism was a call to arms for Gaitskell. It answered his questions and pointed the way forwards. It also gave him an intellectual framework and self-confidence, which meant he was never afraid to discuss political matters with those who held different views to his own. He threw himself into the 1926 general strike, however, and it was then that politics took centre stage for him. He always

---

390 Rodgers, op. cit., p. 19 seq.

391 Ibid., p. 20.

392 Brivati, op. cit., p. 31.

393 Rodgers, op. cit., p. 23.

described it as the chief turning-point in his life; from now on, he declared, 'my future is with the working class'.[394]

After Oxford, Gaitskell worked briefly for the Workers' Educational Association (WEA) in Nottinghamshire, and then took a teaching post at University College London. In London, he played an active role in the Cole Group – which continued for thirty years, and which Margaret Cole describes as 'forming the climate of Labour opinion' – and he also came to the notice of Hugh Dalton, Member of Parliament for Bishop Auckland.

Gaitskell made one failed attempt to get elected to Parliament at the 1935 general election, and then, in 1938, he moved to the National Institute of Economic and Social Research, where he headed the department for political economy. When war broke out, he worked as a civil servant in Hugh Dalton's Ministry of Economic Warfare, and then at the board of trade, which gave him invaluable experience of government. In 1945, he was selected for the seat of Leeds South, and won it in the subsequent landslide with a majority of more than 10,000.

After only two years on the back benches, he was promoted to junior minister at the Ministry of Fuel and Power, largely as a result of the influence of Dalton. In 1950, at the request of Stafford Cripps, he became Minister for Economic Affairs. Roy Jenkins described him over this period as 'quietly competent'.[395] When Cripps stepped down due to ill health, Gaitskell, aged only forty-four, was appointed Chancellor of the Exchequer. Jim Callaghan commented to Gaitskell at the time: 'There is no one else. That is a remarkable tribute.'[396]

This period was marked by a number of crises. First, Gaitskell had to find funding for the Korean War, which was vastly expensive and required savings from other departments. In his first Budget, he ran into difficulties when he introduced charges for spectacles and dentures on the NHS. It led to a direct confrontation with Aneurin Bevan. Neither would give way and

394 Brivati, op. cit., p. 17.

395 Rodgers, op. cit., p. 117.

396 Brivati, op. cit., p. 104.

Bevan resigned, along with Harold Wilson. It revealed – as the Prime Minister Clement Attlee said afterwards – Gaitskell's strength of character.[397]

Following Labour's defeat in 1951, Gaitskell attempted to get himself elected to the NEC. This was no easy feat. Bevan's views were on the ascendancy among the constituencies, but Gaitskell was never one to flinch from a fight. As Roy Jenkins wrote: 'He disliked the noise, but he never kept away from the place where the guns were firing loudest.' Gaitskell confronted the 'snarling' party conference and was defeated – the first of many tricky, ill-tempered encounters with the party – but, two years later, he challenged Bevan for party treasurer and won. The trade unions had decided Gaitskell was a man with whom they could work. By 1955, he had acquired a hold on the party, moving from a 'desiccated calculating machine' – as Bevan had described him, Attlee and Wilson[398] – to a politician with strongly declared political beliefs.[399]

In 1955, following the retirement of Clement Attlee, Gaitskell successfully challenged both Bevan and Herbert Morrison to become leader of the party. As Jenkins commented, he did so 'at a time when formidable rivals were thicker on the ground than they are today'.[400] The first crisis he faced as leader was Suez. He stood back and observed events, and then realised the way the tide was running. He mounted an impassioned opposition to the government's threat of force, and took the Labour Party and many others with him. He was mocked in the House for his stand, but he had won respect.

Jenkins described Gaitskell's period of leadership as an 'adventurous one in Labour Party history': he fundamentally believed that leading meant making his mind up.

In 1959, with the Conservative government in disarray, it appeared Labour would win the election. Gaitskell was buoyant and confident, but it was not to be. The Labour Party became divided. The familiar picture emerged of

---

397 Rodgers, op. cit., p. 150.

398 Tribune rally at the Labour Party conference, 29 September 1954 – Bevan was referring to a type of leader rather than an individual. See Brivati, op. cit., p. 198.

399 Rodgers, op. cit., p. 117.

400 Ibid., p. 116.

moderates and those on the ideological left. A vote on the abolition of Clause IV was lost, but, subtly, the party began to move in his direction – until, that is, the vote on unilateralism took place in 1960 at the Scarborough conference. Gaitskell lost and became, for a time, a wounded leader, but, typically, he did not accept the defeat. He mobilised a grass-roots campaign, and the decision was reversed at the following conference. Harold Wilson challenged him for the leadership in November 1960, and lost by a ratio of 2:1. Gaitskell's position was confirmed. Throughout that winter he delivered speech after speech, and seemed in the best of health, dominant in the party and reasonably popular in the country. At the 1962 conference, he delivered his verdict on British membership of the EEC – he resoundingly rejected it, and thereby built a significant bridge to the left of the party.[401]

It was mid-December 1962 when Gaitskell first became ill. Initially, it was diagnosed as a chest infection and then viral pneumonia. He was discharged from hospital over Christmas, but, a few days later, he was moved to the Middlesex Hospital for tests. His condition became more serious, and he died at 9.12 p.m. on Friday 18 January 1963.

When Gaitskell had sat down at the end of his speech to the Labour Party conference in 1962, he was the dominant personality in British politics. His speech had forcefully opposed UK membership of the EEC and had united the Labour Party behind his leadership. He had eclipsed, for the first time, the Conservative Prime Minister Harold Macmillan. It was the apex of his political career. But 108 days later, he was dead.

There had been key moments on the road to that speech. During the Suez Crisis of 1956, Gaitskell combined brilliantly with his arch political rival Nye Bevan to dissect the government's duplicity. Many in the British establishment never forgave him for that. After being heavily defeated in the 1959 election, he came out against Clause IV of the Labour Party constitution and against unilateral nuclear disarmament. At the conference of 1960, he was defeated on both fronts. However, he then reversed the unilateralist vote at

---

401 Brivati, op. cit., pp. 349–75, 404–31.

the conference in 1961 and went on to bring unity through his stance on the EEC. His official biographer, Philip Williams, wrote that Gaitskell had finally come to terms with the Labour Party. That phrase is key to understanding Gaitskell as leader of the Labour Party, and it highlights the core question of how to lead the Labour Party, or, indeed, how to lead any reforming political party of what used to be called the left.

When I first published my biography of Gaitskell in 1996,[402] some reviewers criticised me for likening Tony Blair to Gaitskell. While acknowledging that there are limits to the comparison, the comparing of the two still offers a good prism for considering Gaitskell as leader and understanding the challenge of leading the Labour Party. Moreover, the turn of the millennium has made the dialogue between Gaitskellite revisionism in the 1950s and the Blair–Brown modernisation project even more interesting. This comparison also throws light on the challenges faced by Ed Miliband. In short, the Blair–Brown project highlighted important structural constraints on the Labour Party in power, when it is led from the right. These constraints would have been much the same for a Gaitskellite government, and were very much in evidence in the opposition that Gaitskell encountered to his own modernising project. After a significant period of Labour in power, one of the central questions of Labour Party studies in the 1980s and much of the 1990s has been answered. The question was: how does Labour win? The answer: by becoming as flexible in the pursuit of power as the Conservative Party. The question for the future is whether or not it is possible to lead the Labour Party to victory from a centre-left position, which does not follow the Conservative path to electoral victory.

The Conservative path to power has often, though not always, historically been through placing the gaining and holding of power at the centre of their political project. In this respect, there are clear comparisons between Gaitskell and Gaitskellite revisionism and the Blair–Brown project. Perhaps there are also marked contrasts with the leadership of Ed Miliband. Under

402 Ibid.

Blair, the Labour Party abandoned any pretence of being interested in using progressive taxation for the redistribution of wealth as distinct from controlling consumer demand. The long-running battles over public ownership, which were for so long central to Labour's ideological direction, now appear to have been no more than bickering over inessentials, and a profound confusion of means and ends. Moreover, the other long-running internal battle over the global position of Britain, expressed either in a desire to see Britain dominant through political leadership (Atlanticism and multilateralism) or through moral leadership (unilateralism), appear to have been complacent and delusional about Britain's developing position in the world. The essence of Labour's victories in 1997, 2001 and 2005 was the abandonment of the notion that economic intervention was superior to market allocation as a means of managing the economy. The central faith of Hugh Gaitskell's life was that economics mattered and that planning was capable of correcting market failure. In both these respects, he agreed much more with all his major political opponents during his own lifetime than he would do with the contemporary generation of leaders of the Labour Party. However, on another level, the contemporary state of British politics would have given him a temporary pause for reflection, and a certain enjoyment – though, here too, the great distances that the Labour Party and the world have travelled would quickly become apparent (more so if Gaitskell had ever formed a government).

The present and the recent past suggest two ways to think about what a Gaitskell government might have been like. They must be thought about with all the caveats that counter-factual history demands. The two dimensions are: public service delivery, and the special relationship with the US.

On public-service delivery, Gaitskell was an early critic of nationalisation, and he famously imposed the first charges on the NHS. He would, in turn, have had no problem with deficit reduction. He would have faced the problem that plagued the Wilson government: how to make the mixed economy deliver. The Blair–Brown governments hit the same structural problems. If the market is not to be the solution to the delivery problem, then what is? Gaitskell had a public-sector workforce that retained a strong sense of the value of public service – but he still faced the problem of motivating the service providers. By the time of his death, Gaitskell lacked convincing answers to the question of how planning would deliver what people wanted.

The second constraint concerns the relationship between a revisionist leader and the party. This would have come into focus for Gaitskell – as it did for Blair – over the special relationship. Williams judged that, in 1962, Gaitskell had finally come to terms with the Labour Party. Michael Foot, reviewing Williams, picked up the point and articulated the left's problem with Hugh:

> For the charge against Gaitskell throughout the years of controversy was not that he lacked honesty or a fine intellect or courage. The charge was that he lacked the imaginative sympathy to understand the labour movement he aspired to lead, and that he was constantly, almost congenitally, seeking to guide it into alien channels.[403]

Foot catches something here: that the self-image of Labour Party members was not reflected back at them by Gaitskell's realist Atlanticism. Anti-Americanism was already widespread in the 1950s; today it is almost universal on the left. Blair suffered the same problem when he articulated his support for the democracies' war against terror, because it connected him to the US. This is not – and was not in the 1950s – an appeal to logic: it is – and was – an emotional response that demands compliance to an oddly Stalinist view of the world, in which America is the evil villain. There was nothing Gaitskell could do in the 1950s and '60s to shake people in the Labour Party out of this hysterical, emotion-driven anti-Americanism, and there was nothing Blair could do in his day either. In both cases, this ensured their leadership would always be contested. Their failure to be mere demagogues, pandering to the anti-Americanism of the crowd, cost them both dearly. It is why Miliband's Labour Party did not have a foreign policy.

---

403 Michael Foot in *The Guardian*, reproduced in Michael Foot, *Loyalists and Loners*, London, Faber & Faber, 2011.

When Hugh Gaitskell found out that he was going to replace Stafford Cripps as the next Chancellor of the Exchequer in 1950, he told William Armstrong – the Chancellor's private secretary – that politics in Britain would gradually become a competition over competence. It would resemble the politics of the United States, and the Labour Party would evolve into a British version of the American Democratic Party. Despite a superficial continuity, the detail of the ideological underpinning of that convergence would have given him equal pause. For Gaitskell in the 1950s, the special relationship was based on the unity of the democracies against the communist world; but the differences between Britain and America remained real, because it was the Labour Party that set the terms of the political debate in the UK, and it was collectivism that set the context within which politics would take place. The party political battle, he firmly believed, would be fought out on the ground prepared by the Labour Party: an interventionist state; a progressive tax system designed to redistribute wealth in the name of greater equality; public ownership of a substantial section of British industry; a global military; and a strategic role as key partner to the US in the anti-communist western alliance.

Labour's ideological position now seems to have developed into something that is neither based on Gaitskell's collectivist faith nor on a full-blown endorsement of neo-liberalism. Labour's third position comprises, roughly, an acceptance of the broad direction of the management of the economy, including complete acceptance of the defeat and irrelevance of public ownership as a form of planning desirable to correct market failure or necessary to promote equality. At the same time, it is a partial rejection of Conservative definitions of austerity and sovereignty. At the heart of Gaitskell's socialism was a belief in equality, and faith that the Labour Party contained the people best able to promote equality through the effective management of the economy, coupled with a deep patriotism: a conviction that Britain was a great country with a global role to play. In the decade after his conversation with Armstrong, Gaitskell fought hard for these principles. With hindsight, his long battles seem slightly unreal. It is difficult to now understand the bitterness that characterised them, and the language in which they were conducted – its emphasis on planning, intervention and social ownership make it seem to belong to a much earlier epoch. The vehemence of the argument between the left and the right of the Labour Party over the extent of public ownership seems quaint – a debate from many decades ago. The 1957 'Industry and Society' policy statement condemned the private sector for its inefficiency and waste, arguing the best way of distributing goods and services was by planning.

The politics Gaitskell espoused is now primarily only of historical interest. The argument in the 1950s was entirely within the terms of collectivism. Gaitskell believed that Labour should govern because the party understood modern economics better than the Conservatives and because modern collectivist economics would solve the problem of distribution. He did not believe in the efficacy of markets; he believed in planning. His opponents within the party went further. In the debate on Clause IV in 1959, Nye Bevan stated that Britain faced an economic challenge from countries that were 'at long last able to reap the material fruits of economic planning and public ownership'. Top of his list was Russia: do not worry about the USA or Germany with their market economies, he said, worry about the command economies. A few years later, Harold Wilson evoked the white heat of technological revolution, so that Britain could keep up with the material and scientific advances of the Soviet Union.[404] But deep in these debates was the belief that there was a key to the successful running of the economy, and that economists held that key. If Gaitskell wanted to dismiss someone, one of his favourite lines was that they were not much good at economics. Faith in the efficacy of the state and in the rightness of the aim of equality permeated political debate then. This faith in economics, in the professional politician, is actually highly characteristic of the Labour Party today. It is based on the idea that you can lead and teach the electorate, and the electorate will follow you.

The 2015 Labour Party leadership did not operate in the intellectual environment it had shaped, nor did it believe it had the economic answers to

404 Brivati, op. cit., p. 342.

contemporary questions: in essence, they were still 'playing catch-up' to a revolution in political economy, instigated by the right. Miliband struggled to find some new way of articulating his endorsement of much of the new economic settlement in the reduced state of the coalition. Collectivism was largely a dead political idea, planning was no longer seen as economically relevant, and the market mechanism was seen as the economic 'truth', despite the many bailouts of banks and so on. The economic ambitions of the Miliband-led Labour Party were modest. The emphasis of a Gaitskell government would have been, in the spirit of the times, economically interventionist. The shadow of the Attlee governments fell over Gaitskell's years as leader, for the achievement of those years underpinned his faith in what he was doing. Miliband's Labour Party operated in the shadow of the Thatcher revolution and the financial crash. In the long run, historians may well judge the Thatcher revolution to have been partial and limited in scope, but to have achieved one, not inconsiderable, shift: the Labour Party abandoned equality as an objective and, in doing so, resembled the 'historic' Labour Party founded in 1900 in name alone. In all these respects, the differences between the party of Gaitskell and that of Miliband tended to be more profound than the continuities, but similarities in their styles of leadership are evident.

Gaitskell would have resembled Thatcher in some ways: his dedication to work, his clarity of objectives and his pedantic attention to detail would have 'given him many of the strengths and the weaknesses of a Thatcher-style premier'. However, the leader he resembled more, as John Campbell has pointed out, was the Conservative Prime Minister Ted Heath. They shared that mid-century technocratic love of the machinery of state and, in Gaitskell's case, the mechanics of economic policy. They shared a positivist faith in the ability to find solutions to human problems. Gaitskell might not have been able to bend to the wind of industrial militancy in the way Heath did, but then the context would have been different. There is clearly a vast, though contested, difference in context of the UK economy today from that of the 1950s. Much of the underlying argument for the shift away from nationalisation, use of progressive taxation, support for universal benefits and so on comes from the notion of the global economy. Though the impact of this global economy, particularly the free and instantaneous movement of capital, is contested and frequently used as a political cover for inaction, nevertheless it would be ludicrous to argue that the Labour Party should, or could, have stayed still in 1963, or indeed that Gaitskell's own beliefs would not have changed and evolved had he lived. However, similarities of approach between Miliband and Gaitskell do exist. They share modernising instincts – and, of course, Gaitskell tried and failed to ditch Clause IV in favour of a new statement of aims: he was the first moderniser. One of Miliband's great political heroes was the moderniser, revisionist and champion of Gaitskell, Tony Crosland. The style of the two leaders also invites comparison.

When Jean Monnet tried to convince Gaitskell that Britain should join the European Union, he failed. After hours arguing, Monnet finally said, 'You must have faith.'

Gaitskell replied, 'I do not believe in faith, I believe in reason.'[405]

One can imagine Miliband making the same response, and many of his speeches were reasoned expositions, reminiscent of Gaitskell. It seems that he also had that Gaitskellite passion to change the terms of political discourse.

Gaitskell was an intriguing human being, who expressed, in the conflict between his public and private lives, a central dilemma – some would say crisis – of masculinity. He tried throughout his life to maintain the separation of the personal and the political, and the gap between the dry, Wykehamist minister and the warm, passionate friend and lover was the central paradox of his life. Occasionally the barriers were breached, and his intense feelings flooded into the political sphere with electrifying effect, but more often the two were kept strictly apart. This sense of self and conflict is very common among male politicians: the number of what we might call integrated personalities in politics is actually very small. Indeed, the search for love that drove Gaitskell in his private life was connected to the forcefulness that propelled him in public life, although the surprising thing is not that Gaitskell was a

405 Brivati, op. cit., p. 412.

divided self, but that others around him (such as Nye Bevan) were so much more of a piece. To account for this conflict requires an understanding of the culture and class from which Gaitskell came. However, what is striking about contemporary politicians such as Gordon Brown and Ed Balls is the extent to which psychological conflict remains a part of politicians' make-up. The politicians of today did not grow up in the social and emotional world of Edwardian Britain, yet they seem to echo the kind of tortured self reflected in aspects of Gaitskell's character – also the defining characteristic of some of his contemporaries, especially Eden and Macmillan.

Gaitskell embodied a strand of British politics now extinct. He never stopped struggling with his upbringing, his class and, finally, the constraints of the public life he had chosen. Initially he sought ways of escaping his background by rebelling against it; later he rebelled against the constraints his political life had placed on his ability to have fun, by making a point of having it. Personally, this seeking out of fun took the form of a love of food, alcohol, jazz and dancing. At times, the intensity of his pleasure-seeking could draw criticism, and the closeness of his relationship with women – such as his lover Ann Fleming – provoked some to question his commitment to the working class. However, more often people remarked on his capacity for friendship, and his extraordinarily warm private persona. Politically, every time it appeared he had found his level, he transcended it, confounding people's expectations. He slowly resolved a number of deep-rooted private battles – for instance, between the demands of the Wykehamist code, summed up by Crossman,[406] and his deep emotional needs – and he seemed to be on the threshold of fulfilling a life of intense hard work when he died suddenly.

At the beginning of this chapter, the questions of what might be meant by the Labour Party and by its leadership were asked. The votes on unilateralism, Clause IV and Europe illustrate the different answers one might give to

406 Brivati, op. cit., p. 8.

these questions. There are, in the end, two political propositions, and therefore two kinds of leadership.

There is the proposition that says: 'This is what I believe in, now follow me.' In this political model, the job of leaders is to persuade their party, and then the electorate, that what they believe is right; that how they see the world is how the world actually works; that their economic approach is the right one.

The second proposition says: 'Tell us what you want and we will try to give it to you.' In this political model, the ideology and manifesto of a party is adapted to the times and context in which the party is operating. Both are kinds of leadership.

The other question is: what is the Labour Party? Either the Labour Party is an idea about the way the world should be, or the Labour Party is a vote-maximising machine in pursuit of power. Most leaders of Labour who win elections believe the party is a machine – they ask people what they want and try to give it to them – Ramsay MacDonald, Tony Blair (on domestic policy) and Harold Wilson are perhaps the best examples, but Attlee was very much the same. The key difference for Attlee was that the people and the dominant ideas of political economy were, for that brief moment, absolutely in tune with the idea of the Labour Party. If they had not been, Attlee would have simply done something else. Neil Kinnock tried very hard to maximise the votes for Labour and so win power. It is only Gaitskell who, though hoping that Labour was a vote-maximising machine, also believed that the electorate should follow him, rather than he follow the electorate – which is why, for many, Gaitskell was the last great democratic socialist leader of the Labour Party.

CHAPTER 13

HAROLD WILSON

THOMAS HENNESSEY

Harold Wilson first entered Parliament in 1945 as the MP for Ormskirk, aged twenty-nine. He was promoted to the Cabinet in just over two years, holding the position of president of the board of trade. Wilson fought Hugh Gaitskell to be leader in 1960, but lost. He became leader of the Labour Party in 1963, however, after Gaitskell's sudden death, beating George Brown and James Callaghan in the leadership contests. Wilson went on to win more general election victories than any other Labour leader, winning office four times (1964, 1966 and twice in 1974) and losing only once (in 1970), before announcing his shock resignation while still in office, in March 1976. This record, Thomas Hennessey argues, sets Wilson apart as Labour's most successful leader in terms of the primary function required of a major party leader – winning power. His premierships can be criticised for being besieged by economic crises (and Wilson's policy errors exacerbated these), however, Wilson inherited challenging conditions at the start of his two terms in office, and eventually made significant contributions towards putting Britain on the path to economic recovery, as well as holding the party together during the EEC membership referendum.

• • •

Assessing Harold Wilson, and his reputation as Labour leader, is as thorny an issue as the man himself. Bernard Donoughue, Wilson's special advisor 1974–76, recalled that Wilson always operated on several different levels concurrently: 'He was perhaps the most complex character I have met in my life.'[407] Donoghue was an eyewitness to the stresses his Prime Minister faced in trying to govern a party that seemed itching to tear itself apart, and he admired the skills Wilson employed to preserve the uneasy truce between right and left in Cabinet – which was also complicated by the tremendous egos therein. Wilson exhibited 'consummate skills in holding together a fissiparous party, which was increasingly just a loose coalition of different and often conflicting interests and beliefs'. He was similarly impressive as chairman of the Cabinet, giving every opportunity to voice a view, always 'seeking consensus, maintaining unity'. Added to this were Wilson's personal qualities – of great relevance to his success as party leader. He was 'accessible, warm, kind and humorous, which drew the affection and loyalty of those who worked for him'. He had none of the pretentions or assumptions of grandeur that sometimes accompanied high office. Indeed, at the end: 'He remained middle class, middlebrow, provincial in the best sense of the word, and a Nonconformist, grammar school, "Little Englander".'[408]

THE ROAD TO LEADERSHIP

A proud Yorkshireman, and devotee of Huddersfield Town Football Club, Wilson was born on 11 March 1916, into a lower-middle-class family: his father was a works chemist, and his mother a schoolteacher before marriage. Famously, aged eight, he had his picture taken by his father outside No. 10, and, at twelve, he wrote an essay in which he saw himself as Chancellor of the Exchequer, about to levy a tax on gramophones and records.[409] A bright, hard-working undergraduate at Oxford, he became a don at twenty-one and a high-flying civil servant during the war. In 1945, he was, aged twenty-nine,

407 Bernard Donoughue, *Downing Street Diary. With Harold Wilson in No.10*, London, Jonathan Cape, 2005, p. x.

408 Ibid., p. 11.

409 D. J. Heasman, 'The Life and Times of Harold Wilson', *International Journal*, 20(1), winter 1964/65, pp. 104.

elected a Labour MP, and, as a result of his administrative reputation, went straight to the government front bench as parliamentary secretary to the Ministry of Works. After a stint as secretary for overseas trade, he became, at thirty-one, president of the board of trade – the youngest Cabinet minister of the century.

Within the Labour Party, Wilson made his name as a man of the left when he resigned, with Aneurin Bevan, from the Cabinet in 1951 in protest to Chancellor Hugh Gaitskell's decision to introduce prescription charges. After Bevan's death, feeling that he was the only left-wing challenger, Wilson ran against Gaitskell for the party leadership in 1960. He lost. (And he lost again when he challenged George Brown for the deputy leadership in November 1962.) Gaitskell, nevertheless, kept Wilson within his shadow Cabinet, appointing him to the key position of shadow Chancellor.[410]

Gaitskell's untimely death in 1963 provided Wilson with another shot at the leadership. His primary opponent was George Brown, from the right of the party, but there were reservations and concerns about Brown: his electoral appeal both in the party and nationally; his capacity to unify the party given his right-wing convictions; and his temperament, particularly his reputation for drinking.[411] Crucially, the entrance of James Callaghan into the fray – as a potential compromise candidate – drew support from Brown. After Callaghan was eliminated, Wilson required a mere eight votes from the Callaghan first-ballot supporters, while Brown needed thirty-four, and when Callaghan endorsed Wilson, the latter was crowned leader.[412] Thereafter he dominated the intellectual confrontation with the Conservatives, attacking the 'stop-go' affliction of the British economy and offering as an alternative a 'science plan', based on the 'white heat' of 'scientific management' and a planned economy.[413]

---

410 Ibid., pp. 106–9.

411 Timothy Heppell, 'The Labour Party Leadership Election of 1963: Explaining the Unexpected Election of Harold Wilson', *Contemporary British History*, 24(2), 2010, p. 159.

412 Ibid., pp. 161–2.

413 Glen O'Hara, 'Dynamic, Exciting, Thrilling Change': the Wilson Government's Economic Policies, 1964–70, *Contemporary British History*, 20(3), 2006, pp. 384–5.

PRIME MINISTER 1964–70

Labour started the 1964 general election campaign as firm favourites, but the result was a close-run affair. The increase in the Labour vote was no more than 0.3 per cent, from 43.8 to 44.1. However, as the Conservative vote was down from 49.4 to 43.4, there was a net swing from the Tories to Labour of 3.15 per cent. Labour emerged with 317 seats, the Conservatives with 304, and the Liberals with nine.[414] So, on 16 October 1964, Wilson staggered over the line with a majority of four in the House of Commons – Labour was in power after thirteen years in the wilderness. Now, constructing his Cabinet, the key appointments were heavyweights – and former rivals – James Callaghan, as Chancellor of the Exchequer, and George Brown, as Secretary of State for the new Department of Economic Affairs (DEA). The economic legacy was alarming, with Wilson inheriting a balance-of-payments deficit and huge pressure on sterling: this was a period of fixed exchange rates, established by the Bretton Woods Agreement, in which governments intervened in the market to prop up their currencies at a fixed value.

When Wilson, Callaghan and Brown held the first of many meetings in the Cabinet Room on 17 October the first item on their informal agenda did not take long to dispose of. It was to decide formally whether or not to devalue the pound: 'We did not need to call in the officials, for each of us knew before the Prime Minister began what our answer would be,' remembered Callaghan, 'and we quickly reached a unanimous conclusion to maintain sterling's exchange rate.'[415] This was the key economic decision taken by the new government – to keep sterling pegged at US$2.80. The consequences were profound.[416] Why did Wilson and his colleagues not devalue? As the Treasury put it: devaluation was 'a major act of state that can only be taken when the alternatives have clearly and demonstrably failed, or are equally clearly and demonstrably

414 Heasman, op. cit., p. 112.

415 James Callaghan, *Time & Chance*, London, William Collins, 1987, pp. 161–3.

416 O'Hara, op. cit., p. 386.

intolerable'.[417] So, to avoid devaluation being forced upon them, Wilson's government would, if necessary, have to commit vast sums of money to maintain the value of the pound at US$2.80. And the only way this could be done was using the Bank of England's reserves or borrowing vast sums from the International Monetary Fund (IMF) and the world's central banks.

Labour had been elected on a programme of raising social benefits – such as higher pensions and the abolition of prescription charges – and these were introduced in the first Budget. While more than balanced out by higher taxes and insurance contributions, these measures 'caused irritation abroad', and the announcement of a proposed corporation tax and capital gains tax caused confusion in the City.[418] The result was increased pressure on the pound, and the first sterling crisis (November 1964) set a pattern for Wilson, until devaluation was forced upon him in a humiliating fashion in 1967.[419] In November 1964, the bank rate was raised to an unprecedented post-war level,[420] and Wilson appealed personally to President Lyndon B. Johnson for financial support – the Federal Reserve was prepared to support sterling up to a maximum of $250 million, with a further $250 million from the US government, and $100 million from the Canadian government. The Governor of the Bank of England was also tasked with securing further massive support from the European central banks.[421] This credit was drawn upon periodically over the following three years to defend the sterling rate – which in turn blunted the government's domestic policy, as Wilson attempted to appease the 'Gnomes of Zurich' (as he referred to the international bankers and speculators).

In the meantime, the big economic idea of the incoming Labour government was the role of planning in the form of the DEA, with Brown at its helm.

417 National Archives, T 312/1485, 'Devaluation', 23 April 1964.

418 National Archives, PREM 13/866, Lord Kahn committee report of the enquiry into the position of sterling, 1964–5.

419 National Archives, PREM 13/261, conclusions of a meeting at Chequers, 21 November 1964.

420 National Archives, PREM 13/866, Lord Kahn committee report.

421 National Archives, PREM 13/261, note of a meeting held at 10 Downing Street on 24 November 1964.

Wilson, Callaghan and Brown agreed that it should be assumed for industrial planning and public presentation that gross domestic product (GDP) would increase by 25 per cent between 1964 and 1970. The growth in public expenditure would be fixed at 4 per cent a year.[422] The main source of savings would be the containment of the defence budget within the figure of £2,000 million at 1964 prices for the entire Parliament – effectively a cut.[423] However, under pressure to reassure the markets about increasing productivity and to address the problems of the British economy, Wilson introduced a prices and incomes policy. The onus for this largely fell on Brown, who reached an agreement with representatives on both sides of industry on a joint statement of intent on productivity, prices and incomes.[424] The incomes policy, however, increasingly took up much of Brown's time, to the detriment of the National Plan, which Wilson ultimately abandoned in all but name.

In fact, the decline in economic fortunes was rapid: on 15 July 1965, Callaghan presented plans to the Cabinet for projected additional expenditure of £240 million in 1969–70.[425] But, within days, another sterling crisis produced a *volte face*, as Wilson, together with Callaghan, drew up a plan for public expenditure cuts of £45 million in a full year.[426] The only possible alternative to cuts was devaluation – also referred to in Treasury circles as the 'unmentionable', because of Wilson's opposition to it: for example, when, in March 1966, a group of the government's economic special advisors all put their names to a paper recommending devaluation (by up to 15 per cent), Wilson's response was hostile.[427]

Wilson had gone to the polls in 1966, with Labour winning a 96-seat majority. The breathing space generated by that result was short-lived. Once

---

422 National Archives, CAB 128/39, Cabinet conclusions, 28 January 1965.

423 Ibid.

424 National Archives, CAB 128/39, Cabinet conclusions, 15 December 1964.

425 National Archives, CAB 128/39, Cabinet conclusions, 15 July 1965.

426 National Archives, CAB 128/39, Cabinet conclusions, 27 July 1965.

427 National Archives, PREM 13/852, Mitchell to Prime Minister, 29 March 1966.

again, under pressure from the markets to address the balance-of-payments deficit, in mid-1966, Wilson persuaded the Cabinet to approve a series of measures amounting to a £500 million reduction in demand – cuts and tax increases – in the private and public sectors. The demand for imports was curtailed and capacity for production for exports was released by the measures, which were unprecedented by the standards of the time.[428] But this too failed to convince the markets, and Operation Patriarch was the codename for the devaluation of sterling on 18 November to a new fixed parity of $2.40 to the pound.[429] It was a humiliation for Wilson: the political damage to his reputation was compounded by his ill-judged television broadcast, in which he claimed the 'pound in your pocket' did not represent a loss of purchasing power for consumers.

Following devaluation, Callaghan resigned as Chancellor, moving to the Home Office, while Roy Jenkins moved in the opposite direction to No. 11, producing a scheme of major expenditure cuts for the financial year 1968–69, which bore sharply on both overseas defence spending and on civil programmes at home. As Jenkins informed the Cabinet, 'We faced a difficult situation as regards confidence abroad.' He warned that only:

> A massive switch of resources would enable us to earn a substantial balance-of-payments surplus in 1969 and 1970. It was then that we should be feeling the full benefits of devaluation and it was essential that we should secure surpluses in those years sufficient to enable us to meet our obligations for repayment of debt and to build up our reserves and strengthen our borrowing rights so as to deal with any balance-of-payments difficulties that might recur in later years.[430]

There began a marathon series of Cabinet meetings on the cuts, 'which was Wilson's chosen tactic'. Between 4 and 15 January 1968, there were eight

428 National Archives, CAB 128/44, Cabinet conclusions, 20 July 1966.

429 National Archives, CAB 128/42, Cabinet conclusions, 16 November 1967.

430 National Archives, CAB 128/43, Cabinet conclusions, 20 December 1967.

separate meetings lasting a total of thirty-two hours.[431] Cuts were forced through – including the reintroduction of prescription charges – and certain taxes were raised to redirect consumer demand away from imported goods. The major policy decision was the withdrawal of British military forces from 'East of Suez', effectively ending the UK's world role: Wilson was informed by Foreign Secretary George Brown that the latter's US counterpart, Dean Rusk, begged for the decision to be reversed with the words: 'For God's sake, be Britain.'[432] Even after devaluation, throughout the rest of the year, an international gold crisis threatened a catastrophic flight from sterling, and Wilson had to approve a doomsday plan (Operation Brutus) that proposed the imposition of draconian exchange controls, though it would have effectively ended Britain's status as a trading nation and introduced a siege economy.[433]

Wilson also found himself confronting a number of other issues that became prominent on his watch – and they were to remain pronounced throughout the 1970s and '80s. In 1966, a national docks strike convinced him that trade union militancy was becoming an issue he had to address. Britain seemed to lead the industrial nations in terms of 'wildcat' unofficial strikes. Wilson tasked his Employment Secretary Barbara Castle with remedying the situation: the result was 'In Place of Strife' – a White Paper advocating the balloting of union members before strike action, with legal penalties in reserve. An infamous meeting with union barons, resistant to the proposals, at Chequers in June 1969 led, at one stage, to threats of mass strike action from Hugh Scanlon, who also suggested the Prime Minister might be seeking 'another 1931'. Wilson reminded him sharply: 'I was not a Ramsay MacDonald, but in the context of his previous comment I wasn't a Dubcek either.'[434] He was defeated in his efforts by a combination of the unions and, in Cabinet, James Callaghan.

---

431 Roy Jenkins, *A Life at the Centre*, London, Macmillan, 1991, p. 226.

432 National Archives, PREM 13/2454, telegram from Foreign Secretary, 11 January 1968.

433 National Archives, CAB 130/497, Brutus.

434 National Archives, PREM 13/2726, note of a discussion at dinner, Chequers, 1 June 1969.

That same year, Wilson had to take the far-reaching decision to commit British troops to the streets of Northern Ireland as 'The Troubles' erupted. With the rise of Scottish and Welsh nationalism, his period of office signalled the beginning of a slow electoral realisation that the UK was not an extension of 'Greater England'. Coupled with the ongoing economic crisis, it was easy to forget that Wilson's premiership signalled a dramatic reform of social legislation, with the passing of the Race Relations Act, the reform of homosexuality and divorce laws, the legalisation of abortion, and the abolition of the death penalty. Wilson's support for these reforms is, perhaps, the greatest legacy of his 1964–70 governments.

Wilson's decision to end Britain's world role was ironic to say the least, especially as, from 1964 to 1968, he strove to assert the UK's position on the international stage. When he led a delegation to meet President Johnson in December 1964, the Americans were told that, of the 'three main roles we undertook – our nuclear deterrent, our presence on the continent of Europe in support of NATO, and our worldwide deployment outside the NATO area … the general view of the Cabinet had been that we should give the highest priority to the third of these'. With the American military commitment to south-east Asia about to escalate dramatically, Wilson opposed the idea that a few soldiers in British uniforms in South Vietnam, for example, would have great psychological and political significance – as Johnson had hinted in none too subtle a manner.[435] At this stage, the fact that Wilson had inherited a 'secret war' from the previous Conservative government – the 'Confrontation' with Indonesian aggression to dismantle the Malaysian Federation – was his trump card in Washington: there were 8,000 British troops in Borneo and a total of 20,000 in Malaysia. The British commitment was comparable to that of the United States in Vietnam.[436] When the Confrontation ended in 1966, Wilson continued to resist a British commitment to Vietnam.

435 National Archives, PREM 13/104, Record of a meeting at British embassy, Washington, and later at the White House, 7 December 1964.

436 National Archives, PREM 13/104, Record of a meeting at the White House, 8 December 1964.

Wilson's strategy was to support the US's activity in South Vietnam and, while working to call an international conference to settle the conflict, take no action to call such a conference until the United States indicated that they were ready for it.[437] The pressure Wilson experienced was as much domestic as from Washington: Vietnam was *the* foreign policy issue that galvanised opinion on the left throughout the 1960s. As the Prime Minister explained, his government could live with the posture of the United States, which was 'namely that of a stick in one hand and an olive branch in the other. We could probably live with any degree of toughening up of United States responses, provided there was also a public recognition of a readiness to negotiate in parallel.'

But, as Wilson once warned the US ambassador, events in Vietnam 'could well lead to the biggest difficulty between Britain and the United States for many years, possibly since Suez'.[438] And it almost did, when Wilson publicly dissociated the British government from Washington's Vietnam policy – much to the anger of Johnson – following US bombing action. This reflected the internal Labour Party pressure the Prime Minister was under, but it was also something he could use to his advantage, as, during a visit to Washington in 1965, Wilson showed Johnson a letter he had had from sixty-eight Labour MPs, protesting over US policy in Vietnam. While Johnson disagreed with some of the diagnosis in the letter, he was very understanding about his guest's internal political problems.[439]

But Wilson was also keen to demonstrate the asset he, and Britain, could be: thus, in June 1965, he proposed the idea of a three-man Commonwealth peace mission on Vietnam.[440] As he argued, it was 'bound to be a winner', whether or not the mission succeeded, in terms of the propaganda value to

437 National Archives, PREM 13/692, meeting between the Prime Minister and Dean Rusk, 29 January 1965.

438 National Archives, PREM 13/693, record of a conversation between the Prime Minister and David Bruce, 12 March 1965.

439 National Archives, PREM 13/686, record of a conversation at lunch at the White House on Friday, 17 December 1965 (note by the Prime Minister).

440 National Archives, PREM 13/690, Commonwealth peace mission diary.

London and Washington.[441] In 1967, during Soviet Premier Kosygin's visit to London, Wilson once again tried to help Johnson by attempting to use his long-term relations with Moscow to broker a breakthrough on Vietnam.[442] Wilson's efforts on Vietnam came to nought, and seemed to illustrate Britain's declining influence on the world stage – a view reinforced when his support for British membership of the EEC (to which he committed himself and the government in 1966/67) were dealt a death blow by General de Gaulle's rejection of UK membership a mere week after the humiliation of devaluation.[443]

1970–76

By the time of the 1970 general election, it appeared that the Labour government's tough measures following devaluation had worked, delivering a consistent balance-of-payments surplus. The defeat to Edward Heath was, therefore, all the more surprising to Wilson. In the interregnum of 1970–74, dissatisfaction with the record of the Labour governments in the previous decade, coupled with Wilson's disengagement from internal policy processes, witnessed the strengthening of the left's hold on alternative economic strategies. The fact that, after Labour scraped home as a minority government in the February 1974 general election, Wilson just ignored party policy aggravated his critics on the left even more, fuelling their demands for more nationalisation and control of the economy.[444]

But upon returning to office, Wilson found the country confronting an economic situation that 'might well be the worst ever faced in peacetime'

---

441 National Archives, PREM 13/690, note for the record Commonwealth mission on Vietnam, 15 June 1965.

442 National Archives, PREM 13/1918, Prime Minister's personal telegram, serial no. T24/67, 11 p.m., 6 February 1967; PREM 13/1918, Prime Minister's personal telegram: serial no. T26/67, 11 p.m., 10 February 1967.

443 National Archives, PREM 13/2646, Paris to Foreign Office telegram, no. 1192, 27 November 1967.

444 Mark Wickham-Jones, 'The challenge of Stuart Holland: the Labour Party's economic strategy during the 1970s' in Lawrence Black, Hugh Pemberton and Pat Thane eds, *Reassessing 1970s Britain*, Manchester, Manchester University Press, 2013, pp. 125–42.

– and it was deteriorating. Inflation was running at over 10 per cent; the balance-of-payments deficit was at around £1,500 million; the borrowing requirement was £4,000 million; and growth virtually came to a halt by the end of that year. The three-day week had multiplied the problems, reducing GDP by 10 per cent during the first two months of the year, and resulting in a cut in industrial output of 20–30 per cent. As in 1968, it was necessary to shift resources from private consumption to the balance of payments and investment – but not so rapidly as to dislocate the economy or lead to large increases in unemployment.[445]

But this was a different Harold Wilson to the one who had been Prime Minister previously. Bernard Donoughue noted how, by 1974, Wilson – old for his fifty-eight years, tired and often unwell – saw nothing left to prove as a politician, other than to achieve certain records of time in office.[446] He recorded Wilson's lament: 'I am so exhausted.' The Prime Minister began to talk about how, in 1964–70, he used to take his dog for a walk to the pub, but no longer managed that. He also used to play a lot of golf, but didn't any more: 'I don't get any relaxation … I'm so tired.' And he saw no way out of the problems facing the UK, noting how the West German Chancellor Helmut Schmidt had described Britain to him as 'useless and ungovernable'.[447]

But despite this dire economic situation, Wilson was forced to point out that all policy proposals, including proposals for legislation, had to be considered against the background of 'this was not a government that had a firm parliamentary majority and could look forward to a long tenure of office', so a relatively early general election was regarded as likely – although, if possible, at a time of the government's own choosing.[448] Wilson announced the new government was to move smoothly from the previous administration's statutory pay controls to voluntary methods.[449] Partly as a result,

---

445 National Archives, CAB 128/54, Cabinet conclusions, 14 March 1974.

446 Donoughue, op. cit p. 11.

447 Ibid., p. 594.

448 National Archives, CAB 128/54, Cabinet conclusions, 28 March 1974.

449 National Archives, CAB 128/54, Cabinet conclusions, 2 May 1974.

the annual rate of wage increase, which had been 13.5 per cent in the first quarter of the year, rose to over 18 per cent by the third. Early in the New Year, the National Union of Mineworkers received a much-publicised increase of 35 per cent.[450]

The result was drift, and it was only well after the second 1974 election in October, when Labour won with a majority of three, that Wilson was forced to face the realities of the economic situation Britain faced. In February 1975, the ministerial committee on economic strategy reviewed the government's counter-inflation policy and agreed upon a new drive to get down the rate-of-pay increases. This posture meant that the government would have to provide more leadership on pay.[451] The economic situation was desperate, with Denis Healey, the Chancellor of the Exchequer, warning the Cabinet that the 'country was living beyond its means', running an external deficit equal to 5 per cent of GDP. This deficit was financed by overseas borrowing, but the United Kingdom's credit was low and falling. The reason for this was that the UK's rate of inflation was twice that of the other countries in the Organisation for Economic Cooperation and Development (OECD). This affected the balance of payments and the public sector borrowing requirement. The balance-of-payments deficit was also the highest of all countries in the OECD. The public sector borrowing requirement for 1974–75 was put at £7,500 million.[452] Healey's first deflationary Budget was in April 1975 – income tax was raised, a higher rate of VAT was introduced, and cuts were announced in public expenditure (especially food subsidies).[453]

It was only in the summer of 1975 when Wilson finally accepted the case for a serious counter-inflation policy – the target being to get the rate of domestic inflation down to 10 per cent by the third quarter of 1976, and

450 Michael Artis, David Cobham and Mark Wickham-Jones ed., *Twentieth-Century British History, Vol. 3*, 1992, pp. 43–4.

451 National Archives, CAB 128/55, Cabinet conclusions, 27 February 1975.

452 National Archives, CAB 128/56, Cabinet confidential annex, 25 March 1975.

453 Artis et al., op. cit., p. 44.

down into single figures by the end of 1976.[454] The social contract was employed in order to reach a voluntary agreement with the unions to limit pay increases to £6 per week.[455] Coupled with this was Wilson's support for Healey's decision to apply for two borrowings totalling £975 million from the IMF[456] – but it was bought at a price: a reduction in public expenditure of £3,750 million in 1978–79.[457] This decision scraped through Cabinet by a small majority, as the opposition therein was led by Tony Benn, who advocated a retreat to a siege economy, and 'believed that senile industries, like infant industries, needed a wall behind which the necessary restructuring could take place'.[458] By the beginning of 1976, however, Wilson and Healey's policies appeared to be working, with inflation falling fast, the balance of payments improving and public expenditure being brought under control.[459]

In contrast to his ambivalent position in the 1960s, Wilson now advocated unequivocal retention of the British 'independent' nuclear deterrent, on the grounds that it represented an insurance against a breakdown in the credibility of the US strategic nuclear guarantee. He also claimed that: 'If we abandoned our deterrent, France would be the only country in Europe with a strategic nuclear capability', and this was not committed to NATO.[460] Possession of the deterrent was one of the few manifestations of Britain as a great power, after the country had withdrawn from East of Suez. Wilson's commitment to updating the deterrent was taken in defiance of an increasingly powerful, unilateralist segment of a party already divided over Europe. And it was the fissures over Europe in the party that, more than anything, demonstrated Wilson's skill in navigating hostile political waters – or his ability 'to wade

454 National Archives, CAB 128/57, Cabinet confidential annex, 1 July 1975.

455 Artis et al., op. cit., p. 44.

456 National Archives, CAB 128/57, Cabinet confidential annex, 6 November 1975.

457 National Archives, CAB 128/57, Cabinet confidential annex, 13 November 1975.

458 National Archives, CAB 128/57, Cabinet confidential annex, 6 November 1975.

459 Artis et al., op. cit., p. 46.

460 National Archives, CAB 128/55, Cabinet confidential annex, 20 November 1974.

through shit' and hold Labour together on the common market question (as the Prime Minister himself described the experience of leading the country to a 'yes' vote in the 1975 EEC membership referendum).[461] Wilson's solution to overcoming a split on Europe was ingenious, and was revealed in Cabinet on 21 January 1975, when Wilson drew on the 1932 National Government's 'agreeing to differ' precedent on the question of free trade versus tariffs. 'Harold', recorded Barbara Castle, 'announced a fundamental change in our constitutional convention as casually as if he had been offering us a cup of tea.'[462] Having held the party together, and being eager to leave on his own terms, Wilson resigned as Prime Minister in March 1976.

CONCLUSION

Harold Wilson is, arguably, Labour's most successful leader ever: his record of winning four out of five general elections ensures this claim is taken seriously. Admittedly, he did only squeak home in three out of the four he won – but he won nevertheless, which is a feat that has eluded many other Labour leaders before and since. In assessing his leadership, it has to be recognised that there were two Harold Wilsons as Prime Minister: the first Harold (1964–70) was a dynamic, positive and ambitious leader, who relished the challenges before him; the second Harold (1974–76) was a weary, relatively uninterested leader, who had stayed too long as head of a party that was increasingly fractious. In between, and during his second stint of office, Wilson had to contend with a party on the verge of rupture. Wilson, often accused of deviousness, demonstrated his Machiavellian strategy to keep the Labour Party together during the 1975 referendum campaign by bending the constitutional rules. It worked, and the party did not tear itself apart; keeping the Labour Party united was yet another feat that was to elude other leaders.

---

461 Peter Hennessy, *The Prime Minister: The Office and its Holders since 1945*, London, Allen Lane, 2000, p. 365.

462 Ibid., p. 367.

If one is to judge Wilson's two tenures as Prime Minister – and the criticism levelled at him – then the fundamental factor governing the 1964–76 period is that of almost perpetual economic crisis. When Wilson became Prime Minister in 1964 and 1974, he inherited, on both occasions, the worst economic conditions since the war. Yet on both occasions – after what, admittedly, can be seen as serious policy errors – Wilson took decisions that set Britain on the road to recovery: restoring the UK's balance of payments to a healthy position by 1970, and introducing a counter-inflation policy that brought wages and prices under some sort of control by the time he left office in 1976. The perceived wisdom that Wilson should have devalued the pound upon entering Downing Street in 1964 does not stand up to detailed scrutiny: it is doubtful his government could have survived had he done so. As subsequent events showed, devaluation would have required severe deflation to succeed, and nearly all the advice to Wilson – from the Treasury, the Bank of England, the US Federal Reserve and the White House – was to oppose devaluation at all costs. In 1975, Wilson and Healey set in motion a credible counter-inflation policy (the IMF crisis after Wilson left office was produced by Treasury forecasts that were incorrect by billions).

If, on both occasions he left office, others made errors of judgement that led to economic shocks to the system, these errors cannot be laid at Wilson's door. Wilson's political tragedy, and that of the Labour Party, was that he was unable to lead his government and party in a period that would have allowed a better judgement of his leadership qualities. But, under huge political pressure, he did as well as any of his rivals might have done, or indeed did do subsequently. As Roy Jenkins observed:

> One of his great qualities was that he had a very good nerve in a crisis. He never recriminated in a crisis and he never panicked in a crisis, and those are two very high qualities in a Prime Minister. It was when things were going better that he got suspicious and difficult.[463]

---

463 Hennessy, op. cit., p. 362.

CHAPTER 14

JAMES CALLAGHAN

PETER KELLNER

James Callaghan became leader of the Labour Party and Prime Minister in 1976, following the shock resignation of Harold Wilson and his victory in the leadership election that followed. Callaghan defeated Michael Foot, Roy Jenkins, Tony Benn, Anthony Crosland and Denis Healey in the contest, which went to a third ballot of the parliamentary party. He remained leader for only three years, however, losing a vote of 'no confidence' in the House of Commons in March 1979. He was then defeated in the May 1979 general election by Margaret Thatcher's Conservatives, who claimed a seventy-seat majority. Peter Kellner argues that, although Callaghan could boast notable policy achievements as a minister, his time as party leader and Prime Minister was a failure. Callaghan inherited a government without a majority in the Commons, a divided party and a weak economy – and initially he weathered the early storms well. However, he then went on to make strategic errors in the second half of his premiership. Moreover, Callaghan was no great reforming leader, offering no great agenda for political change in Britain and little more than the aim of 'keeping the show on the road' for Labour.

• • •

James Callaghan's career can be summed up in two contrasting ways. One suggests towering success; the other, ultimate failure. On the one hand, he remains the only person ever to hold all four of the great offices of state (Prime Minister, Chancellor of the Exchequer, Home Secretary and Foreign Secretary), and he was also one of Labour's most effective politicians at winning party battles, including, at a low point in his premiership, holding a divided Cabinet together. On the other hand, he felt obliged to resign as Chancellor because of the humiliation of devaluation; he thwarted a major attempt to reform Labour's relations with the trade unions; and he lost the only general election he fought as party leader.

To make sense of Callaghan's record at the top of British politics, let us start by briefly tracing his journey to the summit. Born in 1912 and brought up in Portsmouth, he had the exam grades but not the money to go to university. Instead, he joined the Inland Revenue in 1929 as a clerk. He was soon active in the Inland Revenue Staff Federation (IRSF), becoming a full-time union official in 1936. One of his earliest challenges was to find common ground between left-wingers in the IRSF, who wanted to side with the Republicans in the Spanish Civil War, and those who opposed all union involvement in such matters. Callaghan brokered a deal under which the IRSF gave humanitarian aid, but nothing more. It was an early example of his ability to navigate successfully the shark-infested waters of factional left-of-centre politics.

In 1940, Callaghan volunteered for the Royal Navy. Though rising by 1944 to the rank of lieutenant, he saw little action – partly because he was diagnosed with tuberculosis and assigned, for the latter stages of the war, to desk duties in Whitehall. Back in Britain, he narrowly won selection as Labour's candidate for Cardiff South, which he captured from the Conservatives in the Labour landslide of 1945. Two years later, at the age of thirty-five, he joined Clement Attlee's government as a junior transport minister. In 1950, he moved to be parliamentary and financial secretary at the Treasury, where he spent a year, before Winston Churchill led the Conservatives back into government.

During Labour's thirteen years in opposition, Callaghan rose to become one of the party's leading figures in both the shadow Cabinet and the NEC. He also became one of the first politicians to embrace television; his fluent, avuncular manner was popular with viewers (at least television producers thought so, for they kept inviting him back). Callaghan was less popular with his fellow MPs. It wasn't that he was actively disliked; more that he developed only a limited body of strong enthusiasts. He came last in contests for both the deputy leadership in 1960 and, following Hugh Gaitskell's death in 1963, the party leadership.

However, Labour's new leader Harold Wilson confirmed Callaghan as shadow Chancellor (a post he had held since 1961), and, on winning the 1964 election, quickly appointed him to run the Treasury. Two early decisions greatly limited Callaghan's freedom of manoeuvre. The first, within hours of Labour returning to power, was the decision to maintain the value of sterling instead of responding to dire balance-of-payments figures by devaluing the pound. Throughout his three years at the helm of Britain's finances, Callaghan faced a succession of economic crises and the need to curb Labour's ambitions to increase public spending. Secondly, Wilson – who did not completely trust either Callaghan or the party's deputy leader George Brown – set up a new ministry, the DEA, to rival the Treasury. In the end, Callaghan saw off the DEA, which was eventually wound up in 1969. However, in the case of sterling, he could not defy the laws of economic gravity for ever. In November 1967, the pound was devalued, from US$2.80 to $2.40. Callaghan felt he had to step aside as Chancellor, not simply because of his failure to maintain his policy of sustaining the pound's value, but also because, in the frantic days leading up to devaluation, Callaghan had had to lie to Parliament, saying that devaluation was not being considered (when, in fact, plans for it were well advanced, but necessarily being kept secret).

Callaghan and Roy Jenkins swapped jobs, with Callaghan becoming Home Secretary. His two and a half years in that post were notable for three things: his decision to send British troops to Northern Ireland to deal with civil unrest; the imposition of major new curbs on immigration; and his opposition to a White Paper, 'In Place of Strife', intended to provide a new framework for trade union laws.

The troops decision might be regarded as one of the more fateful government decisions of the post-1945 era, given that the army spent three violent decades patrolling the province and becoming disliked by many in the nationalist communities. In 1969, however, they were seen as saviours in those communities: soldiers sent to protect people from the divisive policies and vicious policing of the province's Unionist government. Callaghan's strategy might have been flawed, but his motives were plainly decent.

The 1968 Commonwealth Immigrants Act was the opposite: highly controversial at the time; less so in the decades that followed. This was an era when the Conservative MP Enoch Powell was acquiring a large following, not least from many traditional working-class Labour voters, for his opposition to immigration. Into this toxic atmosphere came the prospect (to use a less emotive word than 'threat') of the arrival of large numbers of Kenyans from east Africa. Callaghan later justified the bill on the grounds that he needed to close a loophole in the existing rules in order to 'preserve a proper sense of order in this country'. In the circumstances, his was not necessarily an objectionable policy, even if he did sound like he was conjugating an irregular Latin verb: 'We preserve order'; 'You yield to popular emotions', 'They are dreadful racists'. Meanwhile, the new law enhanced Callaghan's public appeal.

Callaghan also courted controversy in his battles with Barbara Castle (Wilson's First Secretary of State and the government's Employment Secretary) over 'In Place of Strife'. At the heart of the White Paper was a proposal to require trade unions to hold proper ballots of their members before taking strike action. Callaghan, who had never lost his own union connections, sided with the leaders of the main trade unions, and led a Cabinet revolt against Castle. Eventually, Wilson and Castle were forced to back down. (Callaghan's relations with Castle never recovered. When he became Prime Minister in 1976, one of his first acts was to sack her as Health Secretary.)

Viewed from the vantage point of almost half a century later, Callaghan's stand seems somewhere between ridiculous and grotesque. Strike ballots became compulsory in the 1980s, and the principle behind them (as distinct from specific arguments about turnout rules) is now almost universally accepted. And, in the end, Callaghan himself may have regretted his stance, for the unreformed power of union leaderships played a significant role in Labour's defeat ten years later in 1979.

At the time, however, Callaghan strengthened his position within the labour movement – not just in the trade unions, but also in the (then large) segment of the Labour benches in Parliament that wanted no curbs on trade union power.

Though strong enough to challenge Wilson on policy, Callaghan did not feel strong enough to challenge the Prime Minister for his job. He was tempted, though: by then he despised Wilson – and so did Jenkins, who also wanted to move to 10 Downing Street. The trouble was that both Jenkins and Callaghan also hated each other, and both feared that, by moving against Wilson, they would end up handing power to their rival. That was why (as both men confirmed to me separately, many years later) they decided to tolerate Wilson instead of challenging him.

Callaghan's relations with Wilson softened during the years of opposition between 1970 and 1974. Callaghan declined to challenge Wilson for party leadership after the party's defeat in 1970; and when Jenkins resigned as Labour's deputy leader in 1972 because of Wilson's caution on Europe, Callaghan was content to toe the party line. Callaghan received his reward on Labour's return to power in 1974, when Wilson appointed him Foreign Secretary. More vitally, shortly before Christmas 1975, Wilson told Callaghan that he intended to step down on his sixtieth birthday the following spring – a secret Wilson kept from the rest of his Cabinet.

This advance warning allowed Callaghan to burnish his image with his party, and the wider public, as an experienced and capable national – indeed, international – leader. He had already sought to quell crises (such as Turkey's invasion of Cyprus, and the simmering issue of confronting South Africa over its apartheid policies), rather than take big risks, and he used every opportunity to show himself as a reliable friend, if not true equal, of the US Secretary of State Henry Kissinger. With the US finally pulling out of Vietnam in 1975, this association caused less trouble inside the Labour Party than it might have done some years earlier. While Callaghan's future rivals for Labour's leadership – who did not, at this time, know of Wilson's plans to step down – fought often narrow battles in Westminster, Callaghan occupied the world stage, apparently effortlessly. By the time Wilson announced his resignation, Callaghan was unstoppable.

Knowing this, Callaghan fought perhaps the most remarkable campaign of anyone seeking the leadership of a major party in a democracy. That is, he did not campaign at all – at least, not openly. He delivered no speeches and made no promises. In order to impress the relevant electorate – his fellow Labour MPs – he simply carried on as Foreign Secretary. On one of the days leading up to the first ballot, he dominated the news: first by welcoming Andrei Gromyko, the Soviet Foreign Minister, to London; then by standing at the despatch box in the House of Commons to warn the white rebels running Rhodesia (Zimbabwe) that they were leading their country towards 'death and destruction'.

It took Callaghan three ballots to see off his five rivals. His fellow Welsh MP Michael Foot – the runner-up, who had, in fact, led narrowly in the first ballot – subsequently became deputy party leader.

In order to assess Callaghan's three years as Prime Minister, we must take full account of the political and economic conditions he inherited. Labour had returned to office in March 1974, seventeen seats short of an overall majority. A second election, in October 1974, produced an overall majority of just three – Labour won 319 seats out of 635. A by-election loss in June 1975 reduced the majority to just one by the time Callaghan became Prime Minister. Governing at all was an uncertain business, not least because of the power of Labour's left wing – far greater then than it is today. Governing became even harder when Labour lost four further by-elections and its majority in just over a year. Callaghan was destined to pay far more attention than most twentieth-century prime ministers to the daily challenge of winning votes in the House of Commons.

Britain's economy was also weak. Inflation, though down from its mid-1975 peak of almost 30 per cent, was still well over 10 per cent. So were mortgage rates. Unemployment was 1,500,000 – then considered scandalously high – and rising. The pound had just fallen below $2 for the first time ever.[464]

---

464 In the early 1970s, a floating system of exchange rates had been established. This replaced the previous regime of fixed rates.

The numbers, both parliamentary and economic, would haunt Callaghan throughout his premiership.

Tactically, he handled both with great skill, until the final few months. The government did not fall until almost five years after the October 1974 election, and Callaghan contained the huge tensions that Britain's struggling economy provoked inside his party and Cabinet. There was much loose talk in the '70s of Britain – 'the sick man of Europe' – being ungovernable. This economic sickness was hard to refute, but government carried on. I was a young journalist on the *Sunday Times*. Frequently, my jewelled prose was distributed to only parts of Britain, or not at all, because of industrial (in) action by the print unions. For twelve months, starting in late 1978, *The Times* and *Sunday Times* were off the streets altogether. Frustrating? Absolutely. A breakdown in civil society? Not really. Strikes in this and other sectors should not be confused with ungovernability, just as a bad cold should not be confused with terminal cancer.

Callaghan's first serious crisis as Prime Minister erupted in September 1976. It occurred during Labour's annual conference in Blackpool. On the Tuesday, in his first conference speech as party leader, Callaghan announced the end of Keynesianism – or, to be more precise, its simplified version. In one of his two most celebrated remarks (the other came during the winter of discontent), Callaghan said: 'We used to think that you could spend your way out of a recession, and increase employment by cutting taxes and boosting government spending. I tell you in all candour that that option no longer exists.'

These words, drafted by Peter Jay, Callaghan's son-in-law, were controversial enough. Worse was to follow within hours. Denis Healey, the Chancellor, had left the conference to attend another one in Hong Kong, but had to turn back at Heathrow to deal with the sterling crisis that was erupting. The news overshadowed the conference, for it seemed to threaten the government's entire economic strategy. To calm frayed party nerves, Healey spoke to the conference; however, under the unbending party procedures of the day, he had to do so as an ordinary party delegate for a maximum of three minutes. Healey was at his combative best, but, sweating under the hot lights of the Winter Garden as he made his way through a scrum of delegates, he looked like a man in trouble – which, of course, he was. (He was also voted off Labour's NEC that week – a decision that did nothing to enhance his or the party's reputation.)

That episode provided only the overture to weeks of fraught negotiation between Healey and the IMF, and within the Cabinet. An IMF team came to London and insisted on sharp cuts in public spending as the price for a big enough loan to allow the UK to overcome its crisis. Callaghan realised that he could not simply steamroller his Cabinet. Critics of the IMF included not only Tony Benn, the left-wing Energy Secretary, but also Anthony Crosland, the Foreign Secretary, whose objection was not that of a left-winger but of a continuing believer in Keynesian economics. Peter Shore, the Environment Secretary, also opposed cuts – he was, like Crosland, a committed Keynesian, but, unlike Crosland, a firm opponent of British membership of the common market, too. Benn and Shore proposed an 'alternative strategy', including reflation and import controls. In their different ways, Benn, Crosland and Shore were not only big-hitters; they represented significant strands of thinking within the party.

Callaghan held a series of extra Cabinet meetings, at which he encouraged the arguments to be aired in full. In the end, Crosland decided that loyalty at such a fraught moment trumped everything. He understood that the consequences of his resignation would be catastrophic, so instead fell in line with Callaghan and Healey. Shore and Benn also submitted eventually to the, by now overwhelming, Cabinet majority. The Cabinet agreed to the IMF terms. Callaghan had managed the politics of the situation with skill and sensitivity.

In due course, it became clear that the spending cuts were not needed: Britain's economy and the government's finances had already turned the corner. In any event, by the end of the year, the crisis had passed.

The public mood took longer to lift. From the day Callaghan became Prime Minister in April 1976 until Labour's dramatic conference week almost six months later, the party was roughly level-pegging with the Conservatives. Afterwards, the Tories went into a clear lead. Between November 1976 and April 1977, the Conservatives gained four seats in by-elections and Labour lost its Commons majority. To continue governing, Labour needed to reach beyond its ranks.

Fortunately, the Liberals were receptive to an approach. They were in trouble for a completely separate reason. In May 1976, their leader Jeremy Thorpe resigned amid a scandal that led to his trial, in 1979, for conspiracy to murder male model Norman Scott. (Thorpe and his co-defendants were all acquitted, but the political damage had been done.) The Liberals' new leader David Steel would eventually become an electoral asset, but, at the time of Callaghan's IMF crisis, his party was doing badly in polls and by-elections. The last thing Steel wanted was for the government to collapse and provoke a fresh general election. Callaghan and Steel needed each other – and, in March 1977, they agreed to a Lib–Lab pact, whereby Labour ministers would agree to consult with their Liberal counterparts on economic strategy or before major decisions. In return, the Liberals announced they would support the government in any vote of confidence.

The arrangement fell well short of a coalition – there were no Liberal ministers – but, for the first time since 1931, a British Prime Minister relied for his political survival on a party not in government. Logically, neither Steel nor Callaghan had much alternative; however, negotiations were smoothed by a good personal relationship. Again, Callaghan managed the tactics of a sensitive situation with great skill.

The pact continued until August 1978. By that time, the parliament was almost four years old. The economy had stabilised. Inflation was down, and real wages were rising again. Labour had recovered in the polls. Callaghan was widely expected to call an autumn election, and the Liberals felt they needed time to re-establish their distinct personality.

However, Callaghan defied expectations and announced in early September that there would be no autumn election. He feared that Labour would be unable to secure a clear victory, and hoped that another six or twelve months would entrench the recovery in both the economy and Labour's fortunes. Meanwhile, there would be little final-year legislation, and (he calculated) Labour would be able to survive as a minority government. In the light of what subsequently happened, this proved to be a serious misjudgement (rather like Gordon Brown's decision not to call an election soon after he became Prime Minister in June 2007). But, at the time, it was more defensible.

Callaghan's larger and less defensible misjudgement concerned wage controls. Between 1974 and 1978, the government had sought to restrain wages in cooperation with the trade unions. The policy had largely succeeded, but, by 1978, it was fraying. In January 1978, Callaghan had suggested a 5 per cent limit for wage rises in the 1978–79 pay round. At a time when inflation was nearer 10 per cent, a number of union leaders said this was unrealistic. Within weeks of Callaghan announcing there would be no election in the autumn of 1978, the policy began to unravel. It was rejected on a card vote at Labour's annual conference. Then workers at the Ford Motor Company went on strike when the company offered a pay rise in line with Callaghan's policy. After three weeks, Ford capitulated and gave its workers a 15 per cent raise.

As the first major settlement of the winter pay round, Ford's decision presented Callaghan with an acute dilemma: should he continue an essentially voluntary strategy, and risk his pay policy disintegrating, or should he ask Parliament for powers to impose it, and risk the hostility of the unions? He chose the second option. But, with the Lib–Lab pact having ended, he did not have the votes to get his way. On 13 December, by 285 votes to 283, MPs rejected his proposal to give the government powers to impose sanctions on employers who breached the 5 per cent limit.

This was bad enough, but worse was to follow. Other employers agreed double-digit pay deals, including the BBC with its technicians. One anonymous government aide was quoted as saying: 'We sold our pay policy to have *The Sound of Music* on Christmas Day.' The New Year witnessed walkouts and aggressive picketing by lorry drivers, oil-tanker drivers, ambulance drivers and a wide range of local government workers. Petrol stations ran out of fuel; rubbish was uncollected; bodies went unburied.

On 10 January, on his return from a global economic summit on the Caribbean island of Guadeloupe, Callaghan's normal facility for wise and soothing words deserted him. Amid a scrum of journalists, microphones and cameras, he was asked about the 'mounting chaos' in Britain. He replied: 'Well, that's a judgement that you are making. I promise you that if you look at it from outside, and perhaps you're taking rather a parochial view at the moment, I don't think that other people in the world would share the view that there is mounting chaos.'

In a way, he was right: compared with the acute poverty, disease and starvation in much of the world, Britain remained relatively well off. But to his domestic audience it sounded horribly complacent. The following morning, *The Sun* encapsulated his response with its celebrated headline: 'Crisis, What Crisis?'

From then on, the government's only practical option was to surrender on the best terms it could. On 21 February, local government workers settled for a 9 per cent increase, broadly matching inflation. A similar deal for hospital workers soon followed. A new, fine-sounding, but not easily enforceable concordat was agreed with the TUC, covering picketing, the closed shop and strike ballots. But, in contrast to the commitment of Margaret Thatcher, the Conservative leader, for tough trade union reform, Callaghan's position looked feeble.

Opinion polls added to the government's humiliation. The Conservatives jumped from level-pegging to a twenty-point lead. Thatcher's ratings overtook Callaghan's. The government's reputation for handling the economy, employment, the cost of living and even health care slumped.

Callaghan had one hope left: he could remain in office until the autumn (the latest possible date for a general election was October 1979), and use the spring and summer to restore his fortunes. But, given that he now led a minority government, this depended on sufficient support from minority parties.

His hope was badly dented by Scotland's voters on 1 March. A referendum on devolution had been promised following the Scottish National Party's breakthrough in October 1974, when it won seven seats. The referendum legislation required not only that more people vote 'yes' than 'no', but that the total 'yes' vote had to be at least 40 per cent of the total electorate.

In the event, 33 per cent voted 'yes', 31 per cent 'no', and 36 per cent did not vote. The 'yes' vote was not large enough for devolution to go ahead. Bitterly disappointed by this outcome, the SNP announced it would vote against the government in a vote of confidence. Thatcher duly tabled a confidence motion, which was debated on 28 March. Despite gaining the support of three Welsh nationalists and two Ulster unionists, Labour was defeated by a single vote: 311–310.

Callaghan was forced to call an immediate general election and, on 4 May, Thatcher became Prime Minister. Labour would not return to government for eighteen years.

How, then, should we assess Callaghan's three years as Prime Minister? Were we to stop the clock at the midway point, in the autumn of 1977, we would be able to list items on both the credit and debit side.

On the credit side: Callaghan held his Cabinet and party together during a period of exceptionally tough political and economic conditions. With Healey, he had steered the economy towards calmer waters. He had worked with the main trade union leaders to bring down inflation. He had gradually gained widespread public respect. In October 1977, Gallup found that 59 per cent approved of Callaghan's performance as Prime Minister – a figure Thatcher would never match, even in her moment of victory at the end of the Falklands War.

On the debit side: Callaghan had done little to tackle the underlying problems of Britain's economy and changing society. Trade unions remained unreformed. Strikes could be called far too easily. Nationalised industries remained lumbering, inefficient giants. Council house tenants were unable to buy their homes. Taxes stayed high. Callaghan seemed to be stuck in the mindset with which he had entered Parliament in 1945, when the way to improve the lives of workers lay in collective provision and social protection, rather than the increasing wish of Labour voters to make their own way in the world, with their own cars, homes and foreign holidays.

Whether the credit or debit side was more impressive is a matter of judgement. However, the second half of Callaghan's premiership surely tips the overall scale to the debit side. On pay policy, his relations with the unions, and his decision not to call an election in the autumn of 1978, Callaghan's tactical prowess deserted him. He had a perfectly honourable argument for not reforming the unions – that more good could be done through cooperation than confrontation – but that argument depended on cooperation delivering the goods. In the winter of discontent, it failed spectacularly to do so. In the general election of 1979, the biggest swing against Labour was among skilled workers. Even though most of them were trade union members, they increasingly resented the power of union leaders, and they were attracted by Thatcher's vision of lower taxes, council house sales and trade union reform.

But behind the tactical failures of Callaghan's final months as Prime Minister lay something more fundamental. He seemed to regard his wish to keep the show on the road, in terms of both party management and economic policy, as an end in itself.

Let's imagine that Callaghan had: (a) proposed a more flexible pay policy in 1978; and (b) called, and won, a general election that autumn. Would Callaghan have then launched the radical reforms Britain's economy needed? A pro-Callaghan optimist might argue that he would have been compelled to do so by the changing character of Britain's economy and society, that he would have made the changes in a far more consensual way than Thatcher did, and that Britain would have reached the end of the 1980s with an economy just as flexible as the one it did, but achieved with far less unemployment and social division.

The trouble with this happy, counter-factual history is that there is nothing in Callaghan's career to suggest that, given the time and the chance, he would have been a great reforming Prime Minister.

He was a steady-as-we-go leader, seeking to heal wounds rather than amputate limbs. At other times, such steadiness could have been a great virtue: it is no mean skill, or ambition, to bring a nation together. Callaghan's misfortune was to reach the top of the greasy pole at a time when that was not enough. When Attlee lost in 1951, after six years as Prime Minister, he did so having won the big arguments of the time – those about the character of post-war

Britain. His reforms endured. When Callaghan lost office in 1979, he could make no such claim. Labour was a party that had not only lost votes, but lost the argument about the role of the state. It took a decade for the party to come fully to terms with this fact, and further years in opposition to persuade voters that it had come to terms with modern Britain and the reforms of the Thatcher era.

A more plausible defence of Callaghan's premiership is that he had no real alternative. Given the political and economic conditions he inherited, any attempt to be more radical would have led to imminent disaster, with the unions turning hostile and the left–right tensions inside the Labour Party provoking a formal party split. At least Callaghan avoided that fate – or, perhaps, deferred it until the creation of the Social Democratic Party (SDP) in 1981. The conclusion from that counter-factual perspective is not that Callaghan's failings let him, Labour and Britain down, but that the circumstances of his premiership made true success, in the form of both electoral success and reforming economic strategy, utterly impossible.

In the end, Callaghan's premiership was a failure. The debate that may never be finally settled is how to allocate blame for that failure: to his own shortcomings, to the hand he was dealt, or to a mixture of both?

Towards the end of his life, Callaghan himself offered an intriguing insight into his own career. I asked him what achievement, looking back, gave him his greatest satisfaction. He replied, without hesitation, that he was proudest of his decision to install cat's eyes in roads throughout Britain when he was a junior transport minister in the late 1940s. These clever, cheap, low-tech devices reflect light back from vehicles' headlamps at night, and so enable drivers to see the side and centre of roads in murky conditions at night. Cat's eyes have saved countless lives down the decades. I think he knew he could make no such claim for anything he did as Prime Minister.

CHAPTER 15

MICHAEL FOOT

KENNETH O. MORGAN

Michael Foot, from a famous West Country Liberal family, was the first Labour Member of Parliament to be elected for Plymouth Devonport in 1945, which he held until 1955. He returned to Parliament in 1960 for Ebbw Vale, after the death of its MP Aneurin Bevan. After decades as a backbencher, he served as a minister in the Wilson and Callaghan governments of 1974–79, before being elected leader in the wake of the 1979 general election defeat, thus opposing the newly elected Prime Minister Margaret Thatcher at the despatch box. Under Foot, Labour led in the national opinion polls during the first two years: in December 1980, MORI gave the party a 24 per cent lead over the Conservatives. The lead crumbled after that point, however, in the aftermath of the Falklands War and in an improving economy. Labour suffered a huge electoral defeat in 1983. Kenneth O. Morgan shows that Foot's period of party leadership was therefore an unhappy and very unsuccessful one. But, in Foot's defence, he faced internal party challenges that few other Labour leaders in history could have resolved. Instead, Morgan argues, we should look elsewhere for Foot's major contribution to the party's leadership: he wrote many texts that provided intellectual inspiration (including the famous pamphlet 'Guilty Men' in 1940 and a two-volume biography of Nye Bevan); he was a remarkable communicator in the press and on the platform; he carried through legislation as a minister in the '70s that strengthened trade unions and improved workers' living conditions. He also pioneered devolution. He may have contributed little to Labour's winning or retaining power, but his contribution to the party and the socialist movement in cultural, historical and other respects was substantial.

• • •

The words 'Michael Foot' and 'leadership' appear to have little connection with each other. Foot's entire career suggests a politician of protest, not one at ease with operating power. Before 1974, he had never held any position of public responsibility – and he was, at that time, nearly sixty-one. Until then, as a journalist from 1938 and then as an MP (with one interval) after 1945, he had essentially been a critic – frequently of the Labour Party's leadership. He was a major figure in every dissident body – Keep Left, the Bevanites, the Tribune Group, the Campaign for Nuclear Disarmament (CND) – and, in 1961, he was expelled from the PLP for voting against the whips on the issue of nuclear weapons and army estimates. He seemed to be a permanent rebel – with or without a cause. He did not look or sound like a credible leader, though. Peter Jenkins wrote a sharp vignette denouncing Foot – his clothes shabby, his hair untidy, his facts wrong – as the very symbol of permanent opposition. When he was leader, he was derided in *Private Eye* as the television character 'Worzel Gummidge'. Nothing did his image more harm than his appearance at the Cenotaph on Remembrance Sunday in November 1981, when he was dressed in an unusual coat, described in the tabloid press as a donkey jacket, worn by manual workers. It was, in fact, a smart new coat, bought for him by his wife Jill, and it did meet with the warm commendation of one of Foot's friends, the Queen Mother: 'That's a nice warm coat you've got there, Michael.'[465] The damage was done, though.

There were critics within Foot's own party too, like the former whip Walter Harrison, who attacked the bohemian *litterateur* of a leader for looking 'like an out-of-work navvy', when the other party leaders were in their Sunday best. Foot often seemed most at home not in mundane politics, but in erudite talk on his favourite authors – notably Swift, Hazlitt and Byron. In the

465 Interview with Michael Foot: he and the Queen Mother had a shared interest in dogs, especially Tibetan Terriers and Welsh Corgis.

disastrous 1983 general election campaign, a high point for Foot came when a young student brought him a copy of *Gulliver's Travels* to sign.

Foot had become party leader most unexpectedly. After Labour's election defeat in 1970, he had agreed, with encouragement from Harold Wilson, to run for the shadow Cabinet, and became spokesman for fuel and power, moving on to industrial relations more generally. When Labour narrowly returned to government in March 1974, Wilson, on the advice of Jack Jones, made Foot Secretary of State for Employment. Here he proved to be surprisingly effective, confounding civil service prophecies and passing no fewer than six pieces of major legislation. When Wilson resigned unexpectedly in March 1976, Foot felt compelled to stand for leadership as the main spokesman for the old left of the party, and he polled well, coming in a strong second to Jim Callaghan. Over the next three years, he was to serve Callaghan with exemplary loyalty as deputy leader, especially in championing an incomes policy he had for decades resisted. It added significantly to his stature in the party. But it was not anticipated that he would stand for the leadership in October 1980 when Callaghan resigned, since Peter Shore was in the field as a supposed left-wing candidate and was very hostile to membership of Europe. However, Michael did stand – characteristically announcing his candidature on returning from Dublin, where he had been lecturing in St Patrick's Cathedral on the topic of Jonathan Swift. In a strong field, Foot, to much surprise, came home with 139 votes to 129 for the front-runner Denis Healey. Labour's lurch to the left was thus confirmed, though it was at least the old left of Bevanite memory, not the extra-parliamentary hard left of Benn and Militant Tendency.

Precisely why Foot broke the habits of a lifetime and stood for the leadership in 1980 was much debated by journalists. Clearly there were many among his colleagues – not only soft-left figures like Neil Kinnock, but many of the centre, such as Bruce Grocott – who felt that an amiable, emollient figure like Foot would have a healing effect on his fractious comrades. By contrast, the brilliant but abrasive Denis Healey had no close group of friends or supporters, and his talent for ripe personal abuse had done him no favours. In the leadership vote, it was known that at least three MPs who were shortly to join the SDP (Tom Ellis, Neville Sandelson and Jeffrey Thomas) deliberately voted for Foot in the hope that it would speed up the disintegration of the Labour Party and leave the way open for a new party of the moderate left to emerge. One factor at very close hand was the encouragement of his devoted wife Jill, who had her own understandable ambitions for her gifted but ageing husband in the latter stages of his career.

But the decisive factor was surely neither the persuasion of parliamentary colleagues nor encouragement from Jill, but rather pressure from Foot's leading backers in Labour ranks, namely the trade union leaders with whom he had worked so closely at the Department for Employment. Clive Jenkins, Moss Evans, Bill Keys and even the right-of-centre David Basnett all backed Foot as the custodian of the social contract with the unions, and at least as a caretaker leader before someone younger (Benn, many hoped) could take over.

Dick Clements, editor of *Tribune* – walking down Pilgrims Lane in Hampstead, where Foot lived – saw Clive Jenkins of the Association of Scientific, Technical and Managerial Staffs (ASTMS) walking the other way, carrying a bunch of fuchsias.[466] Jenkins bearing fuchsias meant that something was up. And so Foot accepted the poisoned chalice and was duly elected with a majority of just ten votes. As is all too well known, his subsequent period of leadership to May 1983 was an unhappy and supremely unsuccessful one. Beginning with a strong lead in the opinion polls (Conservative support stood at only 27 per cent in March 1981 – a time of monetarist finance and rapidly rising unemployment), Labour fortunes soon went into swift decline. After a tormented period with an almost ungovernable Labour Party – riven first by the defection of over twenty MPs to the new SDP and then savage internal battles over policy and the deselection of candidates, led by Militant Tendency and a variety of other left-wing groups encouraged by Tony Benn – Foot's leadership was constantly under challenge. His resignation was anticipated in the press, as it was clear the public had no confidence in him

466 Interview with Dick Clements, 16 November 2004.

as a conceivable Prime Minister. He ended up, in 1983, with Mrs Thatcher triumphant at the polls, Labour getting their worst result in terms of seats (209) since 1931, and the party balloting its worst proportion of the vote since it had come into being as a coherent national party in 1918 (28.3 per cent). Its share of the vote was only slightly above that of the fledgling Liberal–SDP alliance, although it was a margin thought to be decisive in the future. Commentators like the Marxist historian Eric Hobsbawm encouraged the belief that Labour was in long-term, inexorable decline.

Foot was widely thought to be the main reason for this decline. That is perhaps not wholly fair. There were signs in the opinion polls through late 1982 that the economy was showing evidence of recovery, partly because the Thatcher government began to moderate some of the more extreme aspects of its monetarist policy, and unemployment began to fall. Some of its policies, such as the sale of council houses, were undeniably popular. This, naturally, was reflected in growing support for the government. In addition, victory in the Falklands War was a huge bonus for Mrs Thatcher. Whatever the shortcomings that led to war in the first place, she had shown a steely resolve in military command that was inconceivable from an old 'peacemonger' like Michael Foot. In the background, as noted above, the Labour Party at this period in its history was in a deep trough of internecine conflict and ideological division. Militant Tendency, with covert support from the Bennites (many of whom re-emerged as pristine centrists under New Labour in 1997), was an immense handicap for the Labour Party on the doorstep, as the present writer can testify: he witnessed an apparently impregnable Labour stronghold in Oxford East being lost to the Conservatives. To the wider public, the Labour Party appeared hopelessly divided, and was felt to be unelectable. The vicious contest for deputy leadership between Healey and Benn in 1981 was a particular low point, and would have undermined any leader. Nor was Foot helped by a feeble campaign committee, which seemed to lack all sense of political reality at times. Thus, Foot and his young assistant Sue Nye were sent to confront a rowdy posse of fox-hunters in Yorkshire – a category of electors it would have been unimaginable to see ever becoming Labour voters.

The leadership was, of course, saddled with a hopeless, over-long election manifesto – the notorious 'longest suicide note', in Gerald Kaufman's words, that highlighted policies such as mass nationalisation, departure from Europe, and unilateral nuclear disarmament, all of which were certain vote-losers.

But Foot's own leadership cannot be acquitted either. His style and approach, declamatory and bookish at the same time, seemed hopelessly out of date in the modern hi-tech age of political campaigning. On economic themes, he seemed particularly weak. In a meeting in Oxford town hall, before a large audience of enthusiastic young voters, he went on at some length recalling the famous 'Munich' Oxford by-election, won by Quintin Hogg (later Lord Hailsham, serving in Mrs Thatcher's government) – an event that occurred many years before most of the audience were even born. Because of episodes such as this, Bob Worcester of MORI believed that Labour would never have won under Foot, anywhere, at any time. After the results were declared, Foot departed as he had arrived: at the behest of trade union leaders. Clive Jenkins and Moss Evans told him he had to go, and he pushed off. Jenkins told his ASTMS executive the next day, before it was public knowledge. Michael, Clive Jenkins and their wives then went off to the cinema to see a political satire dealing with the re-writing of history after the Falklands War.[467] It was not an unfitting epitaph on the long twilight of Foot's career.

Clearly, Michael Foot's contribution to Labour leadership did not lie in his role as formal party leader between 1980 and 1983 but has to be found elsewhere. Indeed, there are many notable long-term achievements. First, were Foot's books. He wrote twenty in all, of varying length and varying style, of which the most thorough by far was *The Pen and the Sword*, a serious and compelling study of the politics of Queen Anne's reign, as seen through the role of Swift in bringing about the downfall of the mighty Duke of Marlborough. But that was for scholars. Two others stand out as most important in the history of the Labour Party.

---

467 Kenneth O. Morgan, *Michael Foot: A Life*, London, Harper Press, 2007, pp. 434–5.

Firstly, there was his devastating pamphlet, 'Guilty Men',[468] penned – under the pseudonym Cato – in harness with Frank Owen and Peter Howard in three days of early June 1940 (during the London Blitz and just after the fall of Dunkirk). Written in personal, polemical style, it proved to be a sensation – the most effective political tract since the days of John Wilkes. It went through seven reprints very rapidly, and sold 220,000 copies in all for its publisher Victor Gollancz.[469] It was a ferocious attack on the appeasers of the 1930s, especially Stanley Baldwin and Neville Chamberlain. It was also a highly selective attack, since it totally omitted at least two of Foot's heroes: David Lloyd George, who had visited Hitler in Berchtesgaden in 1936 and called him the 'George Washington of Germany'; and Max Aitken (Lord Beaverbrook), Foot's patron and employer at the *Evening Standard* and a passionate supporter of the policy of appeasement until well after Munich. Towards Chamberlain, umbrella and all, Foot and the others made no attempt to be fair. For the rest of time, the Prime Minister and his colleagues were to be identified as symbols of folly and cowardice; their military failures in Norway and at Dunkirk were mercilessly exposed. The stereotype stuck.

Ironically, Bush and Blair, at the time of the Iraq invasion in 2003, were some of those who turned to the 1930s as pointing to the moral of the follies of appeasing dictators. More directly, it meant that patriotism in foreign policy, however unjustifiably, was appropriated as a theme by Labour, whose own approach towards re-armament and collective security had been very hesitant throughout the '30s. This served the party well. Foot – a pacific man but not a pacifist, fired by childhood memories of stories of the freeborn seamen of Plymouth and the West Country, defending England against foreign threat from the Spanish Armada – could, when he wished, bang Drake's Drum, even when acting as leader of the CND. During the Falklands invasion in 1982, Foot was to make his last notable parliamentary speech in denouncing

468 Cato, 'Guilty Men', London, V. Gollancz, June 1940. This was written under the pseudonym 'Cato' by Michael Foot, Frank Owen and Peter Howard.

469 Morgan, op. cit., 2007, pp. 76–80.

the Thatcher government's feebleness, and calling for the Falkland islanders to be protected by British arms. He even defended the highly controversial sinking of the Argentine cruiser the *Belgrano*. Since Labour has always been thought to be weakest on foreign and defence issues, the impact of 'Guilty Men' (and the moral imperatives of the patriotism it conveyed) has been salutary indeed.

Foot's other notable book was his brilliant two-volume biography of Aneurin Bevan.[470] Like 'Guilty Men', it is an unashamedly partisan book. Bevan emerges as a kind of Celtic giant – like something from the medieval saga of the *Mabinogion*. His death in 1960 is chronicled as the fall of a mighty oak, hacked down wantonly in full leaf. It is far from being a wholly reliable book, especially its second volume, where Foot's personal hostility towards Gaitskell makes Bevan more resistant to the leadership of the party than was actually the case. Through his life, Foot was reluctant to see in the Wykehamist Gaitskell anything other than a traitor to socialism, which was, in fact, a parody.

Foot's account of Bevan as a socialist tribune in his early years, and especially his pioneering creation of the National Health Service, is a magnificent account of heroic achievement. Most of all, Foot's book, as perhaps no other Labour biography does, conveys, in vivid terms, what it means to be a socialist and what the values and aspirations of that elusive creed really are. Its impact on the political sensibilities of the British left has been incalculable.

'Guilty Men' and the life of Bevan are Foot's two major literary contributions to his party and its message. But perhaps a brief word might be spared too for *Debts of Honour*,[471] a study of miscellaneous radicals (including his father Isaac, Conservatives like Disraeli and Randolph Churchill, a duchess, and even a dog) that is a literary *tour de force*. It appeared in 1982, following his retirement as party leader, and is a work worth recalling now. Some scorn was expressed when my book[472] showed the young Tony Blair, the recently

---

470 Michael Foot, *Aneurin Bevan: A Biography*, London, MacGibbon & Kee, 1963.

471 Michael Foot, *Debts of Honour*, New York, Harper & Row, 1981.

472 Morgan, op. cit., 2007.

defeated candidate at Beaconsfield in May 1982, writing to Foot in praise of his book's merits and inspirational quality. To me, it is a rather touching letter by an enthusiastic, naive young man, searching for a political faith, and seeing in Foot's book the kind of humane, non-Marxist creed of ethical socialism for which he was searching – 'a treasure trove of ideas that I never imagined existed'.[473] Foot took books very seriously; like his father, he was a voracious bibliophile and a far more prolific author. Respect for his writing, from whatever source, would have been immensely satisfying to him.

Secondly, Foot was a remarkable communicator at all levels: on the public platform; at demos; and certainly in Parliament. He could be a wonderful performer in the Commons, with powerfully effective speeches to his credit on the House of Lords (non-)reform and the Falklands invasion. Indeed, it was a brilliantly funny Commons speech in October 1980 that helped him towards leadership. He compared Sir Keith Joseph with a conjurer from his childhood at the Palace Theatre, Plymouth, who had smashed the watch of a member of the audience, and then confessed: 'I am very sorry. I have forgotten the rest of the trick.'[474] Essentially, he was a maverick freelancer on the back benches: many of his Commons triumphs were won at the expense of his own party leaders, as when he scuppered the House of Lords reform (in partnership with Enoch Powell) in 1969. But Foot's powers of communication came over above all through the written word. He took over, and enhanced, *Tribune* after 1945, when its reputation was already very high after its distinguished wartime years. For half a century thereafter, it became a uniquely influential crusading organ for the Labour left – a voice for Bevanite socialism, colonial freedom and nuclear disarmament. From 1958 onwards, its banner headline read: 'The paper that wants to ban the bomb' – which some readers felt might be taking an *idée fixe* rather too far. It prided itself, under Foot's editorship, for its high literary quality. Earlier on, Foot was able to call on writers like George Orwell and Arthur Koestler to grace its pages.

---

473 Blair to Foot, 28 July 1982 (Foot Papers, private).

474 Hansard, 5th ser., 991, col. 601–9, 29 October 1980.

Foot contributed massively to the free press because he believed in it. He was a lifelong member of the National Union of Journalists. He thus came under fire for his 1975 Industrial Relations Bill, which suggested imposing a closed shop on newspapers and periodicals, with critics claiming it would restrict the civil freedom of journalists. Foot took up arms against this charge. He argued that, on the contrary, it would strengthen journalists and their collective rights against their employers. He debated these issues at close quarters with newspaper proprietors, journalists and lawyers, and argued them down successfully. He felt he had been able to show that the issue was really about extending journalists' rights in restraint of trade, as they had traditionally existed since 1871, and therefore defending their professional status.[475] In his confrontation with the newspaper bosses, backed by the House of Lords, Foot proved to be the best communicator of them all.

Thirdly, Foot played a very important role in the Labour governments of the 1970s. He gave, in his own way, new force to the solidarity of the movement, especially the links between the parliamentary party and the trade union movement (Keir Hardie's Labour Alliance thus attained its most tangible form). Foot's industrial legislation at the Department for Employment in 1974–76 was highly controversial, but it had long-term legacies: an effective Health and Safety Act; enduring conciliation services; and measures to assist with race relations and sex discrimination in the workplace. His two major industrial relations measures – the Trade Union and Labour Relations Act 1974, and the Employment Protection Act 1975 – passed after much contention in both Houses of Parliament. They owed much to the learned labour lawyer Professor Bill Wedderburn, and were praised by Lord Scarman in the High Court for making much clearer the legal framework for industrial relations. He stated that it fulfilled the original intention of Campbell-Bannerman's Trade Disputes Act of 1906.[476] The Conservative front-bench spokesman – the studiously moderate James Prior – declared that Foot's Trade Union and

475 Lord Wedderburn, *The Worker and the Law*, London, Sweet & Maxwell, 1986, pp. 586ff.

476 Discussions with Lord Wedderburn, 2005.

Labour Relations Act would henceforth serve as 'the basis for labour law'. His performance as a minister won the strong respect and moral support of his civil servants, who also felt great affection for him. Much of Foot's time in government thereafter was spent battling with increasingly undisciplined trade unions, trying to maintain a prices and incomes policy, and prevent wage inflation running riot. The replacement of the commanding Jack Jones with the mediocre Moss Evans as general secretary of the TGWU left the government at a huge disadvantage. The winter of discontent proved to be a hard, disillusioning experience for Foot, as for James Callaghan, and their defeat led directly to the triumph of Thatcherism in the 1979 general election and onwards.

Much of Foot's legislation was emasculated by the Thatcher government, and the Blair/Brown governments after 1997 showed no inclination to bring it back. It was noticeable that New Labour reviewers of my biography of Michael Foot, while generous about the book in general, actually welcomed the diminution of trade union power and the marginalisation of the trade unions that took place under Labour governments as much as Conservative. The result has been that this legislative about-turn, along with the impact of ferocious depression and heavy unemployment after 2010, has led to much weaker trade unions being seriously marginalised in our society. Writers like Will Hutton have linked the undermining of the unions with the soaring growth of inequality in Britain, far greater than in most other industrialised countries. The rights and opportunities for working people have been sacrificed by the Tories and New Labour alike, through 'the reduction of trade union power in the name of promoting free market flexibility'.

The Frenchman Thomas Piketty's influential work *Capital* has linked the inexorable inequality that a low-growth capitalist economy generates with the declining power of organised labour in the last forty years. Keynes's hope for a fairer, more equal capitalism is no longer feasible, because inherited wealth inevitably grows faster than output and income.[477] The loss of

477 Will Hutton in *The Observer*, 19 January 2014; Thomas Piketty, *Capital in the Twenty-First Century*, Cambridge MA, Harvard University Press, 2014, passim.

Foot's beneficent legislation, attempting to redress the social balance between capital and labour, is thus one key to the structural injustices of modern globalised capitalism.

But industrial relations were not the whole of his work as a minister. In 1977–78, as Leader of the House, he took up the cause of Scottish and Welsh devolution, and got separate measures on both through Parliament. He had not been particularly sympathetic to devolution before – his hero Nye Bevan had, after all, moved from early neo-syndicalism to become a strong centraliser, opposing any concession to Scottish or Welsh nationalism. He had accepted the idea of a Secretary of State for Wales with great reluctance. Nor did Foot show much interest in the technical legal details of a devolution settlement – according to his chief civil servant Sir Michael Quinlan – despite Welsh devolution being within his area of responsibility in 1977–78.[478] He was said to have cast an eye at the test match on the television in his office during the discussion of the more arcane details of the Scottish and Welsh bills. But Foot, a former Liberal who subsequently sat for a Welsh constituency at Ebbw Vale, negotiated the government's tiny majority with aplomb, and got a joint devolution measure for both nations through Parliament. Devolution was thus put before the Scottish and Welsh voters in referendums on 1 March 1979, St David's Day. The result, of course, was calamitous: Welsh devolution was humiliatingly brushed aside; Scottish devolution failed to gain a strong enough proportion of Scottish voters to be put into effect. At least it can now be said that devolution would not go away as an issue thereafter. It was confidently carried in Scotland in September 1997, and very narrowly, but sufficiently, in Wales. Since then, a more pluralist United Kingdom has emerged as part of a raft of fundamental constitutional reforms. The proposal for Scottish independence was defeated in a referendum in September 2014, but the issue remains on the agenda. But it is not the least of Michael Foot's claims to fame that he proved to be an important constitutional pioneer.

Finally, Foot's contribution to Labour's doctrines of leadership when he

478 Interview with the late Sir Michael Quinlan, 1 September 2004.

himself was leader in 1980–83 can be rapidly passed over. As noted at length above, it was a disastrous period, and Labour's depressing defeat in 1983 led to a dark, cantankerous period, greatly in need of rehabilitation and rescue (for which Neil Kinnock rightly received great credit). However, there is one thing to be said for Foot's role at this time. Despite many grim periods – the bitter contest between Healey and Benn for the deputy leadership in 1981, many close calls on the party NEC, Peter Tatchell's disastrous selection and defeat in the Bermondsey by-election of 1983 – Foot did manage (just) to keep the flame of democratic socialism alive. Given the SDP defected though, he did not succeed as party leader in holding the party together. But probably no one could have done so – certainly not Denis Healey, whose capacity for tactful persuasion was not one of his dominant qualities.

Foot championed his cause with methods he understood: attempted persuasion in debate, out loud and in print. He demonstrated, thereby, what Barbara Castle called, somewhat sardonically, the basic rationality of 'the collective Foot type' – all the family products of West Country Methodist Gladstonianism, and the heritage of the seventeenth-century civil wars.[479]

Foot's 'My Kind of Socialism' (1982) defended the 'parliamentary' approach of the 'legitimate left', which he contrasted with the extra-parliamentary – indeed, anti-parliamentary – socialism of the hard left.[480] Foot's argument, buttressed characteristically by much recourse to history from the Levellers of the 1640s onwards, was for an evolutionary, tolerant, pluralist and humane form of socialism that could be viewed from many different perspectives. Like Keir Hardie, Foot saw that there were vigorous alternatives on the left and right within the movement. Like Hardie, therefore, he argued for 'free play between the sections', and he upheld the idea of divided sovereignty. If Foot was the pragmatic Aristotelian, Benn's rhetorical works (devoid of a sense of history) were Platonic in their dogmatism. Moreover, while Foot was the cultured man of letters, who relished books and the theatre and spent his

479 Morgan, op. cit., 2007, p. 410.

480 Michael Foot 'My Kind of Socialism', *The Observer*, 1982, p. 5.

vacations with Jill enjoying the paintings of Titian and the music of Vivaldi (in what he told me was 'matchless Venice'), Benn, the sea-green incorruptible, was noted by journalists as showing no interest in the arts at all.

Foot's argument did not have the same impact within the inbred ranks of political commentators, but it did give a beacon of hope to those comrades alarmed at the intolerance and sense of threat coming from the Bennites and left-wingers in the constituencies (some of whom subsequently became models of orderly propriety in the Blair–Brown governments). Foot, in particular, gave new heart to the centre left: those who associated with his protégé Neil Kinnock and those who moved to the centre ground on industrial policy, defence and Europe proved decisive in rescuing their party from near anarchy. Tony Blair rightly took the credit for Labour's re-emergence as a party of government with a massive majority in 1997, but the seeds, many of them unfruitful, were first sown under Michael Foot sixteen years before.

Nor did Foot's contribution here rest on speculative or literary activity. He did, very reluctantly, take some action. He had a phobia against party discipline; he had long been the victim of the whips and their standing orders himself. His pamphlet 'Parliament in Danger' (1959) was a polemic against the extreme rigidities of party control.[481] He was hostile to acting against the far left on the NEC, even against near-Stalinists such as Frank Allaun. Yet Foot was compelled to take the first faltering steps against Militant, the group that openly preached a doctrine of revolutionary socialism, in which Parliament should be brushed aside. In the end, five members of Militant were expelled from the party, just before the Bermondsey by-election in 1982. It was very meagre and small-scale, but, under Michael Foot, it was a start. Subsequently, opinion polls were taken asking how other Labour leaders, other than Tony Blair, might have fared against the Tories in 1997. The verdict was that even Michael Foot, so much derided, would have won the election then. Perhaps this is true. But, at the very least, his courage and persistence kept the party alive and made the 1997 revival possible.

---

481 Michael Foot, 'Parliament in Danger', London, Pall Mall Press, 1959.

Michael Foot contributed little or nothing to Labour winning power, though. His natural habitat was the march and the demo. The CND, which, in its time, challenged the party leadership almost as fundamentally as Militant Tendency, was perhaps the cause to which he was most devoted. It saw him working closely with non-political personalities like Bertrand Russell, Canon Collins of St Paul's, and the veteran author J. B. Priestley – several of whom had little or no sense of the strategies required to win power and influence in politics. It was amusing to party aides that Foot was once called upon to brief a group of CND journalist activists about the details of the government's defence policy in the late 1970s (which included nuclear weapons like Chevaline and potentially cruise missiles on Greenham Common).[482] He wrote little on Labour policy-making and had scant interest in the details of administration – and not much more on economics, where his ideas had scarcely moved on since his tutorials on Keynesian policies at Wadham with Russell Bretherton as an Oxford undergraduate in the early '30s. On foreign policy, Foot engaged too often in stereotypes; he was often too uncritical of the Soviet Union, and prejudiced against the United States as the stronghold of capitalism. He was hostile to European union – until he changed his mind after his retirement, when he was converted by Jacques Delors's Social Charter and by the doctrines of solidarity preached by European comrades like Francois Mitterrand in France, Gonzales in Spain and Papandreou in Greece.

His historical interest lies elsewhere – in the typology he illustrates. Above all, he is fascinating as a twentieth-century update of the Edwardian man of letters in public life – another Augustine Birrell or John Morley. His was a comfortable patrician background and he drew on the literary and cultural heritage of the nineteenth century – or, even more, the eighteenth. He favoured classical pseudonyms like 'Cato' and 'Cassius'. His intellectual hinterland contained multitudes. The mordant journalism of Swift in Queen Anne's reign was an ever-present model. So, too, was the cool *politique*-type scepticism of Michel de Montaigne in sixteenth-century Bordeaux. His interest in history

482 Interview with Lord McNally, 17 January 2006.

focused heavily on the seventeenth-century civil wars and the Cromwellian era, beloved of his dear father. The reign of Queen Anne was appealing, too, but the movements of industrial labour two centuries later were not – he wrote nothing on those. His was a socialism of the book. It was the social critiques of H. G. Wells and Arnold Bennett that got him into the Labour Party, as he read them on the trams of Liverpool in 1935. His personal library in Pilgrims Lane was strongly literary and of immense cultural fascination.

This made him a particular kind of crusader, from the Socialist League in the 1930s to the defence of Croatia sixty years later – the latter was as remarkable an initiative as the venerable Gladstone's campaign on behalf of the massacred Armenians in 1896. Michael Foot always embodied the centrality of culture, especially literary culture, in Britain as a society, alongside the civilising and enlightening role of history for its citizens. In a harsh political world, he was a scholar, a man of learning and a paid-up citizen of the republic of letters. He relished learned discourse, with great Oxford academics like Siegbert Prawer, on such themes as Heine and Byron. Specialists in eighteenth-century politics found his analysis of the politics of Queen Anne's reign a real contribution to historical understanding.

The impact of his death was remarkable. He was not sentimentalised as a national treasure in the way Tony Benn was, a self-centred socialist whose loyalty to the movement was minimal compared to his own, but simply acclaimed as an intellectually honest and personally respected idealist. He was always his own man in public life. There was a characteristic episode when he was in his eighties and tried to enter Selhurst Park football ground to see his beloved Plymouth Argyle play Crystal Palace. A steward asked him whether he was carrying a dangerous weapon, to which he replied that he was, and showed the man a copy of John Milton's brilliant tract of 1644 written in defence of a free press, *Areopagitica*. It did the trick. As always, they let him in.

CHAPTER 16

NEIL KINNOCK

MARTIN WESTLAKE

Neil Kinnock was party leader from 1983 to 1992. Martin Westlake argues that defeat in two consecutive general elections masked his great achievements in saving, and then reforming, the party, and taking it towards office under difficult circumstances. Kinnock inherited a disillusioned and divided party, and had to deal with the threat of the SDP and a Conservative government emboldened on the back of victory in the Falklands War. By March 1990, not only had Kinnock maintained Labour as the main party of opposition and withstood leadership challenges, but the party looked set for office – only for events, most notably the change in Conservative leadership (itself a sort of backhanded compliment), to turn against him.

• • •

Neil Kinnock's UK political career[483] can be divided into four periods. The first was his south Wales political apprenticeship. He was born on 28 March 1942 in Tredegar – a coal and iron town – as the only child of a former miner father and a district nurse mother, who were determined that he should escape manual labour. Tredegar was Nye Bevan's constituency, and the young Kinnock, whose parents were staunch Labour voters, was imbued with the romantic and political lore of the Welsh mining community. At fourteen, Kinnock started talking politics with a local

483 His subsequent career as a member, and then vice-president, of the European Commission, and his time as chairman of the British Council are not considered here.

miner and Labour councillor Bill Harry, and this led him into a discussion group and early Labour Party membership. He won a place at Cardiff University to study industrial relations and history, and was active in the university debating society, the student union, the socialist society and the anti-apartheid movement. Early on, he met his future wife, fellow student Glenys Parry (an activist with impeccable Labour pedigree). In 1965, Kinnock was elected president of Cardiff University's student union on a reformist ticket. In 1966, he became a tutor organiser for the WEA and, together with Glenys, was a passionate member of the young Bevanites. Chance, design, and his already evident oratorical powers combined to land him selection to the super-safe Labour seat of Bedwellty, which he won with a 22,729-vote majority in the June 1970 general election, aged twenty-eight.

The second period in Kinnock's political development was his time as a young Westminster backbencher and 'left-wing firebrand'. The high number of written questions he tabled in 1970–74 attests to the frustrations of opposition back-bench life, but, once Harold Wilson had led the party back into government in 1974, Kinnock, critical of the managerialism that Wilson and later Callaghan's small majorities imposed upon their administrations, consolidated his left-wing credentials. He was a member of the Tribune Group, and, as an early member of the Campaign for Labour Party Democracy, was supportive of calls to widen the franchise for the election of party leader. With the exception of a brief period as Michael Foot's private parliamentary secretary, Kinnock steered clear of the traditional political career ladder, winning his spurs as a robustly independent backbencher who opposed membership of the then EEC and Welsh devolution. The 1 March 1979 Welsh devolution referendum result (a resounding defeat for the Labour government's proposal) was a vindication of Kinnock's principled position, and such campaigns 'at last began to prove his capacity for the grind of politics'.[484] During this period, Kinnock, an increasingly charismatic and witty orator, also honed his speaking and journalistic skills. A ready and frequent speaker at grass-roots events,

484 Robert Harris, *The Making of Neil Kinnock*, London, Faber & Faber, 1984, p. 106.

and liked by the unions, Kinnock was soon being identified as a rising star within the party. In 1978, at the age of thirty-six, he was elected to the NEC.

The third period began with the 3 May 1979 general election, which saw Labour ousted by a 5.2 per cent swing to the Margaret Thatcher-led Conservatives (the largest swing since 1945). Kinnock always saw this, and not the crushing 9 June 1983 result, as the crucial turning point. The acute political sense he had developed told him that the 1979 result was more than a simple swing of the electoral pendulum. A sea change was occurring. It was 'put up or shut up time'.[485] On 18 June, he was appointed shadow education spokesman. His decision to stand for election to the Cabinet signalled a breaking of ranks with the left. A rousing October party conference speech consolidated Kinnock's popularity in the party. But, significantly, he was also 'starting to speak as though he might one day be in government'.[486] Over the next four years, as the fractious Bennite left and the Campaign for Labour Party Democracy embarked on a very public fratricidal struggle, Kinnock became increasingly critical of what he generally called 'impossibilism': 'It was almost as if sections of the party measured the purity of their socialism by the distance they could put between it and the minds of the British people.'[487] On 26 March 1981, in reaction to what they saw as Labour's increasingly suicidal leftward leanings and ungovernability, the 'gang of four' – two of them sitting MPs – founded the SDP. On 2 April 1981, as if confirming their impression, Tony Benn announced that he would be challenging the incumbent deputy leader of the party, Denis Healey. Kinnock, arguing that this was a harmful error, decided he could not support Benn's bid. He and fifteen others abstained in the second round, narrowly depriving Benn of victory. It was a turning point in the party's history and consolidated Kinnock's status as a potential candidate for leadership. One other significant, though less public, development occurred in this period, too. In February 1981, Kinnock took

485 Neil Kinnock on *Kinnock: The Inside Story*, London Weekend Television, 1992.

486 David Owen, *Time to Declare*, London, Michael Joseph, 1991, pp. 430–31.

487 Neil Kinnock, 'Reforming the Labour Party', *Contemporary Record*, 8(3), winter 1994, p. 535.

on his first full-time research assistant – Charles Clarke. Until then a 'gregarious loner', Kinnock rapidly developed a close, symbiotic relationship with Clarke, and the result was a powerful political pairing. Indeed, Clarke became the linchpin of the modernising movement.[488]

Over the next two years, the party's internecine warfare continued. Meanwhile, a successful conclusion to the 1982 Falklands War and an economic recovery boosted the popularity of the Conservative Party and its leader. Thatcher called a general election for 9 June 1983. Labour's notorious manifesto and a confused and incompetent campaign led Labour to a crushing defeat. The Labour vote fell by over 3,000,000 from 1979, and the party lost sixty seats. Ominously, although it received considerably fewer seats, the SDP–Liberal alliance polled only a few hundred thousand votes behind Labour and gained over 25 per cent of the popular vote – the largest such percentage for any third party since the 1923 general election. Michael Foot resigned as leader, and Kinnock – young, radical, popular, principled, loyal, on the reasonable left, backed strongly by the unions and untainted by office in the discredited 1974–79 government – became the favourite to succeed him. On 2 October 1983, Kinnock was elected leader, taking 71.3 per cent of votes cast. The unsuccessful centre-right leadership candidate Roy Hattersley meanwhile saw off a strong challenge from Michael Meacher to be elected deputy leader, creating a 'dream ticket'. Thus, the fourth period of Kinnock's career began, ending with him standing down eight years and nine months later, on 18 July 1992. In retrospect, in addition to his innate political gifts, the essential qualities that got Kinnock to the leadership position were those with which his parents had imbued him, and which proved essential in the years to follow – principles, loyalty, duty, conscientiousness, and the sheer grind of hard work. Looking back, he described his decision to stand for the leadership as 'almost like being called up. What I believed in and wanted to thrive was in peril and I had to do what I had to do to try to defend it.'[489]

---

488 Martin Westlake, *Kinnock: The Biography*, London, Little, Brown, 2001, pp. 202–3.

489 *Kinnock: The Inside Story*, 1992.

NEIL KINNOCK'S STATECRAFT

As Table 15.1 shows, in purely electoral terms, much progress was made under Kinnock's leadership. In 1987, Labour increased its share of the vote by 3.2 per cent from 1983, winning an additional twenty seats while the Conservatives lost twenty-one. In 1992, the party increased its share of the vote by a further 3.6 per cent from 1987, winning an additional forty-two seats while the Conservatives lost forty. Nevertheless, put starkly, the Labour Party under Neil Kinnock fought and lost two general elections. According to a literal definition of statecraft – 'The art of winning elections and achieving a necessary semblance of governing competence in office'[490] – Kinnock failed.

TABLE 16.1: THE 1983, 1987 AND 1992 GENERAL ELECTION RESULTS.

Date	Seats	Change	UK vote share (per cent)	Votes (millions)
9 June 1983	Con 397	+58	42.4	13.0
	Lab 209	-60	27.6	8.5
	Lib/SDP 23	+12	25.4	7.8
11 June 1987	Con 376	-21	42.3	13.8
	Lab 229	+20	30.8	10.0
	Lib/SDP 22	-1	22.6	7.3
9 April 1992	Con 336	-40	41.9	14.1
	Lab 271	+42	34.4	11.6
	Lib Dem 20	-2	17.8	6.0

Source: Author, compiled from Rallings and Thrasher, British Electoral Facts (2006), pp. 50–53.

However, despite his own self-deprecating judgement on his achievements as leader, Kinnock manifestly did *not* fail, for his success cannot only be measured in terms of general elections won. Kinnock's successes include: the disappearance of the SDP from the table in 1992; the 3,100,000 additional votes won between 1983 and 1992; the Conservative Party's decision to eject its most successful leader ever in 1990; and, above all, the figures in the same

490 Jim Bulpitt, 'The Discipline of the New Democracy: Mrs Thatcher's Domestic Statecraft', *Political Studies*, 34(1), 1986, p. 21.

rows and columns for 1997. For, as Tony Blair himself asserted at the party conference in September of that year: 'The mantle of Prime Minister was never his, but I know that, without him, it would never have been mine.'[491] Clearly, to argue and explain this requires an adapted version of Bulpitt's definition. The sticking point would appear to be (general) elections won, but in terms of the other key statecraft tasks set out in Chapter 2, Kinnock achieved considerable success, and arguably could qualify as a great leader in terms of any overall evaluation. In particular, from the shambolic, fratricidal lows of the 1979–83 period: his leadership brought 'a sense of governing competence among the electorate'; he 'managed his party' with great skill and patience; he 'won the battles of ideas on key policy issues'; and he toiled long and hard to drive through 'constitutional changes' within the party that collectively made it easier to lead and to elect. Even with regard to the fifth key task – 'developing a winning electoral strategy' – it could be argued that this was precisely what Kinnock successfully did. Indeed, in their 1999 analysis of the 1997 Labour landslide, Robert Worcester and Roger Mortimer argued that 'in 1997, Labour would probably have won under Kinnock'.[492] Thus, to cater for the specificities of Neil Kinnock's leadership, the definition of statecraft should be extended to include: first, the maintenance of Labour as the main party of opposition; and, second, the maintenance of leadership in order to complete and consolidate the reform processes necessary for the winning of subsequent elections.

THE OMINOUS CHALLENGES FACING KINNOCK

Context is fundamental in evaluating Kinnock's leadership, beginning with the party's 1983 circumstances. An inept, suicidal campaign had

491 Tony Blair's leader's speech at Labour Party conference in Brighton, 30 September 1997, accessed 9 January 2014 (http://www.britishpoliticalspeech.org/speech-archive.htm?speech=203).

492 Robert Worcester and Roger Mortimer, *Explaining Labour's Landslides*, London, Politico's, 1999, pp. 88–91.

resulted in its lowest share of the vote since 1918 and its reduction to just 209 MPs. The party Kinnock inherited had embraced shibboleths such as unilateral disarmament, withdrawal from the EEC, large-scale nationalisation, and the go-it-alone concept of an Alternative Economic Strategy (though, of course, some of these Kinnock had embraced himself). The party had been humiliated and demoralised. Its organisational and presentational skills had been disastrous. Worse, while still far from looking like an alternative government, the Liberal–SDP alliance had begun to look worryingly like an alternative opposition. There was a real prospect of the Labour Party becoming marginalised – a shrinking party of declining areas and populations. For any new leader, this would already have been a uniquely challenging inheritance. Moreover, there was an enemy within: the left-wing 'impossibilism' that Kinnock had bemoaned in the 1979–83 period had coalesced around a proscribed Trotskyist entryist group, Militant Tendency, which had, in particular, come to dominate Liverpool city council. Elected as a reasonable modernist from the left of the party, Kinnock had to steer a delicate course between two competing considerations in order to get the party back to the all-important centre ground on which the sort of parliamentary majorities he aspired to are always built. On the one hand, far-left antics and excesses could only drive more votes out of the party towards the Jenkinsite SDP, thus further splitting the left and confirming the Conservatives in power. On the other, too rapid and obvious an espousal of the more reasonable policies he knew were necessary would lay his leadership open to accusations of opportunism and selling out. Above all, further schism had to be avoided.

As if this were not enough, in his first years as leader, Kinnock – a miner's son and a staunch trade unionist – had to contend with the painful distraction of the 1984–85 miners' strike. It frittered away his 'honeymoon period', made him seem weak and indecisive, confirmed prejudices on both sides of the divide, and reinforced the image of Labour as being out of date. It also simultaneously obscured and symbolised a deeper development that Kinnock had first sensed in 1979 – the socio-economic sea change that was taking place in the British electorate. As Philip Gould put it, the party in 1983 had 'failed to understand that the old working class was becoming a new middle class'.[493]

Lastly, Kinnock had to face a 'novelty in British politics':[494] a post-Falklands-emboldened Conservative government with a coherent and radical political re-ordering project. This was predicated on the socio-economic sea change already under way, which included the dismantling of much of the post-war consensus, and which, in no small part because of the split opposition, was confident of commanding majorities at successive elections. As Kinnock started his uphill quest towards the centre ground, the objective was being shifted further from his grasp; from the collective to the individual, from the state to the market, from the 'nanny state' to de-regulation.

Thus, it is no exaggeration to conclude that the circumstances under which Kinnock took up the challenge of party leadership could hardly have been less favourable. The 'governing context', in statecraft terms, was absolutely foul.

Having witnessed the follies of the 1979–83 period up close, Kinnock had already largely diagnosed the party's ills, and was increasingly determined to develop a game plan and stick to it. At a policy level, he would gradually shift the party away from its more extreme manifesto commitments, with a view to broadening and deepening the party's appeal, thus enabling it to appear as a viable alternative governing party. On EEC membership, Kinnock had already begun to soften the party's stance, even before he was elected leader, aware that the June 1984 European elections would represent his, and the party's, first national electoral test since the 1983 meltdown (in the event, Labour took fifteen seats away from the Conservatives). Another early initiative was to change the party's policy on council house sales. Retrospectively, Kinnock divided such policy changes into three categories: those possible without encountering major resistance (the party's position regarding the

---

493 Philip Gould, *The Unfinished Revolution, How the Modernisers Saved the Labour Party*, London, Little, Brown, 1998, p. 4.

494 Dennis Kavanagh, *The Reordering of British Politics*, Oxford, Oxford University Press, 1997, p. 171–93.

EEC and council house sales, for example); those that could probably be changed with 'greater effort and the right timing' (for instance, antagonism towards trade union ballots and the general policy on nationalisation); and those with 'particularly deep roots that were, in themselves, benchmarks of political disposition within the Labour Party' (chief among which was the issue of nuclear disarmament).[495]

At a party level, he had to take on, and beat, Militant Tendency for three reasons, all necessitating delicate manoeuvring. First, the strong message to the broader electorate was that the leadership was bent on rejecting extremism. There was, thus, no alternative to winning the fight, no matter how tedious and agonising the process. Also, second, to those on the right still within the party, his decision to take on Militant gave them heart and good reason to stay. For them, Kinnock's famous 1985 Bournemouth speech was (and remains) a famous rallying cry. The third objective was to detach the soft left from the extremists, enabling it to coalesce with the centre and centre-right of the party. The longer-term objective of these policy and party objectives was to make the SDP unnecessary, attract back those who had despaired in 1983, and hence build towards an electoral majority.

All of this was work best done – indeed, perhaps only possible – in opposition, but it also required cultural and structural changes. Kinnock transformed Labour's management team through such key appointments as that of Larry Whitty as general secretary of the party and Peter Mandelson as head of communications. He already had a strong relationship with his 'chief fixer' Charles Clarke, and was able to attract other bright talents such as Patricia Hewitt, creating an able, loyal, reformist team that symbolised the leadership's intentions. He sought structural changes – such as an early form of 'one member, one vote' (OMOV), enabling him to appeal to a broader and more balanced party constituency – and joint policy committees, intended to render the party more manageable and coherent. He professionalised the party by concentrating far more on communication and

495 Kinnock, op. cit., p. 540.

polling skills, leading to the 1986 formation of the shadow Communications Agency, and the more systematic use of communications and polling experts such as Mandelson, Philip Gould and Peter Kellner. He gradually centralised power in the leader's office and sought to construct a stable working majority on the NEC. He brought on a generation of able Labour parliamentarians who would not only act cohesively in opposition, but could convincingly appear to be the backbone of a future Labour administration.

Collectively, this set of reforms represented a massive task to be carried out over a limited period of time and with a radical government rapidly shifting the electoral centre ground. Worse, Kinnock had to contend with a number of restraints.

First was the 'supertanker problem'[496] of inertia within the party. The change regarding council house sales, for example, took two years. In addition to those against change on principle, parts of the party were suspicious of, or sceptical about, the need for reform. As leader, Kinnock had to constantly explain, win over or reassure.

The burden of the past was a second important constraint. The paradoxical conservatism of the party and the labour movement was evident in the fierce loyalty towards symbols and traditions (singing 'The Red Flag', for example). As someone from the left, a miner's son and a quintessential party man, Kinnock had the advantage of working from within, but, equally, was vulnerable to charges of betrayal in a way that, say, a middle-class lawyer such as Tony Blair would not have been.

A third restraint, considered above, was the continued internal division and risk of schism, with the Liberal–SDP alliance simultaneously a potent threat and an obstruction on the path to the middle ground.

A fourth was the presence of repeated distractions – the worst being the miners' strike. Others included 'black sections' and the antics of 'loony left' local councils, which sapped energy and momentum and wasted precious time.

---

496 Eileen Jones, *Neil Kinnock*, London, Robert Hale Ltd, 1994, p. 114.

A fifth was the simple fact that: 'There was no traditional or institutional means within the party for the shadow Cabinet or PLP to instigate such changes.'[497]

Lastly, Kinnock was restrained by a consideration instinctively felt by all reformist leaders – defeat on any central issue could not be contemplated, therefore success had to be certain before any issue could be pressed to a decisive phase. The patient construction of majorities for reform took energy and time. The latter ran out on 11 May 1987, when Margaret Thatcher announced she would call a general election for 11 June.

Though he would not have sniffed at a victory (and, at one stage during the campaign, the Tories were clearly rattled), Kinnock had always assumed he would probably need to play a 'two-innings match'.[498] The party's primary aim in the 1987 general election was to see off the Liberal–SDP alliance threat and to re-establish itself as the main, progressive, centre-left alternative to the Conservatives. In this, it was successful. Kinnock had not only 'saved Labour from self-destruction',[499] but he had reasserted its role as the main opposition party. He had, through patient and skilful party management and constitutional change, won significant battles of ideas on key policy issues, and created a sense of governing competence. In this widened approach to assessing a party leader, the 1983–87 Kinnock was a highly successful leader – indeed, he was regarded during the campaign as being his party's major asset.[500]

That the 1987 general election was lost did not come as a surprise; after all, Labour went into the election facing a Tory lead of more than ten points. But the scale of Thatcher's victory, running counter to the sense of progress created by a slick and successful Labour campaign, was unexpected. The Conservatives focused on lower taxes, a strong economy, and defence (Kinnock, and Labour, were meanwhile still saddled with unilateral disarmament

497 Jones, op. cit., p. 114.

498 Kinnock, op. cit., p. 543.

499 Philip Stephens, 'New Image for the New Left', *Financial Times*, 31 October–1 November 1998.

500 Patrick Wintour, 'Labour's Search for a Lasting Unity' (1992) in David McKie ed., *The Election, A Voter's Guide*, London, Fourth Estate, 2000, p. 28.

– a major campaign weakness). The Tories emphasised that unemployment had fallen below three million for the first time since 1981 and inflation was at its lowest level for some twenty years (4 per cent). The tabloid media strongly supported the Conservatives, particularly *The Sun*, which ran anti-Labour articles with headlines such as: 'Why I'm Backing Kinnock, by Joseph Stalin'. The Conservatives were returned to government, having suffered a net loss of only twenty-one seats, leaving them with 376 MPs. Labour returned only 229 MPs to Westminster. This was the Conservatives' third consecutive electoral victory. A Labour parliamentary majority still seemed a depressingly long way off.

Kinnock was determined to use this catalytic experience to good advantage. It enabled him to argue that nothing short of a complete overhaul of the party's policies would do if democratic socialism was 'to be as attractive, as beckoning and as useful to the relatively affluent and the relatively secure as it is to the less fortunate in our society'.[501] He therefore decided on a comprehensive policy review, pushed through seven policy review groups – each shadowed by a member of Kinnock's staff. In 1988, to Kinnock's chagrin, Tony Benn challenged him for the leadership (and Eric Heffer and John Prescott challenged Roy Hattersley for the deputy leadership). He saw the challenges as unwelcome distractions and reminders of Labour's recent fractious past. In retrospect, however, they served Kinnock's statecraft objectives. The crushing defeats of the challengers (Kinnock won 88.6 per cent; Hattersley 66.8 per cent) consolidated Kinnock's leadership, gave a very clear message that the far left was finished as a serious force, and effectively provided the leader with a mandate to proceed unchallenged with the policy review process.

The combination of the 1987 defeat, the 1988 victory, and, in parallel, the 1986 Reykjavik Summit and the subsequent 1987 Intermediate-Range Nuclear Forces Treaty at last gave Kinnock, much aided by Gerald Kaufman, his shadow foreign affairs spokesman, the possibility of gradually jettisoning the party's unilateralist stance. The NEC finally approved the switch, by

501 Neil Kinnock, quoted in Andy McSmith, *Faces of Labour*, London, Verso, 1996, p. 66.

seventeen votes to eight (an unthinkable majority in 1983), and the new multilateral defence policy was subsequently approved by the party conference on 2 October 1989. In abandoning its unilateral policy, the party had removed a major vote-loser, but it had also opened itself up to charges of opportunism. Kinnock believed: 'It was a risk that had to be taken. Not changing policy would have been wrong and tantamount to suicide.'[502] The move was a perfect example of good statecraft.

Another example of Kinnock's statecraft strategy was the way in which, in the post-1988 period, he steered his party into support for the European single market, attenuated by a strong social Europe, support for membership of the ERM, and, by 1991, the principle of economic and monetary union. The presence of Jacques Delors, as a powerful European Commission president, helped Kinnock as he shepherded the Labour Party into the European social democratic mainstream.

The policy review documents – the fruit of eighteen months' work – were published in May 1989, under the title 'Meet the Challenge, Make the Change'. 'Meet the Challenge' was hailed as one of the most comprehensive sets of proposals ever assembled mid-term by a British political party, and was an enduring testament to Kinnock's leadership and statecraft. It was his energy more than anything that had driven the process forward.[503] The progress made was reflected in Labour's strong showing in the 15 June 1989 European elections. Labour overtook the Conservatives for the first time in any election since October 1974, and for the first time ever in a European election, winning thirteen more seats (forty-five to thirty-two). Two further policy documents were subsequently published: 'Looking to the Future' (May 1990) was essentially a mini-manifesto, but it notably included a commitment to the European ERM; 'Opportunity Britain' (May 1991) was a repackaged policy review. By 1990, the Kinnock-reformed Labour Party looked like a potential

---

502 Neil Kinnock, private interview with the author, 23 December 1998.

503 Jon Sopel, *Tony Blair: The Moderniser*, London, Little, Brown, 1995, p. 180.

government in waiting. Therein lay the rub: in retrospect, the party and its leader had peaked too soon.

The introduction of the poll tax had badly damaged the Conservative government's support and Thatcher's popularity. Kinnock, at last, overtook Thatcher in the voters' estimation as the leader best equipped to be Prime Minister. Opinion polls had, in any case, consistently shown that she was less popular than her party, but polls in September 1990 reported that Labour had established a 14 per cent lead over the Conservatives. By November, the Tories had been trailing Labour for eighteen months. Already in 1989, Thatcher had been challenged for the leadership of the Conservative Party by a little-known back-bench MP, Sir Anthony Meyer. In March 1990, Labour won its best by-election victory for fifty years, overturning a 14,000 Tory majority to take Mid Staffordshire. On 1 November 1990, Geoffrey Howe – the last remaining member of Thatcher's original 1979 Cabinet – resigned from his position as Deputy Prime Minister. Michael Heseltine subsequently challenged for leadership. On 22 November, Margaret Thatcher announced her intention to resign, and, five days later, John Major was elected as the new Conservative Party leader, thus becoming Prime Minister.

Put very succinctly, the Tories had shot Labour and Kinnock's fox, and now the political terrain began to shift in damaging ways. The fact that Major was a new leader made Kinnock look an old one. The style Kinnock had evolved to match Thatcher's combativeness was inappropriate to Major's consensual and modest style. Major had his own working-class pedigree. He used his authority as a new leader to end some of the Conservatives' most unpopular policies, including the poll tax. The August 1990 Iraqi invasion of Kuwait left Kinnock with no option but to give full support for the allied action. As John Major noted:

> I reflected on how frustrating the conflict must be for him. Before I became Prime Minister, Labour were well ahead in the opinion polls, but my election had turned them around. Now, when he must have wished to sink his teeth into a new Prime Minister, he was forced to support him. Nonetheless,

> despite a dissenting minority in his party, he did so and rose enormously in my estimation. Neil Kinnock was an old-fashioned patriot.[504]

Thatcher's surprise announcement, on 8 October 1990, about joining the ERM removed a key difference between the parties in their approach to the conduct of macroeconomic policy. Having known only the negative state of opposition since 1979, and wounded by three successive electoral defeats, Labour's psychological and material resources were now at a low ebb – the need to be on a constant electoral footing was pushing the party into debt. In 1990, Kinnock became the longest-serving opposition leader of the twentieth century, and the strain was beginning to tell. Philip Gould recalled: 'Neil was exhausted by constantly attempting to hold together a party threatening to fracture if he moved too far and too fast, and by the need to look restrained and "respectable" for the press and the public.'[505]

A vicious spiral of self-fulfilling prophecies then set in. Doubts about the party's ability to win the next general election led to preparations for the aftermath and the inevitable succession, which, in turn, badly undermined the party's ability to win. Tensions with his shadow Chancellor and probable successor John Smith, particularly with regard to the party's Achilles' heel (tax), further distracted the party from the cohesiveness it needed in order to fight effectively. It was not all doom and gloom, but Kinnock's personal high points of 1987 and 1990 seemed increasingly far away.

On 9 April 1992, the Conservatives won their fourth consecutive general election victory. The scale of the Conservative victory was remarkable: 336 seats to Labour's 271 – John Major's Conservatives had polled a massive 14,000,000 votes. On 18 July 1992, Neil Kinnock stood down as leader.

---

504 John Major, *The Autobiography*, London, HarperCollins, 1999.

505 Philip Gould, op. cit., p. 103.

JUDGING KINNOCK

If this analysis were to have finished on 22 November 1990, then, in statecraft terms, Kinnock would surely have been adjudged a highly successful leader. As George Lucas wrote: 'Kinnock's reputation is tainted by the tortuous 1991–92 period, when he was already spiritually denuded by the years of private combat and public degradation. His main triumphs were already performed.'[506] With great courage and energy, through sheer effort and patience, and with considerable personal sacrifice, he had measured up to and vanquished the threat within (Militant Tendency and the far left) and the threat without (the SDP and the Liberal–SDP alliance). He had also successfully reasserted Labour as the main opposition party, and – through his evident electability and the success of his policy and structural reforms – had scared the Conservatives into getting rid of their most successful leader, although, as expected, he did lose one general election while dragging the party back from the depths to which it had plumbed in 1983.

In Schlesinger's ranking system (which rated leaders as 'Great', 'Near Great', 'Average', 'Below Average' or 'Failure'), Kinnock was surely a 'Near-Great', if not 'Great', leader.[507] In Theakston and Gill's terms,[508] Kinnock demonstrated brilliant leadership skills and sound judgement, and was 'good in a crisis'. If, following Hennessy,[509] presiding over substantial change is a key indicator of successful leadership, then Kinnock was a resounding success – somebody who had made his own political weather, notwithstanding the socio-economic cyclone through which he was navigating his party. His success as a reformer paired with his ultimate inability to win elections is a graphic illustration of Buller and James's contention that leaders can be both a success

---

506 George Lucas, 'A goldfish full of piranhas', *Independent on Sunday*, 9 December 2001.

507 Joseph Schlesinger Snr, 'The US presidents: What makes a President great? Or a failure? The verdict of history provides some answers', *Life*, XXV, pp. 65–74. This is a nuance that raises the question as to whether politicians can only be great leaders if they enter into government, or, further, govern during wars.

508 Theakston and Gill, op. cit., 2006.

509 Peter Hennessy, op. cit.

and a failure.[510] But the nuance referred to above raises other questions. To whom, if we wish to evaluate him in such terms, should we compare Kinnock? Should it be all *party* leaders? Or all *leaders of the opposition*? Or *Labour* leaders of the opposition (see Table 15.2 below)? What about *reforming* party leaders? If a Venn diagram were to be drawn of all of these categories (from 1937 onwards, when the position of Leader of the Opposition became statutory) then Kinnock would figure in the central common ground, together with only Clement Attlee, Margaret Thatcher and Tony Blair. *Nobody else.*

TABLE 16.2: LABOUR LEADERS OF THE OPPOSITION, 1937–2015.[511]

Leader/period in office	Opposition periods	General elections fought	Results (won/lost)
Clement Attlee 20yr,2m	25 October 1935 – 22 May 1940 23 May 1945 – 26 July 1945 26 October 1951 – 25 November 1955	1945, 1950, 1951, 1955	W2, L2
Hugh Gaitskell 7yr,1m	14 December 1955 - 18 January 1963	1959	L1
Harold Wilson 13yr,2m	14 February 1963 – 15 October 1964 19 June 1970 – 3 March 1974	1964, 1966, 1970, 1974 (x2)	W4, L1
James Callaghan 4yr,7m	4 May 1979 – 9 November 1980	1979	L1
Michael Foot 2yr,11m	10 November 1980 – 1 October 1983	1983	L1
Neil Kinnock 8yr,9m	2 October 1983 – 17 July 1992	1987, 1992	L2

510 Buller and James, op. cit., 2012, p. 536.

511 Not including the short interregnums of Herbert Morrison (November–December 1955), George Brown (January–February 1963), Margaret Beckett (May–July 1994), and Harriet Harman (May–September 2010). Also note that James Callaghan and Gordon Brown came to the Labour Party leadership and the prime ministership without having served as Leader of the Opposition and/or leader of the Party. Attlee, Gaitskell, Wilson, Callaghan and Foot had all served in government. Kinnock, Smith, Blair and Miliband had not.

Leader/period in office	Opposition periods	General elections fought	Results (won/lost)
John Smith 1yr, 10m	18 July 1992 – 12 May 1994		
Tony Blair 12yr,11m	21 July 1994 – 1 May 1997	1997, 2001, 2005	W3
Ed Miliband 4yr,7m	25 September 2010 – 8 May 2015	2015	L1

The value of Kinnock's leadership can be measured through responses to other questions. Was there anybody else who was seriously prepared to take on the reform/modernisation task in 1983? Could somebody else have done it, even at a later date? Was anybody better equipped to do it? Could somebody else have done it quicker? The answer to all of these questions is clearly 'no'. Only Kinnock, the incumbent reformer, could have been empowered enough through the 1987 defeat to take the modernisation process still further. A more subtle question would be to consider whether Kinnock was such a good leader precisely *because* he was a (reformist) Leader of the Opposition. The combination of skills and qualities that he brought to the task was certainly unique. These included his oratorical skills, his political courage, his readiness to engage in debate and suasion, his loyalty, his passion and sheer energy levels, his ability to attract and work with talent,[512] his ability to work with his enemies (for as long, at least, as they were good for the cause), and the fact that he came from the left. The reverse of that coin is to ask whether Kinnock would have made a good Prime Minister. Certainly, his subsequent performances as a commissioner

512 Until 1981, 'Kinnock' largely meant the man and his wife alone (one of the great political partnerships). Thereafter, it meant Kinnock and Glenys (with their young family and her teaching job), Charles Clarke, and a gradually widening team of sympathisers and supporters who believed in him and were determined to see his project through. The close-knit nature of these relationships would lead ultimately to charges of tribalism that Kinnock hotly denied. From his point of view, he had put the party's electoral capacity above all else. Loyalty to the cause was thereafter the watch word.

and vice-president of the European Commission demonstrated that he was at ease with complicated briefs and high responsibilities. He would surely have been up to the job.

The post-1990 relative decline and the 9 April 1992 electoral defeat muddy the picture. Of course, Kinnock continued to strive with every sinew for victory, but there are at least two theories that argue that this second defeat was, paradoxically, part of that overall picture. The first considers how: 'Sometimes the political process throws up leaders who identify a need for radical change, use their position of power to bring about that change, but thereafter seem unable to benefit from the change themselves.'[513] Such leaders of transition are necessarily associated with a particular phase of the regime:

> They are associated to such an extent that it is felt that the completion of the transition process and the emergence of a genuinely new regime necessarily involves going beyond the leader of the transition himself. In order for the transition to be consummated, the leaders of transition must be rejected and abandoned. After all, they are tainted by their provenance from the old world and are therefore unsuited to take the regime into the brave new world.[514]

Accordingly, it was only through his defeat and subsequent resignation that the leader's reforms could be fully consolidated. Such leaders, incidentally, always act with reference to a set of higher moral values – the amount of suffering and vilification that Kinnock was prepared to go through would otherwise have seemed irrational. Here is his own description of the democratic loyalist's logic:

> Certainly for me, it was one thing after the other, but you keep going

513 Martin Westlake, 'Neil Kinnock, Loyalist Reformer', in Martin Westlake ed., *Leaders of Transition*, Basingstoke, Palgrave Macmillan, 2000, p. xiii.

514 Westlake, op. cit., 2000, p. 170.

> because of the cause with a capital 'C', and the cause is always to try to address the present and build for the future. That's why you are in democratic politics in the first place.[515]

The leader of transition theory may be considered *post hoc* rationalisation, but, by 1997, Tony Blair – coming after Kinnock and Smith – seemed light years away from 1983, although, in fact, he was first elected as an MP in that general election, and therefore also fought on the basis of 'the longest suicide note in history'.

A second theory argues that, although it certainly didn't feel like it at the time, Labour, and possibly Kinnock himself, was lucky to lose the 1992 general election. As Ross McKibbin has put it: 'By 1992, Labour had largely recovered the ground lost since 1979, though Kinnock never got much credit for this. Labour owes one other debt to him: he lost the 1992 election – one of the few pieces of genuine good luck the Labour Party has ever had.'[516] Space precludes a proper examination of this argument – bound up in complicated speculation about what Labour might have done within the ERM if it had come to power.[517] Put simply, on 8 October 1991, the Conservatives, at Thatcher's insistence, took sterling into the ERM at a unilaterally declared 'macho' parity of 2.95DM – an act that led directly to Black Wednesday, when the Conservative government was forced to withdraw the pound from the ERM, simultaneously blowing an estimated £3.4 billion of Treasury reserves and its reputation as the party of reliable economic governance.[518] Arguably, it was the loss of that reputation, more than anything else, that cleared the way for Labour's victory in 1997. This is, in any case, *post hoc* rationalisation – Kinnock may have had doubts about whether the 1992 general election could be won, but he certainly didn't set out to lose it.

---

515 Neil Kinnock, 'Opportunity Knocks' interview in *Holyrood Magazine*, 3 November 2013.

516 Ross McKibbin, 'Why the Tories Lost', *London Review of Books*, 19(13), 1997.

517 For a detailed discussion, see Westlake, 2001, pp. 503–4.

518 Labour planned to request a revaluation of sterling within the ERM immediately after it had won power.

This account has sought to evaluate Kinnock's leadership using an adapted version of the statecraft approach. It has concentrated, therefore, on the aspects of his leadership that Bulpitt and, later, Buller and James (see Chapter 2) considered important. It has thus, inevitably, neglected aspects that might, given another approach, be considered of greater relevance. For example: his relationship with the media and treatment by the tabloid press; the way his leadership 'evoked strange snobberies that have now largely disappeared from British life';[519] his Welshness as a target of prejudice; the way his increasing pragmatism allegedly suffocated democratic debate within the party; the – almost certainly erroneous – 'Kinnock blew it' schools of thought; the related 'one more heave' school of thought; his alleged aversion, post-reform, to the development of a new progressive ideology; and, at least partly in consequence, arguments that his reforms led almost inevitably led to a 'New Labour' party and to Blair administrations with many aspects of which he felt uncomfortable.[520]

However, the statecraft analysis raises another question. If Kinnock committed errors of judgement towards the end of his time as leader, these were relatively benign. His 1992 loss had more to do with the way the world suddenly changed around him, rather than with gross errors on his part. The real problem was that he had scared the Conservatives into removing the person who had effectively become his best electoral asset – Margaret Thatcher. Enoch Powell once remarked that all political careers end in failure. Is it possible, then, to evaluate Margaret Thatcher's leadership up to, but before, the introduction of the poll tax? Or Tony Blair's up to, but before, the invasion of Iraq? Or Neil Kinnock's up to the March 1990 Mid Staffordshire by-election? In any case, Kinnock's failures, in statecraft terms, were clearly lesser – at the most, sins of omission rather than commission.

In conclusion, an adapted version of the statecraft approach is a useful tool in better evaluating the record of a Labour leader who never won a general

519 Ross McKibbin, 'The Luck of the Tories', *London Review of Books*, 24(5), 7 March 2002, pp. 8–9.

520 McKibbin, ibid.

election but whose work in 'permanent opposition'[521] was vital for the three general election victories that were to follow. He was, to paraphrase Ortega y Gasset, himself and his circumstances. If Kinnock was lucky in rising to the leadership in the *way* he did, he was unlucky in rising to the leadership *when* he did. Surely, in qualitative terms, of all the Labour leaders who were never Prime Minister (Henderson, Lansbury, Gaitskell, Foot, Smith and Miliband), Kinnock achieved the most by far. As argued elsewhere, he was a leader of transition, and a loyalist reformer.[522] Which is why, some eight years after his resignation, when he was presented, in a very different context, with another 'mission impossible', it came as no surprise that he accomplished this new, equally thankless, but nonetheless heroic task with loyalty, duty, conscientiousness, hard work and, ultimately, aplomb.[523] But that was another – the next – story.

521 McKibbin, ibid.

522 Martin Westlake, 'Neil Kinnock 1983-92', in Jefferys, op. cit., 1999; Westlake, op. cit., 2000.

523 Hussein Kassim, 'The Kinnock Reforms in Perspective: Why Reforming the Commission is an Heroic, But Thankless, Task', *Public Policy and Administration*, 19(3), autumn 2004; Hussein Kassim, '"Mission impossible", but mission accomplished: the Kinnock reforms and the European Commission', *Journal of European Public Policy*, 15(5), August 2008, pp. 648–68.

CHAPTER 17

JOHN SMITH

MARK STUART

John Smith entered Parliament in 1970 and served as Secretary of State for Trade under Jim Callaghan's government, and then shadow Chancellor of the Exchequer under Neil Kinnock from 1987 to 1992. He was elected as leader following Neil Kinnock's resignation in the aftermath of the 1992 general election, decisively beating Bryan Gould. Smith was leader for fewer than two years, as he tragically died from a heart attack in May 1994. Mark Stuart argues that Smith was passed a golden inheritance from Neil Kinnock: a centralised party organisation and no unrest among the backbenchers. Moreover, Smith faced a Conservative Party in turmoil, after Black Wednesday and infighting over Europe. Assessing Smith's achievements is difficult because he never faced an election. He was, above all, a cautious leader, however. He preferred not to unnecessarily unveil policy, arguing that it might give the opposition a strategic advantage. He was also keen to avoid conflict with his own party, and was often reluctant to take centre stage in the media. Stuart suggests that Smith played a key role in the 'modernisation' of the party with the introduction of OMOV, but that the absence of further decisive party reform made it unclear whether Labour would have won power with him at the helm.

• • •

John Smith is atypical of the Labour leaders featured in this book. For a start, he is only the second Labour leader never to have faced an election (the other being George Lansbury – see Chapter 10), serving only twenty-two months, from 18 July 1992 until his tragic death on the morning of 12 May 1994. Since his death, historical perceptions of Smith have been tainted by the 'TB/GB' debate, namely which of Tony Blair or Gordon Brown did Smith think should succeed him? Worse still, historians and journalists of the period have mined back into Smith's leadership to find evidence of Blair in the ascendancy as shadow Home Secretary, or Brown controlling the direction of economic policy as shadow Chancellor. In fact, neither was true. Smith was in charge. When he was elected leader, it was very nearly a shoo-in, Smith crushing the only other candidate, Bryan Gould, by 90.9 per cent to 9.1 per cent.

In this chapter, Smith's rise to party leadership will be charted, before assessing the crucial political context in which Smith's leadership operated. The statecraft criteria outlined earlier in this book will then be deployed to determine the success or otherwise of his short period in charge. Lastly, an overall assessment will be made of his achievements, leading to a discussion as to what can be learned from his leadership style.

SMITH'S EARLY CAREER

In later life, Smith was unfairly characterised as an 'Edinburgh lawyer', but, in fact, he was a Highlander, born on 13 September 1938 in Dalmally (a small village located at the northern end of Loch Awe in the county of Argyll). Aged two, his father took up an appointment as headmaster of a small primary school in the coastal village of Ardrishaig. It was an idyllic childhood, Smith learning on his father's knee about the importance of the redistribution of wealth from those who could afford to pay to those in greater need. Essentially, those values never changed in all the time Smith was alive. He was supremely confident that the rest of Britain believed in such values, too. His legendary debating skills were honed at the Glasgow University Union, alongside Donald Dewar. Both were student politicians spotted by Richard Stewart – a leading Scottish Labour trade unionist – and they were given help finding parliamentary seats. In 1970, Smith was elected as MP for Lanarkshire

North (which became Monklands East in 1983). Despite being one of the sixty-nine Labour MPs to defy a three-line whip in favour of Britain's entry into the EEC, Smith achieved promotion. His first two ministerial jobs in the Wilson government saw him work alongside Tony Benn at the Department of Energy. The experience revealed Smith's ability, despite hailing from the right of the party, to maintain a good working relationship with those on the left. Unlike his rebellious colleagues Neil Kinnock and Robin Cook, Smith overcame his initial opposition to Scottish devolution, and ended up defending it in the House of Commons as a Minister of State, alongside Michael Foot. One devolution bill floundered, while another was emaciated by Labour rebels. Nevertheless, Smith reached Cabinet as Trade Secretary, right at the fag end of James Callaghan's government. In the autumn of 1978, he watched in disbelief as Callaghan, whose consensual style of leadership he admired and later emulated, failed to call a general election.

During Labour's first six years in opposition (1979–85), Smith was largely anonymous. While Neil Kinnock struggled to turn his party around, Smith was to be found back at the Edinburgh Bar, using his skills as an advocate (the Scottish term for a barrister) to secure 'not guilty' or 'not proven' verdicts for several nefarious types accused of murder. Kinnock's inner team was irritated by the fact that Smith appeared to sit back while others toiled to try to turn the party around. In truth, as a right-winger, Smith could not get elected to the NEC – then the main power base in the Labour Party. Failure to sit on that body meant that, when he was elected leader in 1992, Smith knew very little about the internal workings of the party. Nor was Smith one of the party's philosophers, like Donald Dewar or Roy Hattersley. The advocate, used to handing back his papers when a case ended, was always anxious to move on to the next matter at hand. But at least Smith stayed in the party at the time of the SDP split in 1981. Had he, and other right-wingers such as Hattersley, gone, then Labour would have been finished.

Smith emerged as a star, from virtual anonymity, during the Westland Affair in January 1986. But the fact that Smith triumphed in the House of Commons, while Kinnock famously flopped, illustrates the differing skills of the two politicians. Whereas Neil excelled on the party conference platform, John was brilliant in the House of Commons. Whereas John was matey, convivial and entirely comfortable in his own skin, Neil was more insecure. They had emerged through separate routes in the party, meaning that, when Kinnock appointed Smith as his shadow Chancellor, they had very little common ground upon which to build a successful relationship.[524] In short, the two men were chalk and cheese.

After recovering from a massive heart attack in 1988, Smith, as shadow Chancellor, was instrumental in trying to persuade the City of London that a future Labour government would not scare off investors – an exercise later derided by Michael Heseltine as 'the prawn cocktail offensive'. The crustaceans did not all die in vain. By the 1992 election, Smith had earned a reputation as a safe, Scottish bank manager-type figure, while his Treasury team had persuaded the *Financial Times*, no less, to support its prudent approach to economic housekeeping.

However, the Labour Party was saddled with a flawed policy review, which included an expensive commitment to increase pensions, child benefits to be funded by a rise in national insurance, and a 50 per cent top rate of income tax to be established. Kinnock took the view that much more time was needed to persuade the public of the need for higher taxation to pay for public services, whereas Smith preferred leaving it until the last minute. In January 1992, Kinnock hosted a dinner for journalists in a restaurant called Luigi's, during which he suggested that there might be a way of phasing in the national insurance increases. Despite suggesting the idea to Smith in advance that morning, the fact that Kinnock had leaked the plan to the media led to its abandonment. Instead, Smith produced his last-minute shadow Budget in March 1992 to lay out the financing of the spending commitments, but it ended up being picked apart, rather unfairly, by the Conservative-dominated press during the 1992 general election campaign. Debates ensued as to whether Smith's Budget had cost the party the election, but an internal post-mortem

524 Mark Stuart, 'The truth about Neil and John', *New Statesman*, 20 June 2005.

by Labour's general secretary Larry Whitty concluded the obvious point: the majority of voters still did not trust Labour.[525]

THE CHALLENGES FACING SMITH AS LEADER

As Chapter 2 has highlighted already, the circumstances in which a leader assumes power are crucial in determining the level of freedom with which they are able to operate. In that respect, the inheritance they are bequeathed from their predecessors is pivotal. At least in organisational terms, Smith's inheritance from Neil Kinnock was a golden one. After nine years of struggle, Kinnock had moved the power base of the party away from the NEC and the party conference, and back into the hands of the shadow Cabinet and the leader's office. In practical terms, that meant Smith could simply walk into the NEC as its chair and win every vote, with only a couple of dissenting voices. Secondly, when Smith chaired the first ever meeting of the National Policy Forum in Hammersmith in November 1992 (another Kinnock creation), he inherited a policy-making structure, with the Labour leader at its helm. Writing in 1993, Peter Shore rightly concluded: 'No previous leader has enjoyed such personal and institutionalised control over party policy.'[526]

Nor was there any serious prospect of a challenge to Smith's leadership from the back benches. Once again, John had Neil to thank for that – this time in terms of the rule change Neil introduced in 1988, requiring 20 per cent of the PLP to sign their names in blood in calling for a contest. In a party where observing the rule book is part of the cultural DNA, setting such a high threshold for challenging the leader meant, in effect, that Smith was totally secure in his position.

But if Kinnock bequeathed a party that the leader now controlled, nine

525 General secretary, 'Report to the NEC: the general election', 21 June 1992 (GS: 21/6/92).

526 Shore, op. cit., p. 180.

years of breakneck change had taken its toll on party morale. Remember, Labour had reformed and modernised almost every aspect of its policies under Kinnock's leadership, and yet it had lost for a fourth successive time. The mood post-1992 was very much, 'If not now, then whenever.' This author has elsewhere characterised Smith's role in his first year as very much healing the wounds caused by Kinnock's relentless but necessary reform of the party.[527] That involved the new leader spending an inordinate amount of time (wasted time, in the view of the modernisers, who wanted faster change) soothing the ruffled feathers of Labour left-wingers, like Dennis Skinner and Clare Short, who welcomed Smith's more consensual style of leadership. Beyond these convivial one-to-one gatherings, the weekly meetings of the PLP were often lively affairs, in which there was vigorous collective discussion on issues such as electoral reform, Bosnia, and the party's stance on the parliamentary ratification of the Maastricht Treaty. In this sense, the PLP acted as a valuable safety valve, allowing ordinary backbenchers room to 'let off steam' in private. The strategy did not always work, as evidenced by high levels of party dissent over Maastricht, but it was predicated in a more relaxed form of leadership that sought to balance competing wings in the party.[528]

Smith's other great advantage in contextual terms was assuming the leadership at a time when the Conservative government, led by John Major, was hit by a virtual Exocet missile in the shape of Black Wednesday (16 September 1992), when Chancellor Norman Lamont was forced to remove the pound from the ERM. Smith took full advantage, excelling in the House of Commons when he labelled John Major the 'devalued Prime Minister of a devalued government'.[529] From then on, the Conservative parliamentary party began to bicker incessantly over Europe, most notably during the prolonged parliamentary ratification of the Maastricht Treaty. Night after night, Conservative rebels voted against the government. In the words of Tristan

527 Mark Stuart, *John Smith: A Life*, London, Politico's, 2005, Chapter 18.

528 Mark Stuart, 'Managing the Poor Bloody Infantry: The Parliamentary Labour Party under John Smith, 1992–94', *Parliamentary Affairs*, 59(2), July 2006, pp. 1–19.

529 HC debs, 24 September 1992, col. 22.

Garel-Jones, the Minister of State for Europe at the time, the Conservative party 'bled to death' for over a year.[530]

As a result of these travails, Smith felt in his bones that the Conservatives were finished. Increasingly, however, critics derided their leader's 'one more heave' strategy. In fact, Smith was a moderniser, though he favoured modernisation at a slower pace than his younger colleagues, notably Tony Blair and Jack Straw. So, while Smith risked the leadership of his party in late September 1993 to secure a version of OMOV (see below), he was unconvinced about reforming Clause IV of Labour's 1918 constitution, fearing it would stir up a hornet's nest. Rather, he believed it should be allowed to 'wither on the vine'. Indeed, when Jack Straw defied Smith by writing a pamphlet calling for the abolition of Clause IV, Smith lost his temper and threw it back in Straw's face.[531] Straw was right. There was a sense that Smith, relieved to win narrowly on OMOV, thought he had done enough to secure a Labour victory. Others were not so sure. As early as November 1992, Nick Raynsford had penned an article for *Fabian Review* entitled 'Sleepwalking into Oblivion?', criticising Smith's soporific leadership and urging a more radical approach.[532] In April 1993, Bill Rodgers, one of the founding members of the SDP, wrote privately to Smith 'in an entirely personal capacity', urging him to make the necessary changes to win at the general election.[533] Similar criticisms had been echoed in a Fabian Society pamphlet in the autumn of 1992, entitled 'Southern Discomfort' and written by Giles Radice. It revealed that 'swing' voters still believed a Labour government would mismanage the economy, and that the party was stuck in the past.[534]

Operating from the sidelines, Philip Gould – the focus-group guru, and a favourite of both Neil Kinnock and Tony Blair – warned, in a series of private

---

530 Mark Stuart, *Douglas Hurd. The Public Servant*, Edinburgh, Mainstream, 1998, p. 299.

531 Jack Straw, *Memoirs of a Political Survivor* (Basingstoke, Macmillan, 2012), pp. 188-190.

532 Nick Raynsford, 'Sleepwalking into Oblivion?', *Fabian Review*, 104(6), November 1992, p.1, p. 3.

533 Letter from Rt Hon. the Lord Rodgers of Quarry Bank to Rt Hon. John Smith QC MP, 16 April 1993. Murray Elder papers, Box 1.

534 Giles Radice, *Inside the Blair, Brown, Mandelson Project* (London I.B. Tauris, 2010) p. 57.

papers to Labour's deputy leader Margaret Beckett, that Labour was not doing enough to win over disillusioned Conservative voters in the south of England. Smith's response was to scoff at focus groups, which he derided as nine people from Watford talking about bringing back hanging. His basic set of Scottish values – enshrined in the idea of the redistribution of wealth, which he had learned on his father's knee in the Highlands – were not necessarily the values shared by 'those voters' (a favourite Smith phrase) 'down south'. Writing in July 1993, Peter Riddell argued (with more than a grain of truth) that, because the Labour leader had grown up in the Scottish Labour establishment, 'Smith believes that everything would be all right if England were like Scotland'.[535]

Smith's over-reliance on allowing the Tories simply to fail in government caught the eye of Andrew Marr in January 1994. Writing for *The Independent*, Marr compared Smith's strategy to that of the Russian commander Kutuzov in Tolstoy's *War and Peace*. Kutuzov became notorious for his lack of enthusiasm for engaging the French in battle, believing that the Russian Army could not destroy the French Army nearly as effectively as the French were destroying themselves. As Marr sagely pointed out, 'Mr Smith clearly believes that the Conservatives are doing a splendid job of self-destruction', but Smith's Labour Party still had some way to go to 'persuade harassed, worried middle-income Britain that it will be better off under socialism'.[536]

Perhaps the only objective, if imperfect, guide as to whether Smith was on course to win in 1997 was the European election, fought under the leadership of the acting leader Margaret Beckett in June 1994 – one month after Smith's death. According to British Election Study data, although Labour 'won' that election in terms of vote and seat share, what is striking is the very high level of abstention by Conservative voters.[537] The intriguing question is: would those Conservatives have returned to the fold by 1997 if Smith, rather than Tony Blair, had been leader?

---

535 Peter Riddell, 'That Missing Spark', *The Times*, 1 July 1993.

536 Andrew Marr, 'Don't read too much Tolstoy, Mr Smith', *The Independent*, 20 January 1994.

537 Anthony F. Heath, Roger M. Jowell and John K. Curtice, *The Rise of New Labour. Party Policies and Voter Choices*, Oxford, Oxford University Press, 2001, p. 103.

It wasn't just Smith's possible lack of appeal to 'southern' English voters that worried observers at the time. At least four people in Smith's office – Hilary Coffman, Delyth Evans, David Hill and David Ward – wrote private missives to their leader, urging him to adopt a higher public profile.[538] But Smith, forever the advocate, never understood the need to repeat political messages over and over again.

Indeed, for a supposedly modern Labour leader, Smith took a rather naive view of the media, thinking that large swathes of the electorate watched BBC Two's *Newsnight*. The 'dark arts' of spin and news management were looked down upon, as evidenced by the fact that Peter Mandelson's services were not welcome under Smith's leadership. (Reporters would be given a stern talking to if they interrupted Smith's weekends in Edinburgh.) Nor did Smith share Tony Blair's later desire to court Rupert Murdoch's News International media empire. According to his long-time secretary Ann Barrett: 'He [Murdoch] was a no-no.' Just before Smith's death, Hilary Coffman arranged for Andrew Neil, editor of the *Sunday Times*, to interview Smith, without first consulting him. Barrett recalled: 'I thought he [John] was going to explode. But he wouldn't have let down his staff by cancelling it, so Andrew Neil became the last journalist ever to interview John Smith.'[539] In short, Smith was an old-fashioned politician who would have thrived in the Attlee era, but might have struggled in the 24-hour news environment.

SMITH AS LEADER

As has already been pointed out, the biggest obstacle in assessing Smith's achievements as leader is that he never faced an election. Moreover, we can only assess phase one of his leadership, in which he was engaged in

538 Stuart, op. cit., 2005, pp. 312–14.

539 Interview with Ann Barrett, 21 June 2003.

cementing party unity and grappling with policy formulation. Phase two – the point in the electoral cycle when Smith would have been required to sell those policies to the wider electorate – doesn't exist. Very often, observers of Smith – including this author – have engaged in speculation about whether, had Smith lived, he would have won the 1997 election, and what kind of government he would have led.[540] Such speculation, though part of an interesting branch of counter-factual history, does not concern us here. Instead, we must judge Smith's ability to formulate policy, both in respect of national policy and in party political terms.

At the heart of Smith's policy formulation was the task of completing the 'unfinished business' of Scottish devolution. Smith supported Scottish devolution because it represented government closest to the people. Speaking at Strathclyde University on 23 October 1992, Smith used the occasion of the Richard Stewart Memorial Lecture[541] to call for a reversal of the process of centralisation through the establishment of a Scottish Parliament and a Welsh Assembly, and by moving towards a different form of regional government in England. Such proposals were part of a broader set of constitutional reforms, such as establishing a Bill of Rights, which guaranteed the rights of citizens against arbitrary government.[542] In addition, in the autumn of 1992, Smith asked Gordon Borrie, the former director-general of the Office of Fair Trading, to chair the Social Justice Commission, which did not report until shortly after Smith's death. But beyond these two major initiatives, the Smith policy cupboard was remarkably bare.

Whenever he was asked to expound his 'big idea', Smith always replied: 'A Labour government.' Here was a pragmatic leader who was unwilling to commit himself to concrete policies too early in the electoral cycle, fearful that they would be stolen by his political opponents. Besides, Smith felt in

---

540 Mark Stuart, 'What if John Smith had lived?', in Duncan Brack and Iain Dale eds, *Prime Minister Portillo and other things that never happened*, London, Politico's, 2003, pp. 313–32.

541 Richard or 'Dick' Stewart was Smith's election agent and the trade unionist who first secured him a seat in Lanarkshire North.

542 John Smith, '*Reforming our Democracy*', Strathclyde, Strathclyde University, 23 October 1992.

his bones that the Conservatives had fallen so far as a result of devaluation and divisions over Europe that there was no way back for them in time for the following general election. Instead, he focused on attack, lambasting the Major government's economic failings – notably its broken promise not to increase taxes. Smith's damning portrayal of John Major's alleged incompetence was exemplified in his description of him as: 'The man with the non-Midas touch.'[543]

However, there was a deeper reason behind Smith's low policy output. As has already been argued, Smith had a clear set of values, learned on his father's knee, from which he never deviated. The problem was that he was so certain of their validity that he never sought to articulate them. It is therefore a curious but telling observation that Smith never verbalised his values in a speech of any note until he became Leader of the Opposition, when he was more or less obliged to do so. In March 1993, Smith set out the moral basis of his beliefs in the Christian socialist R. H. Tawney Lecture, which became known as 'Reclaiming the Ground'. Drawing on the ideas of Archbishop William Temple,[544] Smith claimed that people had an obligation or duty to one another. In politics, that meant a duty to serve one's community and nation. It was a rare foray into the realm of morality politics for a Scots Presbyterian who was more conditioned to keeping such views to himself.

In party political terms, the historical debate has centred on whether Smith was a moderniser in terms of pressing ahead with the internal reforms of his party. Whereas more zealous members of his shadow Cabinet team (such as Tony Blair and Gordon Brown) favoured a faster pace, Smith was naturally more cautious – more of a 'long gamer'. Indeed, he was fond of telling a rather crude joke about two bulls standing in a field, eyeing up some cows on the hillside. The younger of the two bulls says, excitedly: 'Let's run up the hill right now and shag one of them!'

---

543 HC debs, 9 June 1993, col. 292.

544 William Temple, *Christianity and Social Order*, London, Penguin, 1942.

The older, wiser bull replies: 'No, let's walk up the hill – and shag the lot of them.'[545]

Despite his caution, it is a testament to Smith's commitment to modernising the internal processes of his party that he sought to risk his leadership in order to secure the introduction of OMOV in the autumn of 1993. Neil Kinnock had tried and failed to introduce a form of OMOV in 1984, but he had secured an important rule change in time for Smith in 1993, reducing the union block vote at the party conference from 90 per cent to 70 per cent. Yet again, Smith had cause to be grateful for his golden legacy from Kinnock. Figures such as Charles Clarke (Kinnock's former chief of staff) urged Smith to press ahead with OMOV in 1992, instead of waiting a year. However, Murray Elder (Smith's chief of staff) felt that, without the change to the block vote, Smith might have lost an early vote, thereby fatally undermining his leadership at a very early stage.[546]

Allies of Smith cleverly combined the resolution on OMOV at the 1993 Labour Party conference with one supporting the introduction of a quota system for women, requiring half the winnable seats with no sitting Labour MP to choose a woman candidate. The Manufacturing, Science and Finance (MSF) delegation was opposed to OMOV, but had a long-standing commitment to all-women shortlists. Faced with this dilemma, the MSF delegation abstained. Their conversion was crucial in tipping the vote the leadership's way, because they held 4.5 per cent of the votes, and the eventual winning margin was only 3.1 per cent. Smith was also helped by John Prescott's conference speech in favour of OMOV. As ever, no one quite knew what Prescott was saying, but, with his full weight behind it, Smith narrowly won on the day. The change was hugely significant in terms of the Labour Party's image, because it showed that Labour now believed in democratically arrived-at, party conference-made decisions, rather than union barons arrogantly casting millions of block votes on 'behalf' of their members.

---

545 Stefan Stern, 'Labour's Lost Leader. How Smith Threw the Book at Straw', *New Statesman*, 19 April 2004.

546 Stuart, op. cit., 2005, p. 322.

ASSESSING JOHN SMITH

To sum up John Smith's leadership, he was a cautious, pragmatic politician who placed a premium on preserving party unity and was unwilling to reveal all his policy cards long before the general election (which he expected to win). In terms of political context, Smith was dealt a very favourable set of cards indeed, both in terms of the implosion of the Conservative Party from September 1992 onwards, and in terms of the golden legacy he had inherited from Neil Kinnock. In short, Smith could run the party without any of the internal obstacles faced by his predecessor.

His greatest contribution in terms of output was the reform to OMOV in 1993. It was an early signal to middle-class floating voters that the union barons no longer controlled the Labour Party; rather, individual trade unionists were given the democratic right to be balloted on their preference for Labour leader – a privilege exercised for the first time when Tony Blair won the leadership contest in July 1994. Granted, Smith was not willing to jeopardise party unity by reforming Clause IV. However, Smith's OMOV victory cleared the way for Blair's eventual reform of Clause IV, as the hardest battle of all had already been fought and won by his predecessor.

But, above all, Smith's leadership illustrates that there are two different ways of running the Labour Party. The first approach – typified by Hugh Gaitskell, Neil Kinnock and Tony Blair – is to grab the rest of the party by the scruff of the neck. There is no room for, what Kinnock once termed, *salonistas* – people who sit on their backsides and resist change. Smith wasn't exactly a *salonista*, but he did take a much more relaxed view of party management than his predecessor. Sir David Hare, the playwright and Labour observer, tells a true story of an exhausted Neil Kinnock enjoying a precious night out at the cinema with his wife Glenys, after nine gruelling years at the head of the Labour Party. As Neil relaxed into his chair, he spotted John Smith, the new leader, sitting a few rows in front, eating ice cream. Supremely confident in his own abilities, and sharing none of the insecurities of his predecessor, Smith felt certain of victory. In terms of party management, Smith belonged to the other approach of Labour leader – exemplified by Harold Wilson, James Callaghan, Michael Foot and, some would say, Ed Miliband – in that he sought to balance competing wings of the party.

The jury is out on which way of running the Labour Party is better. Much depends on circumstances. Rarely in Labour history has one reformer – in this case, Neil Kinnock – been followed by another – John Smith. (The example holds for the less radical Gordon Brown following the breakneck leadership of Tony Blair.) Occasionally, the party needs to pause for breath. The question is whether such a pause sets its face against a more modern understanding of British politics – as exemplified by Philip Gould – whereby parties are organisms that must adapt rapidly to changes in electoral preferences, or else risk death due to ossification.[547]

547 Gould, op. cit.

CHAPTER 18

TONY BLAIR

JOHN RENTOUL

Tony Blair became Labour Party leader in July 1994 (following the death of John Smith), comfortably beating John Prescott and Margaret Beckett in the leadership contest. He led the party to win the 1997 general election by a landslide, with a majority of 179 seats. Further general election victories followed in 2001 and 2005, before he resigned as leader in the summer of 2007. John Rentoul argues that, using the statecraft criteria, Blair can only be judged an emphatically successful Labour leader. With an intuitive feel for public opinion and natural communication skills, he developed a winning electoral strategy by moving Labour policy to the centre. Government was well run under Blair and he won the battle of ideas on many policy areas, such that David Cameron adopted some of them as Conservative policy. Blair's successes in terms of party management and constitutional reform were less clear-cut. But, in the end, as Rentoul argues, Tony Blair was still one of the most successful prime ministers since the UK became a democracy.

• • •

It is almost as if Tony Blair's successors set out to draw attention to his strengths as a leader. Gordon Brown, David Cameron, Ed Miliband and even Nick Clegg have each provided case studies, by means of contrast, for Blair's qualities as party leader and Prime Minister. Let me take the five headings proposed by Jim Buller and Toby S. James in Chapter 2 in turn.

WINNING ELECTORAL STRATEGY

First, a winning electoral strategy. This is one plane on which the assessment of Blair ought to brook no argument. No single party has won elections so convincingly under the universal franchise as Labour did in 1997 and 2001. The argument has, nevertheless, been brooked ever since. It has been said that Labour would have won in 1997 if it had put up a donkey with a red rosette as leader – or, without the insulting implication towards him, if the party had still been led by John Smith. This is a strong theme of revisionist Old Labour history: that it would have been better to have won the 1997 election with a smaller majority but on a more socialist platform.

Blair addressed the question in his memoir *A Journey*: 'I assessed that there were three types of Labour: old-fashioned Labour, which could never win; modernised Labour, which could win and keep winning, which was my ambition from the outset; and plain Labour, which could win once, but essentially as a reaction to an unpopular Conservative government.'[548] Smith's half-modernised party was, what Blair describes as, 'plain Labour'. Smith had no patience with the Bennite checklist of so-called left-wing policies – one-sided nuclear disarmament, withdrawal from Europe, public ownership of industry – but he had frustrated Blair with his reluctance to make a bolder pitch for the centre ground.

There is no doubt, however, that the 'reaction to an unpopular Conservative government' was a powerful one, after the failure of John Major's European ERM policy in 1992. The Conservative Party responded badly to adversity, tearing itself apart on the European question, while Major's leadership seemed weak – although that raises precisely the question now at issue, namely: to what extent can the personal qualities of a leader defy the constraints of history?

Blair's distinctive qualities can be defined more clearly than Major's in this period, which tells us something. He rejected the Smith approach

548 Tony Blair, *A Journey*, London, Hutchinson, 2010, p. 83.

– characterised by Peter Mandelson as 'one more heave' – of relying on the Tories' unpopularity to carry Labour into government. When he became leader, Blair took nothing for granted, and continued to move Labour towards the centre. In part, this was because he too was a prisoner of history: many in the Labour Party, but especially the modernisers around Blair, were scarred by the failure of the opinion polls to pick up the shy Tories and the late swing in 1992. They assumed that Labour's comfortable lead in the polls in 1994 might vanish like a vapour trail when it came to the test, and Blair, in particular, was determined to take no chances. The common view that Labour would have won in 1997, regardless of leader, policy or image, was a retrospective one formed only after the majority of 179 seats was safely counted.

That said, the character of Blair's leadership was quite different from Smith's. Both recognised the importance of reassuring the voters that Labour could be trusted to manage the economy, but Smith placed a higher value on keeping the party, and even the old idea of the wider labour movement, united. His view of party reform, after the modernisers had bullied him into securing 'one member, one vote' for the selection of candidates and 'one person, one vote' for the election of future leaders, was that he wanted 'no more adventures'. And, although Smith would probably have made some of the policy changes that Blair made as Leader of the Opposition, he would not have made all of them.

Thus, there is the risk that a Smith-led government would have been committed to the UK adopting the euro, when the main European currencies were locked together in 1999, and to a Scottish Parliament without a referendum. In both cases, Smith would either have risked problems in the House of Lords – they may have found a way around the Salisbury Convention (whereby the Upper House cannot block a manifesto promise) – or, worse, he might have actually succeeded in carrying through the policies.

Blair showed some skill, therefore, in removing policies that would have not only discouraged people from voting Labour, but would have detracted from Buller and James's second test of leadership – governing competence – to which I shall come in a moment.

Getting the basic policies right was a condition of Blair's success in building a winning electoral strategy, but, on its own, it fails to account for the scale of the triumph. Indeed, Deborah Mattinson's research in 2012 suggested that 'policy', as such, did not feature among the qualities people value in leaders. The qualities identified by her survey were, in order: being a 'strong communicator'; decisiveness; integrity; being a good listener; vision. The research was into political leadership in general, but it offers a good basis for judging Blair's success as an opposition politician.[549]

Since the reaction to Blair really set in among commentators, after 2005 his skills as a communicator have tended to be seen in a negative light. The negative connotations of 'spin' – a label attached to Blair and New Labour during the first term of government – curdled into something more toxic by the time Blair left office. By then, being a 'good communicator' was part of everything that was wrong with his time as Prime Minister.

Before 1997, however, Blair's communication skills were regarded overwhelmingly positively. With his fresh face, plain speaking and young family, he embodied optimism, can-do and compassion. In one line in 1993, *Private Eye* captured his appeal: 'The only member of the Labour Party a normal person could ever vote for.' That he spoke 'normal English' on television was one of his greatest strengths. Indeed, it was for this reason that I thought, when interviewing him for the BBC in 1992, that he would be leader of the Labour Party one day: what I called his 'bipartisan reasonableness' in natural speech 'cut through' on television, which was then, and still is, the dominant medium of mass communication.

Of course, there was nothing normal about him, and, although he sounded natural on television, this was partly an artifice of learned skills and an unnatural degree of self-control. When I first wrote a biography of him, in the months after his election as Labour leader in 1994,[550] I interviewed John

549 Deborah Mattinson, 'What is leadership?', *Britain Thinks*, July 2012, accessed 3 March 2015 (http://britainthinks.com/sites/default/files/WhatIsLeadership-print.pdf).

550 John Rentoul, *Tony Blair: Prime Minister*, London, Faber Finds, 2013.

Lloyd (my former editor at the *New Statesman*), who had been a member of the Hackney South & Shoreditch Labour Party general committee alongside Blair in the 1980s. I said that one of Blair's great strengths was that he was so completely normal. 'Oh, he's not normal at all,' said Lloyd. 'I think he would regard himself as completely exceptional.' So he did, and so he was – as we can now see clearly, especially since his own memoir has offered such an insight into the workings of that unusual mind. Typically, he commented on his own communication skills in *A Journey* as if observing someone else:

> When people say to me, 'Oh, so-and-so, they don't believe in anything, they're just a good communicator' – as a statement about politics, it's close to being an oxymoron, certainly for the top person. At the top, the scrutiny is microscopic. It is soul-penetrating.[551]

Although coming across well on television is partly innate – some people do and some people never will (one of the cruellest lessons of politics) – there are skills that can be taught and can make a big difference. Blair had good teachers in Peter Mandelson, Alastair Campbell, Anji Hunter and – before any of them – Gordon Brown, but he also had a fine understanding of the art of communication himself, and he was always learning. His self-control went far beyond editing out the 'um's and 'er's that disrupt genuinely natural speech; he thought ahead to how words and colourful phrases might be reported by journalists, always eager to report gaffes and splits. To take a small example, in a news conference during the 1987 election, he said Margaret Thatcher's housing policy was the product of 'an unchecked and unbalanced mind'. This was seized on as, 'Labour says Prime Minister is mad.' It was not a mistake he made again. One of the few times his care with words let him down was when he accidentally committed himself to ban fox-hunting on live television. He was always his own best spin doctor.

By contrast, Brown, although he could turn a phrase ('Tough on crime,

551 Blair, op. cit., p. 73.

tough on the causes of crime' being the most celebrated example), could not deliver it. One reason Blair overtook him to become Labour leader in 1994 was that Brown, as shadow Chancellor, was mired in the mechanical delivery of sound bites, and failed to convey a clear message. Much later, Brown was able to turn his uncommunication style somewhat to his advantage, contrasting himself with his polished predecessor as a badge of integrity.

Of the party leaders who followed Blair, Clegg was probably the most like him in his communication style. The Liberal Democrat surge during the 2010 election campaign was driven by a notably Blairite performance in the first of the televised debates. Clegg came across as youthful and energetic, exploiting his position as the emphatically reasonable centrist, and employing a rehearsed gimmick of looking directly into the camera at important points. But Clegg lacked Blair's attention to policy detail, and thus found himself in serious difficulty as soon as he was in government – the U-turn on tuition fees being the most striking example.

Blair's skill as a communicator was not merely as a performer, however. As well as an intuitive feel for public opinion, he had a good understanding of how the media worked. In particular, as Leader of the Opposition, he understood the opportunity offered by the pining of many leading commentators, editors and proprietors for the moral certainties of Thatcherism. He saw his chance to step into a vacuum – a chance Smith was unsuited to exploit. 'That is the Grade I point to understanding the politics of that era and to understanding the genius of Tony Blair,' said Charles Clarke at the time.

Thus it was that Blair's attempt to neutralise the hostility of the *Daily Mail* and *The Sun* – which had been so damaging to Neil Kinnock – was more successful than he could have hoped. The attack of the *Mail* was blunted and *The Sun* even urged its readers to vote Labour. At the 1997 election, Labour, for the first time, commanded the support of more than half the newspapers, in terms of sales. Figures compiled by Stuart Wilks-Heeg, Andrew Blick and Stephen Crone for the Democratic Audit found that Blair was backed by newspapers accounting for 61 per cent of total sales in 1997, 71 per cent in 2001 and 58 per cent in 2005. Before then, Labour's highest share had been 44 per cent at the 1970 election. Afterwards, at the 2010 election, it fell to 15 per cent.[552]

As for decisiveness, Blair – once gently mocked by Jonathan Powell, his chief of staff, as a 'flibbertigibbet' – was flattered by the contrast with his immediate successor. Brown's tenure as Prime Minister was nearly destroyed on the launch pad when he dithered over calling an election in the autumn of 2007. He seemed incapable of understanding how the speculation would take on a life of its own in the media – something that Blair would have felt, almost without thinking. In this dimension of leadership, Blair is more similar to Cameron. Indeed, civil servants who experienced the transition from the Brown government were full of praise for the speed and volume of Cameron's decisions. There has always been a veneration in the 'permanent' side of government for the ability to simply make decisions, regardless of quality. Making decisions and sticking to them is certainly a necessary part of good government, even if it is not sufficient on its own.

Miliband was nearer the Brown pole of decisiveness than the Blair one. As a minister, especially at the Cabinet Office, he had a poor reputation among civil servants for decision-making, and several of his parliamentary colleagues said that he 'cannot make a decision to save his life' as Leader of the Opposition. This did not become evident publicly in the way it did with Brown's election that never was. Miliband's style generally was closer to Smith's 'one more heave' than to Blair's 'permanent revolution', but times change: the Labour brand was strong, whereas in 1992–97 it was ambiguous. Miliband had none of Blair's personal charisma, so maybe it made more sense for Miliband to lead in a lower key.

Mattinson's three other qualities – integrity, being a good listener and vision – are rather less easy to assess. Integrity is one of the central problems of politics, and became more of a problem in Blair's time, after the Iraq War, and in Brown's time, as the MPs' expenses scandal contaminated much

552 Stuart Wilks-Heeg, Andrew Blick and Stephen Crone, 'The Democratic Audit of the UK 2012', Democratic Audit, Liverpool, p. 330, Figure 3.1i.

of public life. 'Being a good listener' stands for the related problem of politicians being seen as 'out of touch' – a problem of which Blair was always acutely aware. Despite his use of opinion research – especially focus groups carried out by Philip Gould, who began as a Labour Party pollster but ended up as a US-style political consultant to Blair personally – Blair seemed to regard the erosion of trust in him as inevitable. His aim was to slow down the process as much as possible, and to try to husband his declining store of 'in-touchedness' for as long as he could.

As for 'vision', that is probably one of those things that the voters say they want until they actually get it – unless it simply means a clear sense of general purpose and character, in which case it is much the same as being a good communicator.

GOVERNING COMPETENCE

The second dimension of leadership in Buller and James's taxonomy is governing competence. Here, again, there is a popular myth – which grew up largely after the event – that Blair, in his arrogance and inexperience, did not understand government, and thus rode roughshod over the principles of sound administration – which was eventually to be his downfall.

It is certainly true that Blair, and most of his Cabinet, lacked government experience. As Blair said in his memoir: 'On 2 May 1997, I walked into Downing Street as Prime Minister for the first time. I had never held office, not even as the most junior of junior ministers. It was my first and only job in government.'[553]

This inexperience caused some problems, although they are not usually the ones that animate Blair's critics. Blair should not have carried on with the Millennium Dome, for example, but it was a Conservative project to which he had agreed in opposition. Nor would a group more seasoned in ministerial

553 Blair, op. cit., p. 1.

office have brought in the Freedom of Information Act in the form in which it was enacted in 2000. Looking back, Blair was stunned by his mistake:

> You idiot. You naive, foolish, irresponsible nincompoop. There is really no description of stupidity, no matter how vivid, that is adequate. I quake at the imbecility of it ... For political leaders, it's like saying to someone who is hitting you over the head with a stick, 'Hey, try this instead,' and handing them a mallet.[554]

But these instances are not what most of his critics mean. For them, Blair was responsible for politicising the civil service with special advisors, running an informal sofa government and therefore making decisions on foreign policy with which they disagreed.

Actually, the Blair governments were pretty well run – well enough run, in any case, to merit re-election twice. The 2001 election is often overlooked. In many ways, it was the most uneventful election in modern voting history. Labour lost six seats, the Conservatives gained one, and Blair's majority was reduced from 179 to 167. Yet, it was also one of the most interesting. Not only had Blair been exceptional at the first aspect of leadership – campaigning for election – but he was good enough at the second aspect – governing competently – to win by a huge margin twice. And, not only that, he governed competently enough to defy entropy, as well as an elite consensus that the Iraq War was a disaster, to be re-elected a third time by a comfortable margin.

Ultimately, there is no objective measure of governing competence except the test of re-election, so this part of the assessment of Blair's leadership qualities also ought to brook no argument. Indeed, the 'sofa government' critique collapses when Blair is compared with his successors as Prime Minister. Brown's weaknesses as an administrator were nothing to do with the supposed politicisation of the civil service, and, if Blair had been accused of informality in decision-making, Brown was to demonstrate what that really

554 Blair, op. cit., p. 516–17.

looked like. Brown's use of personal email in addition to formal paper records, for example, caused confusion.

Then, when Cameron became Prime Minister, he quickly replicated three of Blair's administrative innovations, including the expansion of special advisors (which Cameron and Clegg had criticised fiercely when in opposition). Under Blair, the number of special advisors reached a peak of eighty-four. Under the coalition, the total had reached 107 by its final year. Despite Cameron's promise in opposition to 'cut the cost of politics' by limiting each Cabinet minister (apart from himself) to one special advisor – and also Clegg's promise that 'special advisors will not be paid for by the taxpayer' – the coalition agreement put the limit up to two special advisors per Cabinet minister, with nothing said about their being paid for by the political parties themselves. By 2014, nine Cabinet ministers had three special advisors, and Clegg had hired twenty for himself as Deputy Prime Minister.

Cameron also reinvented the Prime Minister's Delivery Unit – the tiny target-setting and progress-chasing unit run by Sir Michael Barber in Blair's second term – after it had been absorbed into the Treasury and allowed to atrophy under Brown. It was called the Implementation Unit, reporting directly to the Prime Minister and the Deputy Prime Minister, but the idea was the same. Linked to this was Cameron's continuation of Blair's 'stocktakes' – meetings with individual ministers ('making sure that the government is delivering on things we said we would do') that take place outside the formal structure of Cabinet sub-committees. These were complicated by the need, sometimes, to include Clegg, but otherwise followed the Blair template.

A fourth reinvention, which would not have been notable except that the Conservatives had criticised Labour's 'top-down targets' while they were in opposition, was the renaming of targets as benchmarks, metrics or standards. It would be hard to imagine any government operating without setting itself measurable objectives.

In the end, the main test of governing competence, however, lies in securing prosperity and stability for the people, and the avoidance of mistakes. Andrew Graham, the economist who is now chairman of the Scott Trust (which owns *The Guardian*), said, at a Fabian conference before the 1997 election, that the greatest achievement of a Labour government – if elected – would be 'not to mess up the economy'. Well, Blair personally dodged that one. The first cracks in the long-rising slope of economic growth showed a few weeks after he left office in 2007, although the crash, when it came the following year, was his joint property with Brown. Some of the prosperity of Blair's later years turned out to have been built on the sand of a credit boom, and those levels of national income per head have still not been recovered at the time of writing. But much of the rise in living standards was real, and the improvements in public services – the NHS, and schools and universities, in particular – have been sustained. He avoided mistakes on the scale of the poll tax or the European ERM, and it is always worth remembering that, for most voters, the biggest mistake of the Blair government was not the Iraq War, but allowing too much immigration.

PARTY MANAGEMENT

In the end, though, it was party management – the third of Buller and James's tests of leadership – that did it for Blair. He was eventually forced out by a Labour Party that was tired of making the compromises he demanded, although the party mistook voter fatigue – Blair having become over-familiar after eight years at the top – for a willingness to vote for a slightly more 'left-wing' leader and programme. The John Smith thesis, if you like, was finally tested, and found wanting, thirteen years later.

From the moment he was elected Labour leader, Blair had used his party apparatus as a foil to dramatise and reflect his centrism to the voters. The debate over rewriting Clause IV of the party's constitution was a reversal of the truism that divided parties are unpopular. Blair deliberately divided his party, which voted for the change by 65 per cent to 35 per cent in 1995, and secured a substantial dividend from the bank of public opinion. He had taken a risk, shown leadership and won the argument.

The pattern would be repeated in government. Partly because of the size of his majority, but partly because of his permanent drive towards the centre, governing-party MPs rebelled more frequently than they had done before, despite the claim that New Labour was a 'control-freak' government. Even though Blair notionally had a huge majority, he came within five votes of losing in 2004 on tuition fees.

In opposition, when the 'control-freak' label was first applied, Blair's attitude to his party combined ideological distance with micro-management. In opposition, you cannot *do*, you can only *say* – as Blair was fond of saying – but something you *can* do in opposition is fix party organisation, which is why his team devoted an inordinate amount of time and energy to managing Labour Party conferences. However, this may have been a misallocation of resources. Blair might have done better to have focused on promoting local parties as campaigning organisations, and (at the other end of party management) on better succession planning – it may not have prolonged his leadership, but it could have made a difference to what happened after he had gone.

Although Blair and his Labour critics both conspired to present him as a leader alien to the traditions of the party, it should be remembered that he left behind him a parliamentary party (and a party in the country) that was essentially Blairite in outlook. In the 2010 leadership election, party members voted for David Miliband over his brother by 54 per cent to 46 per cent, and Labour MPs by 53 per cent to 47 per cent. It was only because the national machines of the three big unions – Unite, GMB and Unison – used their control over their membership lists to deliver the union vote to Ed Miliband by 60 per cent to 40 per cent that David was defeated. If Blair had not lost interest in organisational reform – admitting sheepishly, when Ed Miliband pushed for individual trade unionist affiliation and the abolition of the electoral college in July 2013, that 'Frankly, I should probably have done it as leader' – David Miliband would have become leader in 2010.[555]

555 Tim Bale, *Five-Year Mission: The Labour Party Under Ed Miliband*, Oxford and New York, Oxford University Press, 2015.

The contrast between Blair and Ed Miliband in party management is striking, although, as Blair's praise for Miliband's changes to the union link demonstrated, they were not polar opposites. And Miliband's assiduous maintenance of party unity was, to an extent, forced on him by the fact that he was not the choice of his own MPs. Nevertheless, Miliband sought to keep the party together by balancing a 'leftier than before' rhetoric with – when forced to choose – some pragmatically centrist policies. How much good that did him, given his failure to construct a strong election-winning strategy, became clear at the 2015 election.

POLITICAL ARGUMENT HEGEMONY

The fourth of Buller and James's tests is the extent to which a leader builds a political argument hegemony. This is a test that Blair knew he was being set when he had watched as Margaret Thatcher was hailed by the fashionable thinkers of the 1980s – led by Martin Jacques, the then editor of *Marxism Today* – for having established a hegemonic dominance over British politics.[556] As Labour's employment spokesman, Blair even wrote an article for *Marxism Today* in October 1991, in which he discussed how the state could become a 'vested interest in itself, every bit as capable of oppressing individuals as wealth and capital'.

Mind you, by the time of that article, Thatcher's 'hegemony' had proved itself to be more fragile than some of the trendy Gramscians had thought, and she had been replaced by the less-than-hegemonic Major.

In any case, it was not clear how much Blair actually learned from Thatcher. The nature of his 'project' (a *Marxism Today* word) was a lot vaguer than her liberal market economics, and he started by building the widest possible support, whereas she had started by asserting herself against

556 See: Stuart Hall and Martin Jacques eds, *The Politics of Thatcherism*, London, Lawrence & Wishart, 1983.

the consensus, arriving at temporary hegemony by force of character and good luck (the Labour opposition split and General Galtieri overreached himself).

However, Blair succeeded in changing the terms of trade. While the *Marxism Today*ers had simply wrung their hands at Labour's apparent powerlessness against the Tory promise of cuts in the basic rate of income tax, New Labour managed to win three times by challenging the Tories on where the public spending axe would fall. Even in 2010, a defence of public spending against fiscal stringency was fought to a draw – except that the Liberal Democrats changed sides after the votes were cast.

Indeed, if the test is the extent to which your opponents feel they have to change to accept your ideas, Blair was hegemonic. Just as Labour had accepted the privatisation of utilities and restrictions on trade union power, the Conservative Party under Cameron accepted the minimum wage, no increase in selective schools, the establishment of academy schools, gay equality, and generous foreign aid. Just as Thatcher did by being in power so long, Blair was able to change the tenor of the times – in his case, towards a moderate social democracy.

BENDING THE RULES OF THE GAME

The final test proposed by Buller and James is bending the rules of the game to make winning elections easier for the leader's party. If anything, Blair appears to be guiltier of the opposite. By designing a workable plan for devolution of power to Scotland, he not only undermined the case for Scottish over-representation in the House of Commons – the number of Scottish MPs was cut from seventy-two to fifty-nine with surprisingly little fuss in 2005 – but he also created a power base for the Scottish National Party, whose impact against the Labour Party's interest was seen in 2015. I say 'appears to be', however, because it seems plausible that devolution merely crystallised a problem that would have needed to be faced at some time or other – perhaps to have denied Scotland devolution at that point might have harmed Labour even more.

Similarly, the creation of a directly elected Mayor of London provided a base first for Ken Livingstone – a left-winger expelled from Labour, who won as an independent in 2000, before being readmitted to the party in 2004 – and then for Boris Johnson, who won two terms as a Conservative from 2008.

Otherwise, there was little system change under Blair. Directly elected mayors in other cities had a patchy take-up, and John Prescott's plans for elected regional assemblies fell at the first hurdle – a referendum in the north-east of England in 2004. The only other change was to the law on political funding – to make donations public, to ban foreign donations, and to cap election spending. The leader most disadvantaged by the new regime turned out to be Blair himself, when loans taken by Labour before the 2005 election to avoid disclosure (donations were disclosable but loans were not – a loophole in the law) embarrassed him in 2006, after he sought to nominate some of the secret lenders for peerages.

The scandal was another weight that dragged Blair down towards setting the final limit on his time as Prime Minister. He had already defied political gravity, leaning heavily on Brown's reputation as Chancellor to get him over the line in the 2005 election, but now an aftershock of the Iraq War – in the form of Blair's support for Israel in the Lebanon – convulsed Labour MPs and forced Blair to announce that that year's party conference would be his last.

He lasted a little longer than ten years as Prime Minister, having won three elections with average majorities greater than Thatcher's (137 to ninety-six), although she outlasted him at No. 10, staying for eleven and a half years. Like her, he was never defeated in an election, but was deposed by his party among fears that the leader had become a liability. Those numbers of prime ministerial longevity and cumulative majorities are crude measures, but they are the main objective index of effective political leadership.

On that basis, he was Thatcher's equal – and comparison with his various successors helps to explain why. Blair was a better communicator than Brown or Miliband, and more decisive than either of them. He was more rigorous than Clegg, and more attuned to public opinion than Cameron. He was, therefore, one of the most successful leaders since the United Kingdom became a full democracy.

CHAPTER 19

GORDON BROWN

STEVE RICHARDS

Gordon Brown was elected to Parliament as MP for Dunfermline East (later Kirkcaldy & Cowdenbeath) in 1983, and joined the shadow Cabinet in 1989 as shadow Secretary of State for Trade, before becoming shadow Chancellor of the Exchequer in 1992. He became Chancellor in 1997, when New Labour won power, and remained at the Treasury for ten years. Despite his time at No. 11, in three electorally successful consecutive Labour governments, Gordon Brown served as Prime Minister for fewer than three years, and he lost the only general election he fought. Steve Richards argues that Brown's electoral fortunes were partly the result of mismanaging the matter of whether or not to call an election in the autumn of 2007, and that the events surrounding this decision derailed an otherwise sound strategy for his prime ministership. Brown was also unfortunate in having to come to power under the most difficult of circumstances.

• • •

In order to make a judgement on a Prime Minister, we must take a close look at the context in which he or she acquired the crown. For reasons I will go on to explain, Brown became Prime Minister under unusually daunting circumstances. What is more, the challenging background was part of a pattern during his long career. Brown never had it easy. By 2007, when he finally entered No. 10, he had been travelling along a thorny path towards the summit for fifteen draining years. What happened in those preceding years was nothing compared with what was to follow once he entered No. 10, but the highly complex challenges he faced when he became shadow Chancellor in 1992 help to make sense of Brown's brief and stormy rule as Prime Minister.

Brown became shadow Chancellor following Labour's fourth successive election defeat. In the bleak post-election meeting of the NEC, the party's polling and focus group guru Philip Gould presented the reasons why Labour had lost yet again. Gould declared gloomily: 'In the end, it comes down to this. Voters do not trust us with the economy. They do not trust us to spend their money. They do not trust us with their taxes.' After all Neil Kinnock's heroic party reforms, Labour was still not trusted in relation to economic policy in general, and 'tax and spend' in particular. This was Brown's dark inheritance.

He realised from day one as shadow Chancellor that he faced a stark conundrum. If Labour were to have a chance of winning next time, he would have to reassure voters that he could be trusted on the economy, while also finding a way of addressing the low levels of government spending on increasingly fragile, and, in some cases, decrepit, public services.

If there were to be a Labour government in the future, voters would expect it to deliver improved public services. Yet voters did not trust Labour to spend a halfpenny, let alone billions of pounds. Consider the challenges Labour faced after its 2015 election defeat, not least the perceptions of economic incompetence. Multiply that by 100 to get a sense of the intimidating mountain Brown faced in 1992.

The fact that, between 1992 and 1997, Brown addressed the conundrum successfully is one of the epic achievements in recent British politics. The fact that he continued to do so in power as Chancellor is an even more titanic achievement. Over the first two terms, at least, Brown managed to increase investment in public services, Labour continued to win elections, the markets remained calm, and newspapers that had regarded public spending as largely a waste of money stayed supportive.

He made the ascent via a number of different, complicated routes. First of all, the partnership with his young advisor Ed Balls was of critical importance, and was largely under-estimated by colleagues, opponents and political observers. Many contemporary commentators and politicians viewed their relationship almost entirely through a distorting prism, choosing to see a couple of toxic bullies bashing around various senior figures in the Labour Party. What actually happened over that period was much more interesting and important. The Brown/Balls relationship will be revisited by historians once everyone has calmed down about the Blair–Brown civil war. When the historians do look again, they will note that, together, Brown and Balls re-wrote left-of-centre economic policy at a point when Labour appeared doomed to eternal opposition because of its approach to the economy.

Brown was the politician who set the framework. His great insight was to recognise that, if he repositioned the party's public pitch to the media, business leaders and the wider electorate, there would be space still to improve public services and, to some extent, address issues relating to inequality. Brown insisted resolutely that Labour could not put up the most familiar taxes – most specifically, income tax – if they wanted to win, and that Labour had to be trusted before it could spend much additional cash. From the day he became shadow Chancellor, he leaped on 'Tory tax rises', and stopped his colleagues from making spending pledges of any kind. In the meantime, he sought out tax rises that would be safe to advocate, such as a one-off tax on the privatised utilities that were making soaring profits. Balls was the young economist, previously a leader-writer on the *Financial Times*, who filled in much of the detailed policy. He had been an advocate of Bank of England independence before he became Brown's advisor, and subsequently worked on how the fundamental reform could be implemented in a way that would grant independence while still giving the elected Chancellor considerable influence. Balls knew that Brown had no political space to propose income tax rises, so he worked on other revenue-raising measures that were less totemic and electorally fatal.

At key moments in the years to come, Balls challenged Tony Blair. Brown did so most days of the week. Blair gave little thought to economic policy in opposition, or while he was Prime Minister. He left it to Brown – a pattern that continued when David Cameron became wholly reliant on George

Osborne to determine his government's economic policy. Later, Blair's admirers expressed bewildered frustration when wondering why Blair never sacked Brown. One of the many reasons was that, in the end, Blair knew no other colleague was qualified to meet the titanic demands. In the post-1992 period, at least, Blair largely appreciated what Brown was doing, and was generous enough to realise that, while he was flourishing as shadow Home Secretary, Brown faced the tougher task.

Nonetheless, Blair became timidly assertive at times. There were key emblematic moments after Blair became leader, when Brown and Balls had to confront what could sometimes be Blair's more shallow and defensive approach to policy-making. I cite two of several. Before the 1997 election, Rupert Murdoch's newspapers were insisting that Labour commit to not putting up the overall tax burden. Blair was minded to respond by making such a pledge. He and Brown had already made a commitment not to increase levels of income tax, and Blair now wanted to go much further in order to appease *The Sun* (in particular), superficially convincing himself that a Labour government could manage without raising the overall tax burden. If he had committed to the pledge, he would not have been able to make the necessary investment in public services he subsequently wanted (and urgently needed) to implement. Blair often proclaimed his boldness, but, in reality, he was more fearful than Brown in challenging their Thatcherite inheritance.

A youthful Balls was the one who took Blair on over making such a sweeping commitment in relation to the tax burden, suggesting at one meeting that such a pre-election pledge would be a lie. For certain, the pledge would have destroyed Brown's political strategy, which was to signal a new, tougher approach to 'tax and spend', while more stealthily raising the tax burden in order to meet the need for higher spending. Blair would not have been able to make his subsequent pledge to raise health spending to the EU average if he had prevailed in his short-term desire to appease right-wing newspapers before the 1997 election.

At various points during his leadership, the EU became Blair's preoccupation. Early on, he saw 'Europe' as his historic mission, ending the UK's ambiguous relationship with the continent (as he put it). Towards the end of his leadership, he regarded the UK's entry into the euro as a counter to his support for the US in Iraq – the pro-Europe Prime Minister as well as the pro-US Prime Minister. By focusing forensically and persistently on the economic consequences of joining the euro, Brown and Balls ensured the preoccupation did not go very far. These were important negative interventions, but, much of the time, their focus was more positive, in that they created new, durable economic policies.

Meanwhile, there was an ongoing debate about the future of public services throughout the period of the Labour government. The debate was complex. Blair was instinctively right in his restless quest for innovation, and right also in the self-serving conservatism of the public sector, but Brown and Balls were correct, too, when they responded by, in effect, stating: 'Hold on a minute; you are telling us to go and find the money to increase spending on the NHS. You then want to introduce reforms where hospitals could go bankrupt, so we are taxing people to pay for hospitals that might close.'

The debates were complicated, sometimes deep and ideological. They revolved around the relationship between state and markets – what works and what appears to work superficially. They were never resolved in the New Labour era, or under the subsequent leadership of Ed Miliband.

More widely, Brown, who was three-quarters social democratic, believed that, after the 1980s (and especially 1992), the social democratic case could not be made as an election pitch. The British media, and parts of the British public in the short-term, would not allow it. He and Blair were in total agreement strategically about the need to keep Middle England and its newspapers on board. Instead, Brown believed that it was possible to extend social democracy by stealth. His approach was to increase public spending discreetly, and then retrospectively say: 'Look at what we've done; the Tories threaten to cut it.' The sleight of hand was smart. Voters approved of the investment once it had been made. Nine years after Labour's slaughter in 1992, Blair and Brown fought the 2001 election on 'Labour's investment versus Tory cuts' – a huge leap forward that would've seemed impossible after its fourth election defeat.

By 2007, when Brown became Prime Minister, he had already been implementing stealthy social democracy for a very long time – so much so that he had become famous for his stealth. Political opponents started to refer regularly to 'Brown's stealth taxes'. For Brown, this was a dangerous contradiction – he was known for being stealthy in the same way that Harold Wilson became famous for being devious. If you're devious, no one should know you're devious. Similarly, if you become well known for raising taxes stealthily, the strategy is blatantly no longer working.

For Brown as Prime Minister, the context was even more complex and daunting than the broader political situation in 1992 when he first become responsible for Labour's economic policies. He had been at the centre of the political stage for too long – the shelf life in the modern era being around ten years. Unnecessarily, he had alienated an army of colleagues in his battles with Blair, mistaking aggressive rudeness for a political weapon. By 2007, Labour was well behind in the polls. Tony Blair's personal ratings were in severe decline. The new Conservative leader David Cameron was getting standing ovations at every meeting of NHS workers he addressed, not because they adored him, but because of the complete chaos surrounding Labour's health policy at that point. Iraq also remained toxic.

Yet, during the so-called 'leadership contest' – the absurd one-man contest in which Brown was the only candidate – the newspapers, which Brown rightly still cared about, were echoing the view of *The Sun*'s editorial: 'The test for Gordon Brown's leadership is whether he sticks to Tony Blair's policies on Iraq and public service reform.'

This was Brown's nightmarish inheritance as Prime Minister. He knew he had to move on from Iraq and he knew he had to reform public services in a different way to Blair, yet he knew also he had to keep on board the same set of newspapers (and the voters whom those newspapers attracted). The so-called Blairites in his party were also closer to *The Sun*'s editorial line. Brown knew that divided parties lost elections. He had to keep the Blairites on board while seeking to move on from Blair.

BROWN IN OFFICE AS PRIME MINISTER

It is a myth that Gordon Brown had no plan for office when he got the job of party leader and Prime Minister. He did – and the thinking was characteristically smart and multi-layered, both fearfully cautious in the short term and more ambitious in the longer term. For the period before the general election, Brown appointed Ara Darzi, a distinguished doctor, to review various NHS services. He had a pretty clear idea of the outcome that he wanted to achieve. In effect, Darzi had a remit to propose reforms that met with internal NHS and patient support, while also reassuring newspapers that reforms were continuing.

Brown also understood that the growing lack of trust in the government, especially after Iraq, was both threatening Labour's election prospects and undermining faith in democratic politics more widely. In response, he launched a characteristically cautious, but, in the view of some (Jack Straw specifically, who was given the remit), potentially radical constitutional reform.

There are other examples of changes that were quite subtle, but significant, such as the slight distancing in chemistry between the UK Prime Minister and George W. Bush on foreign policy.

In all cases – NHS reform, constitutional reform and foreign policy – Brown signalled incremental change. Brown had calculated, sensibly, that it would take a year to get the balance right between a small shift from the last period of Blairism and the keeping-on-board of Blair's supporters in his party and in the newspapers. After an election in 2008, he would have more ambitious plans in all three policy areas (and others), which he would feel able to pursue once he had acquired the authority of winning an election as Prime Minister.

He never won such an election, though. The speculation that erupted about an early campaign soon after he entered No. 10 – which he had not anticipated – destroyed his pre-election calculations. Brown made one fatal mistake: foolishly, he assumed that the speculation about an early election would, in itself, destroy Cameron. Brown calculated that the frenzy of uncertainty would undermine the new Leader of the Opposition and drain him of confidence. A wounded Tory leader would be part of the repertoire that Brown could build on as he moved towards the election he planned for 2008.

Instead, Cameron remained impressively calm. The early election speculation mounted and ran out of control, and then Brown backed down. He did not call the election.

Brown had under-estimated how popular he would be when he became Prime Minister and had not thought deeply about how the honeymoon would lead to near irresistible calls for an early election. Such had been his oscillating ride as a senior politician, he had ceased to predict what might happen next in terms of how voters perceived him. This is not surprising. For a leader who quickly afterwards acquired a simplistic reputation as a loser, it is worth recalling the many ups and downs in his career (before he sank to the deepest depths with his mishandling of the early election frenzy).

In 1994, Brown was internally unpopular as shadow Chancellor, acquiring his reputation for fiscal prudence, so it was Blair who stood for the leadership. Brown had no choice but to stand aside. In 1997, Brown became popular, not least in the media, and many commentators hailed him as the chairman of the board – making the big decisions. After the attacks on the US in 2001, when Blair appeared to be a figure of global significance, Brown was widely dismissed as a marginal figure, doomed never to become Prime Minister. By 2005, Brown was so popular again that Blair had to bring him back to run the election campaign he had planned to run without him. By 2006, Brown was so unpopular that parts of the Labour Party were urging other candidates to stand as Blair's successor. When he became Prime Minister, Brown was so popular that Labour's fortunes in the polls were transformed far more quickly than he had anticipated, and he was under pressure to call an early election. When he failed to call the early election, he became the most unpopular Prime Minister since opinion polls began.

After encouraging speculation about an early election and then not calling one – out of justifiable fear he might lose – Brown was dead politically. The strategy he had planned no longer made any sense. He was not what he wanted to be – the apolitical father of the nation (a contrived position, of course, but one he felt comfortable with as he sought to build a big tent of support). The strategy for incremental policy change up to an election he had planned for around the time of the May local elections in 2008 made no sense any more. Suddenly, everything was out of the window. Almost as importantly, his team of close allies fell out over what had gone wrong and who was culpable. Fully alert to the nightmare, Brown was plunged into gloomy despair.

Instead of a year-long path towards an election, Brown was faced with the nightmare of three years with no strategy. This was emphatically the only course he had never contemplated, generating many wrong accusations that he'd had no idea what to do when he reached No. 10. He had thought about an early election and he had planned for one in a year's time, styling himself as the father of the nation seeking a fresh mandate, having healed some of the wounds from the final phase of Blair's leadership. Suddenly, in October 2007, a few months after acquiring the crown, he had been exposed as a partisan figure, and he had no public voice to accompany his new fragile position. His public voice had always been that of an almost apolitical figure, while he covertly made left-of-centre changes on the side. He never used the term 'redistribution' in public, but quietly redistributed. He never used the term 'social democrat', even though part of his agenda was social democratic. He no longer had a public voice and he was dangerously exposed.

How did he respond to the biggest trauma of a tempestuous career? On the whole, badly. For him, it was the ultimate nightmare. He was never good at coping calmly with problems of any sort or dealing with people, and here he faced a terrible problem in which he needed the support and buttress of many.

REFLECTING ON BROWN AS PRIME MINISTER

In his dependence on a range of individuals – from Peter Mandelson to Alistair Darling, who he had previously regarded as a short-term Chancellor before Balls moved to the Treasury – Brown became powerless.

One of the many tragic ironies of his career is that he had ached to become leader and Prime Minister, tormented by the ambition, but, when he achieved it, he ended up being far less powerful than when he was Chancellor. It is a twist of Shakespearean proportions: when he finally seized the crown, he became relatively powerless.

One of the reasons for the mighty impotence was that he lost control of the Treasury. In opposition, Brown, to his great credit, recognised that he had to seize control of the Treasury. In 1997, he and Balls went in there and dominated as resolutely as Geoffrey Howe had in 1979. In the Treasury, he combined prudence with purpose. Conveniently, the media focused largely on the prudence, singing his praises. But the purpose mattered just as much – social justice, in the form of better public services and help for the poor, largely through tax credits. For the first time, the Treasury, as an institution, was asked to focus on public service outcomes and equality. In 1979, Geoffrey Howe entered the Treasury with his first monetarist Budget already written. Brown was as well prepared and equally radical in intent. In control of the Treasury, he was in control of the government.

The most interesting revelation in Darling's memoir was not the claim about what a monster Brown could be – we all knew that. Darling revealed in his book that, when Brown appointed him as Chancellor, he also told him with admirable candour that ultimately he wanted Balls in that position. Brown could be thuggish towards colleagues, but he was not devious. Brown's moods were all on the surface. He told Darling that Balls would be in the Treasury quite soon and that Darling would only be there for a short time. Once more, we are left to reflect on what might have been. If Brown had killed off speculation about an early election immediately, and instead held one the following year, Balls would have been Chancellor if he had won.

But, after the non-election, Brown lost his authority, Darling became the commanding figure in the Treasury, and Brown never replaced him with Balls – though he was desperate to have Balls there, utterly dependent on their partnership. Even in No. 10, Brown had sharp political instincts, but Balls was the economist who could turn instinct into policy. He was now dealing with Darling, who took a much more orthodox Treasury view, and Brown could do nothing about it, although he had become deeply wary of Treasury orthodoxy.

If somebody had told Brown in the mid-2000s – say, 2005 – that in one of his first reshuffles, he would bring back Peter Mandelson, he would have gone and lain down in a darkened room for about a month at the prospect. Unfairly, he had come to loathe Mandelson for the latter's support of Blair. But Brown had to bring Mandelson back because he was becoming powerless. Actually, that was one of his smarter moves; the return of Mandelson calmed down a partially insurrectionary parliamentary party and had a unifying impact on the Labour Party at a point when many were predicting meltdown.

But then there was meltdown of a different sort. Brown had a period of rotten luck – a quite breathtaking sequence of genuine misfortune that not even his worst enemy could have blamed him for. Brown *was* to blame for some crises, but he was incredibly unlucky as Prime Minister. Everything started to go wrong: various Cabinet ministers were accused of fiddling their expenses (when he had hoped to rebuild trust); officials lost all the child benefit data (when he had hoped to convey solid competence before calling an election); and then there was the global financial crash and the near collapse of the UK economy. Here was a Prime Minister – already in despair because of the non-election and the utter implosion of everything he planned – who now faced the prospect of banks going bankrupt within minutes.

On the whole, his response to the nerve-shredding emergency was impressive. While Cameron was arguing for immediate real-term spending cuts, Brown coordinated a near global fiscal stimulus. He brought the world leaders together for the G20 in London, including statespeople like Merkel, whose every instinct would normally have been against a coordinated fiscal stimulus. By the time of the 2010 general election, the British economy was growing again. No bank had gone bankrupt in a way that would have caused utter chaos; people had still got their money out. Subsequently, David Cameron and George Osborne, with the active support of the Liberal Democrat leader Nick Clegg, claimed that the UK was as fragile as Greece in 2010. This was not the case.

In many respects, it was fortunate for the UK that Brown was PM when the crisis erupted. As a long-serving Chancellor, he was well qualified to rise to the crisis: he knew all the key players and he had been immersed in the politics and policies of the financial sector for more than a decade. Bizarrely, the crisis saved his leadership, giving him a renewed sense of purpose.

Yet, at the most testing moment imaginable for a leader, sections of his party were conspiring to remove him, although he was well suited to lead during this particular form of apocalyptic crisis. There was no one else remotely qualified to become Prime Minister at such a time, and if, following an act of regicide and a bloody leadership contest, David Miliband had become Prime Minister in 2008 or 2009 – when banks were on the verge of collapse, with implications for the entire economy – he would not have known what to do or who to turn to.

Brown's substantial response to the global crisis was, of course, too late to save his career. It was all too late even by October 2007, just months after him seizing the crown. He was doomed by the non-election frenzy. Nevertheless, saving the British economy from collapse and an even deeper recession will go down as a significant achievement in the context of a broader career in which Brown often triumphed against the odds.

Even so, the causes of the crisis marked the end of his version of New Labour, as the war in Iraq sowed the seeds for the fall of Tony Blair. For both Blair and Brown, the seeds of their electoral success grew to destroy them. Blair had concluded that, after the defeats of the 1980s (when Labour was seen as anti-US and soft on defence), a Labour Prime Minister had to be loyal to the US President and be an ally in military missions. In being loyal to President Bush, Blair marched towards his doom. Brown worked on the assumption that a Labour government had to be seen to be close to the thriving financial sector. As Labour Chancellor, he felt he would be trusted if seen in the company of senior bankers. When he wanted to convince the public to accept a tax rise to pay for the NHS, he asked a banker to commission a report into the future funding. Suddenly, bankers were the biggest public enemy in the land. His protective shield made him more vulnerable. In the decade that followed, Labour leaders struggled to escape from Iraq and the banking crisis; Blair and Brown had moved towards Iraq and the banking crisis precisely to escape their party's past.

Viewed from the perspective of the global financial crash – a framing shaped by Cameron, Osborne and Clegg after the 2010 election – Brown's leadership, and his long tenure at the Treasury, looks reckless. But the Cameron–Osborne–Clegg narrative – that Brown's spending triggered the crash – is a highly one-sided account. Viewed from the perspective of when Brown started out on his thorny path in 1992, a different narrative emerges. After four Labour election defeats, Brown worked with some of the post-1979 orthodoxies, rather than seeking to challenge them one more time and risk facing another electoral setback. Within those orthodoxies, he found the cash to build more hospitals, improve public transport and redistribute cash to the low paid, while also presiding over a growing economy and winning elections. After the crash in 2008, he led the economy out of a recession that could easily have turned into a depression.

Brown's departure from No. 10 was as much a part of a pattern as his arrival. Virtually every commentator in the land, as well as a host of Cabinet ministers, had assumed for months – and, in some cases, years – that Brown would be gone on the Friday after the 2010 election, a leader burdened for the rest of his life by a terrible defeat.

As with almost every episode in Brown's long career at the top of politics, assumptions formed with unswerving confidence proved to be wrong. Brown was not going anywhere other than Downing Street on the Friday after the May election, and Labour was still more or less alive as a national force, suffering some terrible losses but also making a few unforeseen advances. The denouement of Brown's career was appropriately complex and ambiguous. Unquestionably, Labour had been defeated at the election – yet no other party had won. Far from becoming immediately irrelevant in the early hours after the 2010 election, Brown and his party were still clinging to power.

The days that followed were a compressed version of his highly charged, nerve-racking career – a career marked by dashed hopes and moments of soaring optimism, fuelled by self-interest and altruistic ambition. As the votes were being counted, Brown was a player again in the midst of historic turmoil. Typically, his control over the levers of power was far from straightforward. For many years, Tony Blair had stood in Brown's way. When Brown finally became Prime Minister, he was, for much of the time, too unpopular and unsure of himself to take full control. David Cameron and Nick Clegg were then preparing to pull levers, too. Brown was used to it, always operating in a tiny amount of space and seizing moments when they arose. Politicians quite often act in the way they do because they have no choice. Great ones make the most of tiny spaces.

Brown had lost and won. He had come second in the contest, but he was still breathing as a leader, and the Conservative leader David Cameron was in no position to claim victory. The Conservatives had won 307 seats, Labour was second with 258, and the Liberal Democrats had fifty-seven. A hung parliament presented possibilities. Brown always seemed to function on frighteningly narrow political terrain. Even though he had lost, he had options – or appeared to. Fleetingly, there was the possibility of a historic coalition with the Liberal Democrats.

It never happened. History took another course, but – in the light of subsequent events – perhaps, for both Labour and the Liberal Democrats, the option should have been explored more extensively than it was. Labour suffered further setbacks in 2015, and the Liberal Democrats were virtually wiped out.

How simultaneously odd and typical that it was Brown, the most tribal of politicians, who was left briefly negotiating with other parties in the hope of forming a coalition, and not Blair, who had envisaged a partnership with the Lib Dems when he became leader in 1994, nor Ed Miliband, who polls had suggested wrongly might lead a coalition after the 2015 election. Brown was making history even when history was passing him by – a Labour leader seeking to work with other parties in government, once again responding to circumstances he had not envisaged.

What he had envisaged in 1992 and then accomplished – making Labour economically credible while having the space to invest in public services – is what makes him a much bigger figure than current orthodoxy allows.

CHAPTER 20

ED MILIBAND

TIM BALE

Ed Miliband, son of the influential left-wing intellectual Ralph Miliband, was elected to the House of Commons in 2005. After Gordon Brown became Prime Minister in 2007, Miliband was quickly promoted to become a minister in the Cabinet Office, and then Secretary of State for Energy and Climate Change. Miliband defeated his brother David in the fourth round of the leadership contest that followed Brown's resignation in the aftermath of the 2010 general election defeat. Tim Bale argues that Ed Miliband was ultimately an unsuccessful Labour leader in statecraft terms. He lost the 2015 general election and saw the number of Labour MPs in Parliament further decline from 2010. However, Miliband faced enormous challenges as leader that should be factored into our assessment. He took over after a crushing defeat in 2010 – which would always have been difficult for the party to recover from – and the increasing fragmentation of the electorate made fostering a winning electoral strategy difficult. He also faced skilled opponents in David Cameron and George Osborne.

• • •

Ed Miliband isn't the first Labour leader never to become Prime Minister. Nor, given that exactly the same thing happened to Neil Kinnock in 1992, is he the first Labour leader to think, on the eve of an election, that he might soon be standing on the steps of No. 10, only for the results on the night to tell a completely different story to the one told by opinion polls, thereby dashing his dreams. Indeed, Miliband's defeat by David Cameron in

May 2015 was every bit as devastating as the one suffered by Kinnock at the hands of John Major almost a quarter of a century before. And it prompted just as many people who had previously kept their doubts to themselves, at least in public, to tell anyone who would listen that they always knew he would lose. History, however, may end up judging him just a little more kindly. This, after all, was a man whose party, only a few months before he took over in September 2010, had slid to one of its worst ever electoral defeats; a man whose legitimacy as leader was contested from the get-go; a man who clearly lacked the kind of charisma seen as a *sine qua non* in our 24/7 multi-media environment; a man whose political opponents probably stooped lower than they had ever stooped in order to prevent him winning. And yet, winning – or, at least, preventing Cameron from winning – was precisely what many pundits and pollsters were predicting Miliband was going to do. How, then – using the idea of statecraft to frame our analysis – do we explain the way in which he appeared to come so near, yet ended up so far away?

BIOGRAPHY

Ed Miliband, for all his faults, always had three things going for him as a person and as politician, namely: self-belief; reasonably good people skills; and a marked facility with numbers. Miliband was always good at the latter, even as a teenager: indeed, it was one reason he got into baseball (after spending some time in the United States when he was growing up) – a game for those who love stats as much as sports. No surprise, then, that mathematics provided one of the A grades that helped get him from his London comprehensive into Oxford to read PPE. No surprise either that, once there, he dropped philosophy and focused on economics – a subject in which he eventually went on to take a Master's at the LSE, the university where his father Ralph had first forged a name for himself as one of the country's foremost left-wing intellectuals. It seemed natural, too, that, after a short stint working as a television researcher, Miliband was drawn not just to Labour, but to its Treasury team.

To his detractors, of course, the fact that Miliband spent over a decade working for Brown, initially as a special advisor and eventually as chair of his Council of Economic Advisors, was little more than a schooling in the top-down, 'government-knows-best' statism so beloved of the so-called 'clunking fist'. Perhaps, but Miliband's long spell at the Treasury proper between 1997 and 2005, when he was elected for the rock-solid Labour constituency of Doncaster North, was also a highly practical education in power. He emerged from the experience convinced that whoever came after Blair and Brown would have to transcend the TB–GBs – the tensions and mistrust between the two men and their camps that threatened to tear apart New Labour from the top down. Miliband also emerged knowing which levers to pull and what buttons to press, both in Whitehall and at Westminster. But he did so, in marked contrast to some of those he worked with, without losing his reputation as a genuinely nice (if slightly geeky) guy – someone able, partly because of that reputation and partly because his older brother David was stranded on the other side, to reach across the Blair–Brown divide. Not for nothing did Ed earn the nickname, among those who worked for Tony rather than Gordon, as 'the emissary from Planet Fuck'.

Ultimately, however, what some see as Miliband's inveterate tendency to want to square circles did not mean he could avoid choosing between New Labour's two rival poles of attraction. Undoubtedly, ideology played a part in him jumping one way rather than the other: Brown was – just about – more his kind of social democrat than was Blair. It was also obvious, at least to anyone who could count, that the Chancellor would sooner or later take over at No. 10. Accordingly, when Brown assumed the premiership in late June 2007, Miliband was immediately rewarded with a place in Cabinet, alongside his brother, making them the first siblings to sit together at the top table for nearly seventy years. True, David (as Foreign Secretary) had a much higher profile, especially since, to begin with, Ed was at the Cabinet Office – not necessarily a backwater, but very much a backroom. The gap in seniority between the two narrowed just a little, though, when, in October 2008, Brown appointed Ed secretary of state at the newly created Department of Energy and Climate Change (DECC).

Reviews of Miliband during his time at the DECC are mixed. To his critics, he mimicked his former master's desire to have it both ways and to delay decisions – the fatal flaw that led directly to Brown bottling the 'election that never was' in 2007, and therefore crashing (along with the economy) to defeat three years later. To his admirers, Miliband was in his element. The brief was one that needed a minister who could do detail, think through competing options, and, yes, add and subtract. As for bold and swift decisions (as his friends protest), he took rather than ducked them. For instance, within a fortnight of taking the job, Miliband confirmed that the government would be legislating for eye-watering cuts in emissions. A few months later, he was announcing targets for carbon capture that effectively ruled out the building of new coal-fired power stations in the UK. Miliband also wrung more green-tinged concessions out of Brown on a third runway at Heathrow than many imagined possible.

Even when global climate change talks ran disappointingly into the sand in Copenhagen at the end of 2009, there was an upside. They had provided Miliband with some much-needed overseas experience, but without involving so much foreign travel that he risked, like his brother David, being stranded too far away from the action at home. Now they were over, he could focus on the home remit further, especially since Brown had charged him with drawing up Labour's manifesto for the coming election. Ed, incidentally, was not one of those front or backbenchers who needed to be elsewhere when the parliamentary expenses scandal broke a year before the election. Indeed, he was one of those MPs who had absolutely nothing to apologise for – or to pay back. That this was the case owed less to his facility with numbers than to his old-fashioned sense of propriety. As a well-paid servant of the crown, living with long-term partner Justine, who, as a lawyer, was capable of earning even more than he was, it simply would not have entered his head to claim for the kinds of things that some of his fellow MPs clearly felt happy to charge to the public purse.

But it was not Miliband's spotless record on expenses that saw him through the 2010 Labour leadership contest – a race he'd decided to enter long before the party lost the election in May of that year. His success – and his conviction that he would be successful – came down, once again, to his underlying assurance, friendliness and ability to count. The relationships Miliband had built with union bosses as he put together Labour's 2010 manifesto were clearly crucial: anyone working out how to win the leadership knew the unions were a vital constituency that needed courting, and the decision of most of them to back him clearly proved crucial. Equally crucial, however, was the fact that, unlike his brother, he'd always taken the trouble to chat happily to colleagues, regardless of their rank. That, along with the fact that his small (but perfectly formed) team ruthlessly framed the contest as one between their 'change candidate' and a Blairite throwback, proved vital when the contest came down, as Ed always figured it might, to a handful of MPs' second preferences going to him rather than David.

Miliband, it is true, under-estimated just how much his brother's wounded sense of entitlement (which eventually saw him quit politics and go off to New York to head up a development charity) would tear them apart. But what choice, one wonders, did he really have? Given how unlikely the party was to elect two Milibands in a row, if he really wanted to be leader (which he did), it was literally a one-shot, zero-sum game. Moreover, it was a game Ed believed he had to win because he was convinced – not altogether unreasonably, perhaps – that he stood a better chance than David of preserving the unity of a party that had traditionally sunk into civil war after any big defeat. He was equally convinced he knew how to move on from New Labour in a way that could both help snatch back Downing Street and move the country away from its traditional short-termist, overly financialised, 'Anglo-Saxon' style of capitalism. He wanted to move towards the more managed yet decentralised version seen in, say, Germany – a country that Miliband, encouraged by his long-time *consiglieri* Stewart Wood, had viewed as something as a model for a social democracy that wants to combine sustainability, efficiency and social protection.

It was this, and his willingness to publicly criticise and interfere in allegedly dysfunctional markets (including the newspaper market), that saw

Miliband branded 'Red Ed' by the media, and almost guaranteed him damaging hostility from many in the business world. Yet – along with his opportunistic opposition to hasty missile strikes on Syria in August 2013 and his commitment to reducing university tuition fees – such interventions not only put Labour onside with majority opinion, but also sent a clear signal to left-leaning, if not centrist, voters that the party was back on their side. And it forced the Tories even further into the 'party of the rich' corner, into which they'd already painted themselves after George Osborne reduced the top rate of tax in his 2012 'omnishambles' Budget. Along with Labour's inevitable focus on the NHS and on opposing the bedroom tax, Osborne's Budget also allowed Miliband to quietly shift Labour's stances on immigration and welfare considerably closer (if not, in the end, sufficiently close) to public opinion than they had been in 2010 – and in such a way as to attract amazingly little internal opposition. And that was also the case when it came to his historic reforms of the party's links with the unions, and his refusal, after flirting with it early on in his leadership, to carry on simply parroting their anti-austerity line.

None of those shifts, of course, did anything to help Labour address its precipitous loss of support to the more self-consciously socially democratic Scottish National Party – a meltdown that ultimately contributed heavily to the failure of Miliband's five-year mission (although, given he was intimately involved in Labour's Scottish Parliament election campaign back in 1999 as a special advisor, he might perhaps have done more to foretell and forestall the meltdown). Nor, however – and much more importantly – did these shifts to the centre (or even the right) do anywhere near enough to undermine the Tories' lead on the economy and their message that Labour couldn't be trusted with the public purse.

Given Miliband's own academic background and his father's Marxism – which, for all the abstruse arguments had with others of his ilk about 'structure versus agency', nonetheless acknowledged the centrality of economic matters – his failure to properly come to grips with Labour's inability to win back voters' trust on the economy is mystifying. But only at first glance. The evidence clearly shows that the UK's ballooning deficit and debt were overwhelmingly accounted for by the global financial crisis rather than Labour profligacy. Whether or not the politician in Miliband might have brought himself to pretend that this was not, in fact, the case, and to say sorry for a crime that had never been committed, is unknown, but the economist in him never could. Besides, the economist in him was also betting that George Osborne would be unable to conjure up a sufficiently steep rise in real wages to see the UK's belated return to growth deliver a 'feel-good factor' tangible enough to get the Conservatives over the line. However, because the economy looked as if it was, at long last, on the up, and because Labour still wasn't trusted sufficiently to run it and to control spending, it was a wager that failed.

Miliband's other big gamble failed, too. He realised (how could he fail to?) that he had severe presentational problems. Maybe because they didn't like how he looked and sounded, or maybe because they saw something unnatural in a younger brother supposedly 'knifing' his older sibling to get what he wanted, voters never warmed to him. Miliband worked hard to up his game, and managed, during the general election campaign, at least, to exceed the public's low expectations of him. But, in the end, he was betting that what he thought of as 'substance' would ultimately triumph over what he dismissed as 'style' – that victory would surely go to the wonkish and well-meaning challenger than to the preternaturally posh 'essay-crisis Prime Minister', who simply looked and sounded the part. As it turned out, his opponent – or, at least, those behind his opponent's campaign – proved every bit as adept with numbers as he was. David Cameron and his Conservative Party ended up with over 2,000,000 votes more than Labour, and an overall majority to boot. Miliband – who had been preparing, indeed expecting, to enter negotiations to form a government, even as the exit poll suggesting things hadn't gone to plan was announced – was just as stunned as almost everyone else. By the next morning, he was gone, leaving his shell-shocked party to pick up the pieces, work out what had happened, and get on with choosing his successor.

WINNING ELECTORAL STRATEGY

By definition, since Labour lost the 2015 general election – and lost it badly – Ed Miliband failed to master this most basic of statecraft's tasks. Even his record in the various electoral contests that took place between the two main events that bookended his five years as leader left rather a lot to be desired – so much so that, although the results he achieved were never quite poor enough to prompt disgruntled colleagues to unseat him, they should probably have rung more alarm bells than they did at the time.

Things began ominously with elections to the Scottish Parliament in 2011, where the SNP captured an amazing 44 per cent of the vote to Labour's measly 26 per cent – a drubbing in what was once Labour's heartland. In retrospect, that should have been taken far more seriously as a harbinger of the harrowing to come. In 2012, things looked a little more promising, at least superficially. In local elections in the rest of the country, which took place not only mid-term, but also in the wake of Osborne's omnishambles Budget, Labour gained over 800 councillors, on what psephologists calculated was a notional vote share of some 39 per cent. Yet Labour's lead over the Tories was only 6 percentage points, and it did not do well in all the areas it would need in order to make a strong comeback and win parliamentary constituencies in 2015. By the 2013 local elections, Labour's notional vote share had dropped to just 29 per cent – still ahead of the Tories (on just 25 per cent), but significantly lower than its ratings in opinion polls, suggesting (especially in hindsight) that the latter might have been overstating the party's actual support. A year later, Labour's notional vote share at the 2014 local elections was only around 31 per cent – a poor result, only disguised, firstly, by the fact that it appeared to be doing reasonably well in areas in which it had target seats, and, secondly, by extensive polling on the part of Tory peer Lord Ashcroft, which suggested that Labour was performing slightly better in marginal constituencies than it was nationally. If that was ever the case, it didn't help Labour much in the European Parliament elections that took place at the same time as the local council contest. Labour (on 24 per cent) was beaten into second place by UKIP (on

27 per cent), with the distribution of votes across the regions suggesting that, as some had begun to predict, Nigel Farage's 'People's Army' might end up causing Miliband as many problems as Cameron. Just as worryingly, perhaps, was that Labour only narrowly beat the Tories (on 23 per cent).

Yet the fact that Miliband's electoral strategy wasn't a winning one doesn't mean he lacked any strategy at all. Indeed, one of the main accusations levelled at him by his critics, both before and after the election, was that he was pursuing what they insisted was a '35 per cent strategy' – derived, they claimed, from the conviction that Labour could scrape a narrow victory by retaining the 29 per cent of voters who voted for them in 2010, and adding another 6 per cent, made up primarily from left-wing idealists who had voted Lib Dem at the last election, but had abandoned the party in disgust at Nick Clegg going into coalition with David Cameron. In truth, while Miliband clearly hoped that something like this could be effected, neither he nor his closest advisors believed they could afford to rely completely on such a combination (even if mobilised by what Labour hoped was a superior 'ground game') getting them over the line. After all, some previous Labour voters were bound to switch to the Tories, and not all those disillusioned with the Lib Dems (even assuming they had come over to Labour early on) would stay put. Besides, Miliband and those around him had high hopes of encouraging significant numbers of previous non-voters and first-time voters to give the party the benefit of the doubt. Nor did they completely give up hope that at least some of those who had supported the Tories in 2010 could be persuaded to move in Labour's direction. Indeed, they were seeing little tangible benefit from any economic recovery, and a serious decline in the performance of the NHS, while Miliband was moving Labour's position on immigration, welfare, and tax and spend much closer to that of the average voter.

WINNING THE BATTLE OF IDEAS

The problem with this electoral strategy was that Miliband had won the leadership in the summer of 2010 by appealing not just to those in the party who wanted to move on from the Blair/Brown era (something many voters were happy enough to do), but to those who regarded the very idea of New Labour as some sort of neo-liberal/colonialist aberration. This, and his desire to lock Lib Dem defectors with a left-populist pitch (which he hoped might also appeal to working-class voters who had become detached from Labour since 1997), prevented him from heading as rapidly and as noisily for the centre ground as he should have. Although it eventually happened – and on immigration, welfare, and (by the end) tax and spend, it is important to stress that it *did* happen – it happened too late, and, for the most part, too stealthily, to make much difference. The desire, if not to ditch, then to at least move beyond New Labour, also prevented Miliband reaching back and reminding people of the party's very real achievements – particularly in health and education, and on the economy – between 1997 and 2010. Moreover, segmenting the electoral market, while it may have seemed sensible, risked blotting out the more fundamental truth that any party hoping to win elections has to win over a more nebulous but ultimately far bigger bunch of voters – the archetypal residents of Middle England, who simply want to get on in life, like to see a bit of leadership, value sound government as well as public services, and worry about others ripping them off.

Ed Miliband did chalk up some noticeable wins as Leader of the Opposition, though. He halted what many voters clearly regarded as an ill-advised rush in the summer of 2013 to strike Syria militarily. He also forced the government to take a tougher stance on press regulation (even if it later managed to wriggle out of it) in the wake of the widespread disquiet over revelations in 2011 that tabloid journalists had engaged in systematic hacking of mobile telephones. But, even if these examples demonstrated considerable courage (and, in the case of Syria, helped to bend the rules of the constitutional game in favour of Parliament and against the executive), in neither case was what Miliband did particularly counter-intuitive. Consequently, they failed to cut through a way that might have led undecided voters to re-evaluate either him or his party – something that badly needed to happen sooner rather than later. In particular, Miliband waited far too long before publicly committing his party to fiscal consolidation. He also failed, once he'd done so, to adopt measures that might have made a few Labour eyes water and therefore would've commanded attention and respect (cancelling HS2 and going back on his early commitment to reduce university tuition fees are only the most obvious examples). As a result, Miliband was simply unable ever to persuade people that he really meant it.

Worse, all the time that this was going on, the Conservatives, and their supporters in the media, were utterly relentless (and highly successful) in persuading voters that Labour was to blame for the country's economic difficulties. They made the case that the sensible response to the latter was to reduce spending on supposedly non-core public services, with particular emphasis on pruning back welfare entitlements for working-age and younger people. This was an easy target given the widespread belief that those in receipt of such benefits were lazy and feckless scroungers, rather than (as is the case for the majority of those concerned) simply ordinary people who have fallen on hard times. By the same token, the Tories did little or nothing to counter the equally widespread (if equally misguided) perception that many immigrants are actually 'benefit tourists', whose number can be reduced if only the EU would allow the UK to clamp down on their ability to claim. Miliband, along with those shadowing the Treasury, the Home Office, and the Department for Work and Pensions, clearly decided Labour would have to recognise that 'perception is reality' and adjust its policies in all three areas. Ed Balls (eventually) committed the party to a fully costed programme that would eliminate the deficit in one parliament, while Yvette Cooper and Rachel Reeves made sure Labour went into the 2015 election promising a much tougher line on immigration and welfare than it had back in 2010.

This meant, of course, that Miliband effectively ceded political argument hegemony to his Tory opponents in three electorally crucial areas; although, given that government rather than opposition is by far the best place to try to shift the terms of the debate, whether he could sensibly have done much else is another matter. Anyone tempted to think he should have played things differently should look at what happened when he tried to do otherwise: his populist rhetoric on predatory business and his promise of price freezes worried rather than enthused swing voters, most of whom weren't convinced he would deliver anyway. Likewise, his commitments on the NHS, while aligned with widespread public support for that institution, were discounted because of concerns that his other policies would mean there would be insufficient resources to fund them.

Finally, Miliband's promise to scrap the bedroom tax, to clamp down on zero-hour contracts, to increase the minimum wage, to raise the top rate back to 50p, to introduce a mansion tax, to reduce university tuition fees, and to scrap 'non-dom' status for rich foreign residents all struck a chord with a British public characteristically concerned about helping those at the bottom of the heap without being taken for a ride by those at the top. But his insistent focus on that agenda may well have made it seem as if Labour, unlike the Conservatives, had nothing much to say to those who weren't at the bottom or at the top, but in the middle – in other words, the vast majority of voters. That said, Miliband is far from the only leader of a European social democratic party to be facing the same problem: all are, in some ways, the victims of a social and cultural change that has eroded and alienated their traditional base, as well as economic circumstances that mean there is no longer enough growth or enough money to ensure all shall have prizes.

PARTY MANAGEMENT

Ed Miliband managed to shift Labour's policies towards the centre and to promote new talent without conveying any serious sense of disunity or indiscipline. Naturally, there were arguments – sometimes heated arguments – behind closed doors. However, they were often as much to do with personalities (and his private office and media operation) as politics, and, even insofar as they were occasionally about ends as well as means, they were rarely, if ever, the product of trench warfare between two opposing factions. Indeed, when it came, say, to promoting and demoting people to and from the front bench, Miliband was probably no less adept than most of his predecessors at maintaining a balance between left, right and centre. It is also important to note that he was courageous enough to demand, and canny enough to win, changes to the PLP's rules, which meant that, unlike his predecessors as Labour Leader of the Opposition, he could appoint his own shadow Cabinet, rather than have people foisted on him by his MPs via elections.

That said, Miliband's critics (especially those who believed Labour had to do more to convince the electorate that it was serious about tackling the nation's debt and deficit) argued, with some justification, that the unity he achieved was more apparent than real. That unity was perhaps only the product of: (a) polling, which suggested that Labour had a chance of winning, and, as a result, helped keep his colleagues either on board or at least quiet; (b) a leader unwilling to make the 'hard choices' that would make voters sit up and take notice, but who would not spark outrage among the party faithful and unions; (c) the leader's ultimately counter-productive penchant for disguising shifts to the centre on immigration, welfare, and tax, his opposition to the bedroom tax, zero-hour contracts and tuition fees, and his undying love for the NHS; and (d) the more-or-less explicit decision by many Blairite ultras that he be allowed to fail so that, if and when he lost, they could claim Blair's alternative had been 'tested to destruction'.

Of course, disunity might have broken out if any of the bad blood created by Miliband's decision in 2013 to re-cast (although not abandon) his party's relationship with the trade unions had ended up on the carpet. However, it did not – thanks to the determination of both the Labour leader and the unions themselves to come to some sort of negotiated solution, rather than risk a stand-up fight so close to an election they were desperate to win. Given that voters are nowadays much less worried about unions (and union influence) than they are about politicians who cannot control their own parties, then the discretion and compromise achieved was surely the better part of valour. Miliband can take credit for diluting general secretaries' influence on future Labour leadership contests by moving away from the three-way electoral college system, which elected him in 2010, to a single 'selectorate', comprising members, affiliated supporters and only those union members who explicitly opt in to affiliated membership. Moreover, he managed to do this at the same time as holding on to the union money that, without public funding, is vital to Labour's day-to-day functioning, never mind its election campaigning.

Miliband was also able, aided by general secretary Iain McNicol, to ensure that the party remained in a reasonable state of repair at the grass roots. The upside of his frequently telling party members at least some of what they wanted to hear was that Labour's membership (possibly boosted by an influx of left-wing Lib Dems) may well have risen during Miliband's time as leader. Miliband also managed to get the approval of members both for changes to the way the party selected its leader and for a policy programme that many of those attending the 2014 National Policy Forum would, in their heart of hearts, have considered far too timid. Certainly, Labour did not lose the 2015 general election through any lack of effort or enthusiasm on the part of its activists on the ground.

GOVERNING COMPETENCE

Projecting governing competence is hard for any party that has just been ejected from office, particularly in the wake of perceived shortcomings in its management of the economy – arguably the key indicator of its overall credibility. If the leader of that party then fails, in opposition, to convince the electorate that he is personally 'up to the job', then voters may be more prepared than perhaps they should be to give the incumbent government the benefit of the doubt. Unfortunately, Labour after 2010 was hit with just such a 'double whammy'. The long leadership contest that the party decided to hold in the summer of 2010 gave the Tories time to destroy virtually all its planes while they were still on the ground, obliterating the narrow lead on 'best party to manage the economy' that Labour had regained in the run-up to the general election. It was an advantage that Labour was never able to win back. Its early criticism of the coalition's austerity programme was skilfully exploited by George Osborne to brand Miliband and Balls 'deficit deniers' and then to challenge their attempts later in the parliament (when the economy began to sputter into life again) to insist that they, too, favoured fiscal consolidation. Indeed, given how easy it was for the Tories to identify Labour's leader with the supposedly profligate and hapless Brown regime, it might have been better, at least in hindsight, if Miliband had not (when Alan Johnson felt obliged to bow out as shadow Chancellor a few months after accepting the job) offered the Treasury portfolio to Ed Balls. Balls, after all, could just as easily be tarred with the same brush, and he was even more convinced than Miliband that the Tories would choke off any recovery and be punished for it by an electorate who would then give him the credit for being right all along.

Meanwhile, Miliband himself never managed to approach anything like take-off speed. Ultimately, of course, party leaders' impacts, especially their impact on the electorate, may have less to do with that they actually *do* than with what they *are* – or are seen to be. In other words, the image they have and the impression they create may matter more than any of the moves they make. Moreover, image and impressions are not as easy to manufacture, nor to manipulate and shift, as some people think – particularly if the politician involved is, like Miliband, unwilling or unable in the early stages of his leadership to provide striking and attractive visual images that can 'cut through' to voters. Apart from the obligatory pre-conference family photos, Ed Miliband tended to rely on words. But they were never quite enough or quite right. His party conference speeches and his newspaper profiles, like nearly all examples of their genre, would often begin with an attempt to show the electorate the 'real him' – the emphasis, in his case, on the message that he was far less weird than his wonkish path to power and easily caricatured appearance suggested. Miliband also showed himself a loyal son, determined to defend the honour of his father against an assault on him by the *Daily Mail* as a Marxist who 'hated Britain'.

None of it, however, seemed to make the slightest impact on the impression the electorate had formed of Labour's leader from the outset. Focus group participants continued to write him off as 'weak' and 'weird', while the numbers derived from surveys always put him on a par with those leaders of the opposition who had gone on to lose, rather than those rarer specimens who had turned out incumbent governments. Voters, even a worryingly large minority of putative Labour voters, simply could not see Miliband as Prime Minister. As a result, the man actually doing the job, David Cameron, always beat him by a decent margin (albeit from a low base) on virtually all the leadership attributes tested by opinion researchers, except on the quality of 'being in touch' and/or 'understanding ordinary people', though even the Labour leader's ratings on that score may well have been more a by-product of his party's more 'caring' brand than the result of anything he himself said or did. In an era of valence politics and in a country where – post-Iraq, post-expenses, and post-global financial crash – voters want someone who radiates competence and looks willing and able to make the tough calls required, this was the final nail in Ed Miliband and Labour's coffin.

CONCLUSION

Ed Miliband can be counted a failure – at least, in terms of statecraft. True, he managed the party reasonably well, achieving some important rule changes and maintaining unity. But he was unable to come up with a winning electoral strategy or to win the battle of ideas, and he never came anywhere near projecting governing competence. His critics, nonetheless, have to confront a few facts before rushing to condemn him completely.

First and foremost, Ed Miliband took over just after Labour had gone down to a defeat that was no less disastrous (at least outside Scotland) as the one it suffered in May 2015. The chances of anyone – even his supposedly sainted brother – turning that around in just one term were always tiny. Second, the difficulties faced by Labour in appealing to a more fragmented electorate – much of which is as concerned by immigration as it is with the economy and public services (and important parts of which do not feel sufficiently inspired to actually vote) – are shared by social democratic party leaders right across Europe. Third, Miliband was facing political opponents who are past masters (and much, much better than their Labour counterparts) at using office – at least, before they are seen to have occupied it for too long – in order to alter the terms of political debate. Finally, the Labour Party as a whole cannot escape responsibility for choosing Ed Miliband as its leader in the first place, and then, having chosen him, sticking with him when it became patently obvious that he would struggle ever to convince voters that he was the man for the job. This is not the first time the party has done so, and it is hard to believe it will be the last. Insanity, they say, is repeating the same mistake over and over and expecting a different result.

CHAPTER 21

JEREMY CORBYN

PETER DOREY

Jeremy Corbyn was elected to the House of Commons in 1983 as MP for Islington North. He had therefore been in Westminster for thirty-two years before unexpectedly being elected leader of the Labour Party in 2015. Corbyn led the party into the general elections in 2017 and 2019, losing both contests. Peter Dorey argues that Corbyn faced numerous challenges in office, such as managing the party during the divisive EU referendum campaign, accusations of antisemitism in the party and a hostile parliamentary party. Corbyn's supporters could point to the rise in party membership under his leadership and the increase in vote share in 2017, which prevented Theresa May from winning a majority. However, the party slumped to defeat in 2019, and Corbyn was cited in polls as one of the main reasons why many voters switched from Labour to other parties. In statecraft terms, Dorey concludes that Corbyn's leadership cannot be judged a success.

• • •

Jeremy Corbyn had immersed himself in left-wing politics since moving to north London in the early 1970s, when he became active in the Urban New Left (UNL). Although his socialism was fiercely critical of the depredations of capitalism and its negative impact on the working class especially, much of Corbyn's political involvement was in campaigns and social movements that actively opposed racism, sexism, colonialism and imperialism. The UNL's primary focus on such issues was not just due to the inherent immorality and dehumanisation of such issues and practices per se but also reflected a cognisance that the British industrial proletariat, which previously provided the bedrock of the Labour Party's electoral support, was in decline due to deindustrialisation, globalisation, technological advances and general economic restructuring, in pursuit of maximising profitability and shareholder value.[557] Hence Eric Hobsbawm's assertion that, by the late 1970s, the erstwhile 'forward march of labour' had been 'halted'.[558]

As Corbyn explained to Labour's left-wing (Socialist) Campaign Group in July 1983, while some in the party thus wanted the Parliamentary Labour Party (PLP) to appeal to middle-class suburban voters, he believed that the prime focus should be 'in inner-city areas where there are no major employers except local government and some public services', and in places where 'there just isn't trade union experience, and school-leavers know nothing about the trade union or labour movement'.[559]

Corbyn became actively involved in the UNL by joining the Hornsey constituency Labour Party and also becoming chair of its 'Young Socialists' wing in the early 1970s, before being elected to Haringey Council in May 1974. By this time, he had abandoned his trade union studies course at North London Polytechnic (now London Metropolitan University) and in 1975 was appointed as a full-time organiser for the National Union of Public Employees (NUPE). He became actively involved in social movements such as the Anti-Apartheid Movement and the Campaign for Nuclear Disarmament and consistently called for a united Ireland and a Palestinian state. Corbyn was also active in the PLP's Campaign Group, formed in 1982, and a regular contributor to the left-wing publication *London Labour Briefing*, founded in

557 These changes and trends are now affecting swathes of the middle class, among whom electoral support for the neo-liberal Conservative Party has consequently diminished, with the Conservatives no longer able or willing to offer continued status, stability and security to white-collar workers and professionals.

558 Eric Hobsbawm, *The Forward March of Labour Halted?*, London, Verso, 1981.

559 Quoted in Tony Benn, *The End of an Era: Diaries 1980–1990*, London, Hutchinson, 1992, p. 304, diary entry for 13 July 1983.

1980.[560] Through these activities, Corbyn met other luminaries of the left in the late 1970s and 1980s, such as Tariq Ali, Tony Benn and Ken Livingstone.

Their radicalism and campaigning zeal were naturally reinforced after, and lent added resonance by, the 1979 election of the first Thatcher government, which embarked on a major programme of public spending cuts, privatisation, restrictions on local government, statutory curbs on trade union activities and rights, and strict immigration controls. Seeking to resist these policies imbued the UNL with added impetus, meaning that its associates and activists were brought into even closer and more regular contact with each other, strengthening their ideological affinity and comradeship.

Corbyn was elected as Labour MP for Islington North in June 1983, and although he proved to be a conscientious and diligent servant of his constituents, he continued to expend considerable time and energy on wider, extra-parliamentary activities and campaigns. In this respect, he was very similar to Benn (quite apart from also being teetotal and vegetarian!), who also believed that 'real politics' is mostly conducted outside of Parliament, via grass-roots activities, social justice campaigns and community activism. Moreover, both men enjoyed almost cult-like adulation among many left-wing activists, both within the Labour Party and beyond. This popularity was equally matched by the disdain and derision they attracted from moderate or mainstream Labour MPs and voters, perhaps unduly influenced by the bitter attacks and character assassination they routinely endured from the pro-Conservative press.

Following its heavy election defeat in 1983, the Labour Party steadily moved back towards the centre ground under Neil Kinnock, John Smith and Tony Blair. Corbyn's left-wing stance was thus increasingly at odds with the party's ideological direction of travel, and this reinforced his focus on extra-parliamentary activities and campaigns. Meanwhile, in the House of

560 Jon Cruddas, *A Century of Labour*, Cambridge, Polity, 2024, p. 212; Rosa Prince, *Comrade Corbyn: A Very Unlikely Coup*, London, Biteback, 2016, chapters 4–7; Nigel Cawthorne, *Jeremy Corbyn: Leading from the Left*, London, Endeavour, 2015, chapters 2–4; Andrew Roth and Byron Criddle, *Parliamentary Profiles A-D*, London, Parliamentary Profile Services, 2004, pp. 615–7.

Commons, he was increasingly viewed as a perennial backbench rebel, due to his criticisms of sundry policies promoted by 'modernising' Labour leaders (which he viewed as betrayals of socialism) and his concomitant willingness to vote against the party leadership in parliamentary divisions. Indeed, Corbyn voted against the PLP's stance and the party whips on 617 occasions from 1983, but with 428 of these voting 'rebellions' occurring under Blair and his successor Gordon Brown.[561]

When Ed Miliband resigned as Labour leader following the 2015 general election, the initial leadership candidates were Andy Burnham, Yvette Cooper and Liz Kendall, all of whom were broadly associated with Blairism or 'modernisation'. Corbyn subsequently announced his candidature, having obtained the requisite thirty-five nominations from other Labour MPs just minutes before the deadline. Some of those Labour MPs who nominated Corbyn certainly did not want him as party leader and blithely assumed that he had no chance of winning, but they also acknowledged that an MP from the left ought to be represented, to facilitate a semblance of intra-party debate about Labour's future policies and ideological identity. Then, when the left's candidate was heavily defeated, the 'modernisers' could cite this as further evidence that red-blooded socialism was redundant. As Tariq Ali noted, Corbyn's candidature 'was intended just to show that there was an alternative to the neoliberal leadership that had ruled the country for the last three decades'.[562] At least half of the Labour MPs who nominated Corbyn subsequently voted for other candidates.[563] Certainly, if Labour's leadership contest had been confined solely to the PLP, Corbyn would have fared poorly.

However, a new system for electing Labour leaders had been established in 2014, which created three new categories of voters: fully paid-up members of

561 Ben Wright, 'Labour's Brexit dilemma', BBC News, last updated 27 January 2017, accessed 28 July 2025 (https://www.bbc.co.uk/news/uk-politics-38769838).

562 Tariq Ali, *You Can't Please All: Memoirs 1980–2024*, London, Verso, 2024, p. 606. See also Jon Cruddas, *A Century of Labour*, Cambridge, Polity, 2024, p. 213.

563 Christopher Hope, 'Half of the Labour MPs who backed Jeremy Corbyn desert to rival candidates', *Daily Telegraph*, last updated 23 July 2015, accessed 28 July 2025 (https://www.telegraph.co.uk/news/politics/labour/11756688/Half-of-the-Labour-MPs-who-backed-Jeremy-Corbyn-desert-him.html).

the party, affiliated supporters (such as members of trade unions affiliated to Labour) and registered supporters, the latter required merely to declare their support for the party and pay a nominal £3 fee, which would then entitle them to vote in leadership elections. When Corbyn's candidature was confirmed, there was a surge in registered supporters, whose motive for registering was precisely so that they could vote for Corbyn.[564] Indeed, he attracted the support of almost 84 per cent of registered supporters, compared to 57.6 per cent of affiliated supporters and 49.6 per cent of party members.

Consequently, Corbyn was elected Labour leader with 59.5 per cent of votes cast overall, but he was much more popular among registered supporters outside Parliament than he was among Labour MPs.[565] Indeed, as soon as his victory was confirmed, several senior Labour MPs announced that they would not serve in Corbyn's shadow Cabinet, including Yvette Cooper, Liz Kendall and future Chancellor Rachel Reeves. It was evident from the outset that Corbyn would struggle to assert his authority over the PLP when so few of its MPs had voted for him.[566]

CHALLENGES FACED AS LEADER

Corbyn's political authority over the PLP was, as discussed, limited from the outset. Not only had the majority of Labour MPs not voted for him as leader, they had voted ABC – Anyone But Corbyn. The fact that he was so popular with predominantly middle-class left-wing activists outside

564 Karl Pike, *Getting Over New Labour*, Newcastle-upon-Tyne, Agenda, 2024, pp. 55–6; Phil Burton-Cartledge, 'Class Politics and the Revenge of the Future', in Mark Perryman ed., *The Corbyn Effect*, London, Lawrence and Wishart, 2017, pp. 171–2; Diane Abbott, *A Woman Like Me: A Memoir*, London, Viking, 2024, pp. 216–7.

565 Peter Dorey and Andrew Denham, 'The Longest Suicide Vote in History: The Labour Party Leadership Election of 2015', *British Politics*, 11(3), 2016; Thomas Quinn, 'The British Labour Party's leadership election of 2015', *British Journal of Politics and International Relations*, 18(4), 2016, pp. 759–78.

566 Steve Richards, 'Leadership, Loyalty and the Rise of Jeremy Corbyn', *Political Quarterly*, 87(1), 2016. 12; Meg Russell, 'Corbyn as an Organisational Phenomenon: A Response to Steve Richards', *Political Quarterly*, 87(1), 2016, p. 21.

Parliament reinforced their view that Corbyn was largely a proponent of student union politics and self-indulgent virtue-signalling in a left-wing echo-chamber. Moreover, his repeated defiance of the party leadership in parliamentary votes under Blair further weakened his political authority as leader, because it meant that many Labour MPs now felt similarly disinclined to display any loyalty to Corbyn.

Throughout his leadership, therefore, Corbyn struggled to impose his authority on the PLP, with ideological divisions and policy disagreements reflecting and reinforcing his apparent lack of a mandate and legitimacy to lead the Labour Party in Parliament. This, in turn, perpetuated the perception of a weak or vacillating Labour leader who lacked political credibility.

Apart from general ideological differences between Corbyn and many of his Labour colleagues, and the personal animosity which some of them felt towards him, he faced two particularly debilitating challenges: Brexit and allegations of antisemitism in the party. Corbyn's ambiguous or equivocating responses to these major issues precipitated a leadership challenge, led to the resignation or defection of several Labour MPs, and reinforced the excoriating public criticism from former Labour leader and Prime Minister Tony Blair and some of his closest colleagues, such as Peter Mandelson. All of these exacerbated the widespread impression of a beleaguered leader constantly struggling to exercise authority over his party and who increasingly appeared out of his depth politically.

Brexit

Corbyn was widely associated with the strand of left-wing politics that viewed the EU (and its predecessor, the EEC) as a 'capitalist club', and he had therefore voted *against* the UK's continued membership in the 1975 referendum.[567] A clear majority of Labour MPs supported continued UK membership of the EU when Corbyn became leader in 2015, as did a majority of Labour voters.

---

567 At the time, Corbyn was not yet an MP, but he was active in left-wing politics and in his local constituency party.

However, a majority of Labour MPs represented constituencies that voted Leave in the 2016 referendum. The issue of how to respond to Brexit, and how to devise a coherent and widely acceptable policy, proved a constant problem for Corbyn in terms of leadership, party management and public perceptions of Labour's stance on the issue.[568] Although Corbyn now felt obliged to express formal support for the UK's continued membership, in accordance with the Labour Party's official policy, he never appeared fully committed or enthusiastic; his critics in the party suspected that he remained, at heart, a Lexiter.[569]

In the 2016 EU referendum, the 52 per cent to 48 per cent split between Leave and Remain compounded the problem of Corbyn's equivocation and the ambiguity of his stance. Quite apart from his own latent Euroscepticism, Corbyn struggled to triangulate between respecting the outcome of the referendum, acknowledging that the vast majority of Labour MPs wanted the UK to remain in the EU and recognising that much of the Leave vote had emanated from the party's erstwhile working-class supporters in 'left-behind' towns in northern England and parts of the Midlands.[570] Indeed, among Labour's electoral supporters, there was a discernible division between the party's predominantly anti-EU working-class voters (many of whom abandoned the party in 2019) and its mostly pro-EU middle-class supporters, often graduates in professional and relatively well-paid jobs. It seemed that whichever stance he adopted, Corbyn was going to alienate one section of the Labour Party and/or its supporters.

Any other Labour leader might also have struggled to reconcile Remainers and Brexiteers by devising a constructive and coherent compromise stance, but the animosity felt towards Corbyn meant that his difficulties and equivocation were effectively weaponised against him, so that he attracted scorn

568 John Curtice, 'Remain in light: What do Labour's many Remain supporters want to happen next?', Institute of Public Policy Research, last updated 12 January 2017, accessed 28 July 2025 (https://www.ippr.org/articles/remain-in-light-what-do-labour-s-many-remain-supporters-want-to-happen-next).

569 'Lexiter' refers to a left-wing supporter of the UK exiting the EU. The term is intended to differentiate the left's opposition to EU membership, on socialist grounds, from the often jingoistic and xenophobic opposition of the nationalist right.

570 Cruddas, op. cit., 2024, pp. 218–9.

rather than sympathy. This was a clear example of how Corbyn's lack of political 'capital' grievously hindered his ability to exercise political authority over the PLP and secure the respect and trust of his colleagues.

Consequently, disagreements and equivocation over Brexit continued throughout Corbyn's time as leader, as he oscillated between pledging to respect the referendum result (the apparent democratic 'will of the people'), disputing the details and terms of Britain's departure from the EU (vis-à-vis Theresa May's 2018–9 withdrawal agreement), and supporting another referendum over the type of Brexit ('soft' or 'hard') to be pursued and with the added option of 'remain in the EU' to be included.[571] Consequently, 19 per cent of people who had voted Labour in 2017 but switched to another party in 2019 cited Brexit as the main reason for their switch. These 'switchers' comprised Leave *and* Remain supporters, with both camps dissatisfied or frustrated with, and feeling betrayed by, Corbyn's equivocal stance.[572]

Antisemitism

The other major issue that highlighted Corbyn's lack of decisive leadership, thereupon further weakening his political authority and credibility, was that of antisemitism in the Labour Party.[573] It was not merely the abhorrent antisemitic comments and social media tropes emanating from sundry Labour politicians and other left-wing activists that made the issue problematic for Corbyn but also his own lifelong support for Palestine. This was interpreted by his intra-party and media critics, and many British Jews themselves, as

---

571 On the problems posed by Brexit under Corbyn's leadership, see Wright, op. cit., 2017; Pike, op. cit., 2024, pp. 82–86; Gabriel Pogrund and Patrick Maguire, *Left Out: The Inside Story of Labour Under Corbyn*, London, Vintage, 2021.

572 Chris Curtis, 'In their own words: why voters abandoned Labour', YouGov, last updated 23 December 2019, accessed 28 July 2025 (https://yougov.co.uk/politics/articles/27022-their-own-words-why-voters-abandoned-labour); Paul Hilder, 'Who Labour lost in 2019 – and why', Labour List, last updated 19 June 2020, accessed 28 July 2025 (https://labourlist.org/2020/06/who-labour-lost-in-2019-and-why/).

573 For overviews, see Tim Heppell, 'The British Labour Pary and the Anti-Semitism Crisis: Jeremy Corbyn and Image Repair Theory', *British Journal of Politics and International Relations*, 23(4), 2021, pp. 645–62; David Kogan, *Protest and Power: The Battle for the Labour Party*, London, Bloomsbury, 2019, pp. 336–69; Pogrund and Maguire, op. cit., 2021, chapter 6; Dave Rich, *The Left's Jewish Problem: Jeremy Corbyn, Israel and Antisemitism*, London, Biteback, 2018.

indicative of an innate hostility towards Israel. This meant that even if Corbyn himself was not deemed to be antisemitic, some of the people he associated or aligned himself with vis-à-vis Middle Eastern politics harboured attitudes towards Israel that either were or could readily be interpreted as antisemitic.

The initial response to emerging allegations of antisemitism in the Labour Party, at all levels, was to establish a formal inquiry, chaired by the human rights lawyer Shami Chakrabarti. When its report was published in June 2016, it asserted that while Labour was not 'overrun by antisemitism ... or other forms of racism', there was an 'occasionally toxic atmosphere' and 'too much evidence of ... hateful or ignorant attitudes'.[574] Needless to say, this ambiguous or equivocal conclusion was cited as vindication by both 'sides' in the increasingly bitter argument about antisemitism in the Labour Party. Corbyn and his allies pointed to the statement that the party was 'not overrun by antisemitism', while suggesting that the 'hateful or ignorant attitudes' were not institutional but held by individuals who should be dealt with accordingly, often through disciplinary action. Some of Corbyn's allies also alleged that claims about antisemitism were being fuelled and weaponised by 'his enemies' in the party: those who were ideologically hostile towards Corbyn and were engaged in a 'conspiracy against him' to destroy his leadership.[575]

Against such claims, critics, including those Labour MPs who alleged that they were victims of antisemitic abuse, took the Chakrabarti report's statement that the party was not 'overrun by antisemitism' as tacitly acknowledging the existence of antisemitism but seeking to downplay its scale or seriousness. Moreover, critics also felt vindicated by the report's claim about the 'toxic atmosphere' and 'hateful or ignorant attitudes' in the Labour Party, which they attributed either to Corbyn's own ideological stance or his weak leadership in tackling these problems.

Allegations and cases of antisemitic comments and conduct continued and even increased during the rest of Corbyn's leadership, to the extent that

574 The Labour Party, 'Report of the Shami Chakrabarti Inquiry', last updated 30 June 2016, accessed 28 July 2025 (https://labour.org.uk/wp-content/uploads/2017/10/Chakrabarti-Inquiry-Report-30June16.pdf), p. 1.

575 Abbott, op. cit., 2024, p. 234.

in February 2019, eight Labour MPs resigned from the party citing institutional antisemitism. Corbyn continued to be criticised for failing to tackle the problem more swiftly and decisively, and although he presided over new intra-party procedures and rules to discipline those found guilty of antisemitism, some of his supporters questioned the definition of antisemitism that was being levelled against him and the party by sundry critics, asking whether the definition was too wide. This, of course, compounded the impression that the leadership was not treating the issue with the seriousness it warranted and its victims with the sympathy which they deserved.[576] Even John McDonnell, the shadow Chancellor and a close ideological ally of Corbyn, criticised him for failing to act more decisively on this issue.[577]

Corbyn's failure to tackle antisemitism more urgently and robustly throughout his leadership reinforced the public perception – already fuelled by his ambiguous stance on Brexit – of an indecisive leader, who would be incapable of providing a strong premiership that could successfully promote and defend Britain's interests in an increasingly unstable geopolitical context.

RESIGNATIONS AND LEADERSHIP CHALLENGES

Corbyn's support base (like that of Tony Benn in the 1980s) lay mainly outside Parliament, among left-wing activists, grass-roots members, sundry social movements and progressive campaign groups. The adulation that Corbyn enjoyed among many left-wing activists and social justice campaigners was mirrored by the disdain and distrust he attracted from much of the PLP throughout his leadership. This meant he was always vulnerable to direct leadership challenges (or speculation about them) and defiance from deeply disgruntled Labour MPs, coupled with continued bitter denunciations

576 Cruddas, op. cit., 2024.

577 Eunice Goes, 'Labour's 2019 Campaign: A Defeat of Epic Proportions' in Jonathan Tonge, Stuart Wilks-Heeg and Louise Thompson eds, *Britain Votes: The 2019 General Election*, Oxford, Oxford University Press/Hansard Society, 2020, pp. 85–6.

from Tony Blair and some of Blair's closest allies. These critics berated every aspect of Corbyn's personality and leadership: his overall ideological stance (far too left wing), his policies (denounced as extreme, outdated, unaffordable or unrealistic), his political naivety and his tendency towards vacillation.

In late June 2016, less than a year after Corbyn had been elected as Labour leader, two-thirds of the shadow Cabinet resigned following his dismissal of shadow Foreign Secretary Hilary Benn. They were joined by eighteen shadow junior ministers, including Keir Starmer. Although they had long been deeply dissatisfied with Corbyn's leadership, the catalyst for the mass resignations appeared to be his lacklustre campaigning in the EU referendum, which his critics deemed partly responsible for the Leave result. Corbyn was criticised for not having promoted the benefits of EU membership more clearly and convincingly. This failure was not solely due to Corbyn's own lack of enthusiasm for the EU but also derived from his general lack of communication and leadership skills; his oratory and rhetoric could galvanise activists and inspire enthusiasm at public rallies or Glastonbury Festival, but in these scenarios, he was preaching to the converted. In broader, mainstream public campaigns, however, Corbyn struggled to enthuse or inspire and was certainly rather less charismatic in the EU referendum campaign than prominent Leave advocates like Nigel Farage and Boris Johnson.

In explaining why they were resigning following the EU referendum result, several shadow ministers cited aspects of Corbyn's leadership – or lack of. For example, Vernon Coaker asserted that Britain 'requires leadership and vision that I do not believe you [Corbyn] are in a position to provide', while Heidi Alexander lamented that Corbyn did not possess the 'capacity to shape the answers the country is demanding'. Particularly scathing was shadow Scotland Secretary Ian Murray, who complained that under Corbyn, the Labour Party was 'barely ready for opposition, let alone an election'.[578]

578 All quoted in Owen Bennett, 'Shadow Cabinet Resignations: Vernon Coaker, Lord Falconer, Karl Turner', HuffPost, last updated 26 June 2016, accessed 19 December 2024 (https://www.huffingtonpost.co.uk/entry/another-labour-shadow-cabinet-member-vernon-coaker-quits-on-day-of-mass-resignations_uk_576ffa0ee4b0d2571149d36c).

With Corbyn defiantly refusing either to resign or change course ideologically, following this mass resignation, a PLP motion of no confidence in his leadership was supported by 172 Labour MPs, with only forty supporting him. Yet Corbyn again refused to resign, insisting that the vote had no constitutional validity and that he continued to enjoy strong support in the wider Labour Party, beyond the House of Commons. This was confirmed when Corbyn faced a formal leadership challenge from Owen Smith in July 2016 and was re-elected by 313,209 (61.8 per cent) votes to 193,229 (38.2 per cent). However, as with his original election as Labour leader, Corbyn continued to preside over a PLP in which only a relatively small minority of Labour MPs supported him.[579] Consequently, his own personal deficiencies as Labour leader continued to be reflected and reinforced by his lack of political authority and legitimacy in the eyes of most of his parliamentary colleagues.[580]

During the 2015 Labour leadership contest, Blair claimed that those whose hearts were with Jeremy Corbyn 'need[ed] a transplant', although it is likely that such trenchant criticism, and the source it came from, enhanced Corbyn's support on the left. Immediately upon Corbyn's election as Labour leader in September 2015, Blair denounced his 'Alice in Wonderland' politics, which operated in 'a parallel reality' where 'emotional impact is king', rather than focusing on practical policies that would appeal to mainstream British voters without alienating the business community.[581] Blair later condemned Corbyn for turning the Labour Party into a 'glorified protest movement' with 'cult trimmings ... marooned on fantasy island', which was the antithesis of a

---

579 Peter Dorey and Andrew Denham, 'Entirely as expected? What the voting data tells us about Corbyn's re-election', British Politics and Policy Blog, London School of Economics, last updated 26 September 2016, accessed 28 July 2025 (https://blogs.lse.ac.uk/politicsandpolicy/labour-2016-voting-data/).

580 Andrew Scott Crines, David Jeffery and Timothy Heppell, 'The British Labour Party and leadership election mandate(s) of Jeremy Corbyn: patterns of opinion and opposition within the parliamentary Labour Party', *Journal of Elections, Public Opinion and Parties*, 28(3), 2018, pp. 361–79.

581 Richard Osley, 'Tony Blair attacks Jeremy Corbyn's "Alice In Wonderland" politics', *The Independent*, last updated 30 August 2015, accessed 28 July 2025 (https://www.independent.co.uk/news/uk/politics/labour-leadership-contest-tony-blair-attacks-jeremy-corbyn-s-alice-in-wonderland-politics-10478524.html).

'credible government' in waiting.[582] He subsequently reiterated that Corbyn had been 'a classic protest politician completely unsuited to leadership, let alone to governing', adding that he was 'radical, but not sensible' and had dragged the Labour Party 'to the far left'.[583]

These trenchant criticisms were strongly echoed by Peter Mandelson, probably Blair's closest and strongest ally in the New Labour 'project'. By electing Corbyn as leader, following Labour's defeat under left-leaning Ed Miliband in the 2015 general election, Mandelson claimed that 'the general public now feel we are just putting two fingers up to them, exchanging one loser for an even worse one'. However, Mandelson also counselled against seeking to topple Corbyn at this stage, suggesting that it would be better to wait until 'he demonstrates to the party his unelectability at the polls'.[584]

Two years later, with Corbyn still *in situ*, Mandelson admitted: 'I work every single day to bring forward the end of his tenure in office. Every day I try to do something to rescue the Labour Party from his leadership.'[585] Mandelson subsequently believed that some of Starmer's early difficulties as Labour leader were a legacy of the Corbyn era, which had alienated many mainstream or moderate voters who nonetheless harboured progressive or liberal values. Under Corbyn, according to Mandelson, the party had 'disappeared into a weird ideological netherworld'.[586]

---

582 'General election 2019: Blair attacks Corbyn's "comic indecision" on Brexit', BBC News, last updated 18 December 2019, accessed 28 July 2025 (https://www.bbc.co.uk/news/election-2019-50829352).

583 Tony Blair, 'Without total change, Labour will die', *New Statesman*, last updated 11 May 2021, accessed 28 July 2025 (https://www.newstatesman.com/politics/uk-politics/2021/05/tony-blair-without-total-change-labour-will-die).

584 'Lord Mandelson: Don't rush to oust Jeremy Corbyn', BBC News, last updated 25 September 2015, accessed 28 July 2025 (https://www.bbc.co.uk/news/uk-politics-34355545).

585 Mikey Smith, 'Peter Mandelson says he is "working every day" to topple Jeremy Corbyn', *Daily Mirror*, last updated 21 February 2017, accessed 28 July 2025 (https://www.mirror.co.uk/news/politics/peter-mandelson-says-working-every-9860086).

586 Anoosh Chakelian, 'Peter Mandelson: "I'm afraid Keir Starmer has come badly unstuck"', *New Statesman*, last updated 4 September 2021, accessed 28 July 2025 (https://www.newstatesman.com/encounter/2021/05/peter-mandelson-i-m-afraid-keir-starmer-has-come-badly-unstuck).

ASSESSING JEREMY CORBYN'S RECORD AS LABOUR PARTY LEADER

There are several academic models for evaluating the success of political leaders, with each schema adopting specific criteria. Examples include Fred I. Greenstein's,[587] Leonard Stark's,[588] and Thomas Quinn's – this one developed as an updated adaptation of Stark's.[589] However, in order to ensure consistency with other authors in this volume, we will rely primarily on Jim Bulpitt's seminal model of 'statecraft' as the criteria for successful leadership, entailing a winning electoral strategy, evident governmental competence, skilful party management and political argument hegemony.[590] The utility of Bulpitt's criteria has been acknowledged in this volume (Chapter 2) and elsewhere by Toby S. Jones and Jim Buller.[591]

Clearly, according to these criteria, Corbyn's leadership of the Labour Party from 2015 to early 2020 must be judged a failure. His supporters would naturally point to the enormous increase in Labour's membership under his leadership (and, indeed, the boost it received when he announced his candidature); the enthusiastic crowds that often attended his public speeches and rallies; the extent to which he crafted a policy platform that marked a sharp break from Blairism by offering a programme which was much more akin to socialism, particularly with regards to economic and industrial policies, public services and wealth redistribution; and the wholly unexpected boost in Labour's electoral support in 2017, which deprived Theresa May's Conservatives of a parliamentary majority.

587 Fred I. Greenstein, *The Presidential Difference: Leadership Style from FDR to Clinton*, New York, Martin Kessler Books/The Free Press, 2000.

588 Leonard Stark, *Choosing the Leader: Leadership Contests in Britain from Macmillan to Blair*, Basingstoke, Macmillan, 1996.

589 Thomas Quinn, *Electing and Ejecting Party Leaders in Britain*, Basingstoke, Palgrave Macmillan, 2012.

590 Jim Bulpitt, 'The discipline of the New Democracy: Mrs Thatcher's Domestic Statecraft', *Political Studies*, 34(1), 1985, pp. 19–39.

591 Jim Buller and Toby S. James, 'Statecraft and the Assessment of National Political Leaders: The Case of New Labour and Tony Blair', *British Journal of Politics and International Relations*, 14(4), 2012, pp. 534–55.

Yet a greatly increased membership and enthusiastic, well-attended rallies (often entailing joyful chanting of the leader's name) are largely irrelevant if the conviction and passion are not shared by either the party in the House of Commons or – much more importantly – the wider electorate. Corbyn's popularity among Labour's grass-roots and mostly younger left-wing activists was in inverse proportion to his popularity among Labour MPs, the vast majority of whom had voted for other leadership candidates in summer 2015. Corbyn thus led a divided and fractious PLP, which never accepted his political authority, did not view him as a credible or competent leader or likely election winner, considered him ideologically extreme or out of touch, and was repeatedly frustrated at his equivocation over vital issues like Brexit and eradicating antisemitism in the party.

Meanwhile, his 'success' in the 2017 general election was clearly a one-off, due to unique circumstances. By 2019, his political stock had greatly depreciated, for all the reasons discussed in this chapter. Indeed, that Corbyn had proved relatively successful in 2017, to everyone's surprise, merely ensured that thereafter, his critics, both in the Labour Party and the press, redoubled their efforts to denigrate and discredit him, thereby ensuring that he would not fare as well in the next general election. Of course, his dithering over Brexit and tackling intra-party antisemitism also greatly weakened his political authority and popularity from 2017 onwards.

All of these factors prevented Corbyn from developing political argument hegemony, for he could scarcely inspire the enthusiasm and trust of the wider British electorate for his radical economic programme or persuade mainstream or wavering voters of his leadership competence when he was so publicly disparaged and disavowed by many of his fellow Labour MPs. Certainly, the constant mutual distrust between Corbyn and the PLP was the very antithesis of socialist values such as comradeship, fraternity and solidarity.

In the 2019 general election, Corbyn was cited as the main reason why many voters switched from Labour to other parties; 35 per cent of those who had voted Labour in 2017 attributed their abandonment of the party to Corbyn's leadership – or perceived lack of. Some of this was a personal dislike of Corbyn and some of it was because of specific issues like antisemitism and Brexit, but for many Labour 'switchers' in 2019, Corbyn was also variously viewed as ideologically extreme, an advocate of unrealistic or unaffordable policies (such as abolition of student tuition fees), a risk to national security, unpatriotic and generally *not* prime ministerial.[592] These constituted a toxic cocktail of disdain and distrust, and they were the antithesis of successful statecraft.

592 Curtis, op. cit., 2019; Hilder, op. cit., 2020; Michael Ashcroft, ***Diagnosis of Defeat: Labour's turn to smell the coffee***, London, Biteback Publishing, 2020.

CHAPTER 22

KEIR STARMER

PATRICK DIAMOND

Keir Starmer assumed the role of Labour Party leader in 2020. He enabled the party to win the 2024 general election with a landslide majority, reversing a trend of four successive general election defeats. Patrick Diamond argues that Keir Starmer's attributes and achievements in steering the vessel of his party have been undeniable. Drawing on the statecraft approach, Starmer has proved adept at party management while devising a winning electoral strategy. In opposition, he was able to mobilise political support, demonstrating that his party had fundamentally changed and could now be trusted to manage the British economy. He was ruthless in exposing the incompetence of successive Conservative prime ministers. Yet the paradox is that the attributes required to be a skilful opposition leader are not necessarily those needed to be an effective Prime Minister. It is not yet clear whether Starmer has the qualities necessary to make a success of the premiership.

• • •

The current Prime Minister, Keir Starmer, defies conventional wisdom as to the elusive qualities required for leadership success in politics. Starmer's hastily acquired reputation as the 'unpolitical politician' epitomises his legal background, long career of public service and late entry into elected politics. He is judged, even by many of his own MPs, to possess few of the conventional attributes of effective political leadership.

Yet this assessment does not accurately reflect Starmer's achievements and strategic acumen. He acquired the leadership in 2020, despite the apparent dominance of the Corbynite left within the party. Starmer manoeuvred Labour through the arduous grind and ordeal of opposition, exploiting political opportunities when they arose, notably the collapse in Conservative support following the debacle of the Truss premiership. He repeatedly proved himself a wily, ruthless opponent of ineffectual Tory prime ministers. And as Leader of the Opposition, he achieved a landslide election victory on a scale only Clement Attlee and Tony Blair have matched.

If he is not truly a political leader, Starmer has nevertheless been remarkably successful in the art of statecraft, attaining and exerting power by responding to unanticipated events in order to 'make the weather' in British politics. What is less apparent is whether Starmer has the governing strategy necessary to make a success of his premiership. The paradox is that the capacities that make a leader effective in opposition – seizing the agenda, mobilising electoral support and making an impact in the media while maintaining party morale – are largely redundant, and become potentially counter-productive, when the challenge as Prime Minister is manipulating the levers of state authority to reform British society.

EXPERIENCE AND EARLY CAREER

Keir Starmer does not come from the background traditionally associated with leaders of the British Labour Party. Although his father, Rodney, was a self-employed toolmaker, Starmer was by no means a horny-handed son of toil, a direct descendent of the English working class. He grew up in the southern English town of Oxted on the Surrey–Kent border, a community far removed from the industrial heartland of British labourism. In this way, Starmer scarcely conforms to the traditional proletarian stereotype of Labour's leadership.

Yet his background was undeniably humble. The family owned a modest, pebble-dash three-bedroom semi. Starmer himself recalled that 'my mum and dad were scared of debt' and were not always able to pay the bills.[593] Money was tight. His upbringing was not without adversity due to his mother Jo's ill health. She had severe inflammatory arthritis – a condition known as Still's disease – and was constantly admitted to hospital. Meanwhile, Starmer's relationship with his father was, according to his biographer Tom Baldwin, emotionally barren, a not-infrequent occurrence among political leaders who embark on a search for psychological validation in adulthood.

As such, passing the eleven-plus examination for entry to the prestigious Reigate Grammar School (which shortly afterwards became an independent fee-paying institution) was a crucial stepping stone in advancing young Keir's prospects. As a teenager, Starmer developed an interest in political affairs, subsequently joining the East Surrey Young Socialists, although he was more obsessed with football. His politics at the time were of the 'non-aligned, conscience-driven left'.[594] Affable and intelligent, friends speculated as to whether Starmer might one day be Prime Minister.

Yet Starmer's first career was nothing directly to do with politics. He established himself as one of the leading human rights barristers of his generation. Starmer initially read law at the University of Leeds, graduating with first-class honours. He undertook postgraduate study at the University of Oxford, though reputedly kept well away from student politics. After qualifying, Starmer was appointed as a bencher at the Middle Temple and in 1990 became a founding member of Doughty Street Chambers, specialising in human rights and public law. At the age of thirty-nine, he was appointed Queen's Council (QC).

As a practising lawyer, Starmer made an outstanding contribution to advancing human rights legislation. He was named QC of the year in 2007 for his work on human rights, particularly pro bono cases that objected to

---

593 Tom Baldwin, *Keir Starmer: The Biography*, London, HarperCollins, 2024.

594 Heather Stewart, 'Keir Starmer had no enemies. Can he keep it that way?', *The Guardian*, last updated 27 March 2020, accessed 28 July 2025 (https://www.theguardian.com/politics/2020/mar/27/keir-starmer-profile-labours-non-aligned-leadership-frontrunner).

the use of the death penalty in Uganda, Kenya, Malawi and the Caribbean, alongside those that challenged the unjustified use of control orders for terrorist suspects. Starmer served as a human rights advisor to the Policing Board of Northern Ireland, helping to forge cross-community support for law and order. He was described by his Doughty Street colleague Jonathan Cooper as 'probably the first high-level human rights activist to attain the upper reaches of government in this jurisdiction'.[595]

Starmer's integration into the British legal establishment was affirmed by his appointment as Director of Public Prosecutions (DPP) and Head of the Crown Prosecution Service (CPS) in 2008. It was perhaps a surprising choice given Starmer's track record in judicial activism and human rights, although he was regarded as an efficient administrator and would have been appointed to serve a further term. Friends nevertheless speculated that for Starmer the law was 'never enough'.[596] The allure of the Labour Party and the bearpit of the British Parliament proved irresistible, compelling Starmer to fast acquire the attributes of political leadership.

ENTERING POLITICS

For the departing DPP, the attraction of elected politics in the early 2010s was that Ed Miliband might well become Prime Minister, enabling Starmer to become an influential minister. Having departed the CPS, Starmer was selected as the parliamentary candidate for Frank Dobson's former constituency of Holborn & St Pancras, which he won in 2015 with a majority of over 17,000. Even then, with the Labour Party in post-election turmoil, Starmer had such a public reputation that supporters urged him to stand to replace the defeated Miliband. He wisely declined, choosing to

595 Cited in Ben Silverstone, 'Meet the Director – Keir Starmer', *Counsel Magazine*, 31 January 2009.

596 Baldwin, op. cit., 2024.

bide his time and support Andy Burnham for the leadership, who was then defeated by Jeremy Corbyn.

Starmer had to forge his political career in a party convulsed by Corbyn's unanticipated elevation to the leadership. His politics were by no means of the Corbynite left, although he had little obvious association with the Blair and Brown era and, initially at least, could accommodate himself to the Corbyn dispensation. He was appointed shadow Home Office minister with responsibility for immigration policy, working diligently to fulfil his front-bench duties. It has been said that 'lawyers make good politicians because they know the law'.[597] Starmer's legal background proved particularly beneficial during the early years of opposition.

Remarkably, however, within a year Starmer, along with dozens of colleagues, had resigned from the front bench in protest at Corbyn's failure to fight for Remain in the 2016 Brexit referendum, as well as his allegedly ineffectual leadership style. Starmer made his feelings plain: 'It is simply untenable now to suggest we can offer an effective opposition without a change of leader.'[598]

Corbyn survived the inept leadership challenge of the shadow Cabinet minister Owen Smith. With Corbyn's authority restored, Starmer was compelled to adjust his strategy to survive in the highest echelons of Labour politics. Strengthened by his new mandate, the Labour leader somewhat surprisingly appointed Starmer as shadow Brexit Secretary. Yet it was this position that enabled Starmer to emerge as a viable contender to lead his party. He exploited the European issue, skilfully cultivating a base of political support among Labour MPs, as well as the grass-roots membership.

Even so, Starmer was required to embark on a supremely intricate balancing act. For one, the Brexit negotiations had proved tortuous and politically turbulent. Theresa May and then Boris Johnson struggled to negotiate a viable post-EU trade deal. The process of EU withdrawal in the wake of the

597 Max Weber cited in Paul Duran, 'Max Weber and the Making of Politicians: A Sociology of Political Responsibility', *Max Weber Studies*, 9(1–2), 2009, pp. 51–93.

598 Stewart, op. cit., 2020.

referendum was muddled, messy and chaotic. As the threat of 'no deal' with the EU loomed, Labour faced mounting pressure to support the arrangement the Conservative government had negotiated. Key figures in Corbyn's inner circle were initially persuaded, although there was inevitably much confusion and equivocation. Yet Starmer held out, becoming a stronger and more vocal supporter of a second referendum with Remain as an option on the ballot paper. At the 2019 party conference, a resolution demanding that Labour back Remain in a future referendum was defeated, although it required the block votes of Corbyn's allies in the trade unions. Seumas Milne, then Labour's communications director, suspected that Starmer was already on manoeuvres to secure the leadership, telling allies he profoundly distrusted Starmer's motives.[599]

It is simply not credible to claim that Starmer backed a second Brexit referendum entirely out of political self-interest. He evaluated the polling evidence that 'core' Labour voters – younger university graduates, Muslim and minority ethnic voters, alongside working-class women – had shifted decisively in favour of Remain since the Brexit referendum. Analysis indicated that a pro-Brexit stance would lead to the loss of forty-five seats in a forthcoming general election. Although Labour was heavily defeated in 2019, the result would have been worse had it adopted a policy of actively supporting Britain's departure from the EU.

Yet there is little question that Starmer's handling of the Brexit issue indicated a streak of political acuity and guile. He acknowledged that Corbyn's subsequent position of supporting a second referendum while maintaining a neutral stance on the outcome was an effort to overcome national divisions over Brexit yet declared in an interview: 'I personally think it is better to campaign for Remain.' Within months, Starmer established himself as 'the standard bearer for the people's vote campaign', occupying a position

599 Michael Savage, 'How cross-party talks left both sides frustrated', *The Observer*, last updated 7 April 2019, accessed 28 July 2025 (https://www.theguardian.com/politics/2019/apr/07/how-cross-party-brexit-talks-left-both-sides-frustrated-labour-tories).

of leadership in a party whose activist base was emotionally pro-European to its core.[600]

BECOMING LEADER: THE MOST 'UNPOLITICAL' POLITICIAN WE HAVE EVER KNOWN?

Starmer's positioning on Europe proved supremely adept. Indeed, it transformed him into a first-rank leadership candidate. Corbyn's younger, left-leaning supporters, who believed 'another Europe [was] possible' began to coalesce around Starmer, as did increasing numbers of Labour 'moderates' dismayed by their leader's incompetence. When Corbyn eventually resigned following Labour's crushing defeat in the 2019 election – its fourth loss in nine years – Starmer was prepared to seize the leadership mantle. Well before the election, key allies in the PLP, notably Jenny Chapman and Carolyn Harris, had been carefully preparing the organisational infrastructure for a leadership bid, with input on strategy coming from an advisor called Morgan McSweeney, then director of the think tank Labour Together.

However, at the outset, Starmer's victory was far from certain. *The Guardian* regarded Corbyn's ally Rebecca Long-Bailey as the strong favourite, not least because she was supported by the most powerful trade union, Unite. There was also a prevailing view that the next leader of the Labour Party ought to be a woman. Nevertheless, Long-Bailey, Emily Thornberry, Lisa Nandy and Jess Phillips (who withdrew days into the race), had limited impact at a series of pedestrian hustings with members around the country. The Long-Bailey campaign then all but imploded amid far-left infighting. Sensing the political opportunity, Starmer made his move with ruthless efficiency. His pitch for the leadership centred on disavowing New Labour's inheritance of foreign wars and neo-liberal economics while projecting his

600 Tom Baldwin, op. cit., 2024, p. 145.

appeal as a prospective Prime Minister with the gravitas and experience to win a general election.

The internal coalition Starmer assembled had astonishing ideological breadth. Long-standing Corbyn associates such as Laura Parker, the leader's former private secretary, Simon Fletcher, one-time aide to Ken Livingstone, and the journalist Paul Mason endorsed Starmer on the basis that he would retain Corbyn's radical policies, forge a credible electoral appeal and seek to undo the damage of Brexit.

The pitch was crystallised in Starmer's ten 'leadership pledges', which included scrapping university tuition fees, renationalisation of rail and the Post Office, abolishing the House of Lords, an end to foreign military intervention and a guarantee of full voting rights for EU citizens. Concurrently, Starmer fought to win the votes of Labour's centre-right. He promised to lead the party in the tradition of Attlee, Wilson and, tacitly, Blair, ensuring Labour was a viable party of government, not merely a social movement rooted in activism and protest. He pledged to remove the stain of antisemitism and the taint of political extremism. Remarkably, Starmer then won the leadership on the first round with 56.2 per cent of the vote.

Starmer's rise to the apex of the Labour Party had been achieved in the space of just five years. His ascent was positively meteoric. Starmer's advisor, now-MP Chris Ward, speculated that his former boss was ultimately successful as he had never been 'beholden to a particular faction of the Labour Party'.[601]

THE HARD GRIND OF OPPOSITION

Starmer understood immediately that the position from which he secured the prize of the Labour leadership was not one from which he could hope to achieve a general election victory. Ward acknowledges that Starmer won the leadership from the 'soft left' but sought 'to lead [the party] from

601 Cited in Baldwin, op. cit., 2024.

the centre-right'.[602] He was on a journey to re-establish Labour as a party capable of power.

In so doing, Starmer faced formidable constraints, both internal obstacles within the Labour Party itself and the unfavourable nature of the external political environment the party confronted in the wake of four successive election defeats. Labour was riven with factionalism, while the culture of extremism and antisemitism was believed to have cultivated a 'hostile environment' for the Jewish community inside the party.[603] Meanwhile, Prime Minister Boris Johnson was still relatively popular with the electorate, having 'got Brexit done' in December 2020.

A year after Starmer won the leadership, the party was heavily defeated in the Hartlepool by-election and the local election results were distinctly underwhelming. Most commentators accepted he had steadied the ship, yet Starmer was accused of failing to 'cut through'. He was yet to elaborate a compelling vision for the party's future. Labour had an apparently insurmountable mountain to climb following the 2019 defeat, its worst since 1935. The party's reputation for economic competence had not recovered from the 2008 global financial crisis, exacerbated by the leadership failures of Miliband and Corbyn. Voters palpably did not believe that Labour was a safe pair of hands. They feared that in government, ministers would be profligate, public debt would balloon and taxes on ordinary workers would soar.[604] The fallout from the Covid pandemic and various geopolitical shocks, most notably the war in Ukraine, reinforced the pressure on Labour to demonstrate it was a trustworthy manager of the economy.

The list of strategic vulnerabilities was daunting: a decade of defeat, the inevitable descent into factionalism, the shock of the 2016 EU referendum, the remorseless rise of Scottish nationalism and constituencies lost in northern

---

602 Baldwin, op. cit., 2024.

603 'Margaret Hodge Launches Attack on Jeremy Corbyn', *The Independent,* last updated 28 September 2018, accessed 29 July 2025 (https://www.independent.co.uk/news/uk/politics/labour-party-antisemitism-conference-jeremy-corbyn-jewish-margaret-hodge-andrew-marr-a8553131.html).

604 Jane Green and Will Jennings, *The Politics of Competence: Parties, Public Opinion and Voters*, Cambridge, Cambridge University Press, 2017.

England that had been in Labour hands since the First World War. When Starmer was elected leader, the party was in the grip of an existential crisis. It had no coherent strategy to win a governing majority in the UK's first-past-the-post electoral system. Then the eruption of the pandemic demanded a bipartisan response, suspending the normal 'cut and thrust' of parliamentary politics. Starmer evidently lacked vital capacities: for one, he was not a natural media performer, nor a charismatic orator. Twice during the initial period of his leadership, Starmer contemplated resignation. With justification, Neil Kinnock has described being Leader of the Opposition as 'pure purgatory' and easily the toughest job in British politics.[605]

And there were inevitably further bumps in the road. Starmer had to deal with a political crisis over demands for a ceasefire in Gaza following the seizure of Israeli hostages by Hamas. He fuelled consternation in the Labour Party by telling Nick Ferrari on his LBC radio show: 'Israel has the right to do everything it can to get those hostages back safe and sound. Hamas bears responsibility.' Starmer apparently implied that it was acceptable to withhold water and power from civilians, although he emphasised that any military intervention must be compatible with international law.[606] Many politicians were perturbed by the stance taken on the conflict. In November 2023, fifty-six Labour parliamentarians, including members of the front bench, rebelled, voting for an SNP motion demanding an immediate ceasefire.

Yet the Labour leader demonstrated he was able to deal, politically and psychologically, with the arduous grind of opposition. Under pressure as opinion polls failed to move in his favour, Starmer stuck to the strategy of pivoting Labour to an election-winning position through internal organisational reform followed by a wide-ranging review of party policy. His determination to force through the necessary changes was self-evident, telling the *New*

---

605 Editorial, 'Keir Starmer's Big Question: What is Labour for?', *Evening Standard*, last updated 8 June 2021, accessed 30 July 2025 (https://www.standard.co.uk/comment/comment/keir-starmer-poll-boris-johnson-labour-drops-b939348.html).

606 Asher McShane, 'Israel "has the right" to withhold power and water from Gaza, says Sir Keir Starmer', LBC, last updated 11 October 2023, accessed 28 July 2025 (https://www.lbc.co.uk/news/sir-keir-starmer-hamas-terrorism-israel-defend-itself/).

Statesman even before he became leader: 'I reject wholeheartedly any notion of a Labour Party that is not committed to returning to power at the first opportunity. Of course that needs to be principled power. But standing on the side-lines looking for the purest ideology is a dereliction of the duty for any Labour member.'[607]

He managed the party assertively, appointing David Evans as General Secretary with an organisational mandate to root out antisemitism. When shadow Cabinet minister Rebecca Long-Bailey reposted an article on social media that referred to an antisemitic conspiracy theory, Starmer dismissed her immediately from her post. He implemented the recommendations of the statutory inquiry undertaken by the Equality and Human Rights Commission (EHRC), using the report as a pretext to expel the former leader. When Corbyn implied the EHRC's findings on antisemitism were exaggerated, Starmer suspended his membership and removed the whip. Labour's leader identified the strategic opportunity to project and reinforce the symbolic break with Corbynism.

Inevitably, it took time for these efforts to bear fruit politically. Yet as circumstances shifted, Starmer brutally seized the advantage. Johnson soon became unpopular after he was accused of lying to Parliament about breaches of Covid lockdown regulations. When Starmer himself was investigated for an alleged breach, he pledged to resign immediately if he was fined by Durham Police, a clear dividing line with the government. Following Johnson's defenestration, he was replaced by Liz Truss, who within days presided over the greatest economic crisis for the Conservatives since the UK's premature exit from the Exchange Rate Mechanism in 1992. After alarming the bond markets by proposing unfunded tax cuts in Kwasi Kwarteng's 'mini-Budget', the Bank of England was compelled to hike interest rates, with negative repercussions for mortgage holders and businesses. The government's poll ratings promptly collapsed.

607 Julia Rampen, 'Keir Starmer MP: Choosing ideological purity before power is a dereliction of duty', *New Statesman*, last updated 24 July 2016, accessed 28 July 2025 (https://www.newstatesman.com/politics/2016/07/keir-starmer-mp-choosing-ideological-purity-power-dereliction-duty).

The disintegration of Tory support increasingly made the forthcoming election Labour's to lose. Yet the party would seize the advantage only if regarded as a credible alternative government. The Labour leader abandoned the aim of party unity and his triangulating between Blairism and Corbynism, while eschewing the 'one more heave' approach previously associated with John Smith's leadership (1992–4). Starmer sought to drag the party decisively to the revered 'centre ground', chiefly by insisting Labour could be trusted with the task of economic management. He used his establishment status, having been knighted in 2013, to prosecute the case that his party could be relied upon to govern responsibly and diligently.

Meanwhile, Starmer demonstrated strategic skill, deftly sidestepping the bear trap of Brexit by whipping his party to support the trade deal the Conservative government had negotiated, despite disquiet among Remain-leaning MPs. By doing so, he acknowledged the prevailing mood in the country: a desire to move on from the bitterness of the post-referendum years, overcoming division between Remain and Leave. While Johnson's trade deal was inadequate and unlikely to resolve the European question for the long term in British politics, voting against it and enabling 'no deal' would have courted political disaster.

Indeed, endeavouring to vote down the deal would have damaged Labour in so-called 'Red Wall' seats in the north and Midlands, where many supported Brexit in the EU referendum. Starmer's approach was influenced by the polling expert Deborah Mattinson. In her book *Beyond the Red Wall*, Mattinson construed Red Wall seats as 'old coal, steel and manufacturing constituencies regarded as the home of the traditional Labour vote … where long-standing class loyalties mattered much less now'.[608] Similarly, Starmer's policy advisor Claire Ainsley authored a book entitled *The New Working Class*, which included recommendations as to how Labour should reconnect with

608 Deborah Mattinson, *Beyond the Red Wall*, London, Biteback Publishing, 2020.

the interests of 'new' working-class voters.[609] Restoring trust and emphasising patriotism and respect for English identity was the driving purpose of Starmer's political project.

To more cogently define his political vocation, the Fabian Society published Starmer's credo, a pamphlet entitled *The Road Ahead*. Its analysis drew on conversations with voters across the country. Yet the paper also embraced the 'towering achievements' of previous administrations. The Attlee government epitomised the drive for radical reform in the aftermath of the Second World War. The Wilson era 'began the modernisation of Britain'. After 1997, Starmer reflected, 'Labour understood that a more liberal, tolerant country was being born alongside the old one … it set about … fixing the gaping holes left by Thatcherism, with proper public services, constitutional reform and leadership in Europe.'[610]

Meanwhile, Starmer used his address to the party faithful to underline that his government would restore the mantle of fiscal responsibility: 'There will be no promises we can't keep or commitments we can't pay for.'[611] Writing in the *New Statesman*, the political commentator Philip Collins remarked: 'The shift in the polls is significant, and feels like an abiding change, not a fleeting verdict.'[612] Labour also achieved notable by-election victories, including spectacular wins at Selby & Ainsty, Kingswood and Wellingborough, seats at the pulsating heart of Middle England. Starmer was judged to be an increasingly effective leader. However, it was unclear how far the attributes acquired by Starmer in opposition would then enable the far more arduous task of governing.

---

609 Claire Ainsley, *The New Working Class: How to win hearts, minds and votes*, Bristol, Bristol University Press, 2018.

610 Keir Starmer, *The Road Ahead*, London, Fabian Society, 2021.

611 Keir Starmer, '"We can win the next election" – Keir Starmer's Labour conference speech', Labour List, last updated 29 September 2021, accessed 15 January 2025 (https://labourlist.org/2021/09/we-can-win-the-next-election-keir-starmers-labour-conference-speech/).

612 Philip Collins, 'Events have conspired to give Labour another chance. Will Keir Starmer seize it?', *New Statesman*, last updated 19 January 2022, accessed 25 January 2025 (https://www.newstatesman.com/politics/labour/2022/01/events-have-conspired-to-give-labour-another-chance-will-keir-starmer-seize-it).

WINNING A LANDSLIDE

After four and a half years of hard slog, the general election was called on a cold, wet day in late May 2024. Starmer's party campaigned on a platform of five 'missions', initially launched in February 2023 and elaborated in the party's manifesto as 'first steps'. Labour's programme was quintessentially moderate and social democratic, no doubt familiar to centre-left parties across Europe. It emphasised responsible economic management and an extension of workers' rights, alongside measures to improve public services, tackle the climate emergency and restore trust in democratic institutions. The prospectus was rather more sober, cautious and robustly costed than in 2019.

The election campaign itself was curiously muted. There was an absence of substantive debate about the choices ahead in domestic and international policy. The Institute for Fiscal Studies accused both the main parties of refusing to spell out the difficult decisions on taxation and public spending awaiting the next government. Labour explicitly ruled out tax rises for 'working people', claiming it would not be a 'tax-and-spend' government. Meanwhile, the mendacity of Conservative ministers dominated the election coverage. The Tory campaign almost imploded after figures in the Conservative Party were alleged to have placed illegal bets on the date of the election, while Rishi Sunak stoked controversy by leaving D-Day commemorations for veterans in Normandy prematurely. Live debates with the Prime Minister proved a more demanding test for Starmer. Yet in the face of the atrophy of Conservative support, a Labour victory appeared all but inevitable.

The party's victory was little short of breathtaking. Labour won its second-largest parliamentary majority ever on a huge swing, taking 411 seats. To appreciate the scale of the triumph, it is important to acknowledge the depth of Labour's previous predicament. In 2019, Starmer's party suffered its worst defeat in eighty years. Five years later, the Conservatives won just 121 seats, their worst-ever performance, battered by accusations of serial incompetence. Labour recovered impressively in Scotland and won seats in England it had never previously held, even in the Blair landslide of 1997. Victories in which Labour wins power from opposition with a decisive majority are rare events indeed. There have been only three occasions over the course of the last century: 1945, 1997 and 2024. Starmer thus joined the pantheon of election-winning Labour leaders.

CAMPAIGNING IN POETRY, GOVERNING IN PROSE?

Campaigning in opposition is a relentless and unyielding task with few obvious rewards. Yet if they are fortunate enough to actually win a general election, a leader soon discovers that governing is at least twice as hard. The strategic skill set honed in opposition proves less impactful in government.

The first major test Starmer confronted was an outbreak of disorder and racist rioting in northern English towns. A hotel near Rotherham in South Yorkshire housing vulnerable asylum seekers was set ablaze. During the crisis, Starmer understood the imperative of projecting prime ministerial power, using the pulpit of his premiership to enforce the government's authority. The administration acted swiftly, exhorting the criminal justice system to punish wrongdoing: within days, 400 arrests were made and many rioters received heavy prison sentences.

After the rule of law was restored, Starmer made a speech from 10 Downing Street condemning the 'shocking scenes' and 'mindless minority of thugs ... smashing up communities and terrifying minorities ... under the pretence ... of legitimate protest'.[613] Yet the Prime Minister also acknowledged that 'these riots didn't happen in a vacuum. They exposed the state of our country [and] revealed a deeply unhealthy society.' The more difficult tasks for Starmer's premiership lay ahead, namely tackling the root causes of the

---

613 Keir Starmer, 'Keir Starmer's speech on fixing the foundations of our country: 27 August 2024', Gov.uk, last updated 27 August 2024, accessed 3 February 2025 (https://www.gov.uk/government/speeches/keir-starmers-speech-on-fixing-the-foundations-of-our-country-27-august-2024).

unrest and addressing anxieties about immigration through a robust 'national conversation' about migration policy.[614]

Although there was trouble domestically, Starmer used the first months of his premiership to travel outside the UK, recasting Britain's influence and role in the world post-Brexit and proclaiming the return to 'responsible global leadership'. Within days of arriving in Downing Street, Starmer attended the NATO summit in Washington and shortly afterwards, the G20 meeting in Brazil. The UK government hosted the European Political Community of almost fifty leaders at Blenheim Palace, making the case for more effective cooperation on illegal migration, border controls and energy security.

In July and August, Starmer held bilateral meetings with Olaf Scholz in Berlin and Emmanuel Macron in Paris. In September, Starmer flew to meet President Joe Biden. He visited Italian Prime Minister Giorgia Meloni to discuss Ukraine and illegal immigration, and he attended the UN General Assembly, securing an important bilateral meeting with Donald Trump (then a presidential candidate) in New York. He was the first British Prime Minister since Winston Churchill to attend the Armistice Day celebrations in France, heralding the 'European moment'.

Inevitably, Starmer's diplomacy attracted criticism from right-wing newspapers, but his engagement with the world beyond Britain was about national leadership. The question remained what strategy the Prime Minister should pursue in redefining the UK's relationship with Europe. There was a cogent rationale for creating a revitalised security partnership, given the threat posed by Putin's Russia and indications that the Trump administration's commitment to European security was waning. The British government confirmed that defence spending would reach 2.5 per cent of national income. Yet at least as important was the UK's future trade relationship with Europe, given Britain's continuing economic stagnation. Starmer was scheduled to host

---

614 Martin Kettle, 'Starmer is being tough on the rioters, but history shows that preventing further unrest is the real challenge', *The Guardian*, last updated 7 August 2024, accessed 6 February 2025 (https://www.theguardian.com/commentisfree/article/2024/aug/07/keir-starmer-rioters-unrest-immigration-fears).

further meetings with EU leaders, and in May 2025 agreed detailed proposals for a 'reset' and a new partnership between the EU and the UK.

Another landmark event in the early months of his premiership was the Chancellor of the Exchequer's Budget in October. The political pressure ahead of the statement was considerable: in seeking to pin the blame on the previous Conservative government for the UK's economic inertia, Rachel Reeves was accused of framing an excessively gloomy narrative, reinforced by the decision in July 2024 to scrap winter fuel payments for those not in receipt of pension credit. The Budget itself had been delayed for several months following the election, encouraging criticism that the new administration had no coherent economic strategy.

Battling to correct course, Reeves's Budget committed an extra £20 billion to public services in the next financial year, with £40 billion pledged in subsequent years. Large increases were promised for the NHS, alongside the justice, education and local government departments, subsequently confirmed in the 2025 spending review. The increases in employer's National Insurance contributions and changes to inheritance and capital gains tax made it cumulatively the largest tax-raising Budget since Norman Lamont's in 1993.

With the approval of mainstream economists, the Chancellor announced extra borrowing for public sector capital investment: the additional £25 billion a year would ensure UK net public sector investment was broadly flat rather than falling. The Office for Budget Responsibility believed such measures could enhance the productive capacity of the UK economy, albeit over the next decade (well beyond a single parliament). The Budget measures strengthened the government's pursuit of economic growth, but the real impact on the economy would take time to materialise. There was a risk too that having maintained relatively little headroom, the Chancellor's fiscal rules could be breached if the public finances deteriorated further, representing a blow to the government's economic credibility and making the next spending review even tighter.

Meanwhile, Starmer came to understand the exposure that inevitably accompanies the Prime Minister of the UK. His government almost immediately became embroiled in a scandal over 'sleaze' when it was revealed that Starmer accepted personal donations while Leader of the Opposition. He was gifted £16,200 of clothing and temporary use of a London penthouse by the Labour peer Lord Alli.[615] Gifts of clothing were also made by Alli to Labour's deputy leader, Angela Rayner. It later transpired that Alli had been issued with a No. 10 security pass. Meanwhile, members of the shadow Cabinet accepted free tickets to music concerts. The ensuing row threatened to derail the administration's first months in office, muddying Starmer's promise to provide a 'government of service'. The Prime Minister's poll ratings plunged to record lows.

Yet the fundamental task confronting Starmer's administration in setting the agenda of statecraft was how to enact policy commitments in a heavily constrained fiscal environment, where the capacity of the government and public sector bureaucracy in Britain had atrophied. There was an acceptance that the fortunes of the government hinged on whether it could secure an improved rate of economic growth that increased the living standards of ordinary workers, while also ending the crisis over waiting lists in the NHS. Yet like previous prime ministers, Starmer discovered that the levers of power at the centre of British government are brittle.

Where Starmer's leadership proved particularly inadequate was in failing to ensure Labour was well prepared for government – in particular, priming public opinion for the tough fiscal decisions ahead. Too much attention was focused on consolidating internal party reform at the expense of coherent thinking about Labour's strategy in government. The Leader of the Opposition betrayed his lack of political experience, outsourcing the task to Sue Gray, his then chief of staff. Gray, a former civil servant, was an adept Whitehall bureaucrat but not a strategist able to subtly integrate the art of policy-making with the politics of power. Preparations for government are often necessarily

615 Anna Gross and Jim Pickard, 'Keir Starmer faces backlash over early failure to disclose £16,200 in donor-funded clothing', *Financial Times*, last updated 19 September 2024, accessed 29 July 2025 (https://www.ft.com/content/ddb7600f-f417-4948-9e4b-8d666e15846f).

fraught, since no opposition wishes to appear as if it is taking the election for granted, metaphorically measuring the curtains in No. 10. Yet that can hardly be an excuse for ineffectual planning.

Starmer evidently lacked the intellectual perspective to rigorously assess economic strategy ahead of the election. The accusation is that he did not provide a sufficiently robust political challenge to his Chancellor from the outset. The effective conduct of British economic policy relies on frank exchanges between No. 10 and the Treasury, which was too often absent, leading to notable blunders including the withdrawal of the winter fuel allowance for all but the poorest pensioners and ill-conceived reforms of the welfare state in the summer of 2025. Moreover, insufficient work was done on the long-term issues that would inevitably confront a Labour government, notably the future of social care provision and the financial viability of the higher education sector. 'Safety first' was enough to win an election against an unpopular Conservative incumbent, yet unlikely to form the basis of a long-term governing agenda.

In the run-up to the election, it proved tempting for Labour politicians to claim that Britain's economic problems could be blamed solely on their Conservative predecessors. Yet UK economic growth proved elusive with Labour at the helm too, while the structural and geopolitical headwinds that had buffeted the British economy over the last decade, now exacerbated by President Trump's tariffs and uncertainty in the global economy, significantly constrained Labour's ability to revitalise public services.

On entering 10 Downing Street, Starmer and his team had not resolved the fundamental question bedevilling Labour politicians since the 2008 financial crisis: how to forge a social democratic settlement when there is less public expenditure available to fund the future needs of Britain's ailing public services? Unable to significantly increase investment in the NHS and state education, what exactly was Labour's core purpose in government? Answering that question has proved fiendishly difficult for centre-left parties around the world. But Starmer was culpable for his inability to exercise political leadership in framing a coherent statecraft strategy on the road to power.

FINAL ASSESSMENT

Coming to a definitive verdict on Keir Starmer's qualities as Labour leader is scarcely a straightforward task. Any assessment is necessarily provisional since Starmer remains party leader and is, at the time of writing, just over a year into his premiership.

Nevertheless, a distinctive portrait is fast emerging. Evaluating Starmer against the leadership criteria elaborated by Toby James and Jim Buller in the introductory chapter, Starmer's attributes and achievements in steering the vessel of his party are unquestionable. Judgements that criticise his technocratic worldview, ponderous communications style and lack of political agility are wide of the mark. Starmer has so far been, by any historical benchmark, an extraordinarily successful Labour leader. In overhauling his party, Starmer accomplished in four years what it took Neil Kinnock, John Smith and Tony Blair to achieve in fourteen. Drawing on Jim Bulpitt's statecraft model, Starmer has proved dextrous at party management while devising a winning electoral strategy.[616] Historically, the mark of a skilled leader has been that although they inevitably encountered impediments, 'they took their chance when it was given to them'.[617]

What is as yet unclear is whether Starmer has the qualities necessary to make a success of the premiership. In his first days in No. 10, the new Prime Minister appeared remarkably 'at ease with power'.[618] Yet the essential issue was whether he had a strategy to alter the future trajectory of his country, not merely his party. In Bulpitt's terms, it remains to be seen whether Starmer can fulfil the statecraft objectives of 'political argument hegemony', 'governing competence' and another 'winning electoral strategy'. The paradox is that the capacities which make an opposition leader effective in mobilising

---

616 Jim Bulpitt, 'The Discipline of the New Democracy: Mrs Thatcher's Domestic Statecraft', *Political Studies*, 34(1), 1986, pp. 19–39.

617 Peter Clarke, *A Question of Leadership: From Gladstone to Thatcher*, London, Penguin, 1991, p. 12.

618 Patrick Maguire and Gabriel Pogrund, *Get In: The Inside Story of Labour Under Starmer*, London, Bodley Head, 2025, p. 420.

electoral support and gaining profile in the media are largely redundant when the unremitting task is securing changes in the policy and institutions of the British state, necessitating the relentless 'strong, slow boring of hard boards'.[619] Without such leadership, as Peter Clarke remarks, 'nothing can be done in democratic politics, and the finest potential for statesmanship will run to waste'.[620]

Even so, the pervasive pessimism about Starmer's prospects among political commentators is difficult to fathom. He has an almost unparalleled parliamentary majority, which affords the UK political stability that other liberal democracies, notably France, Germany and even the US, palpably lack. Starmer is almost certain to govern for a full parliamentary term, geopolitical shocks and his own appetite for leadership notwithstanding. Meanwhile, the opposition he confronts is irreparably divided between the Conservatives and Reform UK.

The threat that Reform pose is taken seriously, not least by Starmer's chief of staff Morgan McSweeney, appointed in the wake of Gray's defenestration. There are hints the government is pivoting towards a 'Blue Labour' agenda centred on cutting immigration, reclaiming patriotism (not least through a commitment to strong defence in Europe) and rebuilding the industrial base of the British economy.

Yet the de facto leader of Reform, Nigel Farage, is still not perceived by the majority of Britons to be a credible contender for the premiership. Meanwhile, the Conservatives under Kemi Badenoch are drifting ever further to the right. The party has little to say on voters' pre-eminent concerns about the state of public services and deteriorating living standards. Emphasising their determination to cultivate a 'hostile environment' on migration, the Conservatives are bolstering their credentials as the nasty party while simultaneously undermining the breadth of their electoral appeal. As Professor Robert Ford explains: 'A Tory push into radical right terrain could make

---

619 Max Weber, 'Politics as a Vocation', in *Weber: Selections in Translation*, Cambridge, Cambridge University Press, 1978.

620 Peter Clarke, op. cit., 1991, p. 6.

them unacceptable to otherwise winnable liberal professional voters, with the spectre of Farage boosting anti-Conservative local campaigns.'[621] Meanwhile, as Ford himself attests, for Starmer: 'Chasing Reform puts at risk the large cohort of voters floating between Labour and the cluster of parties – Liberal Democrats, the SNP, the Greens – on its liberal left flank.' Yet in these circumstances, there is no compelling reason why Labour could not sustain a governing majority if the British economy and public services have been shown to have improved by the time of the next election.

For the Prime Minister, the question remains what governing legacy he will bequeath. Leaders make an impact when 'their own outlook and gifts chime with the contemporary mood'.[622] Starmer has a generational opportunity to forge a post-Brexit settlement in UK politics. Britain is a country that confronts an existential threat on the borders of Europe, where vital services struggle to function, where the population is ill-prepared for the challenges wrought by new technology, where politics itself appears broken.

In the face of the global populist insurgency, Starmer's project should offer determined problem-solving leadership in the national interest. He must operate purposefully and be willing to challenge the status quo, taking risks and acting boldly while tackling inevitably complex problems in society and the economy. To be successful, today's political leaders must be 'heroes … in a very sober sense of the word. [They] must arm themselves with that steadfastness of heart, which can brave even the crumbling of all hopes.'[623] Britain requires a Prime Minister with consistency, toughness and resolve. For Keir Starmer, his success in politics will be, as ever, a question of leadership.

---

621 Robert Ford, 'Nigel Farage has been a threat to every recent UK prime minister. But this is something new', *The Observer*, last updated 8 February 2024, accessed 29 July 2025 (https://www.theguardian.com/politics/2025/feb/08/nigel-farage-reform-uk-labour-conservatives).

622 Peter Clarke, op. cit., 1991, p. 5.

623 Max Weber, op. cit., 1978.

PART III

LEADERSHIP PERSPECTIVES

CHAPTER 23

BREXIT AND THE LABOUR PARTY: SQUARING THE CIRCLE

VICTORIA HONEYMAN

The Labour Party has, in order to gain power in an era of changing voting dynamics, attempted to appeal to varied groups with different aims and, often, different world vision. Traditional Labour voters have often been focused in particular geographical areas and specific sectors of the British economy. Their views and interests are often at odds with 'New Labour' voters, those who the party has courted since the 1990s, who tend to be located in different geographical areas and have different policy views. This contradiction causes the party issues and was particularly contentious during the Brexit referendum campaign and in the aftermath of the decision to leave the EU. The party has generally tried to maintain a middle line between these two large voting blocs, but this has been increasingly difficult and has often led to voters from both groups becoming disillusioned.

This chapter will focus on the leadership of Jeremy Corbyn and Keir Starmer. The leadership of Corbyn was contentious for a number of reasons, but his views on Brexit and the enthusiasm, or lack of, he showed during the Brexit campaign and his appointment of Starmer as shadow Brexit Secretary hugely affected the passage of Brexit-related bills through a divided House of Commons. This chapter will focus on the difficult dynamics of the party in relation to the EU and how Corbyn and Starmer tried, in their different ways, to find a solution to the problem – how they tried to square the circle. Ultimately, it will conclude that the process of the UK leaving the EU and the political views which underpinned this meant that the party was

unable to satisfy the majority of its supporters, something which was evident in the collapse of the 'Red Wall' seats. However, the underlying cause of those losses was far deeper than simply the Brexit issue.

• • •

The European Union has always been a difficult issue for both the main political parties in the UK. Due to the extensive nature of the EU's remit, covering domestic and foreign policy, economic and social policy and a myriad of other issues besides, there are few natural allies to be found anywhere. While individuals may agree on, for example, trade policy, they may easily find themselves opposed on issues relating to an EU army or the union's response to climate change. The notions of 'right' and 'left' cannot hope to do justice to the plethora of policy positions that the political parties found themselves grappling with in the EU.

An already complex situation was made considerably worse by the lack of knowledge in the UK of the EU and its functions. There are multiple reasons behind this, but this lack of knowledge was further exacerbated by the need to discuss the issue in more one-dimensional terms for electoral purposes. Few members of the public wish to have an encyclopaedic knowledge of the organisation, and not many more have a detailed knowledge of policy areas, as this simply wouldn't be realistic. UK in a Changing Europe noted, using data from the British Electoral Survey, that 31 per cent of voters with low educational attainment levels (GCSE or below) voted in support of the UK remaining in the EU, while 69 per cent of those with high educational attainment (at least a Bachelor's degree) voted to remain in the EU. Politicians from all parties needed to explain complicated issues in a simple way to an audience who might agree with them on one policy area but vigorously disagree on another. This was the battleground which UK MPs found themselves in while the UK was a member of the EU, and it was made considerably worse by the Brexit referendum in 2016, when these issues came to a head.

For the Labour Party, there were specific problems in discussing the EU and its policies. Inevitably, there was much disagreement on policy, but underlying this was a bigger and more important issue that the Labour Party, like the Conservatives, would need to face head on. Who were they? Who were their electorate? The old certainties of the post-war period had gone. Loyal voters in specific regions, who historically would vote for the party come rain or shine, were now disloyal, and traditional groups were shattered. Instead, the party needed to consider what it was and who it was, and that struggle extended beyond the scope of the EU debate and into the scope of the leadership. This chapter will consider the leaderships of Corbyn and Starmer in relation to the EU, how they saw the party faithful and how that shaped their response to the EU referendum, relations with the EU and their wider leadership tenures.

THE PARTY FAITHFUL

The Labour Party is often described as a 'broad church'. Partially, this is due to its origins, which lie in a coming together of different groups, including trade unions and individuals from all parts of the political left: communists, trade guilds, intellectuals and even some religious figures. Since its creation, the party has inevitably developed and morphed, but some of those links remain today – perhaps most importantly, those with trade unions. That link is not only important for the party financially. Trade union leaders can have a big impact on policy, do have a big role to play in the election of the party leader and often represent the link between the party and the working class in the UK, particularly the white working-class vote.

Until the 1980s, many constituencies in the north of England and Wales, particularly those that were dominated by manufacturing and mining, voted Labour. What became known later as the 'Red Wall' was made up of dozens of constituencies where working-class individuals voted for the Labour Party almost automatically. To vote Conservative in some mining towns and villages would have been almost unthinkable. To those individuals, the Labour Party was their natural home – it understood them, it represented them, it *was* them. For their part, trade union members paid their political subs and partially funded the party, and their leaders contributed, to some degree, to discussions within the wider party framework. The level of influence depended on the trade union leader. Some were more powerful than others, and union influence did wane as the second half of the twentieth century rolled on.

However, the Thatcher years changed much of the political landscape. Those close-knit mining and manufacturing villages and towns were often decimated by the Thatcherite economic revolution. Factories and mines closed, jobs were lost and communities crumbled, as those that could often moved away to gain employment elsewhere.

With economic and industrial change came a change in established voting patterns. When Tony Blair swept to victory in 1997, part of his success came from those old Labour towns – but only part. As Maria Sobolewska and Robert Ford argue: 'The "catch-all" New Labour created by Tony Blair and his reformist allies marked a major departure from earlier patterns of party competition, which was more focused on class conflict, with Labour as the vehicle for the mobilisation and representation of working-class interests.' By the 2010s, those same 'safe' seats were beginning to look considerably less safe, and bubbling frustrations, often driven by socio-economic deprivation and a lack of investment, as well as competition for votes from other parties, meant that the votes which Labour had traditionally relied upon to gain power were now looking considerably less reliable.

These changing voting patterns are a key issue when considering the Brexit referendum and the issue of the EU generally. For the Labour Party, their core voters did not have a settled, unified view of the EU. For some, the EU was vital for trade, vital for jobs, a vital part of Britain's international identity. For others, it was a remote, undemocratic monolith, which had abandoned them and ignored them. Bound into these criticisms were often criticisms of domestic government policy, but often the two were indistinguishable from each other. The Conservative Party faced its own difficulties around this issue, largely due to the all-encompassing nature of the EU, but for the Labour Party, the problems pointed to a bigger issue – who were they? Were they the party of old, the party that represented the working class and often members of minority ethnic groups? Or were they representing New Labour voters – more middle class, more liberal in their thinking, often university educated, with jobs in tertiary sectors rather than manufacturing or mining?

These two groups, while not homogenous, did often differ in their outlooks, and this certainly applied to their views on the EU. How could Labour appeal to the diverse and often vehemently opposing views of its electorate? How could it hold on to one group without losing the other? As David Cutts et al. argued:

> For much of the past two decades, studies have pointed to a tension at the heart of Labour between seeking the metropolitan middle class (whose size as a group in the electorate has been growing over the last thirty years) whilst retaining support in its traditional, working-class heartlands (whose size as a group has diminished over time).

For the Labour Party, caught between these two rather stark groups, there were a myriad of other potential groups to claim votes from, some Labour loyalists, some floating voters. The key issue was obviously the relationship of the UK to the EU, whether that be the UK as a member state of the EU or the relationship of the UK to the EU bloc as an outsider nation. What lay beneath that issue were bigger, more abstract views on what the role of the UK was in Europe and the world more widely, plus how important, how relevant and how powerful the UK was vis-à-vis other nations.

Matt Goodwin argues that voters fell into two categories on the issue of identity. The first group were those with 'a more socially liberal outlook on the world, which saw ethnic diversity as a core strength, actively supported religious, racial and sexual minorities, saw national identity as an issue of civic attachment rather than ethnic ancestry and thought that individual freedoms mattered more than communal values'. The second group held a more 'nationalistic and communitarian outlook', comprising 'those white, working-class and economically marginalised voters'. For that group, 'national identity is linked to ancestry and birthplace, not just institutions and civic attachments, and a much greater value is placed upon order, stability and tradition'.

These questions of identity were and are political kryptonite, as they feed into issues of nationalism, national pride and British exceptionalism, as well as often evoking opinion on Britain's past as well as its future. For those who wished to maintain a strong relationship with the EU, it was vital to argue that Britain was strong, economically successful and politically stable while, at the same time, arguing that that the UK needed the EU – a difficult balancing act to pull off. For those who wanted a more distant and decisive break from the EU, they had to argue that Britain was so strong, so economically successful and so politically stable that it didn't need the EU – something which was extremely difficult to prove.

The dilemma is one that successive party leaders have attempted to deal with. There are two stark choices open to any leader – either attempt to find a middle ground that is only mildly annoying to each group and potential floating voters, thereby keeping most of your voters relatively happy, or pick a distinct position and lose the other group of voters and potentially a large group of your floating voters. In the case of Corbyn and Starmer, both leaders attempted to hedge as much as possible in order to maintain their electorate, although both hedged in different ways, appealing to one group more than another. For Corbyn, his antipathy towards the EU meant that his attempts to engage with and encourage continued EU membership appeared unconvincing to many pro-EU potential Labour voters. For Starmer, his natural support for the EU meant that his views on the post-Brexit EU–UK relationship were viewed by some as a being a way of circumventing the Brexit vote. This chapter will consider the leadership of both and how they attempted to handle the thorny issues of Britain's relationship with the EU and Brexit.

THE CORBYN LEADERSHIP

Jeremy Corbyn was a polarising figure for the Labour Party. For those who supported him, there was little he could have done for them to lose their faith in him. For those who disliked him, there was little he could have done for them to have any faith in him. His election as leader, following Labour's 2015 general election defeat, surprised many, and as attention turned to the forthcoming Brexit referendum, his personal views on the EU increasingly appeared at odds with the party's previous stance. For referendums, generally political parties suspend any party line for members and allow MPs to campaign based on their conscience and personal viewpoint. That was the case during the 2016 Brexit referendum. However, the Labour Party's official position was to support the continued membership of the UK in the EU. The party had, under the Blair and Gordon Brown premierships and the Ed Miliband leadership, been supportive of the UK's role in the EU, even suggesting at certain points that the UK performed an important role in the organisation, such as when Blair described the UK as a bridge between the US and the EU.

Corbyn had traditionally adopted a sceptical attitude towards the EU, something which was not uncommon among those on the left of the party. When he became party leader, his views were amplified, and he appeared to be out of step with many of his frontbench colleagues.

This was unsurprising, as Corbyn found himself in a minority in his own shadow Cabinet. While he was able to recruit some of his closest political allies to key positions (such as John McDonnell as shadow Chancellor 2015–20 and Diane Abbott as shadow Home Secretary 2016–20), he had to fill many positions with individuals who did not share his political views. Indeed, for some, they did not seem to particularly like each other (for example, Tom Watson, his deputy leader 2015–19). Corbyn was continually plagued by rumours of dissent within the party and the shadow Cabinet, but certain issues brought those disagreements into the open, including the debates on Brexit and Corbyn's role in the referendum campaign. As the leader of a party with an official stance that it was in the UK's best interest to remain in the EU, it would have raised unanswerable questions had Corbyn taken an opposing stance. Therefore, he needed to appear, in public at least, supportive of the UK remaining in the EU, but how could this position be squared with his widely known Eurosceptic views? This was a question that every journalist who interviewed Corbyn in the run-up to the referendum, and many months afterwards, asked Corbyn, and his answers were unsatisfactory to many.

During the campaign, the focus for the 'Leave' and 'Remain' campaigns inevitably focused on the official groupings and the MPs and famous faces that supported each group. For David Cameron and Corbyn as party leaders (and as Prime Minister in the case of Cameron), their positions were important but not entirely central to the campaign. Their role was to represent their party positions and their own views, providing a lead for some voters and supporters.

Cameron was, of course, a key figure as Prime Minister, but Corbyn, as a relatively new and not entirely popular Labour leader, had a less visible role. Throughout the campaign, Corbyn was criticised for his lack of enthusiasm and lack of engagement. However, there is a question over whether that lack of engagement and activity was real or more of a perception perpetuated by the British press. In the minds of the British public at least, Corbyn appeared to be, at best, a very unenthusiastic accepter of the UK as an EU member, rather than an enthusiastic supporter. One of Corbyn's most famous TV appearances during the Brexit campaign was on the popular comedy show *The Last Leg* on Channel 4. When asked by presenter Adam Hills what score he would give the EU out of ten, he said he would give it a seven or a seven and a half – hardly a ringing endorsement for an organisation that he was officially campaigning for the UK to remain a member of.

The result of the Brexit referendum did not mark the end of the issue, as some had hoped, but instead opened up Pandora's box. Now that the UK had voted to leave the EU, a pathway to do so had to be found, and there were a myriad of issues and problems to tackle in a short period. While the main focus was inevitably on the Conservative government, which, after the resignation of Cameron, needed a new leader, the Labour Party also came into sharp focus. While the Conservative government did have a twelve-seat majority following the 2015 general election, such a contentious issue coupled with such a slim majority meant that the government were going to need the support of the opposition parties, particularly Labour, in order to get their legislation through the House of Commons. In normal times, that support might have been difficult to secure (as cross-party support is always hard to reach), but on such a wide-ranging, contentious and emotionally rooted issue, that agreement was almost impossible to even envisage, let alone achieve.

What began after the 2016 referendum could be described as little more than chaos in the UK governing system. Brexit became the only policy area of note as the Conservative government made repeated efforts (largely unsuccessfully) to agree some kind of trading deal with the EU. This deal obviously had to be agreed with the EU negotiators, headed by Michel Barnier, but then also had to be approved by Parliament. If the negotiations with Barnier were complex and difficult (which they were), they were child's play in comparison to the passage of those bills through the House of Commons. This already impossible situation was exacerbated by different views within the political parties (particularly the Conservative and Labour parties) on what the end point of the negotiations should be and how that end could be achieved. No leader, whether it be Theresa May for the Conservatives or Jeremy Corbyn for Labour, could guarantee the votes of their members on any one issue relating to Brexit, let alone the whole web of issues involved in the UK leaving the EU. For Corbyn, his difficult relationship with his parliamentary party added another layer of complexity to this situation (although May had some of the same issues in the Conservative Party).

Keir Starmer was appointed as shadow Brexit Secretary in October 2016. Starmer was clearly an extremely capable individual, with a long legal career behind him before entering Parliament in 2015. He had held the position of shadow Home Office minister from September 2015 to June 2016, meaning he had become a member of the shadow Cabinet almost immediately upon entering the House of Commons. The speed of Starmer's rise to the front bench demonstrates both his ability (and the recognition of this ability more widely) but also the lack of pre-2015 MPs who were willing to work for Corbyn. Indeed, Starmer only remained in the role until June 2016, when he resigned from the position in protest at Corbyn's leadership (or perceived lack of) during the EU referendum.

With that background, his appointment as shadow Brexit Secretary four months later was extraordinary. Starmer had backed Britain's continued membership of the EU during the referendum and then resigned in protest at his leader's actions during the campaign, but he was now largely in charge of the Labour Party's policy on the deal being negotiated with the EU to achieve Brexit. This would not only bring Starmer into inevitable conflict with his leader (and potentially his party) but would also potentially lead to deadlock between Corbyn and Starmer in a continual battle over whose voice was dominant in this policy area. The natural answer should have been Corbyn as leader, but in practice, the answer was often Starmer.

STARMER AS SHADOW CABINET MINISTER

The 'Vote Leave' group, which campaigned for the UK to leave the EU, was, like most political campaigns, very light on the detail of how to achieve this aim. That isn't surprising, as the purpose of any political campaign is to win the ideological argument and secure an electoral majority where required. The campaign achieved this, but the complexity of achieving what they had committed to was enormous. Additionally, the slogans and campaign discussion meant that there was no agreed version of 'Brexit' – and there were many versions which could be pursued. One example of this came just days after the referendum, when Nigel Farage, a key figure in the Brexit campaign, was asked about the signage on the Brexit bus that stated: 'We send the EU £350 million a week. Let's fund our NHS instead.' Farage stated that it was a 'mistake' and claimed he had never made such a commitment. Different individuals and different groups wanted different versions of Brexit and made different commitments, meaning Brexit could be all things to all people. However, for those trying to work out what the future of the UK should look like, this gave very little insight on what was and was not acceptable to the electorate or what was possible in terms of an agreement with the EU.

The Labour Party followed the lead of new Prime Minister Theresa May in July 2016 by creating a new position of shadow Brexit Secretary. This role was initially taken by Emily Thornberry, who was the shadow Foreign Secretary (with the roles running concurrently), before Keir Starmer took over the role in October of that year. While the pressure was obviously on the Tory government to secure a deal with the EU that was agreeable to Parliament, with a general election possible at any time due to the precarious position of the government, the Labour Party needed to ensure it was appealing to its electorate – both pro-European and pro-Brexit. This was an impossible square to circle, so the party reverted to its long-held position of picking a middle line and trying to appeal to all groups.

This was the job of Starmer – support a deal with the EU that wouldn't be too damaging to the UK but also ensured enough division between the EU and the UK that they could not be accused of circumventing the will of the people. For any politician, and any party, this was simply impossible. Starmer had to be very careful, given his support for Remain, not to give any indication that he would thwart the 'decided will of the people'. One example of this came in July 2017, when Starmer was accused of hypocrisy over his role as a legal advisor to the law firm which brought legal action against Theresa May's triggering of Article 50. Starmer later turned down an offer to become a permanent advisor for the firm.

Initially, both the party and Starmer needed to maintain a public presence on the issue while not being involved in the negotiations with the EU. This was not easy, as questions were raised continually on what might be done or what the party might do differently – though these are the bread-and-butter questions a politician might be expected to tackle. The Conservative government, meanwhile, initially tried to head off some potential trouble by suggesting that they should agree any negotiating strategy without House of Commons approval. However, they were forced by the Dominic Grieve amendment to ensure that Parliament was given the final say on any agreement, something which was bound to create political havoc when the deal reached the floor of the Commons. What began was a period of huge political uncertainty, with the government repeatedly losing votes and multiple amendments being put forwards, which also tended to fail. These votes tended to focus on the terms of a deal, or what 'no deal' would mean, resulting in multiple votes with multiple outcomes being considered in fairly quick succession.

Under normal circumstances, losing a Commons vote might well be considered such a fatal blow for a government that the leader, or even the entire government, would fall. Bronwen Maddox argues that it was 'hard to overstate the significance' of the government losing the Commons vote on their deal in 2019, coming on the back of so many other defeats. However, so unusual were the times that multiple loses were survivable. This was due to both a lack of a workable alternative leader or party of government and the necessity of avoiding the paralysis that the fall of a government or leader would cause. A deal was needed sooner rather than later, and the entire parliamentary system needed to function to make that happen. Party discipline was largely forgotten, as each vote created a different kaleidoscope of supporters and opponents depending on the specific details.

Eventually, the chaos became too much, and May resigned as Prime Minister. This led to the election of Boris Johnson as party leader (and Prime Minister) and the proroguing of Parliament in September 2019, which was challenged in the Supreme Court and shortened considerably.

While it might be assumed that the Conservative Party were the only victims here (and they certainly were involved in an internal battle), the Labour Party also had deep divisions. Different MPs had different views on what could and could not be achieved and what was and what was not beneficial.

In addition, different constituencies had voted in different ways, and therefore their MP needed to be very careful when voting to consider what the views of their direct electorate might be. For an MP in a pro-Brexit seat, to vote against a deal or even to vote against no deal might be perceived as being too pro-European and therefore could store up electoral issues for them in the future.

During the summer break, Hilary Benn proposed the Benn Bill to break the deadlock. This bill ruled out a no-deal Brexit and required the government to either find a deal which Parliament could accept or extend the deadline. The bill was passed, despite official government opposition. While this wasn't the end of the Brexit debate – indeed, there has been no end. as the process of Brexit continues to the point of writing due to the extreme complexity and vital importance of the UK–EU relationship – the Benn Act did mean that a no-deal Brexit was ruled out, which was a key issue for many MPs, and many members of the public. Starmer's role in this parliamentary soap opera was key. His role, as shadow Brexit Secretary, was to provide the official opposition's view on different proposals and to offer up suggestions for action. The Benn Act was supported by Starmer on behalf of the Labour Party. However, discipline was impossible to maintain, and often opposition voting groups were bolstered by members of the Conservative Party, as well as some Labour MPs voting with the government on specific bills. Party discipline was also undoubtedly hampered by Corbyn's own lukewarm views on the EU.

THE CONCLUSION? STARMER AS PARTY LEADER AND PRIME MINISTER

Corbyn resigned as party leader following the December 2019 general election defeat and Starmer was elected leader in the early days of the Covid pandemic. His previous positions as director of the Crown Prosecution Service and as shadow Brexit Secretary were used by his opponents to criticise him, both during the campaign and once he was established as leader.

For Starmer, his primary aim was to win the next general election, which was due to be held in 2024, and to do that he needed to diffuse the Brexit bomb with the Labour faithful. He needed, again, to tread that very careful line of indicating that the UK would not rejoin the EU (which would be unthinkable for those Labour voters who supported Brexit) but also indicating that he did want a good relationship with the organisation (which was essential for those who were still supportive of the EU, regardless of whether they wanted the UK to rejoin or not). With Johnson as Prime Minister, a partial agreement had been reached with the EU, with some of the contentious issues agreed on and others postponed with temporary agreements. This at least eased some of the pressure on Starmer, whose attention inevitably swung to the Covid outbreak and domestic lockdown arrangements. Brexit continued to be a thorn in the side of both political parties, with Starmer indicating that Britain, which exited the EU on 31 January 2020, now needed to focus on the future rather than the battles of the past.

The 2024 general election focused on a number of issues, but Brexit was not a key battleground, unlike the 2019 general election. This was partly due to exhaustion from both the public and politicians on the issue and a desire to move away from such a contentious debate. Starmer was expected to win the election, and he did, with a large majority.

Having gained power for the first time in fourteen years, the attention of the government turned to issues beyond Brexit. When the matter was raised, the Starmer line was that closer relations with the EU as a non-EU member were important, but there was no debate on the UK rejoining the organisation. Starmer and the Labour Party had not survived the Brexit fallout unscathed, but they had managed to diffuse the issue enough to return to Downing Street. However, the impact of Brexit and the debate surrounding the UK's role in Europe and the world have not gone away, and the Labour Party, and Starmer, will need a strategy for dealing with the issue in the future. Ignoring it won't make the issue go away permanently.

BIBLIOGRAPHY

Tony Blair, 'The Full Text of Tony Blair's Speech to the European Research Institute', *The Guardian*, last updated 23 November 2001, accessed 31 January 2025 (https://www.theguardian.com/world/2001/nov/23/euro.eu1).

Owen Bowcott, 'Johnson's Suspension of Parliament Unlawful, Supreme Court Rules', *The Guardian*, last updated 24 September 2019, accessed 31 January 2025 (https://www.theguardian.com/law/2019/sep/24/boris-johnsons-suspension-of-parliament-unlawful-supreme-court-rules-prorogue).

David Cutts, Matt Goodwin, Oliver Heath and Paula Surridge, 'Brexit, the 2019 General Election and the Realignment of British Politics', *Political Quarterly*, 91(1), 2020, pp. 7–23.

Matt Goodwin, 'Brexit: Causes and Consequences', Japan Spotlight, Japan Economic Foundation, November/December 2017, accessed 31 January 2025 (https://www.jef.or.jp/journal/pdf/216th_Recent_JEF_Activity_02.pdf).

Victoria Honeyman, 'The 2024 UK General Election and the absence of foreign policy', UK Election Analysis, 2024, accessed 31 January 2025 (https://www.electionanalysis.uk/uk-election-analysis-2024/section-5-policy-and-strategy/the-2024-uk-general-election-and-the-absence-of-foreign-policy/).

Peter Kellner, 'The UK Braces for a Change of Direction', Strategic Europe, last updated 28 May 2024, accessed 31 January 2025 (https://carnegieendowment.org/europe/strategic-europe/2024/05/the-uk-braces-for-a-change-of-direction?lang=en).

Daniel Kraemer, 'Brexit: What does the No Deal Bill say?', BBC News, last updated 4 September 2019, accessed 31 January 2025 (https://www.bbc.co.uk/news/uk-politics-49580500).

Bronwen Maddox, 'The Historic Significance of Theresa May's Defeat', Institute for Government, last updated 15 January 2019, accessed 31 January 2025 (https://www.instituteforgovernment.org.uk/article/comment/historic-significance-theresa-mays-defeat).

Caroline Mortimer, 'Jeremy Corbyn on the Last Leg: enthusiastic about staying in the EU but won't share a platform with Cameron', *The Independent*, last updated 10 June 2016, accessed 17 January 2025 (https://www.independent.co.uk/news/uk/

politics/jeremy-corbyn-says-he-is-enthusiastic-about-staying-in-the-eu-but-won-t-share-a-platform-with-david-cameron-a7075626.html).

Sami Quadri, 'Labour Leader Keir Starmer rules out UK rejoining the European Union', *The Standard*, last updated 14 February 2022, accessed 31 January 2025 (https://www.standard.co.uk/news/uk/labour-leader-keir-starmer-rules-out-uk-rejoining-european-union-b982474.html).

Alessandra Rizzo, 'Starmer Rejects Brexit law firm role after claims of hypocrisy', Sky News, last updated 25 July 2017, accessed 31 January 2025 (https://news.sky.com/story/starmer-rejects-brexit-law-firm-role-after-claims-of-hypocrisy-10961191/).

Elizabeth Simon, 'Educational Attainment and Referendum Voting: Questions and Connections', UK in a Changing Europe, last updated 16 March 2022, accessed 30 January 2025 (https://ukandeu.ac.uk/educational-attainment-referendum-voting/).

Maria Sobolewska and Robert Ford, *Brexitland*, Cambridge, Cambridge University Press, 2020.

Heather Stewart, 'What does Dominic Grieve's amendment mean for Brexit?', last updated 4 December 2018, accessed 23 January 2025 (https://www.theguardian.com/politics/2018/dec/04/what-does-dominic-grieves-amendment-mean-for-brexit).

Jon Stone, 'Nigel Farage backtracks on Leave campaign's "£350m for the NHS" pledge hours after result', *The Independent*, last updated 25 June 2016, accessed 23 January 2025 (https://www.independent.co.uk/news/uk/politics/eu-referendum-result-nigel-farage-nhs-pledge-disowns-350-million-pounds-a7099906.html).

CHAPTER 24

NEIL KINNOCK ON LEADERSHIP, THE LABOUR PARTY AND STATECRAFT THEORY

NEIL KINNOCK, TOBY S. JAMES AND CHARLES CLARKE

This chapter is an edited transcript of an interview with Neil Kinnock[624] to understand his path towards becoming leader, the challenges that he faced, and whether he thinks that the statecraft approach is a useful framework for assessing leaders. Neil Kinnock describes his journey towards becoming leader as being more the result of lucky circumstances than his own grand design. He argues that the statecraft framework is a fair method because it is objective. He suggests that he had some successes in making the Labour Party electable, especially given the difficult challenges he faced managing the party, but that his failure to provide an overall narrative for government was a major mistake, and prevented him from winning office. Kinnock then considers the characteristics leaders need in order to be successful.

• • •

REFLECTIONS ON THE ROAD TO BECOMING LEADER

TOBY JAMES: Going back to the beginning, in some ways – when you won the Labour Party nomination to stand as a parliamentary candidate for

---

624 This interview took place in Fielden House, Little College Street, London, on Friday 24 March 2015.

Bedwellty in June 1969, what were your aspirations and what did you want to achieve?

NEIL KINNOCK: I suppose that you have to go back a little bit further. I was born and brought up in industrial south Wales, and became 'political' by the time that I was about twelve or thirteen. This was simply because my family experience, and what I had witnessed in other people's homes, made me want to make things better. By the time that I was twelve or thirteen, although it would not have appeared in this precise syntax at the time, I realised that, in order to make things better, you had to work with other people and you had to get organised. So I joined the Labour Party, courtesy of the local branch secretary Billy Harry, who was our county councillor. He allowed me to join on 1 January 1957, three months before I was fifteen, so I was illegitimately in the Labour Party.

What did I mean by making things better? I could see poverty. Of course, things were gigantically better than they had been, even ten years before then – let alone twenty years before then. But there was poverty, illness that occurred particularly among people who'd had a poor upbringing, shortages of food, people permanently cold, and people with too little schooling. Around the area, I could see ugliness imposed upon beauty, and considered that all these things could and should be put aside. There was also the inspiration of Aneurin Bevan, who was our Member of Parliament, and who I saw performing compellingly in public several times, even if I only met him a couple of times.

That's the way I became political and that's why I joined the Labour Party. But there was no personal aspiration in it. There was an ambition to secure change, and collective means was the only route available for doing that. I didn't think in terms of running for any sort of office, other than chairman of the Young Socialists, until I went to university. That was meat and drink. I buggered up my degree in the course of doing it, but we had two general elections in 1964 and 1966. I worked my butt off for Jim Callaghan, who I liked very much. He had a real fondness for me, but an even greater fondness for Glenys, who, by that time, was my regular girlfriend.

The opportunity of student politics was an opportunity for organisation. I became chairman of the socialist society, and then president of the union. But the student politics was a sideline. The greatest opportunity was the recruitment and mobilisation of people to whom I had very easy access. We recruited a hell of a lot – we had a very big socialist society – and had a really big impact on the election in Cardiff South East and then in Cardiff North in 1966. That brought home to me the fact that I was articulate, that I could represent other people and could get elected.

Then, after I graduated, I found the dream job, which was to be a tutor organiser at the WEA. Even then, the idea of getting selected for a seat was remote. I would not have said that it was absent – because other people kept on talking about it – but it was barely a light above the horizon. And, in any case, I was very happily married; we had a nice house; Glenys and I had jobs that we absolutely loved. But, in the very nature of WEA, I was doing shop stewards' classes and getting round the valleys, so it was not long before people were saying to me: 'You should fight this seat next time.'

Anyway, the great moment really came at an executive committee meeting in my own constituency of Bedwellty,[625] where I was the minutes secretary (the lowest form of representative life). The sitting MP, who I thought was in his late fifties, but turned out to be in his late sixties, announced under 'any other business' that he was not going to run for the next election. That was in January 1969.

I went down to the pub with the boys and Glenys and said: 'Right – who are we going to run?' And they said: 'You, you silly sod! Of course it is going to be you!' So that was it. I can't say that my real ambition to be a Member of Parliament was born then, but it was only then that it became tangible. I was twenty-seven and I knew that I was going to have an uphill struggle with the selection for this seat – a 22,000 majority and a very established old guard. In the end, I won the nomination by two votes. And, a year later, courtesy of the electorate, there I was in Parliament.

---

625 In 1983, it became the parliamentary constituency of Islwyn.

Ambition after that? Not much, really – being a Member of Parliament was real fulfilment. Maybe it was because I was elected at the time of Labour's defeat, but the idea of being on the front bench, especially given my political disposition (which was the Tribune-ite, Bevanite, Footite left), really didn't feature at all. Maybe it should have. Maybe I would have made some changes to stances that I took. It probably would have been the wrong thing to do in terms of authenticity and being true to myself, but it would have caused fewer bumps in subsequent years. If you calculate like that, though, you're a careerist pain in the bum – and there were enough of those kinds of people among my contemporaries in the PLP at the time.

It wasn't until after the 1974 election, when we got a Labour government unexpectedly and I was asked to be an opening speaker in the debate on the Queen's Speech, that it occurred to me that I was wearing a no. 12 shirt, and, whenever Wilson got the chance, he was going to offer me a place in the government. Even that didn't initially occur to me – it was said to me by others. Leo Abse, George Thomas, Stan Orme, were among the people who said: 'Oh, he's got you marked.'

Glenys and I were then invited to dinner at 10 Downing Street with Lee Kuan Yew and Jeremy Thorpe. We joked, Glenys and I, that it was so Wilson could check whether I knew which knife and fork to pick up. After that, I made several challenges against the government, especially on public expenditure, and, after Wilson's time, on devolution. This blotted my copybook, so the idea of being on the front bench faded further into the background. I was very glad about that, because I was a member of the select committee on nationalised industries, and campaigns of various kinds.

When Jim Callaghan was elected leader, he offered me a ministerial post on two occasions. But, by that stage, with Denis Healey's public expenditure plans and devolution really looming larger, it would have been dishonest of me to have taken the position in those circumstances, when I disagreed with the leadership on both of these major issues. I explained to Jim that it just would not have been sustainable and he could find somebody who was going to be more dependable. So he got Bob Cryer. [*Laughter*]

That was that, apart from getting elected to the party NEC in 1978, until we lost the 1979 election. Jim Callaghan gave me the education portfolio, even though I was the runner-up in the shadow Cabinet elections, at which point, I fortunately encountered the Rt Reverend Charles Clarke.

CHARLES CLARKE: And never looked back!

NEIL KINNOCK: Exactly. That was my rocket take-off – finding him!

TOBY JAMES: When did you develop aspirations to be leader then?

NEIL KINNOCK: In a sense, that was thrust on me. Jim Callaghan resigned as leader in 1980. He talked privately to me about resigning at the party conference in Blackpool that year. He got so frustrated with the antics of the NEC that he was going to resign there and then. I begged him not to go. I said: 'Stay for two years, at least. I know that it is very irksome, but we've got the Conservatives on the ropes.' Thatcher was very unpopular at the time, and the Tories were bumping along the bottom in the polls. I said: 'We've got these buggers on the ropes, despite the winter of discontent and everything.'

CHARLES CLARKE: They almost lost the Southend by-election…[626]

NEIL KINNOCK: Exactly. Teddy Taylor just scraped home by a couple of hundred votes and against *us*! That was how long ago it was.

Jim Callaghan didn't resign in Blackpool in October – he left it a couple of months. I then spoke to Michael Foot about him running, and showed him my score sheet – which I had checked with Phil Whitehead (said to be on the right of the party, but an excellent man) – to demonstrate that, on his absolutely best day, he was definitely going to lose by nine. Philip had him

626 Teddy Taylor won the Southend East by-election on 13 March 1980 by 430 votes, with a 13 per cent swing against the Conservatives.

losing by eight. We had gone through the list separately and together. I told Michael and he said: 'Phough! That's bloody good news! Let's go and have a drink!' He didn't want to be leader.

But Ian Mikardo, Clive Jenkins, Jack Jones and Hughy Scanlon prevailed on him. Over a weekend, he'd changed his mind. He came back from giving a lecture on Swift in Dublin, and they were waiting for him when he got home. Of course, Jill (his wife) was always in favour of him doing it. So he ran. I called him and said: 'You know, Michael, I'm actually against you running. I think that that's your view as well, but I understand the reasons why you're running – so I'll manage your campaign.' That I did, and told a lot of fibs in order to get quite unlikely people to vote for him.

Michael won the leadership election, but, after a year, he was having the most difficult of times. The party was abominable. The Social Democrats had been formed and it was bloody dreadful. I'll never forget. We were in an Indian restaurant in Newport on a Friday night, after the general committee, with Barry Moore, Gwyn Evans and Tommy Williams. Barry actually said: 'You're going to have to sort this out, you know?' I said: 'It's going to take a lot of people to do that.' He said: 'No, when Michael goes, you've got to go for the leadership.'

I can't say that I hadn't thought about it. People like Don Concannon, from the right wing of the party, with whom I had lived for nearly two years in Belsize Park, had suggested it to me. I thought: 'OK, this is going to be it.' Within weeks, Charles and I talked about it. This would have been late 1981, after the crazy conference at which Benn ran against Healey for the deputy leadership. So that was when I took the decision. Looking around, it occurred to me that the only alternative that could have given me real problems was John Smith. But, as the months of party turmoil went on, it was obvious that John could not have done it, and didn't want to.

Michael announced that he was standing down as leader a couple of days after the 1983 election. Clive Jenkins of the ASTMS phoned me while I was on the radio talking about the result. He said that he was going to announce that afternoon that his union was nominating me. I then had to scramble to phone Michael to say what was happening. I asked Clive to delay it for a couple of days for decency's sake. Michael said: 'There is no need for that!'

We – Charles, mainly – then came up with the stunningly brilliant idea of running for the leadership and the deputy leadership, and getting Roy Hattersley to do the same. Roy was initially reluctant to run for the deputy leadership, but, fortunately, Dave Hill persuaded him, so the whole process was a great deal smoother than it otherwise would have been. I actually think that Roy did marginally better in the leadership election, because he demonstrated this generosity of spirit and desire for unity – maybe I did, as well. Nonetheless, we had a very substantial mandate, which we would have liked to have exploited. But along came Arthur Scargill! Then, the months until mid-1985, after the miners' strike ended, were pure hell.

That is the full story. So, if you take Shakespeare literally and think of being leader of the Labour Party as 'greatness', it was not so much thrust upon me, but there was not really an alternative who could do the necessary job in prevailing conditions. I have since reflected that, just a few years before I became leader of the Labour Party (at forty-one years of age), Tony Benn had been politically sane, Shirley Williams was there, Anthony Crosland hadn't died and Denis Healey was four years younger. If Denis Healey had not got older (and he seemed to get older fast, it has to be said), Benn hadn't gone politically crazy, Shirley hadn't defected and Crosland hadn't died, I wouldn't have even had to think about becoming leader. In the absence of those, there was no alternative.

CHARLES CLARKE: I remember that, even as late as the morning of polling day in 1983, Gwyn Evans came up to you and said that he'd spoken to a bookmaker who had very good odds on you being the Labour leader. Gwyn said that he was going to mortgage his house and put the whole of its value on you becoming leader. You completely lost your temper with him because you thought that you couldn't be responsible for him losing his house. This was mostly because, even at that late stage, you were not sure that you'd be a candidate.

NEIL KINNOCK: I said to him: 'Listen! What if I were killed in a bloody car crash?!' And he said: 'Well, the bet would have been off then.'

I gave him a list of other reasons and he was not entirely persuaded. And then, on 13 July, I did turn the car over, and survived – by a miracle. The next day Gwyn phoned me and said: 'Jesus Christ! I *am* glad I didn't bloody bet on you!'

The idea of aspiration, therefore, really dawned with me on 2 October 1983. My aspiration then was to win the election and therefore to become Labour Prime Minister. You can't get to be a Member of Parliament at the age of twenty-eight without ambition. I am not saying that I'm ambition-free or without aspiration. The idea that politics is a ladder, and once you have got on one rung, you climb onto the next, exists, and it is very strong. But, perhaps because of a lack of aspiration or confidence, I never thought in terms of those ladders. I had a series of political ladders falling on me and, somehow, came out with only dust on my shoulders.

REFLECTIONS ON ASSESSING PARTY LEADERS, STATECRAFT THEORY AND HIS OWN LEADERSHIP

TOBY JAMES: You eventually became leader. But by what criteria do you think we should evaluate contemporary party leaders in Britain?

NEIL KINNOCK: I think they should be evaluated, in no particular order, in terms of their quality of leadership and in terms of the benefits they derive for their party, their country and the economy.

Obviously, those leaders who were only in opposition – including the Tory leaders who came and went in quick succession, Ashdown, and myself – can't be judged in terms of what economic impact they had. The main judgement of those who did not become Prime Minister has to be in terms of what they did for their party. However, I suppose the benefits that they offered to the country by providing, or by not providing, serious alternatives to government, and securing, or not securing, a changed attitude among the public towards their party should be taken into consideration.

TOBY JAMES: The framework that we have used in the book is the statecraft approach. This assesses leaders in terms of whether they win elections and are seen as competent in office. Do you think that this is a fair approach?

NEIL KINNOCK: It is. I think that it's a fair method because it's objective, and you have boiled it down to absolutely essential judgements. You can always tag on one or two if they occur to you subsequently, but I think that those criteria are fair *and* illuminating. It is no good them just being fair – they have to reveal insights, as well. But they are objective and they can be generally applied.

TOBY JAMES: Statecraft theory, with its focus on winning elections, was originally put forward because it was thought that the pressures of Westminster politics are such that if leaders don't win elections and demonstrate competence, leaders aren't leaders for long. Is that something that you personally have found or something you think other leaders have faced?

NEIL KINNOCK: In the end, it's about winning elections. There are contributing factors, but, in the end, they are covered broadly by the statecraft criteria. Nothing replaces winning elections.

Cameron has now, with his 'I'm going before 2020' stuff, opened a leadership succession race, and it is quite beyond me why he did that, because he didn't win a majority in 2010. If he'd even had a majority of two – or even if he'd been so substantially the biggest single party, but slightly short of a majority, and had had week-by-week arrangements with the Liberals or other parties – he would have been forgiven by the Tory right. But the fact that he didn't win in 2010 by quite a street, and then felt obliged – under the influence of Osborne – to have a dependable majority by aligning himself with the Liberals, was an unavoidable strategic error, simply by the numbers. The arithmetic really counts. He's had an unsteady premiership, which was the hand he was dealt, but he made it work by being the appeasement Prime Minister. Cameron has never seriously tried to manage his party, and now, with his resignation notice, he's making a pre-emptive strike against insurgency and a coup.

Ill discipline is uncharacteristic of the British Conservative Party – historically one of the most electorally successful parties in western democracies. But, because of the nature of Thatcher's departure, that started to crumble. Major just about held it together despite 'the bastards'. Then they went through the period of weak leadership. After that, they got Cameron, and voted for him because he looked the likeliest one to win in circumstances where the Tories were sick and tired and furious at losing. He then got the degree of support that any Conservative leader can expect from the right-wing press, and he got some quietude – even from the rampaging nutters in his party – through appeasement and the desire to win again. That's how he became the leader – but he felt that he had to mollify them from day one, and has carried on doing so.

TOBY JAMES: Describe the pressures you felt yourself in 1987, after not winning the election.

NEIL KINNOCK: We won the *campaign* in '87. In the wake of '87, more people in the party, including some in the NEC, at last began to learn the lesson of defeat. It took them a hell of a long time. It wasn't for lack of tuition – I preached it; Charles did; Bryan Gould did. All kinds of sensible people who wanted a Labour government for all sorts of good reasons said: 'Without unity there is no victory.' Eventually, enough additional people, in the wake of '87, swung round, some of them quite sharply, to support a different approach. At that point, there was no question of any challenge to my leadership. This was because people expected us to lose, because our campaign was better than anticipated, and because we beat the Social Democrat–Liberal alliance into third place, and were therefore still Her Majesty's Opposition, having gained about a couple of dozen seats.

A leadership challenge came a year later. It wasn't very assertive but it had to be beaten down. I was assisted in beating it down, of course, eventually – and inadvertently – by Tony Benn, and his stupidity in running against me. Even without him doing that, I think those attempting to topple me would have been beaten off. There weren't many, they didn't have the balls to do it openly and they didn't have a credible alternative. There was still a lot of the job to be done, especially in policy terms, and they knew that whatever talents he had – and they were considerable – John Smith couldn't do the slog of party management that was vital. So there wasn't a serious challenge. There would have been had I hung about in '92, but the idea of staying on longer than a few transitional weeks was so bloody abominable to me I couldn't have done it.

CHARLES CLARKE: After the event, I felt that, in 1991, there was a more serious effort by John Smith than I personally had appreciated at the time. Roy Hattersley said that to me after the 1992 election, and I had always asserted that there was no challenge. However, I came to the view afterwards that there *was* a more coordinated effort immediately before the 1992 election.

NEIL KINNOCK: That's right, I discovered that too. Only one guy said it out loud and that – I'm told – was Barry Sheerman. Apparently he said it in New York, and I got a report back from there. Donald Dewar was the moving spirit in trying to encourage Smith to run, and there were a couple of others around. I think the couple of others may have included Gordon Brown, and maybe Tony Blair at the margins – but at the distant margins. As the election approached, John Smith didn't have it – and knew he didn't have it. It's as simple as that, and they didn't have anybody else.

TOBY JAMES: So, turning to the five functions of the statecraft model, what would you say are the difficulties you faced in developing a winning electoral strategy over the course of those two elections?

NEIL KINNOCK: Well, I inherited a party in 1983 that gave every impression that it didn't actually want to win! I've rationalised it since and, in the same way as the Democrats in the USA and the Social Democrats in Germany can win gubernatorial or Länder elections, we were having gigantic success in winning council elections, and elements in the party were pretty happy to settle for that – just as they are in the States and just as they are in Germany. There is a political mentality that wants to win, but only on its own terms, and it believes that the electorate will eventually come to their senses. That certainly was a substantial body of opinion in the Labour Party, certainly in its leadership echelons, at regional and national level – certainly in the NEC. They held the view that we had an extreme government that was oppressive, exploitative, poverty-generating, unemployment-generating and, 'eventually, the proletariat will reject it' – which, of course, was bloody nonsense. That mentality existed. If I had to give a short description of the challenge facing us, that would be it – people who would rather pass a conference resolution or gain an NEC seat than make the effort to win a general election.

It started to change after '83. I continually made the argument: 'You joined this party voluntarily because you had beliefs and principles. It is your duty not to betray the people who depend on us for a better country and emancipation.' I didn't have much difficulty in convincing the rank and file, but, for those who were part of the self-righteous, self-indulgent priesthood, it meant severely adjusting, if not completely changing, their religion. That was the tough bit.

To go through the statecraft criteria, I would put 'manage the party' as objective number one. Divided, irresolute and self-obsessed parties have no appeal to the electorate. That's illustrated by my history, and it's illustrated by the history of David Cameron's election as leader in 2005. It is absolutely essential in order to offer a coherent set of policies and a convincing manifesto to the electorate. If you fall short in that, people are not listening. Full stop. They will vote out of loyalty, but there are never enough loyalists to win an election and there are never going to be.

Managing the party can therefore contribute to a reputation for competence.

The Labour Party's reputation for competence in 1983 was nil. This was despite the fact that, in my shadow Cabinet, I had people of proven and manifest competence. Even those who hadn't been ministers, people knew they were bloody good. Those who had been ministers included, for instance, Denis Healey, Roy Hattersley and Gerald Kaufman: all very good at their jobs; all with, for any rational person, decent reputations. Bryan Gould and Robin Cook were others who exuded competence, even though they had never been ministers. Not all were perfect, but you can't go out and buy them off the shelf, can you?

In opposition, of course, you never get a chance to run the economy, so you aren't judged on running the economy, but you *are* judged on the credibility of your economic policies. In '87, that didn't exist. In '92 it *did* exist. I think, however, that it was weakened more than it need have been by what turned out to be very bad timing in the presentation of economic policy. If we had taken months longer to put near-final detail to the country, we would have had those months for advocacy and rebuttal. That was my view. John Smith, who was shadow Chancellor, disagreed, and I didn't want to risk a really big public bust-up with him, so it didn't happen.

The final announcements were, therefore, delayed, and, by the election, we had three and a half weeks for advocacy and rebuttal, instead of six or seven months. I think that made a difference. I am not blaming John for losing the election – there are many factors in addition to that, including public perceptions of me – but that's certainly one of them. It meant, however, that we didn't develop for ourselves the reputation of credible economic competence that was there to be had with the right effort and timing. The detail was right and our sums added up very effectively.

Coming after that, the criterion of 'win the battle of ideas on key policy issues' is vital and very much mixed in with the idea of economic competence. I don't think that I or my colleagues – but certainly I – sought to really fight the battle of ideas. That was partly because I didn't sufficiently believe in the significance of doing so. I should have believed in that more, especially since, as it turned out, I had eight years to play with. From the start, we thought that winning was going to take 'a two-innings match' – and I should have taken the 'ideas bat' to the crease. Looking at it subsequently, I'm inclined to think that, after the leadership election 2010, the Labour leadership knew they had four and a half years in which to build interest and reputation. And, like us, they didn't. That is one of the reasons we have difficulties now. This is not a mistake that Tony Blair, Alastair Campbell and their associates made. From July 1994, or certainly from conference 1994, they started to build a *narrative*. They knew that they had two or three years to do it, and they did it – helped, as they will acknowledge, by deep Tory weaknesses. I didn't do it, and I think that was, in the end, something I paid the price for.

TOBY JAMES: A narrative for the party, or a narrative for a particular policy?

NEIL KINNOCK: A narrative of our approach to the electorate, our approach to appealing to voters, our approach to winning elections, getting full understanding of the meaning and purpose of our policies. Put together this would have meant that we faithfully presented our view of what Britain could be for itself and in the world. A narrative that, by repetition and the proper choice of language, would have won people over.

The only time that I think I really did this was, ironically, in the 1985 Bournemouth speech. All the coverage came from the 'Militant mauling', but I'd spent the first half of the speech talking about 'the enabling state'. It was the idea the state is an instrument – no more and no less – and that, in stupid and corrupt hands, it will be stupid and corrupt; in honest and generous hands, it will be honest and generous. 'For us, it must be a servant state, at the disposal of the people.' Damn it, even the *FT* has picked that up since.

As people reflected on that, they thought: 'Bloody hell, we have Kinnock's version of social democracy.' Some people, like Norman Buchan, said: 'You've got to make that speech again, because this is where the battle is.' Either because of lack of time, lack of imagination, lack of intelligence, lack of patience – maybe all of that – I didn't do it. If I had sustained that, stepped over the fact that all of the attention on that speech came from the attack on Militant, and reasserted the idea again and again and again and again – with illustrations from real life – it would have worked.

So, we didn't properly engage in the battle of ideas. In the shadow Cabinet, only Roy Hattersley was conscious all the time that we needed to do so. There were people outside of the shadow Cabinet who emphasised it, but only Roy thought it was vital. I should have started doing that straight away from '83. There was the huge interruption of the miners' strike, of course. But, even then, we should have started producing a narrative. Even after '87, we should have learned the lesson that we needed to beat the Tories in part by presenting a broad, appealing, social democratic or democratic socialist alternative to the woman who was doing such damage to our country. We didn't do it; we just didn't do it. A couple of stabs at it, but nothing more than that.

Now, I think that it is absolutely crucial. But it has to start from *day one* if it is going to be effective. Blair understood it and Cameron understood it. The narrative that Cameron chose was 'compassionate Conservatism'. Bull, utter bull, of course. But it didn't matter, because what he had to do was change the appeal of the brand, and he strove to do that. It involved quite a lot of theatricality and superficiality, but that comes naturally to him because he is a PR man. He would have done even worse in 2010 if he hadn't got that idea going, lodged in enough minds.

Attlee had a narrative supported by his personality, without even thinking about it. It wasn't a conscious development – because, back then, nobody thought in those terms, not only in the Labour Party. I guess the first person to do it in modern politics was Harold Macmillan. Heath did it with 'Selsdon' policies, and then had to abandon it, to his credit, because he realised that it was completely up the bloody creek. Thatcher did it under the guidance of Keith Joseph from day one; even when people derided it. That was because she was prepared to be, unusually for a Tory, an ideologue. In a sense, you've got to win the battle of ideas and set out a narrative *without* being an ideologue, so that you can genuinely secure an understanding of, and credit for, being a conviction politician, without being seen as mad. It goes back to

Tawney: 'The Labour Party must prove that its idealism is not madness and its realism is not torpor.' I understood that then; I understand it now. But I didn't bloody act on it in terms of winning ideas.

TOBY JAMES: The statecraft criteria hadn't been developed when you first became party leader. But when you look back now, were these the tasks that you were trying to achieve? Were you thinking, for example, 'I need show that we are competent on the economy'?

NEIL KINNOCK: I should have known it, in any case, whether someone had defined this criterion academically or not.

One of the things that a leader needs is intelligence – political intelligence – which is what we call 'nous'. Nous in '83 told Charles and myself just that. When we set out my manifesto for the leadership of the party in '83, we knew we couldn't be utterly honest, so we had to dilute the kind of changes to policy and disposition we wanted to make – notably on Europe and one or two other basic things, like council house sales.

We had enough nous to know that change had to come, but it also had to be presented in language that would not be frightening to the electorate, i.e. the Labour Party. I should have thought in those terms on 2 October 1983, when I was elected leader. The work we needed was the presentation of our ideas on policy and convictions in a way that wouldn't frighten the party into stasis or schism, or – more importantly – alarm the electorate into rejecting us.

Maybe I did think of that, but, having the constant dilemma of having a party that was so distant from the electorate, including people who actually cherished that distance, meant that, if you appealed, even in modest and convincing terms, to the party, you were going to get caricatured by the press, and therefore misunderstood by the electorate. If you went straight for the electorate, then you were going to get serious frictions and distractions in the party. Even when we established real managerial and political control over the party and made the big changes in the crucial areas of policy by the late '80s, I *still* had to get up at the Labour Party conference and say something like: 'Comrades, one day this conference will be faced with the choice between two versions of socialism, I look forward to that day. In the meantime, we have to manage capitalism better than they do.' And even that elementary realism was rejected by people who accused me of having 'electionitis'. I pleaded guilty, I said, because, without election, we are not capable of giving any help to the people we are supposed to be in politics to represent. In the mid-'80s, if I had spoken in those terms to the Labour Party in conference or anywhere else, there would have been not just reservation, but active opposition, and that wouldn't have helped us at all. I was happy to have confrontation, but the party couldn't afford chronic division. Here was the perpetual dilemma. I don't offer it as an excuse; it is the historic reality, that's all. There is damn all we can do about it now – all the blood has flowed under the bridge. But it must never be repeated by a Labour Party that understands the vital importance of realism and unity.

Even then, I should have been able to find the vocabulary, and I identified some salient objectives that I could gradually use to convince those in the party who were resistant to it. In numerical terms, those putting up resistance were never a majority in the party. It's just that they had the positions in which they could make a difference, whether it be secretary of a constituency party or member of the national executive. Greater speed would have brought greater division – and 'Labour split again' is a lethal headline. That was always the dilemma, and it ensured agonisingly slow progress for our changes.

CHARLES CLARKE: I do think you're slightly unfair on yourself in all this. I think that the negative problems we had to sort out, such as the miners' strike, were very substantial.

I agree with the guilty plea for myself as well, for not focusing on the ideas of the wider population. I think that's true, but I think you're overstating it. I think that the problems we faced were a serious mitigation and we still had a serious problem.

I agree with your point on the timing of the shadow Budget. I remember a meeting in a restaurant in 1992, where it became clear that John really wasn't signed up to this way of thinking. You were so keen – rightly, in my opinion – to avoid a drama.

The criticism I would make, which I don't often make publicly, is that I think neither Tony Blair nor Gordon Brown were ready to commit to the modernisation process in those last two or three years before '92. They would attend the shadow Cabinet meetings, but not really get involved – neither of them – to work together with us. I never really understood that, and I've never really put it to either of them in a serious way. You were doing too much on your own in wanting to do this and it wasn't entirely your fault.

NEIL KINNOCK: That was true. I mean the people I could really, really depend upon in all the twists and turns were Jack Cunningham, Robin Cook, Gerald Kaufman and Bryan Gould. I don't even remember Gordon speaking up in terms of an initiative in shadow Cabinet. I remember Tony a couple of times, but otherwise those two were silent partners really. A couple of other people fortunately distinguished themselves with absolutely solid support, coming up with ideas and answers to problems, instead of just bloody problems.

CHARLES CLARKE: It wasn't their job fundamentally, but it's another reason why you should be less hard on yourself…

NEIL KINNOCK: It is a reason, I guess. The basic point is, however, that being leader is a lonely job. If you assiduously try to make it less lonely, you will be accused of cronyism – even when the ambition is certainly not to make a cadre, but to try to ensure genuine sharing of decision-making and the invitation of ideas. Charles and others in my office – like John Eatwell, John Newbigin, Sue, Jan and Kay – all reduced that isolation in my case.

But unless somebody is extremely lucky – I mean seriously bloody struck with good fortune – it is very difficult to avoid the loneliness, which means a burden of work and focus that, even for geniuses – and I never claimed to be one of those – is very hard. My office team of Stakhanovites was terrific, but obviously that's not the equivalent of having a squad of senior politicians pulling with you.

TOBY JAMES: You spoke about some of the challenges you were facing, particularly from the others. In general terms, are the challenges more difficult for Labour or Conservative leaders?

NEIL KINNOCK: I think, indubitably, Labour, because of the nature of the party – especially in times of change. The Conservative Party, for most of its history, has been pragmatic to the point of oily in its ability to give the impression of handling the shifts and alterations in times, challenges and public attitudes. The Labour Party has gone through the birth of quins every time it has become apparent that a big societal or political change is on. It rarely happens suddenly, of course. It is almost always evolutionary. Getting the party to adapt its behaviour, thinking, attitude, discipline, clarity of objectives and policies to the changes taking place around them, I think, is much more difficult in Labour than it is in the Conservatives. That might be changing with the Tories now, as they succumb to right-wing populism that looks flexible but is actually political arthritis.

TOBY JAMES: One statecraft task that you have not mentioned is constitutional management…

NEIL KINNOCK: When I first entered Parliament in 1970, the question of the constitutional implications of a policy or strategy wouldn't have been asked. Now, you've got to ask it. This is a new idea in British politics – certainly since Ireland in the 1920s or, to a lesser extent, Europe in the '70s. It should be one of the test questions for leaders: is what you are about to do in this innocuous Green Paper going to eventually lead to an absolute car crash?

I give a central example:

In the 1970s, frightened by a couple of SNP by-election wins, Labour developed a London-based reaction to a situation that had a hell of a lot to do with pit closures and incomes policies, and nothing at all to do with secession – as I pointed out at the time. Devolution was then conceived. It was the wrong response to the wrong question. We are going to get badly battered, devastatingly battered, in Scotland in the 2015 election, because nobody asked the constitutional question in 1997 – when the current system was established – without posing or answering the *real* political question about Scotland, Wales, England and the UK. The guy who answered it was Nye Bevan. In *In Place of Fear*[627] in 1952, he said: 'I have no time for the statesmen who constantly want to design constitutions. The constitutions are the clothes on the economic and political reality: they are there because of the political and economic reality.' If everybody had remembered that, and I quoted it repeatedly back in the '79 referendum, then they would have said: 'Wait a minute; should we not deal with the economic and political *reality* instead of going to the tailor's to try to find the cheapest suit of clothes to cover it?'

ON THE CHARACTERISTICS THAT SUCCESSFUL LEADERS NEED

TOBY JAMES: So what are those characteristics that a leader needs? You mentioned political nous. What else?

NEIL KINNOCK: Intelligence – you can't have a stupid leader, but we've had a few.

You need, as I said earlier, political nous – 'political intelligence' – to understand the terrain, the nature of the enemy, the strengths and weaknesses of your own forces, how to build the former and how to diminish the latter. But you also need basic intelligence – insights, comprehension, and

627 Nye Bevan, *In Place of Fear*, London, Heinemann, 1952.

creativity too. Leadership is not for dull people, particularly in a democracy. Totalitarian thugs can, and do, get away with it, of course.

You need courage. You're isolated as a leader, so if you're a cowardly leader as well, it must be absolute bloody hell. The temptation to appease and make friends with people and ideas you detest… 'A coward dies a thousand deaths; a brave man only one.' And that's fundamentally true in politics, which is, as Clausewitz said, war by another means.

You need calmness. This is a characteristic that I didn't have, and still haven't got. I had a form of calmness that, under fire, meant I could be cool. It is when the shooting stopped that I lost my cool. One of the great qualities of Ed Miliband is that he is not cold, but he is calm. I used to think it was his one contribution to the thespian art, but, unlike Tony, there is no actor in Ed Miliband. Over the past four years, I have seen that he really is cool in various testing situations. As long as it doesn't disable you, or interfere with your necessary speed of reaction, it is a real quality.

Obviously, you need calmness more under fire than you do otherwise, but it is better if you have it in general. The polling question that is often posed on the issue of calmness is: would you be good in a crisis? I would have been bloody good in a crisis because I don't flap, but, hopefully, crises wouldn't have occurred more than once a day!

Tony generally had aplomb – that terrific self-confidence and a readiness to consult a tiny number of people (not the hangers-on), who had insights and would be candid with him. As Charles knows, I think one of the most basic attributes of any reasonable leader is to insist to their staff that they are told the bad news, especially before it occurs, if at all manageable. The good news will look after itself; it's the bad news that you need to know. And if people know that you will react to bad news rationally, then they are more likely to give you the bad news honestly. I think Tony encouraged people to give him the bad news without throwing a fit, whereas Gordon – when they eventually worked up the courage to give him the bad news – would apparently be furious. That's not a strength. So, I put quite a premium on calmness in difficulty, and it's even better if it's a more general characteristic.

Empathy is important in leaders. The Italian word for what I want to describe is *simpatico*, but we haven't really got an equivalent in the English language. I mean there are great leaders – certainly, in my view, the greatest Prime Minister, Clement Attlee, was bereft of *simpatico*, but made up for it in being absolutely straight and candid with everybody, great and small. He had the advantage of being head of the Labour Party in very tough times – much of it in very testing circumstances during the war before he became Prime Minister – so his whole life had been training for that, unconsciously. So, I think that maybe there are different kinds of empathy. There is a kind of empathy that makes people know that you want to understand and respect them, but you're not going to patronise them. That's a kind of empathy. There can even be an empathy of fear, although that's very dubious and, of course, very fragile. There can be an empathy of plainness, of manifest directness, which means that what you're getting back from the leader can be bruising, but it is the genuine article and for grown-ups – that says a lot. It means that the leader may be coruscating, but he's treating you and your honesty with respect.

CHAPTER 25

TONY BLAIR ON LEADERSHIP, NEW LABOUR AND STATECRAFT THEORY

TONY BLAIR, TOBY S. JAMES AND CHARLES CLARKE

This chapter is a transcript of an interview that the editors of the book undertook with Tony Blair to gain his views about how leaders should be judged, the challenges they face, and whether the statecraft approach is a useful framework for assessing them. Tony Blair argues that successful leadership requires setting a clear vision for the future of the country and galvanising support for this vision. Such leadership has become increasingly difficult in the new media age. However, he argues that strong leadership – which speaks to the country as a whole and not just a party – is respected and desired by the electorate. Tony Blair goes on to reflect on the challenges he faced, and considers how successful he was in statecraft terms.

• • •

TOBY JAMES: By what criteria do you think we should evaluate recent party leaders in Britain?

TONY BLAIR: I think that the most important criteria is that you have a clear vision for the country and where it goes, and are prepared to locate that vision of the country in an understanding of how the future is going to work. So, for a country like Britain, in terms of domestic policy – how does it maximise its advantages? How does it engage in the process of reform that all countries are having to go through as the role of government changes – as you have to re-direct public spending, reforming your public services and welfare – or a challenge that is as simple as: how do you use technology in the delivery of more effective government?

So, one part of it is that domestic agenda, which is all about reform, modernisation and change. The other is: what is your country's place in the world today? How does it maximise its influence? Without engaging in criticism of the recent leadership, it is hard to see where Britain fits today in the world that is developing – and that is a significant challenge.

TOBY JAMES: In the book that we are working on, we are using a statecraft approach. This ultimately assesses leaders in terms of whether they win elections and achieve a degree of competence in office, or at least move their party in that direction, because if party leaders do not achieve that, then they might not be party leader for very long. Is that a fair test of a leader?

TONY BLAIR: It is an important test of a leader that you are sufficiently politically competent and astute so that you are in a position in which you can lead. If you lose the election, then no one is going to end up asking that question about you particularly.

I do think that the single biggest challenge of leadership today is handling change – how, in a fast-changing world with a slow-changing government, you manage to create the right capabilities in government to effect change for your people. That is why what we were doing – particularly in our second five years, actually – as a government around education, health care, criminal justice reform, welfare – all of those – was also an essential part of leadership.

Of course, you have to win elections, you have to be competent, you have to manage your party, but for me the issue is: do you understand the modern world and can you lead your country in it?

TOBY JAMES: Does the need to win elections force leaders into trade-offs between achieving those bigger visions and staying in office?

TONY BLAIR: Well, I think that there will always be something in politics about being sufficiently competent in the business of politics so that you are able to win, and that will involve compromises, trade-offs and so on. But I don't think that is what defines leadership. What defines leadership is the ability to set a clear direction and to follow it – overcoming those obstacles. For me, the thing about leadership is that you may need to engage in compromises, but those compromises should be tactical. You should never be compromising the big strategic objectives of your government. Otherwise, why are you there?

My theory of politics today is that leadership is very, very difficult because of the noise – the wall of noise (conventional media, multiplied by social media) – and leaders often find it difficult to work out how they lead because there are so many pressures on them not to take difficult decisions to push their country forward. But my theory is that the public in fact understands that is what leadership is about – and wants it.

I can't think of many cases today where strong leaders have lost elections. You might point to Greece and say that the guy in Greece took some difficult decisions… I don't know. But, on the whole, if political leaders show a clear sense of direction and purpose, then the public is more likely to reward than not. Even, by the way, if they don't necessarily agree with the details of the actual decisions.

There is also another phenomenon, which is very different to the past – parties have become more partisan at the same time as the public has become less partisan. You see this in the US; you see this in the UK. One test is, therefore: are leaders prepared to get above their party? They have got to lead them and they have got to be with them and so on, but, in the end, the people don't want a party leader, they want a leader of the country.

That is why Europe has been such a problem for the leaders of the Conservative Party – they have not taken on this anti-Europeanism and defeated it. If they did, I think they would find themselves in a stronger position. I think that, for the next American presidential election, whichever candidate shows that they are not just representing their party – but are, in a very well-defined way, reaching out for the country's interest as a whole – will win.

CHARLES CLARKE: Do you think that that is down to individual weaknesses and failures? I am not asking you to comment on David Cameron, but, to give the example that you just gave, would a different leader of the Conservative Party be able to take a different position on Europe? Is it down to the personal characteristics of the leader, or are there circumstances around – like the overall balance of power or the forces within your own party – that bring you back? Is it about personal qualities, or is it contextual factors that make it very difficult to get out of that situation?

TONY BLAIR: I think it is about a personal quality, but there might be contextual factors that mean you don't succeed. You might never become the leader, or you might become the leader and fail. Contextual factors can be very powerful, obviously.

But I think that, provided you are able to navigate those two things, the point I am making is that the single most important element of leadership in today's world is an ability to shape and change and form a country in a way that gives it a sense of what it is for the future. You can say that about virtually any country in the world today. A really important thing for a country is that it has got to know its place in the world. It is what, while I was in government, I used to call the 'What's it all about, Alfie?' question! What are we trying to do here? For a country like Britain, what are its strengths? They are its creativity, the English language, its history – and its people are, on the whole, pretty decent, strong-minded and enterprising. So how do you then create a domestic policy agenda that allows those attributes to develop? That is why the education agenda is so important in a country like the UK.

The other question is: how do you go out and form alliances in the world that help to maximise your influence and power around the attributes that you have? This is why being anti-immigration is so crazy for a country like Britain, because if you are a creative, open-minded nation, then that is a resource. And to be isolationist in foreign policy is a disaster, because the whole point of your USP is that you are out there in the world.

My point about British politics at the moment is that the kind of, what I would call, strong centre-ground position is not reflected among the political parties as much as it is among the public. What is the role of the leader in those circumstances? It is to try to bridge that divide.

Now, maybe I was lucky. One of the things I often wonder about is what if I had been leader of the Labour Party when they spent four years in opposition. It might have been a different task! After eighteen years of opposition, all but the dumbest could work out that we were obviously doing something wrong. So the space was there for someone to say: 'Look, I know where we are going; we are going this way.' And it seemed to work; people were more-or-less happy to go virtually anywhere.

I still think that, in your assessment of leadership, the context – as Charles described it – in which leaders operate today makes it more difficult to take tough decisions. But, actually, the public, in my view (partly because they understand this world), are very confused and uncertain – they want that leadership.

TOBY JAMES: The statecraft theory suggests that leaders will need to achieve five tasks if they are to be successful in winning elections. One of those is developing a winning electoral strategy. You are talking about some of the challenges that leaders face in that area. Are there other challenges they face in terms of winning elections?

TONY BLAIR: Interest groups are always challenges. I think they have the challenge of spotting, too, where opinion is evolving. I think one thing that's really interesting – which I know you deal with a bit – is looking at the Attlee government: why didn't it deliver two terms? It is an interesting question.

CHARLES CLARKE: I was reflecting on the chapter on Attlee by Nicklaus Thomas-Symonds in this book. I didn't realise how tight the decision to have a general election was. There did not have to be a general election in 1951. He had one because he was worried about the health of his members going through the lobbies. He was worried about some of them dying at a difficult time. The King wanted one as he was going on a foreign trip to Australia and he wanted it all sorted out before he went off. Attlee was a deep loyalist to the monarch. Thomas-Symonds therefore takes the view that, despite his general geniuses as a leader, he got some core points wrong on the managing of Toby's constitution test, but also on the winning electoral strategy test.

I would say that – for you – you were always focused on winning the next election, as was Neil Kinnock. I would not have said John Smith was always focused on winning the next election. I think that you had an exceptional commitment to – to quote Toby's statecraft theory – 'developing a winning electoral strategy'. I don't think it is at all obvious that all leaders think like that. The perception of the public is often that this is all we are about. But, actually, there is a group of the public who think that great leaders are not necessarily very good party leaders – Churchill being the great example. He did not develop a winning electoral strategy in 1945 for the Tories. He thought that he would win it automatically. And others are not ready to focus on the winning side of it – Ed Miliband being a good case in point.

TONY BLAIR: With Attlee, you see, I don't think they noticed early enough that the public was moving on from the rationing era after the war. They did not quite get that the public did not just want a continuation of the time when 'the state must protect us'. Six years on from 1945, the public had moved on from that, frankly.

TOBY JAMES: What would you say were the biggest challenges you yourself faced in developing a winning electoral strategy during your time as leader?

TONY BLAIR: Bits of the party wanted to pull me off it, I think – probably!

Look, the tragedy of the Labour Party is that in 2010 – in my view – we could have won if we had, after 2007, taken New Labour to a new level. We drew the opposite conclusion – which was that the public had had too much of it – and it therefore needed to be dampened down. But, in fact, there was no evidence from the public that that was what they thought. It was really that the party had become a little exhausted by it all, and therefore wanted something calmer and easier.

The most difficult thing today for political leaders, certainly if you are a progressive political leader, is you have got to get to the centre ground to win – and your party wants to pull you back from that. That is a crude way of putting it.

TOBY JAMES: The second element of the statecraft model is establishing a reputation for governing competence, especially on the key issues of the day – which is, almost invariably, the economy. How central was that for you?

TONY BLAIR: It was absolutely a precondition of winning again. One of the lessons of politics is that you can't achieve a vast amount of change unless you get at least two terms. For the Labour government of 1945, I think that people constantly under-estimated the degree to which it was actually continuing an agenda that had been developed in the war years. If it had been starting from scratch, then six years would not have been enough to see it through.

I was obsessive about the notion that we had to show in the first term; we had to establish the credibility to govern. Therefore, you have to be careful.

What you have to go on to realise is that having the credibility to manage the government at the time is not the same as changing the country. That, I certainly learned. One of the biggest things about modern democratic politics is that you run for office as the 'great communicator', but, once you are in government, you have to be the 'great executor'. Now, that is a completely different skill set. One of the curious things about politics is that it is the only walk of life in the world where you are designated as competent to run a vastly complex bureaucracy on the basis that you've won an election. It is like appointing the next manager of Manchester United by saying: 'We are just going to have a poll of the fans and anyone can stand' – and then that person gets put in charge of the team. Newcastle United would probably go for that system! Suppose you just have a really passionate fan – they are now in charge of the football club? They have got to choose the team, work out the formation, choose the right training regime, and buy the players. That is an insane way of running things! But in politics, what happens is that you put people there like that. That was the first and only ministerial position I had held: Prime Minister. So, establishing your competence to govern is really important, because there will be a natural reluctance to make an inexperienced person Prime Minister.

CHARLES CLARKE: In 1991, I had a conversation with Richard Ryder, who had worked for Margaret Thatcher and then been a minister and Chief Whip, about what to do if Labour won in 1992. (He had previously suggested appointing someone like William Whitelaw as Deputy Prime Minister and chair of key Cabinet committees, and this process had allowed Thatcher to get on and do the communication, while allowing Willie to manage the process of government.) His advice to me was that Neil, if elected, should get somebody in – and his suggestion was Gerald Kaufman – to play that role in government, i.e. a progress-chaser/pusher/resolver of problems. Although I am not a great fan of John Prescott, I do think that, in that role of chair of the domestic affairs sub-committee, he often played an insufficiently regarded role in resolving certain kinds of problems in your favour.

TONY BLAIR: Absolutely. He was very important in managing the government because of the relationships with the party, yes.

TOBY JAMES: What was the biggest challenge that you faced in terms of being competent in office, but also demonstrating that competence to the public?

TONY BLAIR: It was very different in the second and third terms to in the first term. I was very clear in the first term that it was about making sure that, having *won* an election as a different type of Labour Party, you *governed* as a different type of Labour Party. It was important to minimise any sense that the party was reverting or doing things to please itself. By the time I got the second term and the third term, I had decided that I kind of knew how things work, so I actually wanted to do something with it. I wanted to do that in the first term, too, but later I had a far clearer idea of how the machinery of government worked. I would say that the main challenge then was getting able people in charge of policies – those who could drive the thing through.

TOBY JAMES: The third element of the statecraft model is managing your own party. What were the key challenges there, and how successful do you think you were in that particular area?

TONY BLAIR: I think that we were quite successful in managing the party and I do think that John Prescott played a real part in that. As time went on, we brought more people into senior positions within the Cabinet (like Charles), who were able to have both the party and the public argument. We also made certain changes about the way that the party conference operated, which made a difference, too. I think that we were more successful at managing the party than people sometimes think.

CHARLES CLARKE: I think so, but the big case people would make against that would be your departure from office. The party divisions and concerns came back and, at the end of the day, they led to you not being able to continue – or led to your opponents being able to mobilise enough support to undermine you. That was a consequence, critics might suggest, of the failure to manage the party in important respects.

Obviously, it was far better than the Callaghan government, for example – where the party divisions were a massive issue for him. A massive issue for Neil Kinnock in his leadership was trying to get the party in the right place, which was very problematic. I certainly think you can correctly say that you overcame some – or most – of those issues by the various things you did. The question of what happened towards the end, however, is where there is criticism of you as a party leader. I would be interested to hear how you assess that criticism.

TONY BLAIR: I did rely enormously on public support for my basic position, to neutralise some party opposition. As time went on, especially post-Iraq and so on, it became more difficult, and that method of disciplining the party became less successful.

I always felt it was better – as Gordon became my main opponent – to have him within the tent.

I also think that managing the party is something you should always be doing. One of the things that happens to you after you have been in office for a long time is that you are so interested in doing what you are doing for the country, that you become a bit impatient with that side of things. But I'm afraid that you have to be eternally patient with it.

CHARLES CLARKE: And a key issue for you was the trade union relationship with the party. You said after leaving office that you wished, at some point, that you had taken it into a new setting. Taking your point about the leadership of change – at the end of the day, it just wasn't worth the candle at the time you were there, because whether you were running the trade unions or running the country was not really an issue. But a problem not addressed at the time becomes a problem further down the line for you.

TONY BLAIR: I would agree with that. I think that, in retrospect, I would have made the change with the unions.

TOBY JAMES: The fourth statecraft task is winning the battle of ideas on the key policy issues of the day. Is that an area you feel you succeeded in? Did you change the country's position on issues such as the economy or the NHS, for example?

TONY BLAIR: Yes, we did have a strong policy agenda that became, in my view, stronger over time. New Labour was a concept, but it took proper policy form more in the last six years than in the first three or four. We did pretty much dominate the political agenda, and some reforms have stayed. If you take things like minimum wage and some of the constitutional changes (people forget that we introduced the Mayor of London and all that) on a whole set of issues like civil partnerships – these changes were not reversed.

One of the things that I think is good about the country today is that there are not – between the main political parties, at any rate – any real rows about race or sexuality; things that, frankly, in the '70s and '80s were very prominent political issues. I do think that we created a new consensus around that.

I feel reasonably confident on that – although I do think that we should have deepened the support for those New Labour ideas within the party. We did as much as we could.

CHARLES CLARKE: I still think that, if you'd polled the Labour Party members in 2010, let alone 2005, in terms of their attitude to these types of things, you'd find that there was a large agreement with where we were.

TONY BLAIR: Yes, I felt that we were dominant. I always say that the thing that should worry you as a government is when you feel an idea of power coming at you. In 1979, there was such an idea. I don't think that in any of the elections up to 1997 the Tories were really threatened by an idea. New Labour was that different idea.

I didn't feel threatened in any of the three elections I fought. I realised that I could lose, of course, but I didn't feel that there was a potent force coming at me that I was having to work at to gravitate around. On the contrary, I felt that we were still the central gravitational pole.

TOBY JAMES: Going back to Attlee again, some of the praise that was heaped on him and his government was that they changed the contours of British politics and set positions on policy issues for decades onwards. I have sometimes heard it said that one of the successes of your governments was that David Cameron felt he had to modernise the Conservatives. Do you feel that yourself?

TONY BLAIR: Yes, I do think that there is a certain truth in that – although, to be fair, we were also very clear that we were not undoing the Thatcher changes. That was a very powerful starting point for us, actually. The election of 1997 was also an acceptance, by a large part of the public, that they wanted to always be moving on and not moving back. The Attlee government in 1945 embodied the spirit of collectivism that was there at the time. But what was interesting was that the Labour Party then found it extremely difficult to retain that spirit and keep it in tune with the modern times, and it got somewhat into a position of stasis with what that meant in policy terms.

What is interesting to me about the Attlee government is that, once they created the National Health Service and the many other really important things they did, there was not much sign that they foresaw the rise of a more aspirational working class on the back of the very collective changes they had ushered in.

TOBY JAMES: The final component of the statecraft model is constitutional reform, and there was, of course, enormous constitutional reform under your governments. What were the longer-term consequences of these for yourself as leader, and the longer-term electoral fortunes of the Labour Party?

TONY BLAIR: The constitutional reforms obviously covered a number of different areas. I did feel that we made a mistake on devolution. We should have understood that, when you change the system of government so that more power is devolved, you need to have ways of culturally keeping England, Scotland and Wales very much in sync with each other. We needed to work even stronger for a sense of UK national identity.

But I don't accept the idea that we should never have done devolution. If we had not devolved power, then there would have been a massive demand for separation – as there was back in the '60s and '70s.

Elsewhere on the constitution, I think, I would have gone further on mayors – still would.

CHARLES CLARKE: One of Toby's other areas of research is on electoral participation – how we vote – and there was a whole series of reforms on voting, some of which were tried under our office, but were not particularly successful. These include voting at the weekends, compulsory voting etc. It would be interesting to hear your reflection on this from the Labour point of view – that increasing participation would be beneficial to Labour (which I don't necessarily think is true, by the way). Do you have any reflections on that side of things?

TONY BLAIR: One reflection I had was that I think it is odd, when the technology exists, that we don't do voting in a far more modern and inclusive way.

CHARLES CLARKE: We tried experiments…

TONY BLAIR: Did we ever…?

CHARLES CLARKE: Yes, there were some small experiments with people voting from their phones and stuff. All very small. There is also the issue of individual rather than household electoral registration.

TONY BLAIR: Yes, I think it is really interesting to look at. I just find it very odd sometimes that it just insists things have to be done, particularly when the rest of the world is changing. I would make it as easy as possible for people to vote. 'We all have to go to the polling booth on the Thursday because that is how it is meant to be…' Why? In no other walk of life would it be like that.

Where I disagree with many is that I don't think people are uninterested in politics today. I do agree that there is a lot of cynicism about our politics – and there is a whole other story about why that is – but people are not uninterested. They just lead different lives, and I don't see why it's not made as easy as possible to participate.

TOBY JAMES: What is missing from the statecraft framework, if anything? Are there other tasks that leaders need to achieve to win elections, or is anything else missing?

TONY BLAIR: It might be that the other factors you describe add up to this, but I am not sure they do really. But, as I said at the very beginning, leadership has to have a strong galvanising vision behind it to succeed. I do think that is very important. But I don't think that it is just about a set of mechanical tasks. When I think about leadership, I do not just mean the business of leading – I mean leadership as opposed to drift, as opposed to followership. In terms of the success of leaders, most leaders have that. If they don't, then they might be good managers of the status quo, but they are not really changing anything.

BIBLIOGRAPHY

ACADEMIC ARTICLES

Rudy B. Andeweg and Jacques Thomassen, 'Pathways to party unity: Sanctions, loyalty, homogeneity and division of labour in the Dutch Parliament', *Party Politics*, 17(5), 2011.

Fabio Angiolillo, Martin Lundstedt, Marina Nord and Staffan I. Lindberg, 'State of the World 2023: Democracy Winning and Losing at the Ballot', *Democratization*, 31(8), 2024, pp. 1597–621.

Nancy Bermeo, 'On Democratic Backsliding', *Journal of Democracy*, 27(1), 2016, pp. 5–19.

Pierre Bocquillion, Suzanne Doyle, Toby S. James, Ra Mason, Soul Park and Matilde Rosina, 'The Effects of Wars: Lessons from the War in Ukraine', *Policy Studies*, 45(3–4), 2024, pp. 261–81.

Stephen Brooke, 'The Labour Party and the 1945 general election', *Contemporary Record*, Vol. 9, 1995.

Jim Buller and Toby S. James,

'Integrating Structural Context into the Assessment of Political Leadership: Realism, Gordon Brown and the Great Financial Crisis', *Parliamentary Affairs*, 68(1), 2015.

'Statecraft and the Assessment of National Political Leaders: The Case of New Labour and Tony Blair', *British Journal of Politics & International Relations*, 14(4), 2012.

Jim Bulpitt, 'The Discipline of the New Democracy: Mrs Thatcher's Domestic Statecraft', *Political Studies*, 34(1), 1986.

Christopher Byrne and Kevin Theakston, 'Understanding the power of the prime minister: structure and agency in models of prime ministerial power', *British Politics*, Vol. 14, 2019, pp. 329–46.

Andrew Crines and Tim Heppell, 'Rhetorical style and issue emphasis within the conference speeches of UKIP's Nigel Farage 2010–2014', *British Politics*, Vol. 12, 2017, pp. 231–49.

Andrew Scott Crines, David Jeffery and Timothy Heppell, 'The British Labour Party and leadership election mandate(s) of Jeremy Corbyn: patterns of opinion and opposition within the parliamentary Labour Party', *Journal of Elections, Public Opinion and Parties*, 28(3), 2018, pp. 361–79.

David Cutts, Matt Goodwin, Oliver Heath and Paula Surridge, 'Brexit, the 2019 General Election and the Realignment of British Politics', *Political Quarterly*, 91(1), 2020, pp. 7–23.

Peter Dorey and Andrew Denham, 'The Longest Suicide Vote in History: The Labour Party Leadership Election of 2015', *British Politics*, 11(3), 2016, pp. 259–82.

Jun Du, Emine Beyza Satoglu and Oleksandr Shepotylo, 'How Did Brexit Affect UK Trade?', *Contemporary Social Science*, 18(2), 2023, pp. 266–83.

Paul Duran, 'Max Weber and the Making of Politicians: A Sociology of Political Responsibility', *Max Weber Studies*, 9(1–2), 2009, pp. 51–93.

David Erdos, 'Charter 88 and the Constitutional Reform Movement Twenty Years On: A Retrospective', *Parliamentary Affairs*, 64(4), 2009.

Edward Fieldhouse, Ralph Scott, Christopher Prosser, Jack Bailey and Jonathan Mellon, 'Who lacks voter identification? The electoral implications of the Elections Act 2022', *Parliamentary Affairs*, December 2024.

Steven Fielding, 'What did "the people" want? The meaning of the 1945 general election', *Historical Journal*, Vol. 35, September 1992.

Alan Finlayson, 'YouTube and Political Ideologies: Technology, Populism and Rhetorical Form', *Political Studies*, 70(1), 2020, pp. 62–80.

Roberto Stefan Foa and Yascha Mounk, 'America after Trump: From "Clean" to "Dirty" Democracy?', *Policy Studies*, 42(5–6), 2021, pp. 455–72.

Neil T. Gavin, 'Television News and the Economy: The Pre-Campaign Coverage', *Parliamentary Affairs*, 45(4), 1992.

Neil T. Gavin and David Sanders, 'The economy and voting', *Parliamentary Affairs*, 50(4), 1997, pp. 631–40.

Rachel Gibson, Esmeralda Bon, Philipp Darius and Peter Smyth, 'Are Online

Political Influencers Accelerating Democratic Deconsolidation?', *Media and Communication*, 11(3), 2023, pp. 175–86.

Andrew M. Guess et al., 'How do social media feed algorithms affect attitudes and behaviour in an election campaign?', *Science*, 381(6656), 2023, pp. 398–404.

Glen O'Hara, '"Dynamic, Exciting, Thrilling Change": the Wilson Government's Economic Policies, 1964–70', *Contemporary British History*, 20(3), 2006.

D. J. Heasman, 'The Life and Times of Harold Wilson', *International Journal*, 20(1), winter 1964/65.

Richard Heffernan, 'Prime Ministerial Predominance? Core Executive Politics in the UK', *British Journal of Politics and International Relations*, 5(3), 2003, pp. 347–72.

Timothy Heppell,

'The Labour Party Leadership Election of 1963: Explaining the Unexpected Election of Harold Wilson', *Contemporary British History*, 24(2), 2010.

'The British Labour Pary and the Antisemitism Crisis: Jeremy Corbyn and Image Repair Theory', *British Journal of Politics and International Relations*, 23(4), 2021.

Eric J. Hobsbawm, 'The forward march of Labour halted?', *Marxism Today*, September 1978.

Toby S. James,

'Electoral Administration and Voter Turnout: Towards an International Public Policy Continuum', *Representation*, 45(4), 2010.

'Political Leadership as Statecraft? Aligning Theory with Praxis in Conversation with British Party Leaders', *British Journal of Politics and International Relations*, 20(3), 2018, pp. 555–72.

'Assessing the Policy Effects of Political Leaders: A Layered Framework', *Policy Studies*, 42(5–6), 2021, pp. 437–54.

'The effects of Donald Trump', *Policy Studies*, 42(5–6), 2021, pp. 755–69.

'Real Democracy: A Critical Realist Approach to Democracy and Democratic Theory', *New Political Science*, 46(3), 2024, pp. 228–58.

Bob Jessop, 'The Organic Crisis of the British State: Putting Brexit in its Place', *Globalizations*, 41(1), 2016, pp. 133–41.

Ron Johnston, Charles Pattie, Danny Dorling and David Rossiter, 'Fifty Years of Bias in the UK's Electoral System', paper presented to the American Political Science Association Conference, 2001 (http://sasi.group.shef.ac.uk/publications/2001/johnston_et_al_50_years.pdf).

Michael David Kandiah, 'The Conservative Party and the 1945 general election', *Contemporary Record*, Vol. 9, 1995.

Hussein Kassim,

'"Mission impossible", but mission accomplished: the Kinnock reforms and the European Commission', *Journal of European Public Policy*, 15(5), August 2008.

'The Kinnock Reforms in Perspective: Why Reforming the Commission is an Heroic, But Thankless, Task', *Public Policy and Administration*, 19(3), autumn 2004.

Neil Kinnock, 'Reforming the Labour Party', *Contemporary Record*, 8(3), 1994, pp. 535–54.

David Lukowitz, 'George Lansbury's Peace Missions to Hitler and Mussolini in 1937', *Canadian Journal of History*, 15, 1980.

Gary McCulloch, 'Labour, the left, and the British general election of 1945', *Journal of British Studies*, Vol. 24, October 1985.

Michael P. McDonald and Samuel L. Popkin, 'The Myth of the Vanishing Voter', *American Political Science Review*, 95(4), 2001, pp. 963–74.

Ross McKibbin,

'Arthur Henderson as Labour leader', *International Review of Social History*, Vol. 23, 1978.

'The Economic Policy of the Second Labour Government', *Past and Present*, Vol. 65, 1975.

'The Luck of the Tories', *London Review of Books*, 24(5), 7 March 2002.

'Why the Tories Lost', *London Review of Books*, 19(13), 1997.

Marta Miori and Jane Green, 'The Most Disproportionate UK Election: How the Labour Party Doubled its Seat Share with a 1.6-Point Increase in Vote Share in 2024', *Political Quarterly*, 96(1), 2025, pp. 37–64.

Henry Pelling,

'The 1945 general election reconsidered', *Historical Journal*, Vol. 23, 1980.

'The Politics of the Osborne Judgment', *Historical Journal*, Vol. 25, 1982.

Thomas Quinn, 'The British Labour Party's leadership election of 2015', *British Journal of Politics and International Relations*, 18(4), 2016, pp. 759–78.

Nick Raynsford, 'Sleepwalking into Oblivion?', *Fabian Review*, 104(6), November 1992.

Steve Richards, 'Leadership, Loyalty and the Rise of Jeremy Corbyn', *Political Quarterly*, 87(1), 2016, pp. 12–17.

Royal Holloway Group PR3710, 'British MPs on British PMs: Parliamentary Evaluations of Prime Ministerial Success', *Politics*, 35(2), June 2015.

Meg Russell, 'Corbyn as an Organisational Phenomenon: A Response to Steve Richards', *Political Quarterly*, 87(1), 2016, pp. 20–22.

Joseph Schlesinger Snr, 'The US presidents: What makes a President great? Or a failure? The verdict of history provides some answers', *Life*, XXV.

The Scotsman, 22 January 1907, 2 May 1910, 4 October 1915, 3 January 1939.

Scottish Review, spring 1917.

John Shepherd, 'A Life on the Left: George Lansbury (1859–1940): A Case Study in Recent Labour Biography', *Labour History: A Journal of Labour and Social History*, No. 87, November 2004.

Alastair Smith, 'Election Timing in Majoritarian Parliaments', *British Journal of Political Science*, 33(3), July 2003.

John Smith, 'Reforming our Democracy', Strathclyde, Strathclyde University, 23 October 1992.

Jack Straw, 'New Labour, Constitutional Change and Representative Democracy', *Parliamentary Affairs*, 63(2), 2010, pp. 356–68.

Mark Stuart,

'The truth about Neil and John', *New Statesman*, 20 June 2005.

'Managing the Poor Bloody Infantry: The Parliamentary Labour Party under John Smith, 1992–94', *Parliamentary Affairs*, 59(2), July 2006.

'Ranking Twentieth-Century British Prime Ministers', *British Journal of Politics and International Relations*, Vol. 8, 2006.

'The Post-War Premiership League', *Political Quarterly*, 82(1), January–March 2011.

Kevin Theakston and Mark Gill, 'The Postwar Premiership League', *Political Quarterly*, 82(1), 2011, pp. 67–80.

Andrew Thorpe, 'Arthur Henderson and the British Political Crisis of 1931', *Historical Journal*, 31(1), 1988.

James Tilley and Sara Hobolt, 'Brexit as an Identity: Political Identities and Policy Norms', *PS: Political Science & Politics*, 54(4), 2023, pp. 546–52.

BOOKS

Diane Abbott, *A Woman Like Me: A Memoir*, London, Viking, 2024.

Michel Aglietta, *A Theory of Capitalist Regulation: The US Experience*, London, Verso, 1979.

Claire Ainsley, *The New Working Class: How to win hearts, minds and votes*, Bristol, Bristol University Press, 2018.

Tariq Ali, *You Can't Please All: Memoirs 1980–2024*, London, Verso, 2024.

Matthew d'Ancona, *Post-Truth: The New War on Truth and How to Fight Back*, London, Ebury Press, 2017.

Robert Page Arnot, *A History of the Scottish Miners*, London, Allen & Unwin, 1955.

Michael Artis, David Cobham and Mark Wickham-Jones ed., *Twentieth-Century British History, Vol. 3*, 1992.

Clement Attlee, *As It Happened*, London, Heinemann, 1954.

Tom Baldwin, *Keir Starmer: The Biography*, London, HarperCollins, 2024.

Tim Bale, *Five-Year Mission: The Labour Party Under Ed Miliband*, Oxford and New York, Oxford University Press, 2015.

George Nicoll Barnes,

From Workshop to War Cabinet, London, Herbert Jenkins, 1923.

History of the International Labour Office, London, William & Norgate Ltd, 1926.

Karl Marx, London, The Labour Party, 1910.

Reginald Bassett, *Nineteen Thirty-One: Political Crisis*, London, Macmillan/New York, St Martin's Press, 1958.

Laura Beers, *Your Britain: Media and the Making of the Labour Party*, Harvard University Press, 2010.

Anne Olivier Bell and Andrew McNellie eds, *The Diary of Virginia Woolf*, Harmondsworth, Penguin, 1982.

Caroline Benn, *Keir Hardie*, London, Hutchinson, 1992.

Tony Benn, *The End of an Era: Diaries 1980–1990*, London, Hutchinson, 1992.

Nye Bevan, *In Place of Fear*, London, Heinemann, 1952.

Lawrence Black, Hugh Pemberton and Pat Thane eds, *Reassessing 1970s Britain*, Manchester, Manchester University Press, 2013.

Tony Blair, *A Journey*, London, Hutchinson, 2010.

Neal Blewett, *The Peers, the Parties and the People: General Election of 1910*, London, Macmillan, 1972.

Duncan Brack and Iain Dale eds, *Prime Minister Portillo and other things that never happened*, London, Politico's, 2003.

Noreen Branson, *Poplarism, 1919–1925: George Lansbury and the Councillors' Revolt*, London, Lawrence & Wishart, 1979.

Asa Briggs and John Saville eds, *Essays in Labour History 1886–1923*, Hamden CT, Archon Books, 1971.

Brian Brivati, *Hugh Gaitskell*, London, Richard Cohen Books, 1996.

Fenner Brockway, *Inside the Left: Thirty Years of Platform, Press, Prison and Parliament*, London, 1942.

K. D. Brown ed., *The First Labour Party, 1906–1914*, London, Croom Helm, 1985.

Jim Buller, *National Statecraft and European Integration*, London, Cassell, 2000.

Alan Bullock, *The Life & Times of Ernest Bevin: Vol. 2: Minister of Labour 1940–1945*, London, Heinemann, 1967.

James MacGregor Burns,

Leadership, New York, Harper & Row, 1978.

Transforming Leadership: A New Pursuit of Happiness, New York, Grove Press/Atlantic Monthly Press, 2004.

Alan Campbell, *The Scottish Miners, 1874–1939: Trade Unions and Politics, Vol. 2*, Aldershot, Ashgate, 2000.

David Cannadine ed., *The Speeches of Winston Churchill*, London, Penguin, 1990.

Thomas Carlyle, 'The Hero as Divinity', in *Heroes and Hero-Worship*, London, Chapman & Hall, 1840.

Cato (psuedonym for Michael Foot, Frank Owen and Peter Howard), *Guilty Men*, London, V. Gollancz, June 1940.

Nigel Cawthorne, *Jeremy Corbyn: Leading from the Left*, London, Endeavour, 2015.

Charles Clarke, *The 'Too Difficult' Box*, London, Biteback, 2014.

Harold D. Clarke, David Sanders, Marianne C. Stewart and Paul Whiteley,

Performance Politics and the British Voter, Cambridge, Cambridge University Press, 2009.

Political Choice in Britain, Oxford and New York, Oxford University Press, 2004.

Peter Clarke,

The Keynesian Revolution in the Making 1924–1936, Oxford, Clarendon Press, 1988.

A Question of Leadership: From Gladstone to Thatcher, London, Penguin, 1991.

Mary Ann Clawson, *Constructing Brotherhood: Class, Gender and Fraternalism*, Princeton NJ, Princeton University Press, 1989.

John Robert Clynes,

Memoirs, Vol. 1, London, Hutchinson, 1937.

Memoirs, Vol. 2, London, Hutchinson, 1937.

G.D.H. Cole, *A History of the Labour Party from 1914*, London, Routledge & K. Pau, 1948.

Maurice Cowling, *The Impact of Labour 1918–1924*, Cambridge, Cambridge University Press, 1971.

Robert Crowcroft, *Attlee's War: World War II and the Making of a Labour Leader*, London, I.B. Tauris, 2011.

Jon Cruddas, *A Century of Labour*, Cambridge, Polity, 2024.

Iain Dale ed., *Labour Party General Election Manifestos, 1900–1997*, London, Routledge, 2000.

Hugh Dalton,

The Fateful Years: Memoirs, 1931–45, London, Muller, 1957.

High Tide and After: Memoirs 1945–60, London, Muller, 1962.

Bernard Donoughue, *Downing Street Diary: With Harold Wilson in No. 10*, London, Jonathan Cape, 2005.

Roy Douglas, *Land, People and Politics: A History of the Land Question in the United Kingdom, 1878–1952*, London, Alison & Busby, 1976.

Arthur Power Dudden, *Joseph Fels and the Single-Tax Movement*, Philadelphia, Temple University Press, 1971

Patrick Dunleavy, Alice Park and Ros Taylor, *The UK's Changing Democracy: The 2018 Democratic Audit*, London, LSE Press, 2018.

Wil Jon Edwards, *From the Valley I Came*, London, Angus & Robertson, 1956.

Mark Evans, *Charter 88: Successful Challenge to the British Political Tradition?*, Aldershot, Dartmouth, 1995.

Mary Fels, *Joseph Fels: His Life Work*, New York, B. W. Huebsch, 1920.

Frank Field, *Attlee's Great Contemporaries: The Politics of Character*, London, Continuum, 2009.

Michael Foot,

Aneurin Bevan: A Biography, London, MacGibbon & Kee, 1963.

Debts of Honour, New York, Harper & Row, 1981.

Loyalists and Loners, London, Faber & Faber, 2011.

Parliament in Danger, London, Pall Mall Press, 1959.

Rob Ford and Matthew Goodwin, *Revolt on the Right*, London, Routledge, 2014.

Alfred George Gardiner, *Prophets, Priests and Kings*, London, Rivers, 1908.

Edward George, *From Mill-boy to Minister: The Life of John Robert Clynes*, London, T.F. Unwin, 1918.

Bruce Glasier, *J. Keir Hardie MP: A Memorial,* Manchester, National Labour Press, 1915.

Philip Gould, *The Unfinished Revolution, How the Modernisers Saved the Labour Party*, London, Little, Brown, 1998.

Thomas N. Graham, *Willie Graham*, London and New York, Hutchinson, 1948.

E.H.H. Green and Duncan Tanner eds, *Political Leaders, Moral Values and the Reception of Economic Debate*, Cambridge, Cambridge University Press, 2007.

Jane Green and Will Jennings, *The Politics of Competence: Parties, Public Opinion and Voters*, Cambridge, Cambridge University Press, 2017.

Fred I. Greenstein, *The Presidential Difference: Leadership Style from FDR to Clinton*, New York, Martin Kessler Books/The Free Press, 2000.

Stuart Hall and Martin Jacques eds, *The Politics of Thatcherism*, London, Lawrence & Wishart, 1983.

Mary Agnes Hamilton, *Arthur Henderson: A Biography*, London, W. Heinemann, 1938.

Keir Hardie,

From Serfdom to Socialism, London, 1907.

The ILP and All About It, London, Independent Labour Party, 1909.

The Red Dragon and the Red Flag, Merthyr, Independent Labour Party, 1912.

My Confession of Faith in the Labour Alliance, London, Independent Labour Party, 1909.

Kenneth Harris, *Attlee*, London, Weidenfeld & Nicolson, 1984.

Robert Harris, *The Making of Neil Kinnock*, London, Faber & Faber, 1984.

Roy Hattersley and Kevin Hickson, *The Socialist Way: Social Democracy in Contemporary Britain*. London, I.B. Tauris, 2013.

Alan Haworth and Dianne Hayter, *Men Who Made Labour: The Parliamentary Labour Party of 1906 – The Personalities and the Politics*, London, Routledge, 2006.

Anthony F. Heath, Roger M. Jowell and John K. Curtice, *The Rise of New Labour: Party Policies and Voter Choices*, Oxford, Oxford University Press, 2001.

Arthur Henderson,

The Aims of Labour, New York, Headley Bros, 1918.

British Finance and Prussian Militarism, London and New York, Hodder & Stoughton, 1917.

Peter Hennessy, *The Prime Minister: The Office and its Holders since 1945*, London, Allen Lane, 2000.

Tim Heppell, *Choosing the Labour Leader*, London, I.B. Tauris, 2010.

Tim Heppell and David Seawright eds, *Cameron and the Conservatives: The Transition to Coalition Government*, Basingstoke, Palgrave Macmillan, 2012.

Kevin Hickson, *The IMF Crisis of 1976 and British Politics*, London, Tauris Academic Studies, 2005.

Eric Hobsbawm,

The Forward March of Labour Halted?, London, Verso, 1981.

The Age of Extremes: The Short Twentieth Century 1914–1991, London, Michael Joseph, 1994.

David Howell, *MacDonald's Party: Labour Identities and Crisis 1922–1931*, Oxford, Oxford University Press, 2002.

I. G. C. Hutchinson, *A Political History of Scotland 1832–1924: Parties, Elections and Issues*, Edinburgh, John Donald Short Run Press, 1986.

Ronald Inglehart, *Culture Shift in Advanced Industrial Society*, Princeton NJ, Princeton University Press, 1990.

Toby S. James,

Elite Statecraft and Election Administration: Bending the Rules of the Game, Basingstoke, Palgrave Macmillan, 2012.

UK Democracy Under Strain: Democratic Backsliding and Strengthening 2019–2023, London, Unlock Democracy, 2023.

Anthony Jay ed., *The Oxford Dictionary of Political Quotations*, Oxford, Oxford University Press, 1996.

Kevin Jefferys, *Leading Labour: From Keir Hardie to Tony Blair*, London, I.B. Tauris, 1999.

James B. Jeffreys, *The Story of the Engineers*, London, Lawrence & Wishart, 1945.

Edwin A. Jenkins, *From Foundry to Foreign Office: The Romantic Life-Story of the Rt Hon. Arthur Henderson, MP*, London, Grayson & Grayson, 1933.

Roy Jenkins, *A Life at the Centre*, London, Macmillan, 1991.

Bob Jessop,

The Future of the Capitalist State, Cambridge, Polity Press, 2002.

The State: Past, Present and Future, Cambridge, Polity Press, 2015.

Eileen Jones, *Neil Kinnock*, London, Robert Hale Ltd, 1994.

Dennis Kavanagh,

The Reordering of British Politics, Oxford, Oxford University Press, 1997.

Thatcherism and British Politics, Oxford, Oxford University Press, 1990.

Anthony King ed., *Britain at the Polls 1992*, Chatham NJ, Chatham House, 1993.

Brian Klass, *Fluke: Chance, Chaos, and Why Everything We Do Matters*, London, John Murray, 2024.

William W. J. Knox, *Scottish Labour Leaders 1918–1939: A Biographical Dictionary*, Edinburgh, Mainstream, 1984.

David Kogan, *Protest and Power: The Battle for the Labour Party*, London, Bloomsbury, 2019.

Paul Krugman, *End This Depression Now!*, New York, W. W. Norton & Company, 2012.

Edgar Lansbury, *George Lansbury, My Father*, London, Sampson Low, Marston & Co., 1934.

George Lansbury, *My Quest for Peace*, London, Michael Joseph, 1938.

Brian R. Law, *Oldham Brave Oldham: An Illustrated History of Oldham, 1849–1999*, Oldham, Oldham Council, 1999.

Fred Leventhal, *Arthur Henderson*, Manchester, Manchester University Press, 1989.

Steven Levitsky and Daniel Ziblatt, *How Democracies Die*, New York, Penguin, 2018.

Seymour M. Lipset and Stein Rokkan, *Party Systems and Voter Alignments: Cross-National Perspectives*, *Vol.* 7, New York, Free Press, 1967.

Benjamin Little and Alison Winch, *The New Patriarchs of Digital Capitalism: Celebrity Tech Founders and Networks of Power*, London, Routledge, 2021.

Robert Trelford McKenzie, *The British Political Parties: The Distribution of Power within the Conservative and Labour Parties*, London, Heinemann, 1964.

Ross McKibbin,

The Evolution of the Labour Party, 1910–1924, London and New York, Oxford University Press, 1983.

Parties and People: England 1914–1951, Oxford and New York, Oxford University Press, 2010.

David McKie ed., *The Election, A Voter's Guide*, London, Fourth Estate, 2000.

Andy McSmith, *Faces of Labour*, London, Verso, 1996.

Patrick Maguire and Gabriel Pogrund, *Get In: The Inside Story of Labour Under Starmer*, London, Bodley Head, 2025.

John Major, *The Autobiography*, London, HarperCollins, 1999.

Nelson Mandela, *Long Walk to Freedom: The Autobiography of Nelson Mandela*, London, Hachette UK, 2008.

David Marquand, *Ramsay MacDonald*, London, Jonathan Cape, 1977.

Andrew Marr, *The Making of Modern Britain*, London, Pan, 2010.

Roderick Martin, *Communism and the British Trade Unions, 1924–1933*, Oxford, Clarendon Press, 1969.

Deborah Mattinson, *Beyond the Red Wall*, London, Biteback Publishing, 2020.

Ralph Miliband, *Parliamentary Socialism: A Study in the Politics of Labour*, London, Merlin Press, 1972.

Abe Moffat, *My Life with the Miners*, London, Lawrence & Wishart, 1965.

Janet Morgan ed., *The Backbench Diaries of Richard Crossman*, London, Hamish Hamilton/Jonathan Cape, 1981.

Kenneth O. Morgan,

Keir Hardie: Radical and Socialist, London, Weidenfeld & Nicolson, 1975.

Labour People: Leaders and Lieutenants: Hardie to Kinnock, Oxford and New York, Oxford University Press, 1987.

Michael Foot: A Life, London, Harper Press, 2007.

Kenneth O. Morgan and Jane Morgan, *Portrait of a Progressive: The Political Career of Christopher, Viscount Addison*, Oxford, Oxford University Press, 1980.

Kevin Morgan, *Labour Legends and Russian Gold*, London, Lawrence & Wishart, 2006.

Barry Naughton, 'Deng Xiaoping: The Economist', *China Quarterly*, Vol. 135, 1993, pp. 491–514.

Friedrich Nietzsche, *Beyond Good and Evil*, New York, Random House, 1966.

Pippa Norris and Ronald Inglehart, *Cultural Backlash: The Rise of Authoritarianism-Populism*, New York, Cambridge University Press, 2019.

Joseph Nye, *The Powers to Lead*, Oxford and New York, Oxford University Press, 2008.

George Orwell, *The Lion and the Unicorn: Socialism and the English Genius: Part 3: The English Revolution*, London, Secker & Warburg, 1941.

David Owen,

In Sickness and In Power: Illness In Heads of Government During The Last 100 Years, London, Methuen, 2008.

Time to Declare, London, Michael Joseph, 1991.

Oxford Dictionary of National Biography, Oxford and New York, Oxford University Press, 2004.

Mark Perryman ed., *The Corbyn Effect*, London, Lawrence and Wishart, 2017.

Ann Pettifor, *The Case for the Green New Deal*, London and New York, Verso, 2020.

Karl Pike, *Getting Over New Labour*, Newcastle-upon-Tyne, Agenda, 2024.

Thomas Piketty, *Capital in the Twenty-First Century*, Cambridge MA, Harvard University Press, 2014.

Ben Pimlott,

Hugh Dalton, London, Papermac, 1985.

Labour and the Left in the 1930s, London, Allen & Unwin, 1986.

Ben Pimlott ed., *The Political Diary of Hugh Dalton 1918–40, 1945–60*, London, Jonathan Cape (in association with the London School of Economics and Political Science), 1986.

Gabriel Pogrund and Patrick Maguire, *Left Out: The Inside Story of Labour Under Corbyn*, London, Vintage, 2021.

Raymond Postgate, *The Life of George Lansbury*, London and New York, Longmans, 1951.

Rosa Prince, *Comrade Corbyn: A Very Unlikely Coup*, London, Biteback, 2016.

Adam Przeworski, *Democracy and the Market: Political and Economic Reform in Eastern Europe and Latin America*, Cambridge and New York, Cambridge University Press, 1991.

Thomas Quinn, *Electing and Ejecting Party Leaders in Britain*, Basingstoke, Palgrave, 2012.

Giles Radice, *Inside the Blair, Brown, Mandelson Project*, London, I.B. Tauris, 2010.

Colin Rallings and Michael Thrasher, *British Electoral Facts 1832–2012*, London, Biteback, 2012.

John Rentoul, *Tony Blair: Prime Minister*, London, Faber Finds, 2013.

Dave Rich, *The Left's Jewish Problem: Jeremy Corbyn, Israel and Antisemitism*, London, Biteback, 2018.

Steve Richards, *Whatever It Takes: The Real Story of Gordon Brown and New Labour*, London, Fourth Estate, 2010.

Neil Riddell, *Labour in Crisis: The Second Labour Government 1929–1931*, Manchester, Manchester University Press, 1999.

Daniel Ritschel, *The Politics of Planning: The Debate on Economic Planning in the 1930s*, Oxford, Clarendon Press, 1977.

William Rodgers ed., *Hugh Gaitskell 1906–1963*, Thames & Hudson, London 1964.

Jonathan Schneer, *George Lansbury*, Manchester, Manchester University Press, 1991.

Eric Shaw, *Discipline and Discord in the Labour Party: The Politics of Managerial Control in the Labour Party, 1951–87*, Manchester, Manchester University Press, 1988.

John Shepherd, *George Lansbury: At the Heart of Old Labour*, Oxford, Oxford University Press, 2004.

John Shepherd, Jonathan Davis and Chris Wrigley ed., *Britain's Second Labour Government, 1929–31: A Reappraisal*, Manchester, Manchester University Press, 2011.

Emanuel Shinwell, *The Labour Story*, London, McDonald, 1963.

Peter Shore, *Leading the Left*, London, Weidenfeld & Nicolson, 1993.

Robert Skidelsky,

Oswald Mosley, London and Holt, Rhinehart & Winston, 1975.

Politicians and the Slump: The Labour Government of 1929–1931, London and Melbourne, Macmillan, 1967.

Robert Skidelsky ed., *Thatcherism*, Oxford, Blackwell, 1988.

Lord Snell, *Men, Movements and Myself*, London, Dent, 1936.

Philip Snowden, *An Autobiography, Vol. 2*, London, I. Nicholson & Watson Ltd, 1934.

Maria Sobolewska and Robert Ford, *Brexitland*, Cambridge, Cambridge University Press, 2020.

Jon Sopel, *Tony Blair: The Moderniser*, London, Little, Brown, 1995.

David W. Soskice and Peter A. Hall, *Varieties of Capitalism: The Institutional Foundations of Comparative Advantage*, Oxford, Oxford University Press, 2001.

Nick Srnicek and Alex Williams, *Inventing the Future: Postcapitalism and a World Without Work*, London, Verso, 2015.

Leonard Stark, *Choosing the Leader: Leadership Contests in Britain from Macmillan to Blair*, Basingstoke, Macmillan, 1996.

Keir Starmer, *The Road Ahead*, London, Fabian Society, 2021.

Angus Stevenson, *Oxford English Dictionary* (third edition), Oxford, Oxford University Press, 2010.

Joseph E. Stiglitz, *The Road to Freedom: Economics and the Good Society*, New York, Norton and Company, 2024.

Paul Strangio, Paul 't Hart, James Walter eds, *Understanding Prime-Ministerial Performance: Comparative Perspectives*, Oxford, Oxford University Press, 2013.

Jack Straw, *Memoirs of a Political Survivor*, Basingstoke, Macmillan, 2012.

John Street, *Mass Media, Politics and Democracy*, London, Bloomsbury, 2021.

Mark Stuart,

Douglas Hurd: The Public Servant, Edinburgh, Mainstream, 1998.

John Smith: A Life, London, Politico's, 2005.

Duncan Tanner, *Political Change and the Labour Party, 1900–1918*, Cambridge and New York, Cambridge University Press, 1990.

A. J. P. Taylor, *English History 1914–1945*, Oxford, Clarendon Press, 1965.

Major A. C. Temperley, *The Whispering Gallery of Europe*, London, Collins, 1938.

William Temple, *Christianity and Social Order*, London, Penguin, 1942.

Lawrence Thompson, *The Enthusiasts*, London, Victor Gollancz, 1971.

Andrew Thorpe, *The British General Election of 1931*, Oxford, Clarendon Press, 1991.

Ben Tillett, *Is the Parliamentary Labour Party a Failure?*, London, Twentieth-Century Press, 1908.

H. Hessell Tiltman, *Ramsay MacDonald, Labour's Man of Destiny*, London, Jarrolds, 1929.

Jonathan Tonge, Stuart Wilks-Heeg and Louise Thompson eds, *Britain Votes: The 2019 General Election*, Oxford, Oxford University Press/Hansard Society, 2020.

David Torrance, *The Scottish Secretaries*, Edinburgh, Birlinn, 2006.

Paul Tyler, *Labour's Lost Leader: The Life and Politics of Will Crooks*, London, I.B. Tauris, 2007.

Beatrice Webb, *Diaries 1912–1924*, London and New York, Longman, 1952.

Max Weber, 'Politics as a Vocation', in *Weber: Selections in Translation*, Cambridge, Cambridge University Press, 1978.

Lord Wedderburn, *The Worker and the Law*, London, Sweet & Maxwell, 1986.

Daniel Weinbren, *Generating Socialism: Recollections of Life in the Labour Party*, Stroud, Sutton, 1997.

Egon Wertheimer, *Portrait of the Labour Party*, London, G. P. Putnam's Sons, 1929.

Martin Westlake, *Kinnock: The Biography*, London, Little, Brown, 2001.

Martin Westlake ed., *Leaders of Transition*, Basingstoke, Palgrave Macmillan, 2000.

Stuart Wilks-Heeg, Andrew Blick and Stephen Crone, 'The Democratic Audit of the UK 2012', Democratic Audit, Liverpool, 2012.

Francis Williams, *Nothing So Strange: An Autobiography*, London, Cassell, 1970.

Lord (Thomas) Williams of Barnburgh, *Digging for Britain*, London, Hutchinson, 1965.

Philip Williamson, *National Crisis and National Government: British Politics, the Economy and Empire 1926–1932*, Cambridge and New York, Cambridge University Press, 1992.

J. Havelock Wilson, *My Stormy Voyage Through Life*, London, Cooperative Printing Society, 1929.

J. M. Winter, *Socialism and the Challenge of War: Ideas and Politics in Britain, 1912–1918*, Routledge & Kegan Paul, 1974.

Leonard Woolf, *Downhill All the Way: An Autobiography of the Years 1919–1939*, New York, Harcourt, Brace & World, 1967.

Robert Worcester and Roger Mortimer, *Explaining Labour's Landslides*, London, Politico's, 1999.

Chris Wrigley,

A. J. P. Taylor: Radical Historian of Europe, London and New York, I. B. Tauris, 2006.

Arthur Henderson, Cardiff, GPC Books, 1990.

Winston Churchill: A Biographical Companion, Santa Barbara, CA, ABC Clio Inc, 2002.

MISCELLANEOUS

Attlee Papers,

Clement Attlee to Tom Attlee, 15 July 1931 (fo. 46).

Clement Attlee to Tom Attlee, 18 December 1931 (fo. 45).

Clement Attlee to Tom Attlee, 29 February 1932 (fo. 46).

Clement Attlee to Tom Attlee, 3 April 1933 (fo. 58).

18 May 1945 to 13 August 1945 (MS.Attlee.dep.18).

14–17 August 1945 (MS.Attlee.dep.19).

Letters to Tom, 21 October 1951.

BBC News,

'Churchill "greatest PM of twentieth century"', last updated 4 January 2000, accessed 19 February 2015 (http://news.bbc.co.uk/1/hi/uk_politics/575219.stm).

'Thatcher and Attlee top PM list', last updated 29 August 2006, accessed 19 February 2015 (http://news.bbc.co.uk/1/hi/uk_politics/5294024.stm).

'Churchill tops PM choice', BBC Newsnight, last updated 1 October 2008, accessed 19 February 2015 (http://news.bbc.co.uk/1/hi/programmes/newsnight/7647383.stm).

'Lord Mandelson: Don't rush to oust Jeremy Corbyn', BBC News, last updated 25 September 2015, accessed 28 July 2025 (https://www.bbc.co.uk/news/uk-politics-34355545).

'General election 2019: Blair attacks Corbyn's "comic indecision" on Brexit', BBC News, last updated 18 December 2019, accessed 28 July 2025 (https://www.bbc.co.uk/news/election-2019-50829352).

'"Work of change begins" – Keir Starmer's No 10 speech in full', BBC News, last updated 5 July 2024, accessed 25 July 2025 (https://www.bbc.co.uk/news/articles/crgewjwqqq4o).

Francis Beckett, 'Neil Kinnock: the man who saved Labour', *New Statesman*, last updated 25 September 2014, accessed 23 July 2025 (https://www.newstatesman.com/long-reads/2014/09/neil-kinnock-man-who-saved-labour).

Owen Bennett, 'Shadow Cabinet Resignations: Vernon Coaker, Lord Falconer, Karl Turner', HuffPost, last updated 26 June 2016, accessed 19 December 2024 (https://

www.huffingtonpost.co.uk/entry/another-labour-shadow-cabinet-member-vernon-coaker-quits-on-day-of-mass-resignations_uk_576ffa0ee4b0d2571149d36c).

Mathis Bitton, 'The Estonian Miracle: E-Estonia and the Future of Digital Infrastructure', VR/AR Association, last updated 11 November 2022, accessed 31 July 2025 (https://www.thevrara.com/news2/2022/11/11/the-estonian-miracle-e-estonia-and-the-future-of-digital-infrastructure).

Tony Blair, to Michael Foot, 28 July 1982 (Michael Foot Papers, private).

Leader's speech at Labour Party conference in Brighton, 30 September 1997, accessed 9 January 2014 (http://www.britishpoliticalspeech.org/speecharchive.htm?speech=203).

'The Full Text of Tony Blair's Speech to the European Research Institute', *The Guardian*, last updated 23 November 2001, accessed 31 January 2025 (https://www.theguardian.com/world/2001/nov/23/euro.eu1).

'Without total change, Labour will die', *New Statesman*, last updated 11 May 2021, accessed 28 July 2025 (https://www.newstatesman.com/politics/uk-politics/2021/05/tony-blair-without-total-change-labour-will-die).

Lukas Boer and Malte Rieth, 'The Macroeconomic Consequences of Import Tariffs and Trade Policy Uncertainty', International Monetary Fund, IMF Working Papers,19 January 2024.

Owen Bowcott, 'Johnson's Suspension of Parliament Unlawful, Supreme Court Rules', *The Guardian*, last updated 24 September 2019, accessed 31 January 2025 (https://www.theguardian.com/law/2019/sep/24/boris-johnsons-suspension-of-parliament-unlawful-supreme-court-rules-prorogue).

Stephen Bray, 'Guest Post: The Greatest Prime Ministers of All Time', Iain Dale's Diary, last updated 5 August 2010, accessed 19 February 2015 (http://iaindale.blogspot.co.uk/2010/08/guest-post-greatest-prime-ministers-of.html).

Sally Broughton Micova, 'Systemic Risk in Digital Services: Benchmarks for Evaluating the Management of Risks to Electoral Processes', Centre for Regulation in Europe (CERRE), last updated 24 May 2024, accessed 23 July 2025 (https://cerre.eu/publications/systemic-risk-in-digital-services-benchmarks-for-evaluating-the-management-of-risks-to-electoral-processes/).

Faye Brown, 'Elon Musk brands Starmer "two-tier Keir" and asks "is this Britain or Soviet Union?" over Facebook comment arrest video', Sky News, last updated 6 August 2024, accessed 23 July 2025 (https://news.sky.com/story/elon-musk-brands-starmer-two-tier-keir-and-asks-is-this-britain-or-soviet-union-over-facebook-comment-arrest-video-13191898).

John Burns's diary (British Library, Add.MSS. 46,337).

Anoosh Chakelian, 'Peter Mandelson: "I'm afraid Keir Starmer has come badly unstuck"', *New Statesman*, last updated 4 September 2021, accessed 28 July 2025 (https://www.newstatesman.com/encounter/2021/05/peter-mandelson-i-m-afraid-keir-starmer-has-come-badly-unstuck).

Philip Collins, 'Events have conspired to give Labour another chance. Will Keir Starmer seize it?', *New Statesman*, last updated 19 January 2022, accessed 25 January 2025 (https://www.newstatesman.com/politics/labour/2022/01/events-have-conspired-to-give-labour-another-chance-will-keir-starmer-seize-it).

Jon Crudas, 'George Lansbury: the unsung hero of blue Labour,' Labour Uncut, last updated 5 August 2011, accessed 29 May 2015 (http://labour-uncut.co.uk/2011/05/08/george-lansbury-the-unsung-father-of-blue-labour/).

John Curtice, 'Remain in light: What do Labour's many Remain supporters want to happen next?', Institute for Public Policy Research, last updated 12 January 2017, accessed 28 July 2025 (https://www.ippr.org/articles/remain-in-light-what-do-labour-s-many-remain-supporters-want-to-happen-next).

Chris Curtis, 'In their own words: why voters abandoned Labour', YouGov, last updated 23 December 2019, accessed 28 July 2025 (https://yougov.co.uk/politics/articles/27022-their-own-words-why-voters-abandoned-labour).

Iain Dale, 'Ranking Our 55 Prime Ministers – An Impossible Task, But a Fascinating One', IainDale.com, last updated 12 November 2020, accessed 25 July 2025 (https://www.iaindale.com/articles/ranking-our-55-prime-ministers-an-impossible-task-but-a-fascinating-one).

Peter Dorey and Andrew Denham, 'Entirely as expected? What the voting data tells us about Corbyn's re-election', British Politics and Policy Blog, London School of Economics, last updated 26 September 2016, accessed 28 July 2025 (https://blogs.lse.ac.uk/politicsandpolicy/labour-2016-voting-data/).

Electoral Commission, 'Accuracy and completeness of electoral registers',

2023, accessed 23 July 2025 (https://www.electoralcommission.org.uk/research-reports-and-data/electoral-registration-research/accuracy-and-completeness-electoral-registers).

T. Evans, 'Peace Issue at the 1935 Labour Conference', BBC Sound Archives.

Michael Foot, 'My Kind of Socialism', *The Observer*, 10 January 1982.

Robert Ford, 'Nigel Farage has been a threat to every recent UK prime minister. But this is something new', *The Observer*, last updated 8 February 2024, accessed 29 July 2025 (https://www.theguardian.com/politics/2025/feb/08/nigel-farage-reform-uk-labour-conservatives).

Sam Francis and Hannah Miller, 'Keir Starmer defends praising Thatcher in pitch for Tories', BBC News, last updated 3 December 2023, accessed 23 July 2025 (https://www.bbc.co.uk/news/uk-politics-67604830).

Friendly Society of Iron Founders, 'Monthly Report', January 1903.

Glasgow Herald, 24 February 1936.

General secretary, 'Report to the NEC: the general election', 21 June 1992 (GS:21/6/92).

Mark Gill and Kevin Theakston, 'The league table of post-war leaders of the opposition according to academics', LSE, last updated 13 July 2021, accessed 25 July 2025 (https://blogs.lse.ac.uk/politicsandpolicy/post-war-leaders-of-the-opposition/).

Bruce Glasier's diary (University of Liverpool Library).

Matt Goodwin, 'Brexit: Causes and Consequences', Japan Spotlight, Japan Economic Foundation, November/December 2017, accessed 31 January 2025 (https://www.jef.or.jp/journal/pdf/216th_Recent_JEF_Activity_02.pdf).

Anna Gross and Jim Pickard, 'Keir Starmer faces backlash over early failure to disclose £16,200 in donor-funded clothing', *Financial Times*, last updated 19 September 2024, accessed 29 July 2025 (https://www.ft.com/content/ddb7600f-f417-4948-9e4b-8d666e15846f).

Hansard, April 1948, October 1980.

Keir Hardie to Bruce Glasier, 8 October 1907 (Independent Labour Party Archive, London School of Economics Library).

Keir Hardie to Bruce Glasier, 7/8 January 1908 (Glasier Papers).

Keir Hardie to Rose Davies, 1914 (Glamorgan Record Office, Cardiff, D/Dxik, 30/27).

Keir Hardie, 'The Sunshine of Socialism', speech delivered at the twenty-first anniversary of the formation of the Independent Labour Party in Bradford, 11 April 1914, accessed 29 May 2015 (http://labourlist.org/2014/04/keir-hardies-sunshine-of-socialism-speech-full-text).

Victoria Honeyman, 'The 2024 UK General Election and the absence of foreign policy', UK Election Analysis, 2024, accessed 31 January 2025 (https://www.electionanalysis.uk/uk-election-analysis-2024/section-5-policy-and-strategy/the-2024-uk-general-election-and-the-absence-of-foreign-policy/).

Christopher Hope, 'Half of the Labour MPs who backed Jeremy Corbyn desert to rival candidates', *Daily Telegraph*, last updated 23 July 2015, accessed 28 July 2025 (https://www.telegraph.co.uk/news/politics/labour/11756688/Half-of-the-Labour-MPs-who-backed-Jeremy-Corbyn-desert-him.html).

Hope Not Hate, *State of Hate 2024: Pessimism, Decline and the Rising Radical Right*, accessed 23 July 2025 (https://hopenothate.org.uk/wp-content/uploads/2024/03/state-of-hate-2024-v15.pdf).

House of Commons Library, last updated 1 March 2013, accessed 24 July 2025 (https://commonslibrary.parliament.uk/research-briefings/rp13-14/).

Institute for Public Policy Research, 'Up to 8 million UK jobs at risk from AI unless government acts, finds IPPR', last updated 27 March 2024, accessed 23 July 2025 (https://www.ippr.org/media-office/up-to-8-million-uk-jobs-at-risk-from-ai-unless-government-acts-finds-ippr).

Miss W. H. Irwin to Ramsay MacDonald, 4 May 1899 (National Archives, MacDonald Papers, 5/6).

Danielle Jefferies, Dan Wellings, Jessica Morris, Mark Dayan and Cyril Lobont, 'Public satisfaction with the NHS and social care in 2023: Results from the British Social Attitudes Survey', King's Fund, last updated 27 March 2024, accessed 23 July 2025 (https://www.kingsfund.org.uk/insight-and-analysis/reports/public-satisfaction-nhs-social-care-2023).

Peter Kellner, 'The UK Braces for a Change of Direction', Strategic Europe, last updated 28 May 2024, accessed 31 January 2025 (https://carnegieendowment.org/europe/strategic-europe/2024/05/the-uk-braces-for-a-change-of-direction?lang=en).

Martin Kettle, 'Starmer is being tough on the rioters, but history shows that preventing further unrest is the real challenge', *The Guardian*, last updated 7 August 2024, accessed 6 February 2025 (https://www.theguardian.com/commentisfree/article/2024/aug/07/keir-starmer-rioters-unrest-immigration-fears).

John Maynard Keynes, 'Sir Oswald Mosley's manifesto', *The Nation and Athenaeum*, 13 December 1930.

Neil Kinnock,

on *Kinnock: The Inside Story*, London Weekend Television, 1992.

'Opportunity Knocks' interview in *Holyrood Magazine*, 3 November 2013.

Daniel Kraemer, 'Brexit: What does the No Deal Bill say?', BBC News, last updated 4 September 2019, accessed 31 January 2025 (https://www.bbc.co.uk/news/uk-politics-49580500).

The Labour Party,

'Report of the Seventh Annual Conference of the Labour Party', 24 January 1907.

'Report of the Eighth Annual Conference of the Labour Party', 20 January 1908.

'Report of the Labour Commission to Ireland', December 1920.

'Report of the Annual Conference of the Labour Party', 1918.

'Report of the Thirtieth Annual Conference', 1930.

'Report of the Annual Conference', 1934.

'Report of the Thirty-Fifth Annual Conference', 1935.

'Report of the Thirty-Sixth Annual Conference', 1936.

'Report of the Forty-Sixth Annual Conference', 1947.

Labour Representation Committee,

'Report of the First Annual Conference of the Labour Representation Committee', 1 February 1901.

'Report of the Third Annual Conference of the Labour Representation Committee', 21 February 1903.

George Lansbury, 'How I Became a Socialist', *Labour Leader*, 17 May 1912. *Labour Leader*, 3 February 1900, 16 June 1900, 2 September 1904, 17 April 1908, 2 October 1913, 23 October 1913.

George Lansbury to Charles Trevelyan, 5 January 1932 (Trevelyan Papers, CPT 145).

George Lansbury to Jim Middleton, September 1935 (Middleton Papers, MID 54).

Harold Joseph Laski, 'Why I am a Marxist', *Nation*, 14 January 1931.

Jack Lawson to Ramsay MacDonald, 1 September. 1931.

Keith Laybourn, '"Suicide During a Fit of Insanity" or the Defence of Socialism?', *The Bradford Antiquary*, 3rd ser., No. 5, 1991.

Steven Levitsky,

'The New Authoritarianism', *The Atlantic*, last updated 10 February 2025, accessed 23 July 2025 (https://www.theatlantic.com/ideas/archive/2025/02/trump-competitive-authoritarian/681609/).

'"Right Now, the U.S. Is Ceasing to Be a Democracy"', *Der Spiegel*, last updated 24 March 2025, accessed 23 July 2025 (https://www.spiegel.de/international/world/harvard-professor-steven-levitsky-right-now-the-u-s-is-ceasing-to-be-a-democracy-a-d6595df5-68a5-4b74-ab09-1dbf5179ddbd).

George Lucas, 'A goldfish full of piranhas', *Independent on Sunday*, 9 December 2001.

Will Lunn to Ramsay MacDonald, 30 August 1931.

Gordon Macdonald to Ramsay MacDonald, 29 August 1931 (MacDonald Papers 1315).

Ramsay MacDonald to Bruce Glasier, 21 July 1906 (Independent Labour Party Archive, London School of Economics Library).

Asher McShane, 'Israel "has the right" to withhold power and water from Gaza, says Sir Keir Starmer', LBC, last updated 11 October 2023, accessed 28 July 2025 (https://www.lbc.co.uk/news/sir-keir-starmer-hamas-terrorism-israel-defend-itself/).

Bronwen Maddox, 'The Historic Significance of Theresa May's Defeat', Institute for Government, last updated 15 January 2019, accessed 31 January 2025 (https://www.instituteforgovernment.org.uk/article/comment/historic-significance-theresa-mays-defeat).

Grahame Madge, '2024: record-breaking watershed year for global climate', Met Office, last updated 10 January 2025, accessed 28 July 2025 (https://www.

metoffice.gov.uk/about-us/news-and-media/media-centre/weather-and-climate-news/2025/2024-record-breaking-watershed-year-for-global-climate).

Manchester Guardian, 29 October 1931, 9 September 1935.

Andrew Marr, 'Don't read too much Tolstoy, Mr Smith', *The Independent*, 20 January 1994.

Deborah Mattinson, 'What is leadership?', Britain Thinks, July 2012, accessed 3 March 2015 (http://britainthinks.com/sites/default/files/WhatIsLeadership-print.pdf).

Merthyr Pioneer, 9 October 1915.

The Metropolitan, New York, June 1912 (copy in Tamiment Library, New York City).

Caroline Mortimer, 'Jeremy Corbyn on the Last Leg: enthusiastic about staying in the EU but won't share a platform with Cameron', *The Independent*, last updated 10 June 2016, accessed 17 January 2025 (https://www.independent.co.uk/news/uk/politics/jeremy-corbyn-says-he-is-enthusiastic-about-staying-in-the-eu-but-won-t-share-a-platform-with-david-cameron-a7075626.html).

National Archives,

CAB 130/497, Brutus.

CAB 128/19, CM (51) 4, Cabinet Papers, 25 January 1951.

CAB 128/19, CM (51) 25-6, Cabinet Papers, 9 April 1951.

CAB 128/39, Cabinet conclusions, 15 December 1964.

CAB 128/39, Cabinet conclusions, 28 January 1965.

CAB 128/39, Cabinet conclusions, 15 July 1965.

CAB 128/39, Cabinet conclusions, 27 July 1965.

CAB 128/44, Cabinet conclusions, 20 July 1966.

CAB 128/42, Cabinet conclusions, 16 November 1967.

CAB 128/43, Cabinet conclusions, 20 December 1967.

CAB 128/54, Cabinet conclusions, 14 March 1974.

CAB 128/54, Cabinet conclusions, 28 March 1974.

CAB 128/54, Cabinet conclusions, 2 May 1974.

CAB 128/55, Cabinet confidential annex, 20 November 1974.

CAB 128/55, Cabinet conclusions, 27 February 1975.

CAB 128/56, Cabinet confidential annex, 25 March 1975.

CAB 128/57, Cabinet confidential annex, 1 July 1975.

CAB 128/57, Cabinet confidential annex, 6 November 1975.

CAB 128/57, Cabinet confidential annex, 13 November 1975.

PREM 13/866, Lord Kahn committee report of the enquiry into the position of sterling, 1964–5.

PREM 13/261, conclusions of a meeting at Chequers, 21 November 1964.

PREM 13/261, note of a meeting held at 10 Downing Street on 24 November 1964.

PREM 13/104, Record of a meeting at British embassy, Washington, and later at the White House, 7 December 1964.

PREM 13/104, Record of a meeting at the White House, 8 December 1964.

PREM 13/692, meeting between the Prime Minister and Dean Rusk, 29 January 1965.

PREM 13/686, record of a conversation at lunch at the White House on Friday, 17 December 1965 (note by the Prime Minister).

PREM 13/693, record of a conversation between the Prime Minister and David Bruce, 12 March 1965.

PREM 13/690, Commonwealth peace mission diary, June 1965.

PREM 13/690, note for the record Commonwealth mission on Vietnam, 15 June 1965.

PREM 13/852, Mitchell to Prime Minister, 29 March 1966.

PREM 13/866, Lord Kahn committee report, June 1966.

PREM 13/1918, Prime Minister's personal telegram, serial no. T24/67, 11 p.m., 6 February 1967.

PREM 13/1918, Prime Minister's personal telegram: serial no. T26/67, 11 p.m., 10 February 1967.

PREM 13/2646, Paris to Foreign Office telegram, no. 1192, 27 November 1967.

PREM 13/2454, telegram from Foreign Secretary, 11 January 1968.

PREM 13/2726, note of a discussion at dinner, Chequers, 1 June 1969.

T 312/1485, 'Devaluation', 23 April 1964.

New Leader, 24 November 1922.

The Observer, 30 June 1918, 19 January 2014.

Office for Budget Responsibility, 'Brexit analysis', last updated 1 February 2025, accessed 28 July 2025 (https://obr.uk/forecasts-in-depth/the-economy-forecast/brexit-analysis/).

Office for National Statistics, 'Population estimates for the UK, England, Wales, Scotland and Northern Ireland: mid-2023', last updated 8 October 2024, accessed 28 July 2025 (https://www.ons.gov.uk/peoplepopulationandcommunity/populationandmigration/populationestimates/bulletins/annualmidyearpopulationestimates/mid2023).

Richard Osley, 'Tony Blair attacks Jeremy Corbyn's "Alice In Wonderland" politics', *The Independent*, last updated 30 August 2015, accessed 28 July 2025 (https://www.independent.co.uk/news/uk/politics/labour-leadership-contest-tony-blair-attacks-jeremy-corbyn-s-alice-in-wonderland-politics-10478524.html).

George Parker, Jim Pickard, Lucy Fisher and Rafe Uddin, 'Keir Starmer enters Downing Street as UK prime minister after historic victory,' *Financial Times*, last updated 5 July 2024, accessed 23 July 2025 (https://www.ft.com/content/9ddccaa8-4b63-4a7a-8192-c65b7318c16e).

Sami Quadri, 'Labour Leader Keir Starmer rules out UK rejoining the European Union', *The Standard*, last updated 14 February 2022, accessed 31 January 2025 (https://www.standard.co.uk/news/uk/labour-leader-keir-starmer-rules-out-uk-rejoining-european-union-b982474.html).

Julia Rampen, 'Keir Starmer MP: Choosing ideological purity before power is a dereliction of duty', *New Statesman*, last updated 24 July 2016, accessed 28 July 2025 (https://www.newstatesman.com/politics/2016/07/keir-starmer-mp-choosing-ideological-purity-power-dereliction-duty).

Peter Riddell, 'That Missing Spark', *The Times*, 1 July 1993.

Alessandra Rizzo, 'Starmer Rejects Brexit law firm role after claims of hypocrisy', Sky News, last updated 25 July 2017, accessed 31 January 2025 (https://news.sky.com/story/starmer-rejects-brexit-law-firm-role-after-claims-of-hypocrisy-10961191/).

Lord (William Thomas) Rodgers of Quarry Bank to Rt Hon. John Smith QC MP, 16 April 1993 (Murray Elder Papers, Box 1).

Andrew Roth and Byron Criddle, *Parliamentary Profiles A-D*, London, Parliamentary Profile Services, 2004, pp. 615–7.

Michael Savage, 'How cross-party talks left both sides frustrated', *The Observer*, last updated 7 April 2019, accessed 28 July 2025 (https://www.theguardian.com/politics/2019/apr/07/how-cross-party-brexit-talks-left-both-sides-frustrated-labour-tories).

Ben Silverstone, 'Meet the Director – Keir Starmer', *Counsel Magazine*, 31 January 2009.

Sky News, 'Brexit stopped Ukraine invasion from succeeding, Jacob Rees-Mogg says', Sky News, last updated 14 May 2023, accessed 17 July 2025 (https://news.sky.com/story/brexit-stopped-ukraine-invasion-from-succeeding-jacob-rees-mogg-says-12880590).

Elizabeth Simon, 'Educational Attainment and Referendum Voting: Questions and Connections', UK in a Changing Europe, last updated 16 March 2022, accessed 30 January 2025 (https://ukandeu.ac.uk/educational-attainment-referendum-voting/).

Matthew Smith, 'David Cameron was the best Prime Minister since Thatcher', YouGov, last updated 10 August 2016, accessed 25 July 2025 (https://yougov.co.uk/politics/articles/16170-cameron-best-prime-minister-since-thatcher).

Mikey Smith, 'Peter Mandelson says he is "working every day" to topple Jeremy Corbyn', *Daily Mirror*, last updated 21 February 2017, accessed 28 July 2025 (https://www.mirror.co.uk/news/politics/peter-mandelson-says-working-every-9860086).

Keir Starmer,

'"We can win the next election" – Keir Starmer's Labour conference speech', Labour List, last updated 29 September 2021, accessed 15 January 2025 (https://labourlist.org/2021/09/we-can-win-the-next-election-keir-starmers-labour-conference-speech/).

'Keir Starmer's speech on fixing the foundations of our country: 27 August 2024', Gov.uk, last updated 27 August 2024, accessed 3 February 2025 (https://www.gov.uk/government/speeches/keir-starmers-speech-on-fixing-the-foundations-of-our-country-27-august-2024).

Philip Stephens, 'New Image for the New Left', *Financial Times*, 31 October–1 November 1998.

Stefan Stern, 'Labour's Lost Leader. How Smith Threw the Book at Straw', *New Statesman*, 19 April 2004.

Heather Stewart, 'Keir Starmer had no enemies. Can he keep it that way?', *The Guardian*, last updated 27 March 2020, accessed 28 July 2025 (https://www.theguardian.com/politics/2020/mar/27/keir-starmer-profile-labours-non-aligned-leadership-frontrunner).

Jon Stone, 'Nigel Farage backtracks on Leave campaign's "£350m for the NHS" pledge hours after result', *The Independent*, last updated 25 June 2016, accessed 23 January 2025 (https://www.independent.co.uk/news/uk/politics/eu-referendum-result-nigel-farage-nhs-pledge-disowns-350-million-pounds-a7099906.html).

Kevin Theakston, 'Academics rate David Cameron among worst post-war prime ministers', The Conversation, last updated 13 October 2016, accessed 25 July 2025 (https://theconversation.com/academics-rate-david-cameron-among-worst-post-war-prime-ministers-66780).

Kevin Theakston and Mark Gill, 'Theresa May joint worst post-war prime minister, say historians and politics professors in new survey', The Conversation, last updated 6 July 2021, accessed 25 July 2025 (https://theconversation.com/theresa-may-joint-worst-post-war-prime-minister-say-historians-and-politics-professors-in-new-survey-163912).

The Times,

16 February 1899, 2 December 1909, 11 December 1909, 31 December 1909, 4 January 1910, 10 January 1910, 12 January 1910, 8 January 1919, 29 November 1922, 16 June 1932, 5 July 1945, 9 October 1967.

Bianca Todd, 'Labour has betrayed its roots by distancing itself from the unions', *The Guardian*, last updated 3 March 2014, accessed 29 May 2015 (http://www.theguardian.com/commentisfree/2014/mar/03/labour-party-unions-left-unity-ed-miliband).

Charles Trevelyan to George Lansbury, 29 October 1931 (Lansbury Papers, Vol. 8, fos 172–3).

Edouard Vaillant to Keir Hardie, 1 August 1912 (Independent Labour Party Archive).

Nigel Walker, 'Brexit timeline: events leading to the UK's exit from the European Union', House of Commons Library, last updated 6 January 2021, accessed 28 July 2025 (https://commonslibrary.parliament.uk/research-briefings/cbp-7960/).

West Fife Echo, 2 February 1910.

Workers' Dreadnought, 16 October 1915 (material in Sylvia Pankhurst archive B/12, Institute of Social History, Amsterdam).

Ben Wright, 'Labour's Brexit dilemma', BBC News, last updated 27 January 2017, accessed 28 July 2025 (https://www.bbc.co.uk/news/uk-politics-38769838).

FURTHER READING ON STATECRAFT THEORY

Nathan Critch, 'Merely the "Art of Winning Elections"? Regrounding the Statecraft Interpretation of British Politics', *British Journal of Politics and International Relations*, 27(2), 2024, pp. 497–509.

Richard Hayton,

'Conservative Party Statecraft and the Johnson Government', *Political Quarterly*, 92(3), 2021, pp. 412–19.

'Conservative Party Statecraft and the Politics of Coalition', *Parliamentary Affairs*, 67(1), 2014, pp. 6–24.

'Ideology and Statecraft: A Reply to Griffiths', *Parliamentary Affairs*, 69(3), 2016, pp. 729–34.

Toby S. James,

Elite Statecraft and Election Administration: Bending the Rules of the Game, Basingstoke, Palgrave, 2012.

'Neo-Statecraft Theory, Historical Institutionalism and Institutional Change', *Government and Opposition*, 51(1), 2016, 84–110.

'Political leadership as statecraft? Aligning theory with praxis in conversation with British party leaders', *British Journal of Politics & International Relations*, 20(3), 2018, pp. 555–72.

Andrew S. Roe-Crines and David Jeffery eds, *Statecraft: Policies and Politics under Prime Minister Theresa May*, Basingstoke, Palgrave, 2023.

INDEX

Abbott, Diane 407
Abse, Leo 420
Adams, Grantley 97
Adamson, William 101–17
  overview 20, 40, 101–2
  performance in general elections 44–7, 49–54, 56, 114
  and 1918 general election 54, 56, 114
  early life and career 103–4, 105, 107–8
  during First World War 110, 112–13
  as leader of Labour Party 113, 114
  as Secretary of State for Scotland 115–16
  values of 116–17
  criticisms of 124–5
Addison, Christopher 147, 149
Adler, Viktor 99
Aims of Labour, The (Henderson) 162
Ainsley, Claire 388–9
Aitken, Max 265
Alexander, Heidi 371
Ali, Tariq 363, 364
Alli, Lord 394
Amalgamated Society of Engineers (ASE) 104–5, 109
antisemitism 368–70, 385, 387
Arab Spring 71
Armstrong, William 223
Asquith, H. H. 162, 177
Attlee, Clement 195–211
  overview 8–9, 20, 40, 195
  and 1945 general election 25–6, 56–7, 201–2
  and 1951 general election 29–30, 56, 209–10
  performance in general elections 44–55, 56–7, 201–2, 208–11, 291
  party management 55, 210
  prime ministerial ranking 58, 59, 60
  ranking as leader 60, 61, 195–6, 200, 210–11
  and Keir Hardie 100
  and Ramsay MacDonald 136
  under George Lansbury 181, 184–5, 186, 188–9, 190, 199
  as Prime Minister 195–6, 203–8
  early life and career 196–9
  during First World War 197–8
  under Ramsay MacDonald 198–9
  becomes leader of Labour Party 199–200
  during Second World War 200–201
  threats to leadership 202–3
  and trade unions 203–4
  and battle of ideas 207, 431
  and 1950 general election 209
  after 1951 general election 210
  electoral strategy 228, 443–4
  Neil Kinnock on 438
Attlee, Ellen 196
Attlee, Henry 196
Attlee, Tom 198
Attlee, Violet 198
Auden, W. H. 216

Badenoch, Kemi 397
Baldwin, Stanley 142, 194, 216, 265
Baldwin, Tom 379
Balls, Ed 328–9, 330, 336–7, 357
Bank of England 189, 204–5, 233, 244, 329, 387
Barber, Sir Michael 320
Barnes, George Nicoll 101–17
  overview 20, 40, 101–2
  performance in general elections 44–5, 47–53
  early life and career 102–3, 104–5
  in Liberal Party 106–7
  and discipline in Labour Party 108
  during First World War 109–11
  resigns leadership 109
  after First World War 112
  values of 116–17
Barnier, Michel 409
Barrett, Ann 305
Basnett, David 262
battle of ideas (political argument hegemony)
  as component of statecraft 29, 34–6
  and Clement Attlee 207, 431
  and Hugh Gaitskell 214, 218–28
  and Neil Kinnock 280–89, 429–33
  and Tony Blair 323–4, 448–50
  and Ed Miliband 351–4
  and David Cameron 431
Bebel, August 99
Beckett, Margaret 304

Benjamin, Carl 36
Benn, Hilary 371, 413
Benn, Tony
under Harold Wilson 242
under James Callaghan 252
under Michael Foot 262
interest in the arts 272
bid for deputy leadership 277, 422
challenges Neil Kinnock for leadership 286, 427
and John Smith 299
comparison with Jeremy Corbyn 363
Neil Kinnock on 423
Betjeman, John 215
Bevan, Aneurin 41, 93, 186, 205, 208, 210, 224, 231, 266, 270, 418, 436
Beveridge Report 26, 204
Bevin, Ernest
and Ramsay MacDonald 144, 149
and Arthur Henderson 158, 163, 167
and George Lansbury 190–91, 193, 199
and Clement Attlee 200, 202, 203
as Foreign Secretary 204, 205–6
as Minister of Labour 207
Biden, Joe 392
'Black Wednesday' 32
Blair, Tony 311–26, 439–52
overview 8–9, 19, 20, 40, 311
and battle of ideas 35, 323–4, 448–50
performance in general elections 43, 45–54, 56, 57, 291, 319
ranking as leader 54, 60, 61
electoral strategy 55, 312–18, 444–5
party management 55, 321–3, 434, 447–8
prime ministerial ranking 58, 59, 60
and constitutional change 68, 324–5, 450–51
comparison with Hugh Gaitskell 220–22, 228
and Michael Foot 266–7
and Neil Kinnock 280
as communicator 314–16
media support for 316–17
governing competence 318–21, 445–7
as Prime Minister 318–21
and 2001 general election 319
and Jeremy Corbyn 366, 372–3
traditional labour voters and 404
Neil Kinnock on 437
on statecraft 443–50
and trade unions 448
Blewett, Neal 159, 161
Blick, Andrew 316
Bondfield, Margaret 144
Borrie, Gordon 306
Bouazizi, Mohamed 71
Bowra, Maurice 215–16
Bray, Stephen 60
Bretherton, Russell 273
Brexit
negotiation process 72–3, 411–13
consequences of 72, 73
Jeremy Corbyn's approach to 366–8, 371, 407–8, 409–10
Keir Starmer's approach to 381–3, 388
and Labour Party voters 404–6
Leave campaign 410–11
British Empire 76
Brockway, Fenner 87, 187
Brown, George 231, 232, 233–4, 236, 247
Brown, Gordon 327–41
overview 19–20, 26, 40, 327
performance in general elections 43, 45, 47–54, 57, 339–400
prime ministerial ranking 58, 59, 60
ranking as leader 61
as communicator 315–16
governing competence 319–20
as shadow Chancellor of the Exchequer 328–30
as Chancellor of the Exchequer 330–32, 336
as Prime Minister 332–41
failure to call 2008 general election 333–4
reaction to banking crisis 337–9
and 2010 general election 339–400
and Ed Miliband 345
party management 434
Tony Blair on 448
Buchanan, George 115
Bulpitt, Jim 27n, 374, 396
Burnham, Andy 364, 381
Burns, James MacGregor 196, 211
Burns, John 85, 95
Burns, Robert 104
butterfly effect 71–2

Callaghan, James 245–58
overview 19, 20, 40, 245–6
performance in general elections 43, 45, 47–54, 57, 291
prime ministerial ranking 58, 59, 60
ranking as leader 60, 61
as Prime Minister 97, 249–58
on Hugh Gaitskell 217
1963 leadership bid 231, 247
under Harold Wilson 232, 234, 235, 236, 247–9
early life and career 245–9
economic policy 250–52, 253–5, 256–7
becomes leader of Labour Party 250
Neil Kinnock on 418, 420–21

Cameron, David
  and electoral system reform 37
  influence of Tony Blair on 320, 324
  popularity of 332
  and early general election speculation 333–4
  reaction to banking crisis 337, 339
  and 2010 general election 340
  leadership qualities 358
  and Brexit referendum 408
  Neil Kinnock on 425–6
  party management 428
  and battle of ideas 431
Campbell, John 225
Campbell, R. J. 93
Campbell-Bannerman, Sir Henry 202, 268
Capital (Piketty) 269
Carvel, John 206n
Carville, James 32
Castle, Barbara 236, 243, 248
Chakrabarti, Shami 369
Chamberlain, Neville 201, 265
Chapman, Jenny 383
Churchill, Winston 9, 61, 109, 196, 201–2, 246, 444, 464
Citrine, Walter 149, 203
Clarke, Charles 278, 283, 308, 316, 419, 422, 423
Clarke, Peter 397
Clause IV debate
  and Hugh Gaitskell 214, 218–19, 224, 226
  and John Smith 303
  and Tony Blair 321
Clegg, Nick 37, 316, 320, 337, 339, 351
Clements, Dick 262
climate change 75, 78
Clynes, John Robert 119–33
  overview 10–11, 19, 20, 40, 119
  performance in general elections 44, 45, 46–7, 49–53, 57, 121, 125–8
  electoral strategy 55
  ranking as leader 61
  influence on Labour Party 119–22, 127, 129–31, 132–133
  deposed by Ramsay MacDonald 120, 128–9, 131–2
  early life and career 122–4
  as leader of Labour Party 124–31
  after leadership of Labour Party 124, 129, 131–3, 165, 166
  and 1922 general election 125–8
  under Ramsay MacDonald 137
Coaker, Vernon 371
Coalition Government (2010–2015) 37
Coffman, Hilary 305
Cole, G. D. H. 184, 216
Cole, Margaret 217
Collins, Philip 389
Commonwealth Immigrants Act (1968) 248
Communist Party 102, 179
complete leadership 15–16
Concannon, Don 422
conscience in leadership 9–11, 12, 13, 15–16
Conservative Party
  and 1992 general election 32
  and 1997 general election 32
  and economic management 32
  and ERM 32, 302, 312
  ousting of leaders 33, 34
  and National Government 152
  and 1945 general election 201
  and Clement Attlee 207
  and 1951 general election 209–10
  and 1950 general election 209
  and 1964 general election 232
  and 2010 general election 340
  and 2015 general election 353
  and 2024 general election 390
  and Brexit 408–9, 412
  Neil Kinnock on 426
constitutional change
  and Keir Hardie 90–91
  and Arthur Henderson 160
  and Tony Blair 324–5, 450–51
  and Neil Kinnock 435–6
constitutional management 29, 36–7
Cook, Robin 275, 434
Cooper, Jonathan 380
Cooper, Yvette 353, 364, 365
Corbyn, Jeremy 361–76
  and 2017 general election 4, 375
  overview 19, 20, 361
  press representation of 26–7
  becomes leader of Labour Party 41, 364–5, 372
  performance in general elections 43–4, 46–8, 49, 50–55, 56, 57
  ranking as leader 60
  early political involvement 361–3
  career as backbencher 363–4
  political authority within PLP 365–6, 367–8, 370–73, 375
  as leader of Labour Party 365–73, 381, 407–10
  and Brexit 366–8, 371, 407–8, 409–10
  and antisemitism in Labour Party 368–70, 387
  assessment as leader 374–6
  and 2019 general election 375–6
  as polarising figure 407
  relationship with parliamentary party 409, 410

Craigie, Jill 260, 261, 262, 272, 422
Cripps, Stafford
under George Lansbury 181, 184–5, 186, 188–9, 199
resignation from NEC 192
expelled from Labour Party 200
under Clement Attlee 203, 205–6, 207
and Hugh Gaitskell 217
Crone, Stephen 316
Crooks, Will 154
Crosland, Tony 226, 252, 269
Crossman, Richard 207, 227
Cruddas, Jon 8, 194
Cryer, Bob 420
culture wars 24
cunning in leadership 11–16
Cunningham, Jack 434
Curran, Peter 158
Cutts, David 405

Daily Citizen 178
Daily Herald 25, 178
Daily Mail 316, 357
Daily Worker 25
Dalton, Hugh 100, 184, 188, 192, 203, 206, 217
Darling, Alistair 336–7
Darzi, Ara 333
Debs, Eugene 88, 99
Debts of Honour (Foot) 267–8
democratic backsliding 16–18, 37, 77–8
Deng Xiaoping 64
devolution
and Keir Hardie 98
and William Adamson 115
and James Callaghan 255–6
and Michael Foot 270
and Neil Kinnock 276, 435–6
and John Smith 299, 306
Dewar, Donald 298
digital media *see* social media
Disraeli, Benjamin 176
Dobson, Frank 380
Donoughue, Bernard 229–30, 240
Dreyfus, Alfred 96
Dulles, John Foster 210
Duncan, Charles 109
Duncan Smith, Iain 34, 54
Dyson, Will 178

economic growth *see* regimes of accumulation
Ede, James Chuter 25
Edwards, Wil Jon 100
Elder, Murray 308
Elections Act (2022) 17
electoral strategy
as component of statecraft 28, 29–31
Clement Attlee 55, 228, 443–4
Harold Wilson 55
John Robert Clynes 55
Keir Hardie 55
Keir Starmer 55, 388–9, 390, 396
Kinnock, Neil 55
Tony Blair 55, 312–18, 443–5
Ed Miliband 350–51, 444
John Smith 388, 444
Neil Kinnock 427–8, 444
electoral system 4, 30, 55–6
Ellis, Tom 262
Elvin, Lionel 193
Equality and Human Rights Commission (EHRC) 387
European Economic Community (EEC) membership
and Hugh Gaitskell 219, 226
and Harold Wilson 239, 242–3
and Neil Kinnock 276, 282, 299
European Exchange Rate Mechanism (ERM) 287, 288, 294, 302
European Union membership
as issue within Labour Party 41, 402–3
and Michael Foot 273
see also Brexit
Evans, David 387
Evans, Delyth 305
Evans, Gwyn 423–4
Evans, Moss 262, 264, 269

Fabian Society 87, 89–90, 176, 197, 389
Falklands War 263, 265–6, 278
Farage, Nigel 36, 371, 397, 398, 410–11
Fels, Joseph 94
Ferrari, Nick 386
Fife, Clackmannan and Kinross Miners' Association (FCKMA) 106, 114–15
Finlayson, Alan 36
first-past-the-post electoral system 30
Fletcher, Simon 384
Foot, Michael 259–74
overview 19, 20, 259
and 1983 general election 26, 263–4
performance in general elections 43, 45, 47–8, 50–53, 55, 57, 263–4, 291
ranking as leader 60
on Hugh Gaitskell 222
as deputy leader of Labour Party 250, 261
criticisms of 260–61

becomes leader of Labour Party 261–2
as leader of Labour Party 262–4, 421–2
and trade unions 262, 268–70
writings of 265–7
belief in freedom of press 267–8
oratory skills 267
role of in 1970s Labour governments 268–70
party management 270–71, 272
and devolution 270
socialist beliefs 271–2
historical interests 273–4
resignation of 278, 422
Ford, Robert 397–8, 404
Friendly Society of Iron Founders 154

Gaitskell, Hugh 213–28
overview 11, 19, 20, 213–14
performance in general elections 43, 45, 47–53, 55, 57, 218, 291
ranking as leader 60
under Clement Attlee 207, 208
early life and career 214–17
and battle of ideas 214, 218–28
party management 218–28
becomes leader of Labour Party 218
comparison with Tony Blair 220–22
Gallacher, Willie 116
Gardiner, A. G. 84
Garel-Jones, Tristan 302–3
General and Municipal Workers Union (GMWU) 123
general elections
1900 10
1906 107, 108, 123, 159, 160, 177
1910 109, 159, 160–61, 177
1918 46, 54, 56, 111, 113–14, 123, 138, 163
1922 114, 125–8, 138, 140, 141, 198
1923 141
1924 56, 141, 198
1929 46, 136, 139, 147–8
1931 42, 116, 136, 141, 142, 152, 164, 167, 170, 174, 180–81, 199
1935 141, 194, 199
1945 25–6, 54, 201–2, 211, 217, 230–31, 246
1950 209
1951 29–30, 56, 209–10, 211
1955 210
1959 218
1964 232, 418
1966 234, 418
1970 31, 239, 261, 276
1974 (February) 30, 56, 239, 250
1974 (October) 241, 250
1979 277
1983 26, 263–4, 271, 277, 278
1987 285–6, 426–7
1992 32, 54, 289, 293–4, 300–301, 328, 331
1997 32, 42, 54
2001 319, 331
2010 316, 339–400, 444
2015 56, 343–4, 349–51, 358–9, 409
2017 4, 56, 375
2019 375–6
2024 3–4, 30, 56, 390–91, 414
Labour Party performances in 6, 41–51, 291
George VI, King 25, 209
Gladstone, Herbert 61, 89, 107, 159
Gladstone, William 175–6
Glasier, John Bruce 84, 96, 168–9
global financial crisis 71–2
GMB Union 322
Gompers, Sam 99
Goodwin, Matt 405–6
Gould, Bryan 298, 429, 434
Gould, Philip 281–2, 284, 289, 303–4, 318, 328
governing competence 40
as component of statecraft 28, 31–3
Tony Blair 318–21, 445–7
Gordon Brown 319–20
Ed Miliband 356–8
Graham, Andrew 320–21
Graham, Willie 166, 167
Gray, Sue 394, 397
Grayson, Victor 85, 86
'Green New Deal' 78
Greenstein, Fred I. 374
Greenwood, Arthur 147, 149, 189, 199–200
Grieve, Dominic 412
Gromyko, Andrei 250
Guardian, The 383
'Guilty Men' (Foot) 265–6

Hague, William 54
Hansen, Marion Coates 177
Hardie, Keir 83–100
overview 10, 19, 20, 40, 83
performance in general elections 44–6, 48–53
electoral strategy 55
achievements as leader 83–5
leadership weaknesses 85–7
support for suffragette movement 85, 95–6
creation of Labour Party 87–93
views on political action 90–92
resists anti-clericalism 92–3
entry into Parliament 93–4
and unemployment 94–5

Hardie, Keir *cont.*
and racial equality 96–7
socialist beliefs 97–9
death of 99–100
anti-war views 99
influence of 100
and Liberal Party 169
Hare, David 309
Harris, Carolyn 383
Harrison, Walter 260
Harry, Bill 275–6, 418
Hattersley, Roy 41, 278, 423, 427, 429, 431
Havelock Wilson, Joseph 157
Healey, Denis
on Harold Wilson 9
and leadership of Labour Party 41, 261–2, 271, 423
as Chancellor of the Exchequer 241–2, 251–2, 420
becomes deputy leader 422
Neil Kinnock on 423, 429
Heath, Edward 30, 225, 239, 431
Heffer, Eric 286
Henderson, Arthur 153–71
overview 20, 40, 153
performance in general elections 44–5, 47–53, 167
and Keir Hardie 85, 86
during First World War 110, 162–3
and 1918 general election 114, 163
under Ramsay MacDonald 137
and Ramsay MacDonald 143, 149, 155, 159, 164–5, 179
as Foreign Secretary 146
at 1930 party conference 147
influence on Labour Party 153–4
party management 154–5, 157–64
early life and career 154–7
and trade unions 156–7, 170
as party chairman 157–64, 168–9
and Ernest Bevin 158
and House of Lords 160
as leader of Labour Party 164–8, 169–71, 181–2
and Ireland 167–8
and 1931 general election 167, 170
Henderson, David 162
Heseltine, Michael 288
Hessell Tiltman, H. 131
Hewitt, Patricia 183
Hill, David 305, 423
Hills, Adam 408
Hobsbawm, Eric 67, 263, 362
Hopkins, Katie 36
House of Lords 36, 159–61
Howard, Michael 54
Howard, Peter 265
Howe, Geoffrey 288, 336
Hutton, Will 269
Hyndman, H. M. 110, 176

immigration
prevailing forces 71
and neo-liberalism 77, 78
and James Callaghan 247, 248
and Tony Blair 321
and Ed Miliband 348, 353
and Keir Starmer 391–2
Implementation Unit 320
In Place of Fear (Bevan) 436
'In Place of Strife' 236, 247, 248
Independent, The 304
Independent Labour Party (ILP) 87, 88–90, 100, 123, 142, 144, 148, 176, 187–8, 197
India 97, 206
Inglehart, Ronald 35
Institute for Fiscal Studies 390
international change 68–9
Ireland 91, 139, 167–8

Jacques, Martin 323
Jaures, Jean 92, 99
Jay, Peter 251
Jenkins, Clive 262, 264, 422–3
Jenkins, Roy 217, 218, 235, 244, 247, 249
Johnson, Alan 357
Johnson, Boris 17, 34, 78, 371, 385, 387, 388, 412, 414
Johnson, Lyndon B. 233, 237, 238–9
Johnston, Tom 115, 180
Jones, Jack 261, 269, 422
Joseph, Keith 267, 431
Journey, A (Blair) 312, 315
Journey's End (Sheriff) 146
Jowett, Frederick 114
Judicial Review and Courts Act (2022) 17

Kaufman, Gerald 26, 264, 286, 429, 434, 446
Kellner, Peter 284
Kendall, Liz 364, 365
Keynes, John Maynard 147, 204
Keynesian welfare state 76
Keys, Bill 262
Kinnock, Glenys 276, 418, 419, 421
Kinnock, Neil 275–96, 417–38
overview 11, 20, 275
performance in general elections 43, 45–6, 48–53, 55, 57, 279, 291
electoral strategy 55, 427–8

party management 55, 281, 283–5, 428–30
ranking as leader 60, 61
and Michael Foot 261
early life and career 275–8, 418–21
becomes leader of Labour Party 278, 422–4
statecraft 279–80, 289–95
and battle of ideas 280–89, 429–33
as leader of Labour Party 280–95, 446
and 1987 general election 285–6, 426–7
and 1992 general election 289, 293–4
and Westland Affair 299–300
and OMOV 308
on being Leader of the Opposition 386
on qualities of leadership 424–6, 436–8
and constitutional change 435–6
Kissinger, Henry 249
Korean War 208
Kwarteng, Kwasi 387

Laar, Mart 64
Labour and the Nation 142, 165, 179
Labour Leader 91
Labour Representation Committee (LRC) 88, 89, 107, 123, 156
Lamont, Norman 302
Lansbury, Bessie 176, 189
Lansbury, Edgar 189
Lansbury, George 173–94
overview 8–9, 20, 42, 173–5
and Keir Hardie 86
and Ramsay MacDonald 142, 149, 174, 177, 179
popularity of 173–4
own view of leadership 174–5
early life and career 175–80
as leader of Labour Party 180–90, 199
party management 187–9
resignation 190–94, 199
Laski, Harold 184
Last Leg, The 408
Lawson, Jack 150
leadership
importance of 5–6, 7–8
conscience in 9–11, 12, 13, 15–16
cunning in 11–16
Neil Kinnock on 424–6, 436–8
Tony Blair on 439–43
leadership role 84
Lee Kuan Yew 97, 420
Left Unity 11
Liberal Democrats 37, 316, 340, 351, 352
Liberal Party
and early history of Labour Party 89, 108–9
and George Nicoll Barnes 106–7
and William Adamson 107
decline of 139, 141
and 1929 general election 147–8
and Keir Hardie 169
and George Lansbury 175–6
and 1945 general election 201
and 1950 general election 209
and Lib–Lab pact 253
and Liberal–SDP alliance 263, 278, 281, 426
Liberal–Labour movement 87, 89–90, 139–40, 156, 159
Liberal–SDP alliance 263, 278, 281, 426
Lib–Lab pact 253
life expectancy figures 75
Livingstone, Ken 325, 363, 384
Lloyd, John 314–15
Lloyd, Tony 120
Lloyd George, David 91–4, 94, 102, 113–14, 157, 162, 169, 265
London Labour Briefing 362–3
Long-Bailey, Rebecca 383, 387
'Looking to the Future' 287
Lucas, George 289
Lunn, Will 150–51
Lynams school 214–15

Macdonald, Gordon 151
MacDonald, Malcolm 150
MacDonald, Ramsay 135–52
overview 11, 19, 20, 40, 41, 135
performance in general elections 42, 44–53, 55, 56, 57
prime ministerial ranking 58, 59, 60
ranking as leader 61
as leader of Labour Party 83, 138–9, 149, 228
and Keir Hardie 84, 86
negotiations with Liberal Party 89, 107, 108, 137–8, 159
anti-war views 99, 138
and 1918 general election 114, 163
in National Government 116, 150–51, 152, 180, 187
deposes John Robert Clynes 120, 128–9, 131–2
view of in Labour Party 136–7, 182–3
and 1922 general election 140
party management 142–4, 145, 155
and George Lansbury 142, 149, 174, 177, 179
as Foreign Secretary 146
socialist beliefs 146
reaction to National Government announcement 150–52
expulsion from Labour Party 152
and Arthur Henderson 159, 164–5

McDonnell, John 370, 407
McKibbin, Ross 155, 157, 293
McLean, John 111
Macmillan, Harold 219, 431
McNicol, Iain 356
Macron, Emmanuel 392
McSweeney, Morgan 383, 397
Maddox, Bronwen 412
Major, John
  and 1992 general election 32, 54, 289
  and 1997 general election 32
  as leader of Conservative Party 288, 312
  performance in general elections 289
  rebellions against 302–3
  John Smith on 307
  Neil Kinnock on 426
Making of Modern Britain, The (Marr) 132
Mandela, Nelson 64, 97
Mandelson, Peter 283, 305, 313, 337, 366, 373
Mann, Tom 104
Marr, Andrew 132, 304
Marx, Karl 90, 104, 216
Marxism Today 323
Mason, Paul 384
Mattinson, Deborah 314, 388
Maxton, James 187
May, Theresa 34, 73, 411
May Report 148–9
Meacher, Michael 278
media coverage, importance of 30–31
'Meet the Challenge, Make the Change' 287
Meloni, Giorgia 392
Meyer, Sir Anthony 288
Middleton, Jim 192
Mikardo, Ian 422
Miliband, David 41, 129, 322, 338, 345, 347
Miliband, Ed 343–59
  overview 19, 20, 343–4
  performance in general elections 43, 45, 47–53, 55, 56, 57, 291, 343–4, 349–51
  ranking as leader 60
  decisiveness of 317
  and trade unions 322, 355–6
  party management 323, 354–6
  and 2015 general election 343–4, 349–51, 358–9
  early life and career 344–6
  at Department of Energy and Climate Change 345–6
  becomes leader of Labour Party 346–7
  as leader of Labour Party 347–9
  electoral strategy 350–51, 444
  and battle of ideas 351–4
  governing competence 356–8
Miliband, Ralph 25–6, 344, 357
Militant Tendency 272, 281, 283, 430
Milne, Seumas 382
Milne-Bailey, Walter 148
Monnet, Jean 226
Moore, Barry 422
Morgan, Kenneth O. 159, 169
Morley, John 89, 156
Morrison, Herbert 40, 147, 188, 199–200, 202, 203, 204–5
Mortimer, Roger 280
Mosley, Oswald 140, 143, 148, 180, 187
Mountbatten, Lord 206
Murdoch, Rupert 305
Murray, Ian 371
Musk, Elon 5
My England (Lansbury) 190
'My Kind of Socialism' (Foot) 271

Nandy, Lisa 383
National Council of Labour 188
National Government
  and William Adamson 116
  formation of 136, 150–51, 180
  and 1931 general election 152
  Labour Party opposition to 166, 182–3, 186–7
National Health Service (NHS) 205
National Insurance Act (1946) 205
Neil, Andrew 305
neo-liberalism 76–7, 78
New Statesman 386–7, 389
Northern Ireland 237, 247–8
Nye, Sue 263

Observer, The 123–4
Office for Budget Responsibility (OBR) 73, 393
OMOV ('one member one vote') 303, 308, 309
online influencers 36
'Opportunity Britain' 287
Orme, Stan 420
Orwell, George 11
Osborne, George 337, 339, 348, 349, 357, 425
Osborne Judgement 161–2
Owen, Frank 265

Pankhurst, Sylvia 86, 96, 100
Parker, Laura 384
'Parliament in Danger' (Foot) 272
parliamentary sovereignty 68
party funding 30
party leaders
  importance of 7–8
  assessment difficulties 24–7

party management
  as component of statecraft 29, 33–4
  Clement Attlee 55, 210
  Harold Wilson 55
  Keir Starmer 55, 387, 396
  Neil Kinnock 55, 281, 283–5, 428–30, 433–6
  Tony Blair 55, 321–3, 434, 447–8
  Ramsay MacDonald 142–4, 145, 155
  Arthur Henderson 154–5, 157–64
  George Lansbury 187–9
  Hugh Gaitskell 218–28
  Michael Foot 270–71, 272
  John Smith 307–8, 309–10, 427, 433–4
  Ed Miliband 323, 354–6
  Jeremy Corbyn 365–6, 367–8
  David Cameron 428
  Gordon Brown 434
Pearce, Robert 26
Pearce, Sir William 198
Pease, Sir Joseph 154
Pelling, Henry 26
Pen and the Sword, The (Foot) 264
Peters, Arthur 155
Phillips, Jess 383
Phillips, Morgan 202
Piketty, Thomas 269
Pimlott, Ben 188
Police, Crime, Sentencing and Courts Act (2022) 17
policy areas 66, 68
policy problems 66, 68, 69
political argument hegemony *see* battle of ideas
political institutions 68, 69
Poll Tax 287–8
Ponsonby, Arthur 192
population growth 75
populism 35–6, 37, 71
post-truth 24
Powell, Enoch 248, 267
Powell, Jonathan 317
Prescott, John 286, 325, 446, 447
Prime Minister's Delivery Unit 320
Prior, James 268
Putin, Vladimir 72

Quinlan, Sir Michael 270
Quinn, Thomas 374

Radice, Giles 303
Rallings, Colin 43
Ranshofen-Wertheimer, Egon 138
Rayner, Angela 394
Raynsford, Nick 303
'Red Wall' seats 388–9, 403–4
Rees-Mogg, Jacob 72
Reeves, Rachel 365, 393, 395
Reform UK 4, 397, 398
regimes of accumulation 75–8
Representation of the People Act (1918) 29
Riddell, Peter 304
Roberts, George 163
Robinson, Tommy 36
Rodgers, Bill 303
Royal Commission on the Poor Laws and the Relief of Distress 177
Rusk, Dean 236
Russo-Ukraine War 72
Ryder, Richard 446

Sandelson, Neville 262
Sankey, John 150, 151
Scanlon, Hugh 422
Scargill, Arthur 423
Schmidt, Helmut 240
Scholz, Olaf 392
Scottish National Party (SNP) 56, 348, 350, 435
Scottish Trade Union Congress 88
Shackleton, David 84, 109, 157
Shaw, George Bernard 99
Sheerman, Barry 427
Sheriff, R. C. 146
Shinwell, Emanuel 113, 124–5, 205
Shore, Peter 252, 261, 301
Simon, Sir John 199
Smillie, Bob 88
Smith, John 297–310
  overview 20, 42, 297–8
  ranking as leader 60
  early life and career 298–301
  and devolution 299, 306
  and 1992 general election 300–301
  criticisms of 303–5, 312
  and OMOV 303, 308, 309
  party management 307–8, 309–10, 427, 433–4
  electoral strategy 388, 444
  Neil Kinnock on 427, 429
Smith, Owen 372, 381
Snell, Lord 158
Snowden, Philip 91, 125, 137, 146, 147, 164, 165, 167
Sobolewska, Maria 404
Social Democratic Federation (SDF) 87, 90, 104, 176
Social Democratic Party (SDP) 258, 262, 263, 271, 278, 279, 281, 283, 422, 426
Social Justice Commission 306
social media 5, 24, 30–31, 36
Socialist International 98–9

Socialist Party of America 88
societal structure 66–7, 69
South Africa 96–7
'Southern Discomfort' (Radice) 303
Stark, Leonard 374
Starmer, Jo 379
Starmer, Keir 377–98
  and 2024 general election 3–4, 390–91, 414
  performance in general elections 3–4, 43–4, 46, 48–53, 54, 56
  as Prime Minister 5, 63, 78, 391–5
  on Margaret Thatcher 9
  overview 19, 20, 40, 377–8
  as Leader of the Opposition 54, 384–90
  electoral strategy 55, 388–9, 390, 396
  party management 55, 387, 396
  in Corbyn shadow cabinet 371, 381–3, 409–10, 411, 413
  and legacy of Corbyn era 373
  early life 378–9
  career in law 379–80
  and Brexit 381–3, 388, 409–10, 411, 413
  becomes leader of Labour Party 383–4
  as leader of Labour Party 384–95, 413–14
  assessment as leader 396–8
Starmer, Rodney 378–9
statecraft
  meaning of term 18, 27
  party leaders assessed 19–20
  framework employed 27–38
  governing competence 28, 31–3, 40
  winning electoral strategy 28, 29–31
  constitutional management 29, 36–7
  party management 29, 33–4
  winning the battle of ideas (political argument hegemony) 29, 34–6
  Tony Blair on 443–50
Steel, David 253
Stewart, Richard 298
Straw, Jack 333
Sun, The 285–6, 316, 330, 332
Sunak, Rishi 54, 390
Sunday Times 251
Symons, Margaret Travers 95

Taff Vale verdict 84
Tatchell, Peter 271
Taylor, A. J. P. 173–4, 180
Taylor, Alan 158
Taylor, Teddy 421
Temple, William 307
Thatcher, Margaret
  Keir Starmer on 9
  resignation of 33, 288, 426
  and battle of ideas 35
  and Hugh Gaitskell 225
  as Leader of the Opposition 255, 256
  and 1983 general election 263
  as Prime Minister 263, 363
  and Poll Tax 287–8
  impact on 'Red Wall' seats 404
  Neil Kinnock on 431
Theakston, Kevin 57–8, 59, 60
Third Reform Act (1884) 92
Thomas, George 420
Thomas, Jeffrey 262
Thomas, Jimmy 137, 143, 147, 164, 165, 180
Thornberry, Emily 383, 411
Thorne, Will 123
Thorpe, Andrew 166
Thorpe, Jeremy 253, 420
Thrasher, Michael 43
Tilak, B. G. 97
Tillett, Ben 108–9, 110
Times, The 58, 113, 160, 191, 201, 251
Trade Union Congress (TUC) 88, 144, 148, 149, 150
trade unions
  and Taff Vale verdict 84–5
  and Keir Hardie 87–8, 91
  and George Nicoll Barnes 104–5
  and William Adamson 105–6, 107–8
  links to Labour Party 107–8, 114, 144–5, 161–2, 268, 355–6, 403, 404
  and Arthur Henderson 156–7, 170
  and Clement Attlee 203–4
  and Harold Wilson 236
  and James Callaghan 248–9
  and Michael Foot 262
  New Labour view of 269
  and Ed Miliband 322, 355–6
  and Tony Blair 448
Trades Disputes Act (1906) 84, 268
transformational change 63–79
  potential areas of change 65–9
  challenges of effecting 69–73
  types of change 73–4
  longue durée change 75–8
Trevelyan, Sir Charles 183, 187
Tribune 267
Truman, Harry S. 206
Trump, Donald 16, 70–71, 77–8, 392, 395
Truss, Liz 34, 387
TV debates 31

UK in a Changing Europe 42
UK Independence Party 351

Unemployed Workmen Bill (1905) 94–5
unemployment
  and Keir Hardie 94–5
  and George Nicoll Barnes 103
  and William Adamson 116
  and Ramsay MacDonald 142–3, 148–52
  and Arthur Henderson 166
  and George Lansbury 180, 184
  and James Callaghan 250–51
unilateral disarmament
  and Hugh Gaitskell 218–19
  and Harold Wilson 242
  and Michael Foot 273
  and Neil Kinnock 286–7
Unison 322
Unite 322, 383
Urban New Left (UNL) 361–2, 363

Vaillant, Edouard 99
Vietnam 237–9, 249

Wallace, William 92, 115
Ward, Chris 384–5
Ward, David 305
Watson, Paul Joseph 36
Watson, Tom 407
Webb, Beatrice 9, 113, 138, 177, 184
Webb, Sidney 163, 179
Wedderburn, Bill 268
Westland Affair 299–300
'Westminster Model' 68
Whitehead, Phil 421
Whitty, Larry 283, 301
Wilkie, Alex 107
Wilkinson, Ellen 113, 201
Wilks-Heeg, Stuart 316
Williams, Philip 219
Williams, Shirley 423
Williams, Tom 186, 422
Willis, Vi 182–3
Wilson, Harold 229–44
  overview 8–9, 19, 20, 40, 229
  and 1974 general elections 30, 239, 241
  and 1970 general election 31
  on importance of economic policy 32
  performance in general elections 43, 45–53, 55, 56, 57, 232, 239, 291
  electoral strategy 55
  party management 55
  prime ministerial ranking 58, 59, 60
  ranking as leader 60, 61, 243–4
  challenges Gaitskell for leadership 219, 231
  Bernard Donoughue on 229–30
  early life and career 230–31
  becomes leader of Labour Party 231
  economic policy 232–6, 239–42, 243–4
  as Prime Minister 232–42
  and 1964 general election 232
  and 1966 general election 234
  and trade unions 236
  foreign policy 237–9
  resignation of 243
  Neil Kinnock on 420
Wood, Stewart 347
Woolf, Leonard 190
Woolf, Virginia 190
Worcester, Bob 264, 280